W9-BTJ-222

THE SACRED

WAYS OF KNOWLEDGE
SOURCES OF LIFE

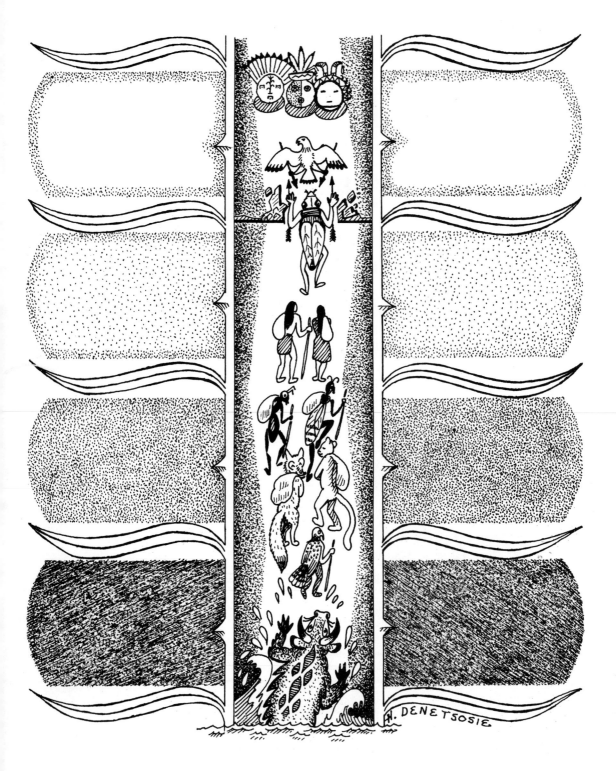

H. DENETSOSIE.

THE SACRED
WAYS OF KNOWLEDGE
SOURCES OF LIFE

Peggy V. Beck
Anna L. Walters

1977

Burgss

E
59
· R38
B43
copy 2

ISBN 0-912586-24-9

Library of Congress Catalog Card Number: 80-123388

Copyright © 1977 by the Navajo Community College Press
Second Printing 1980

Printed in U.S.A.

NAVAJO COMMUNITY COLLEGE PRESS
Navajo Community College
Tsaile (Navajo Nation), AZ   86556

No part of this publication may be reproduced, stored in a retrieval system, or transmitted, in any form or by any means, electronic, mechanical, photocopying recording, or otherwise, without the prior written permission of the publisher.

CONTINUATION OF COPYRIGHT CITATIONS AND ACKNOWLEDGEMENTS OF
MATERIALS UNDER COPYRIGHT REPRINTED IN THIS TEXTBOOK

The authors of this textbook have made every effort to contact authors and publishers of works we have used that have been published under a previous copyright. We gratefully acknowledge the consideration given to us by the following individuals and/or publishing firms.

Bahr, Donald M., *Piman Shamanism and Staying Sickness*, Juan Gregorio, David Lopez, Albert Alvarez, by permission from Tucson: University of Arizona Press, © 1974.
Barrett, S.M., *Geronimo: His Own Story*, edited by S.M. Barrett, © 1970 by Frederick W. Turner III, reprinted by permission of the publishers, E.P. Dutton.
Boas, F., *Religion of the Kwakiutl Indians*, New York: Columbia University Press, 1930, reprinted by AMS Press, 1969.
Bowers, Alfred W., *Mandan Social and Ceremonial Organization*, reprinted by permission from the University of Chicago Press.
Cope, Leona, *Calendars of the Indians North of Mexico*, in California Publications in Archaeology and Ethnology, Vol. 16, No. 44. Published in 1919 by the Regents of the University of California, reprinted by permission of the University of California Press.

(continued on page 369)

Contributors

Arg 84/02/07

ILLUSTRATORS
  Hoke Denetsosie
  Raymond Johnson
  Ed Singer
  Harry Walters

AUTHOR
  Nia Francisco (Chapter Twelve: Navajo Traditional Knowledge)

TYPISTS
  Verda Davis
  Claudia Roanhorse
  Glenda Gayle Morgan

TRANSCRIBER/TRANSLATOR
  Dolly Tabaha

PRINTER
  Fairfield Graphics, Fairfield, Pennsylvania

Acknowledgements

The research, writing, and publishing of this textbook were made possible through a grant award under the Basic Institutional Development Program, Title III, Higher Education Act, 1965, P.L. 89-239, Grant 600-74-08468.

The authors wish to thank the Navajo Community College library staff for their generous assistance.

The manuscript was read by three individuals who evaluated the material specifically for reading level, conceptual content, and visual appearance. They were Dr. Dave Warren, Director, Cultural Studies Division, Institute of American Indian Arts, Santa Fe, New Mexico; Roberta Watts, Education and Reading Specialist, Institute of American Indian Arts, Santa Fe, New Mexico; and Pat Baca, Counselor, Albuquerque Indian School, Albuquerque, New Mexico. Our thanks goes to them for their suggestions, criticisms, and encouragement.

This textbook would not have been written without the help of a great many people. The following individuals aided us with the creation of the textbook either by putting us into contact with other individuals, providing interviews, donating material, identifying photographs, or making suggestions and criticisms.

Herman Agoyo (Tewa, San Juan Pueblo)
Pat Baca (Sandia Pueblo)
Ron Barton (Navajo)
Dr. Roger Buffalohead (Ponca)
Maeve Butler (Minnesota)
Ed Castillo (Cahuilla)
James Cully (Seminole)
Ralph Davis (Navajo)
Hoke Denetsosie (Navajo)
John Dick (Navajo)
John Emhoola (Kiowa)
Corena England (Seminole)
Larry Etsitty (Navajo)
Shirley Etsitty (Navajo)
Nia Francisco (Navajo)
Antonio Garcia (San Juan Pueblo)
Cip Garcia (San Juan Pueblo)
Sam Gardipe, Jr. (Pawnee/Sauk Fox)
Harold Goodsky (Anishnabe)
Marie Hall (Creek/Seminole)
Andrew Harjo (Seminole)
George B. Harjo (Seminole)
Ramona Jones (Dakota)
Amy Kindle (Navajo)
David Kindle (Navajo)

Elsie Lee (Navajo)
Aunt Lucinde (Seminole)
Barney Mitchell (Navajo)
Dale Mitchell (Navajo)
Mike Mitchell (Navajo)
Dr. William Morgan (Navajo)
Andrea Nicholas (Maliseet)
Earl Nyholm (Anishnabe)
Dr. Alfonso Ortiz (San Juan Pueblo)
Peter Paul (Maliseet)
Tom Ration (Navajo)
Loren Sekeyumptewa (Hopi)
Dolly Tabaha (Navajo)
Ronald Theisz (Sinte Gleska College)
Soge Track (Taos Pueblo)
Hulleah Tsinnanjinnie (Seminole/Navajo)
Wullakie Tsinnanjinnie (Seminole/Navajo)
Susan Tureen (Perry, Maine)
Gerald Vizenor (Anishnabe)
Anna Walters (Pawnee/Oto)
John Walters (Navajo)
Dr. Dave Warren (Santa Clara Pueblo)
Manual Watchman (Navajo)
Roberta Watts (I.A.I.A.)
Alfred Yazzie (Navajo)

Contents

CHAPTER 13

CHAPTER 14

REFERENCE SECTION

Table of Maps and Charts

How This Book Is Organized

This textbook consists of fourteen chapters, the first of which is divided into two parts since it is an introductory chapter and is provided to familiarize students with certain *concepts* and ways of thinking about ideas presented later on in the textbook.

Words in the text are in italics for three reasons and if the student has any questions concerning the vocabulary, he/she should consult the instructor or a dictionary. Words are in italics:

1. To indicate that the word is in the glossary at the end of the book.
2. To indicate that the word has more than one meaning or definition.
3. To emphasize a thought, an idea, or a statement.

Certain words in this textbook are used in their original definitions. *Aboriginal, native*, are examples of words that have been misused over the years and have taken on negative meanings. In all cases where such words are used in the text we will try to define them in the context of the material, in footnotes, or in the glossary. Chapter Six: **The Changeable Earth: The Colonizers and Genocide**, for example, discusses many words such as these. Most individuals who are knowledgeable in their tribe's sacred ways choose their words very carefully when they speak of sacred matters. We feel it is important when discussing concepts in religion and history to clear words from the contexts of prejudice or misapplication. Therefore, we have tried to choose the words we use very carefully and to check translations for their correctness.

At the end of the book is a complete bibliography. Listed here are the books, articles, periodicals, etc., from which the textbook was researched. In this bibliography the student can find the source of a quotation that is cited in the text; quotations from interviews are not cited in the bibliography. For example, a quotation will be identified at its completion by, for instance, (Ortiz, 1972: 136). The student can find the source of the quotation by turning to the bibliography and looking under "Ortiz." Here you will find the following listings:

ORTIZ, ALFONSO

1973   "Look to the Mountaintop," **in** *Essays In Reflections*, E. Graham Ward, ed., Boston, Mass., Houghton-Mifflin.

—————————, ed.

1972   *New Perspectives On The Pueblos,* 1st ed., Albuquerque, New Mexico Press.

—————————

1969   *The Tewa World: Space, Time, Being, and Becoming In A Pueblo Society*, Chicago, Ill., University of Chicago Press.

You can find the source of the quotation therefore, by looking on Page 136 in Ortiz's book, *New Perspectives On The Pueblos.*

At the end of each chapter suggestions for further reading are given. The books or articles suggested discuss the material in the chapters in more detail or add to the information about certain specific tribal activities, philosophies, ceremonies, or organizations.

Contemporary films on subjects concerning Native Americans and topics covered in the textbook are reviewed in the reference section too. The films and their distributors are listed alphabetically.

Of course, the most valuable source of knowledge and ideas are The People themselves. The sacred life in every tribal community goes on throughout the day, every day. Learning through experience and work in the community is a basic source of knowledge.

It should also be noted that some of the material in this textbook may be restricted in its use to the winter months of the year. Instructors as well as students should be aware of these restrictions.*

There may be spelling variations when words are written in tribal languages, especially Navajo and the Eskimo languages.

---

* See Chapter Three: **Learning The Way: Traditional Education**, re: restrictions on Storytelling.

Preface

In this textbook, we will be emphasizing the *traditional* characteristics of sacred ways in North America. We feel that the *concepts* and practices at the root of *classic* tribal systems of knowledge continue to describe a basic way of thinking about the sacred in today's Indian communities.

Even contemporary religious *movements* and ways of worship contain elements of classic tribal oral traditions and sacred ways. In addition to the traditional elements in contemporary religious movements, some of these ways have developed partly in response to the present-day conditions of poverty, oppression by racism, and environmental changes that have dominated The Peoples'* lives since colonization. Contemporary sacred ways and religious movements (e.g. Christianity, the Native American Church, and A.I.M. sponsored sacred activities) tend to be *pan-tribal*. Sometimes they overlap many different tribal communities and reach into urban areas that have less distinct tribal centers than do reservations. Sometimes they contain customs and practices that are not native to this continent. But, as we shall point out in this textbook, many of the elements of contemporary sacred practices are *derived* from classic tribal traditions and practices.

Both Native Peoples and non-native peoples are only very recently beginning to understand the fatal impact of certain forms of economic exploitation and unharnessed technology on the *eco-systems* of the Earth. In addition, beliefs of cultural superiority on the part of some segments of the world's population have also caused imbalances and suffering for those they call "inferior." Because of this, we find it helpful and practical to study North American sacred ways and contemporary problems in the light of history as well as in the context of their aboriginal** environments. Perhaps by studying these traditional ways of knowledge the seeds of relearning about the nature of this continent and the relationships of all beings on it can be found.

We urge the student to keep in mind that traditional sacred ways were and are never unchanging. One of the characteristics of Native American sacred ways is their *viability*† or adaptability. Traditions and customs are altered as necessary given the changing conditions or requirements of the community. Some of the strict rules of behavior the Elders required of young people twenty years ago have given way, for example, to a consideration of young peoples' schooling requirements or desires to find employment outside the community. The fact that young men and women return to the community for dance rehearsals, special ceremonies, and important seasonal activities, demonstrates in each community, the strength of its traditional sacred ways.

Nevertheless, it is important to remember that the knowledge *at the core* of most traditional or aboriginal beliefs and practices remains virtually unchanged since our Road of Life has not changed all that much. We are still faced with four traditional enemies: Poverty, Sickness, Fatigue, and Old Age‡ We can still map the sacred boundaries of our world. The seasons

---

* Many groups of Native Americans name themselves, in their own languages, by the term which translates into English as "The People." We will use this term throughout the textbook to mean American Indians, Native Americans, and other names given The People.
** Aboriginal means "native to a region or indigenous" from the Latin, *ab origine* from the beginning.
† Viable—able to take root and grow; likely to live, able to live.
‡ See Part II, 4 of Chapter One, for example. Here, David Kindle, a Navajo Elder, tells one of the stories from the Blessingway, a Navajo healing ceremony and body of knowledge, in which the Twin brothers, sons of Changing Woman, and the Sun meet the last four enemies of The People: Poverty, Sickness, Fatigue, and Body Lice.

continue their cycle of change, and the stars appear as night covers the earth. People are born and people die. The study of these *phenomena* and their relationship with one another is where the study of all North American religions and sacred ways begins.

CHAPTER ONE

H. DENETSOSIE

1 Seeking Life: Definitions of Religion and the Sacred

Part I   Introduction

What I am trying to say is hard to tell and hard to understand...unless, unless...you have been yourself at the edge of the Deep Canyon and have come back unharmed. Maybe it all depends on something within yourself—whether you are trying to see the Watersnake or the sacred Cornflower, whether you go out to meet death or to Seek Life. It is like this; as long as you stay within the realm of the great Cloudbeings, you may indeed walk at the very edge of the Deep Canyon and not be harmed. You will be protected by the rainbow and by the Great Ones. You will have no reason to worry and no reason to be sad. You may fight the witches, and if you can meet them with a heart which does not tremble, the fight will make you stronger. It will help you to attain your goal in life; it will give you strength to help others, to be loved and liked, and to Seek Life.*

This textbook is about the sacred ways of Native American people in North America. Through examples from the oral tradition of The People, through interviews, speeches, prayers, songs and conversations, these ways will be explored.

The material in this textbook will attempt to describe, not intrude by analysis, the meaning, role and function of sacred traditional practices and observances in the lives of The People, individually and collectively. This textbook will perhaps also help to correct the misinformed views on Native American sacred traditions and observances. These views fill the archives, the libraries, the movies, and the textbooks students use throughout the world. By simply letting The People speak we may come to better understand the profoundness of strength, beauty, and vitality of this dimension of American Indian People.

Many Native People find it difficult to explain their ways of life, beliefs, traditions, and observances with the word "religion." Therefore, we tried to find a word that would better describe sources of life and ways of knowledge. For this reason we chose the word *sacred* which we will define in more detail later on in this chapter.

However, since the term religion is used to describe the beliefs and observances of people in other cultures, including the dominant society in North America, we will examine the meaning and definition of this word now.

Like all peoples throughout the world, Native Americans seek their own way to explain origins and destinies—to face the unknown and learn the power and meaning of natural laws and forces. Religions attempt to bring an individual or group closer to the source of these powers and laws. A study of the world's religions would show that many symbols, ways of teaching, and ways of expressing the sacred, are universally shared

---

* An Elder Tewa man from San Juan Pueblo, speaking to Vera Laski, recorded in (Laski, 1959:128-129).

3

by human beings. The point this textbook makes, however, is that in contrast to many organized religions in the world, Native American sacred ways limit the amount of explaining a person can do. In this way they guide a person's behavior toward the world and its natural laws. Many Native American sacred teachings suggest that if people try to explain everything or seek to leave nothing unexplored in the universe, they will bring disaster upon themselves, for then they are trying to be like gods, not humans.

Today, science, psychology, and other behavioral sciences which are examples of the evolution of western thought and ideas, seek to discover such things as origins. They seek to explain the unknown. These sciences are considered to be separate from the religious life of the scientists who study them and who perform the experiments.

Because of this there is an attempt by many people and societies today, to dominate and control the unknown, to overcome human frailty or weakness. This has begun to destroy certain balances and relationships that exist in the world and its ecosystems. By destroying balances of this kind people destroy alternatives—they make it more and more difficult to adapt to change, to crisis, and to the unexpected. One of the great strengths of Native American sacred ways is their viability or adaptability. These ways are *viable* because they were aboriginally, and in many cases still are, *practical* systems of knowledge. The "scientists" of the sacred were holy people working together, arguing, challenging, playing so that life could go on; so that The People could, as far as possible, live well and long.

As we listen to Native Americans speak about life and sacred ways throughout this textbook, we begin to see that originally, sacred ways and practices were at the heart of living and survival. There was not a part of life that was not touched by these traditions. As Peter Paul, a Maliseet from Woodstock New Brunswick, Canada, puts it, "An Indian, as far as religion goes, he lived his religion. He didn't have to go to church to be told just how to live. Everyday life was his religion." Certainly not all Native American people today could admit that their sacred life dominates their day-to-day existence, but some could. And as we said

St. John's river, Tobique Reserve, Maliseet, New Brunswick, 1975. (Photo courtesy of Andrea Bear Nicholas).

View of Tobique Reserve, Maliseet. (Photo courtesy of Andrea Bear Nicholas)

earlier in the preface, the *core* of Native American sacred beliefs and practices remains virtually unchanged from classic tribal times.

Classic tribal sacred ways do not try to explain or control all *phenomena* in the universe. They do not, as organizations, seek to dominate peoples' thoughts or ways of personal worship. This is what makes these sacred ways distinct from "schools" of philosophy in the history of ideas, or "denominations" of organized religions in the history of religion. One of the concepts held by the Elders to be very important is *respect*. Great respect is held for those who protect sacred ways and help them grow. A human being's spiritual life is his/her most important expression of his/her humanity. To respect this is something the Elders teach in almost every tribal community in North America. Native American sacred ways were not, classically, incorporated, *sectarian*, or evangelical. They were just ways of seeking life. We feel that the strength and wisdom within this core of traditional beliefs is a valuable body of knowledge for today's world. How a people come to learn their sacred ways, how they express the sacred, and how these ways reflect the world, is what this textbook is about.

DEFINITIONS OF RELIGION

A dictionary* defines religion as a bond, commitment, an integrated system, and *reverence*. The dictionary goes on to say that religion is *spiritual* and is also connected with "a belief in a superhuman God who created the universe and all life in it."

Reverence is defined as awe or respect. *Spiritual* is defined as an "animating (moving or vitalizing, life-giving) force, or vital principle. It is a *will* that is unseen and *intangible*.

Putting these all together the definitions speak of the basic religious attitude as respect, amazement (awe), and commitment. What is respected is *intangible* and it gives life to everything. Because it is unseen and mysteriously life-giving, we know it with our spirit more than with any other of our senses.

Another attempt to define religion led one individual to describe why religions exist for all human beings. He listed four reasons:

Religions *explain*. They answer questions [about existence]: how the world

came to be, how humans are related to natural species and forces, why human beings die, and why their efforts succeed and fail...

Religions *validate*. Religions [say that there are] controlling forces in the universe that sustain the moral and social order of a people. Ancestors, spirits, or gods reinforce rules and give *validity* and meaning to human acts...

Religions reinforce human ability to cope with the fragility of human life—with death, illness, famine, flood, failure ...religions give security and a meaning in a world which...is unpredictable...

And religion also heightens the intensity of shared experience, of social communion." (Keesing, 1976: 386-387)

Alfonso Ortiz, a Tewa man and anthropologist from San Juan Pueblo, has also defined the term *world view*, a term used in the academic subjects that study different cultures. In Anthropology for instance, this term is used to describe the way a person "sees" his or her world and his or her place in it. Ortiz defines the term *world view* by saying:

The notion "world view" denotes a distinctive vision of reality which not only interprets and orders the places and events in the experience of a people, but lends form, direction, and continuity to life as well. World View provides people with a distinctive set of values, an identity, a feeling of rootedness, of belonging to a time and a place, and a felt sense of continuity with a tradition which transcends the experience of a single lifetime, a tradition which may be said to transcend even time. (Ortiz, 1973:91)

He goes on to explain how the word religion differs from the term World View.

A world view—provides a people with a structure of *reality*; it defines, classifies, and orders the "really real" in the universe, in their world, and in their society...a world view "embodies man's most general conceptions of order." If this is accepted as a working definition, then religion provides a people with their fundamental orientation toward that reality. If world view provides an *intellec-*

---

* *The American Heritage Dictionary of the English Language*, William Morris, ed., New York: The American Heritage Publishing Co., 1973: p. 1099.

tually satisfying picture of reality, religion provides both an intellectually and *emotionally* satisfying picture of, and orientation toward, that reality... religion, as here defined, carries the added burden of [making] endurable such unpleasant facts of the human condition as evil, suffering, meaninglessness, and death...(Ortiz, 1971: 136)

DEFINITIONS OF SACRED WAYS

We have used the word spiritual to help us define the word religion. What makes a religious experience different from what we might call an "ordinary" experience is its spiritual, *intangible*, or unseen aspects. A person or a people may have a guiding vision in common. Those times when they actually experience a hidden meaning in that vision are *sacred* moments. Religions are, at their core, made up of sacred moments and sacred knowledge. Sometimes organized religions lose sight of the emotions and sacred moments that are their guiding vision. Most Native American sacred ways allow for constant individual and collective *revitalization* of the emotions and *mystical* experiences that make up the core of their guiding vision.

A dictionary* defines sacred as "made or declared holy; dedicated or devoted exclusively to a single use, purpose, or person; worthy of reverence or respect."

Sacred means something special, something out of the ordinary, and often it concerns a very personal part of each one of us because it describes our dreams, our changing, and our personal way of seeing the world. The sacred is also something that is shared, and this sharing or *collective* experience is necessary in order to keep the oral traditions and sacred ways vital. As we discuss the sacred, we might say there are two sides to it: the personal, *ecstatic* side that individuals find hard to describe, and the part of the sacred that is shared and defined year after year through oral histories, ritual, and other ceremonies and customs.

Having a guiding vision in common as a people and maintaining it with renewals, ceremonials, rituals and prayers, is what we could call religious *worship* and practice.

One of the ideas that is expressed over and over again by different people throughout this textbook is that their sacred ways are felt to be inseparable from the "ordinary." These people feel that knowledge should be searched for along with something else. Science, psychology, and similar disciplines should not be tasks separate from that of living and of worshipping. Knowledge comes during those moments when one experiences a hidden meaning—*sacred* moments.

WISDOM AND DIVINITY: DAILY AWARENESS

Alfonso Ortiz suggests that life, from the Tewa point of view, and perhaps from the point of view of all sacred traditions, is a double quest (or search) for wisdom and *divinity*. To live, he says, is to seek knowledge and fulfillment on the one hand and to also have touched at the heart of life and death through experiences of the sacred. A person will have problems in life, he suggests, only when a person forgets that these two quests must be kept in balance and harmony. A person will have problems when he/she sacrifices the quest for divinity, or the sacred, for knowledge only.

Perhaps another way of saying this same thing is by listening to a dialogue about life and beliefs between Knud Rasmussen, the late Danish Ethnographer, and Najagneq, an Eskimo man of knowledge and *shaman*.

Rasmussen asked the intense old man, "what do you think of the way men live?" and Najagneq answered:

They live brokenly, mingling all things together: weakly, because they cannot do one thing at a time. A great hunter must not be a great lover of women. But no one can help it. Animals are mysterious in their nature; and [we] who must live on them [must] act with care. But men [strengthen] themselves up with *amulets* and become solitary in their lack of power. In a village there must be as many amulets as possible....

"How did you learn all this?"

I have searched in the darkness, being silent in the great lonely stillness of the

* The American Heritage Dictionary, o p cit. p. 1141.

dark. So I became a shaman, through visions and dreams and encounters with flying spirits. In our forefathers' day, the shamans were solitary men, but now they are all priests or doctors, weather prophets or conjurers producing game or clever merchants, selling their skill for pay. The ancients *devoted their lives to maintaining the balance of the universe: to great things, immense, [mysterious] things.*

"Do you believe in any of these powers yourself?"

Yes, a power that we call Sila, which is not to be explained in simple words. A great spirit, supporting the world and the

The environment of the Southwest Cape, St. Lawrence Island, Alaska, 1922. Farrar Burn. (Courtesy of the Museum of the American Indian, Heye Foundation)

weather and all life on earth, a spirit so mighty that [what he says] to mankind is not through common words, but by storm and snow and rain and the fury of the sea; all the forces of nature that men fear. But he has also another way of [communicating]; by sunlight and calm of the sea, and little children innocently at play, themselves understanding no-

thing. Children hear a soft and gentle voice, almost like that of a woman. It comes to them in a mysterious way, but so gently that they are not afraid; they only hear that some danger threatens. And the children mention it [casually] when they come home, and it is then the business of the [shaman] to take such measures as shall guard against the danger. When all is well, Sila sends no message to mankind, but withdraws into his own endless nothingness, apart. So he remains as long as men do not abuse life, but act with reverence towards their daily food.

No one has seen Sila; his place of being is a mystery, in that he is at once among us and unspeakably far away. (Rasmussen, 1927:383-386)

The responsibility of these Baffin Bay people in their relationship with "the world, the weather, and all life on earth," is to devote their lives towards "maintaining the balance of the universe; to great things, immense, [mysterious] things." Insight into life's meaning was not given to Najageneq—he had to go out and search for this insight. In solitude he put himself at the mercy of Sila and in this way held his communion with the mysteries and the powers. He suggests that our daily awareness of the powers of the universe and the ways we express our relationship to them, for example, by carving special figures, making amulets, composing songs, hunting well, is what makes life worth living, what gives life meaning. We could define this "daily awareness" as religion, but since it is a part of everyday survival and activity necessary to living long and well, we could define it as simply, "seeking life."

It is always a source of wonder that the unseen and intangible tie or hold us to the world that is so visible, filled with different life forms. That is what makes the sacred so difficult to talk about. When you wonder you are silent. There are no words to express this bond to the Great Mysteries.

Part II   Ways of Thinking About The Sacred

> In our ordinary, everyday life we do not think much about all these things, and it is only now you ask that so many thoughts arise in my head of long-known things; old thoughts, but as it were, becoming altogether new when one has to put them into words...
> (Aua, an Iglulik Eskimo shaman)

To acquaint students with some of the basic elements and characteristics of sacred traditions among Native peoples in North America, we will devote the next *six sections of this chapter* to a discussion of *concepts* or ways of thinking about the sacred.

Ordinarily we do not spend much time thinking about or talking about these things. They are things we usually experience and then they disappear into dreams, songs, dances, or just wondering. As we work and play and learn from living in the world, sacred experiences grow with us too. Often, as we shall learn later on in the textbook, there are certain times when a growing individual is given the opportunity to express his/her visions, dreams, or newly discovered experiences. There are also certain Elder people one can go to for instruction and advice.

Often, individuals and students do not share their own traditional experiences of the sacred in discussions. For one thing there may be *prohibitions* about discussing certain aspects of their religion or sacred ways. Another reason is that there is no academic or educational context within which to talk about things like religion or traditional *philosophy*. But people all over the world, at some time or another, meet people from different backgrounds, different cultures. We are all curious. All people throughout the history of the world have been curious.

Often, without the proper discussions and conversations—without clearing the air of prejudice and misconceptions—people grow up with fixed ideas in their heads of what other people are like. As we have said before, the Elders teach *respect* for other people's ways of worshipping; this is a basic tool for living a long and good life. Since one of the purposes of this textbook is to enable students to compare their cultural experiences with those of other cultures, we have provided the following sections as tools for thinking about concepts at the root of the sacred, at the root of Native American sacred ways and practices. Later, in the following thirteen chapters of the textbook each of these concepts will be taken up and discussed again in greater detail. We hope that the student will reflect on his or her own life and tribal experience for this will help put the concepts into perspective, into the context of daily life.

Some of the ways most Native Americans have in common with respect to their sacred ways and practices are seen in the following six concepts:

1) A belief in or knowledge of unseen powers, or what some people call The Great Mystery.
2) Knowledge that all things in the universe are dependent on each other.
3) Personal worship reinforces the bond between the individual, the community, and the great powers. Worship is a personal commitment to the sources of life.
4) Sacred traditions and persons knowledgeable in them are responsible for teaching *morals* and *ethics*.
5) Most communities and tribes have trained practitioners who have been given names such as medicinemen, priests, shamans, caciques, and other names. These individuals also have titles given them by The People which differ from tribe to tribe. These individuals are responsible for specialized, perhaps secret knowledge. They help pass knowledge and sacred practices from generation to generation, storing what they know in their memories.
6) A belief that humor is a necessary part of the sacred. And a belief that human

beings are often weak—we are not gods—and our weakness leads us to do foolish things; therefore clowns and similar figures are needed to show us how we act and why.

1 A Belief In or Knowledge of Unseen Powers*

One thing most Native American people have in common in their traditions of sacred knowledge is the existence of unseen powers. These powers may take the form of *deities* or these powers may be more of a "feeling" that something exists and is sacred and mysterious.

Unseen powers, when they are portrayed as deities, might be worshipped in elaborate ceremonial dances, with intricate precise movements and language. The Hopi and the Zuni people dramatize their relationships to the unseen powers in, for example, the Kachina dances. Various Kachinas portray aspects of life by their masks, their costumes, the movements of their dances, hands and feet. The Pueblo people in general have a complex way of seeing and portraying their universe and the mysteries of life. There are many societies, Kiva activities, intricate designs for body painting, doll-like figures constructed for children to learn the Kachinas' names and of course many prayers, songs, legends, and other sources of knowledge about the sacred powers.

Other tribes acknowledge the presence of unseen powers. Their shamans communicate with the powers in order to learn their ways for their own needs. Some tribes seem to have much simpler or *primitive* ways of seeing the world, their ceremonial life much less sophisticated. We find, however, on closer examination, that their cosmologies and perceptions are, in fact, very complex. (See Chapter Five: *Shamans and the World of Spirits: The Oldest Religion*). Jaime de Angulo, speaking about the Pit River people of Northern California in the 1920s, (see map of California tribes) describes their ways of experiencing the world and its mysteries:

> ...the reader will ask, if they have no religious ceremonies, no priesthood, no ritual of any kind, and not the slightest approach to any conception of [god] how can one speak of their having spiritual or religious values?...I must answer that ...the life of these Indians is nothing but a continuous religious experience... To them, the essence of religion is...the 'spirit of wonder' ...*the recognition of life as power*, as a mysterious, [ever present] concentrated form of non-material energy, of something loose about the world and contained in a more or less condensed degree by every object—that is the [way] of the Pit River Indians. (de Angulo, 1926: 354)

In de Angulo's words, these unseen powers are a non-material energy, something let loose about the world and yet concentrated in every object. A Teton Sioux man says much the same thing in different words. The mystery and power is referred to in the language of the Sioux as *waken*. He tells us:

> It is hard to explain what we believe about this. It is the general belief of the Indians that after a man dies his spirit is somewhere on the earth or in the sky we

---

* See Chapter Five, **Shamans And The World of Spirits: The Oldest Religion**, and Chapter Ten, **The Peyote Spirit**

do not know exactly where, but we believe that his spirit still lives...so it is with Wakan'tanka. We believe that he is everywhere, yet he is to us as the spirits of our friends whose voices we cannot hear. (Densmore, 1916:68-69)

Another Teton Sioux man put it this way. "This earth is under the protection of something which at times becomes visible to the eye; ...its representations appear everywhere..." (Densmore, 1916:69)

Still another Teton man continued the discussion saying:

The most wonderful things which a man can do are different from the works of nature. When the seasons changed, we regarded it as a gift from the sun, which is the strongest of all the mysterious *wakan* powers... We use the words *Taku wakan* for with it prayers may be made and good obtained. We cannot see the thunder, and we say it is *wakan*, but we see the lightning and we know that the thunder and the lightning are a sign of rain, which does good to the earth. Anything which has similar power is *wakan*, but above all is the sun, which has the most power of all. (Densmore, 1918: 157)

These mysterious powers then might be found in objects—thunderstones, charred wood, obsidian, feathers. Each plant has a special power and personality which doctors, medicine people, and other specialists learn to know and speak to. Gifts of power are given by animals and other spirits to individuals who seek them in dreams and during fasting. Visions and dreams are also considered to be powerful possessions.

The mysteries are seen in the way the seasons change, the way day follows night, the way the sun moves across the sky. The changes in the day—from the colors and sounds of dawn through the afternoon to night time—all these changes have personalities. They affect each one of us and we learn to read the signs they show to us. Growth itself, the germination of seeds, are part of the great mystery. Cycles of the kind we are talking about are often marked by collective rituals and ceremonials—a way of recognizing the spirits of the seasons and sharing with them the good they bring. The spirits are also connected with dread, fear, disease, and disaster, and as we have noted before and will discuss later in the textbook, sacred oral tradition deals with this aspect of life and power.

How does a human being know about these unseen powers? What is the source of this "religious feeling" de Angulo talks about? Many Native people say it is the soul of a person that reaches out to touch the mysteries. Dreams and visions are born in the soul, and it is our soul that can *wonder* about things beyond the ordinary world. Aua, an Igluluk Eskimo explained a part of his people's sacred beliefs saying:

We Eskimos living up here do not believe, as you have told us many white men do, in one great solitary spirit that from a place far up in the sky maintains humanity and all the life of nature. Among us, as I have already explained to you, all is bound up with the earth we live on and our life here; and it would be even more incomprehensible, even more unreasonable, if after a life short or long, of happy days or of suffering and misery we were then to cease altogether from existence. What we have heard about the soul shows us that the life of men and beasts does not end with death. When at the end of life we draw our last breath, that is not the end. We awake to consciousness again, we come to life again, and all this is effected through the medium of the soul. Therefore, it is that we regard the soul as the greatest and most incomprehensible of all. (Rasmussen, 1930, Vol. 7 No. 1:60-61)

Najagneq, whom we met before, when asked, "What does a man consist of?" answered:

Of the body; that which you see; the name, which is inherited from one dead; and then of something more, a mysterious power that we call *yutir*—the soul, which gives life; shape and appearance to all that lives. (Rasmussen, 1927:382)

Other people refer to similar beliefs and call the soul, the spirit" as Luther Standing Bear does when he tells us, "living—and all the *intangible* forces that constitute that phenomenon—are brought into being by Spirit, that which no man can alter." (Standing Bear, 1933:247) The soul communicates the personal and individual side of the sacred and the unseen powers. Ikinilik, a Utkuhikjaling Eskimo, was asked what he understood by "the soul." He answered, "it is something beyond understanding, that which makes me a human being." He went on to say:

> The only thing of value in a man is the soul. That is why it is given everlasting life, either in the Land of the Sky or in the Underworld. The soul is man's greatest power; it is the soul that makes us human, but how it does so we do not know. Our flesh and blood, our body, is nothing but an envelope about our vital power. (Rasmussen, 1931: Vol. 8 No. 2:501)

Barney Mitchell, a Navajo, puts the question this way: "How do I come in contact with this *thing*," meaning the world. He explains that the specialist in these problems, persons in contact with the mysteries, must examine the world carefully. They would say that *"the greatest sacred thing is knowing the order and the structure of things."* What does he mean by this? He explains that the medicine people who studied the world and the mysteries over a long period of time found that everything in the world is made up of four elements: earth, water, air, and light (heat, fire). Things stay together or maintain their "shape" by a balance of these elements in their structures. The order of these elements in each plant, animal, or other life is different. To *know* a plant, for example, you have to know its own particular *order* and *structure*: then, Barney Mitchell says, "you know its name." The plant has its own mind that you learn to know. A medicine person who needs to use a particular plant gets to *know* the plant and then, taking it and "asking it by name" uses it, and can give its life for the life of someone needing help in a curing ceremony.

In summary, we have seen some examples of the way different people experience the world around them in a sacred way. The world is mysterious and at the same time changes predictably, as if there were a guiding intelligence. Native American sacred traditions observe both of these phenomena and a great part of sacred worship is to respect these powers and listening silently, learn from them.

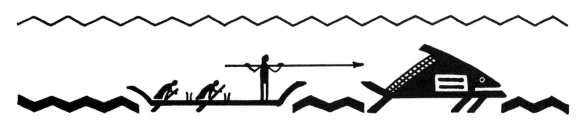

2 All Things Are Dependent on Each Other

Another concept that North American sacred traditions have in common is that *all things in the universe are dependent on one another.* * Everything, though having its own individuality and special place, is dependent on and shares in the growth and work of everything else. This means, for example, that if you take the life of an animal you have to let that animal know why you are doing so and that you are taking full responsibility for your act. Why? For one reason; because it is a way of showing that you understand the balances that exist in all natural systems, or *ecology*. For another

---

* See Chapter Two, **Ritual Drama, Ceremony and Prayer;** Chapter Four, **The Boundaries of the World;** Chapter Five, **Shamans and The World of Spirits: The Oldest Religion;** and Chapter Twelve, **Navajo Traditional Knowledge.**

Hunters with caribou. Photo taken before the turn of the century when caribou became extinct in the Tobique River area. The snowshoes and the sleds are in the traditional Maliseet style except that the sleds have metal runners. (Photo courtesy of Andrea Bear Nicholas)

reason (perhaps harder to see) because human beings and animals have a relationship to one another. Animals, for instance, know when they are in the presence of human beings, and they learn to avoid places where one of their own members has been killed. The elders and the oral histories tell us that long ago we once could speak the language of animals and that our survival depended on maintaining the relationships between animals, plants, rivers, feeding grounds, etc. Keeping this in mind then, the concept of dependency and respect is not difficult to understand. Peter Paul talks about this when he tells us about the word "Moose" in his Maliseet language:

Moose is very important to us... it is the same as buffalo was to Western Indians. The Moose was his [the Maliseet] livelihood—made his clothing, footwear, and he ate his meat.

I should say that he [the Maliseet] made his footwear and clothes from the hide of the moose. And, of course, the meat was eaten. So we go—from that, to most everything that was important. Everything that was important or everything that should be respected had this word *moose* in it.

For instance, grandfather is called *moose ohmps; nokomoose* for grandmother; and love comes from moose too ...*mooseallah*, "I love him," *moosellahm*: "he or she loves me," *moose alt*, he is loved. So moose comes in all these

and then moose comes into medicinal plants and trees too.

The reverse is also true. Together with the knowledge that everything is dependent upon everything else comes a respect which borders on fear. We are all related and therefore must be constantly aware of how our actions will affect others, whether they are plants, animals, people, or streams. Ivaluardjuk, an Igluluk Eskimo explained how the Igluluk understood this relationship:

The greatest peril of life lies in the fact that human food consists entirely of souls. All the creatures that we have to kill and eat, all those that we have to strike down and destroy to make clothes for ourselves, have souls, souls that do not perish with the body and which must therefore be [pacified] lest they should revenge themselves on us for taking away their bodies.

In the old days, it was far worse than it is now. Everything was more difficult, and our customs accordingly much more strict. In those days, men hunted only with bow and arrow and knew nothing of the white men's firearms... It was far more difficult to live then, and often men could not get food enough. The caribou were hunted in Kayaks at the crossing of rivers and lakes, being driven out into the water where they could be easily overtaken in a Kayak. But it was hard to make them run the way one wished and therefore rules were very strict about those places. No woman was allowed to work there, no bone of any animal might be broken, no brain or marrow eaten. To do so would be an insult to the souls of the caribou, and was punished by death or disaster. (Rasmussen, 1930: Vol. 7 No. 1:55-56)

Through this interdependency and awareness of relationship, the universe is balanced. A concept at the root of Native North American sacred tradition* is that all the elements in the universe are paired and balance each other.

---

* And many philosophies and religions around the world, for example, as seen in the Chinese I Ching or Book of Changes, which is one of the Taoist religious texts.

Too much of one thing can lead to an imbalance. In many cases, healing ceremonies are held in which the source of the imbalance is sought and diagnosed and a rebalancing brought about by various means. At the heart of one Navajo healing ceremony, the Blessingway (*Hozhoo ji*) and Navajo tradition in general, is the notion that the world is balanced. Barney Mitchell explains that the Blessingway is like an "engine tune-up." It is prescribed for example, when a man or woman is not "tuned to what's around him—he's not tuned to what he's about, what he encounters. He feels exaggerated. You just don't feel comfortable. . .you think you're going to sleep but you're thinking about things. . .too many memories. The Blessingway is prescribed so you won't feel exaggerated."

MOOSE

One important "pair" is that of male and female. In Navajo philosophy everything you see must be both male and female and within each sex is both male and female (all of us have both male and female within us). A parallel of this among the Plains tribes, Mitchell comments, is the red and blue blanket that is worn—the blue side, like the blue arteries of blood in the body signifies the male, and the red side, like the blood veins, signifies the female.

Other "pairs" that are fundamental to Native American sacred tradition are cardinal directions, night and day, moon and sun, moist and dry, tree and stone, dark and light and others that one hears and learns about in the histories and songs or sees in the sand paintings or body paintings.

Anishnabe man and woman gather wild rice from canoe in Minnesota. (Courtesy of the Minnesota Historical Society)

Many people see religion as mainly concerned with the question of "good" and "evil" in the world. Among the Native American sacred tradition, the idea of good and evil is not as important as the problem of balance and imbalance—or harmony and disharmony. Evil is essentially seen as excess or imbalance, and it can be adjusted and corrected through various means. On the other hand, that which is "not good" or "not beautiful" remains part of the human condition, so naturally we find that this subject is part of Native American oral tradition.

One of the great "pairs" we hear about is the pair of Life and Death—like Fall is to Spring, death is a part of life. Death brings separation and sorrow and is therefore not something that the individual strives for the way one strives for health and long life; but it is inevitable.

Classic tribal sacred teachings, the oral histories, tell us that a two-faced creature like Coyote, Raven, Rattlesnake, or Spider, helped in the creation of our Earth and human beings. But along with these goods that this creature gave human beings, he also gave us death—sometimes as a result of a blunder or joke on his part. Below are two Navajo versions of stories that tell of how Death came to the world:

When the first hogan was finished, everyone rested. The first hogan was occupied by First Man and First Woman. Together they planned how things would appear. They discussed that there should be a sun to mark the day and night. While the people were planning inside the hogan, a couple of others died outside. No one knew what to do; so they asked Coyote. They told him they were leaving it up to him to decide. Coyote decided that he would take a *Tadzootse'* (Black Rock) and go to *Todihil* (Black Water Lake) to reinforce his decision regarding the dead persons. There he would throw the rock into the Lake. If the rock came up and floated, the spirits of the dead persons would go up and there would be no death; if it sank, the spirits would go to the world below and there would be death. When Coyote went to the Lake and threw the rock, it sank. That is why the spirits of the dead always go to the world below. (Yazzie, 1971:20)

The following version explains why death must exist along with life. According to Navajo oral tradition, of the four enemies that remained after the twins Monster Slayer and Born-for-the-Water had destroyed all the monsters, one was Old Age. On his way home, Monster Slayer met Old Age who told him he could not be gotten rid of:

Old Age spoke up, "In spite of all, I am going to live on, my grandchild!" he told him. "You have not the right thing in mind. I see," he told him. "Should you kill me, dying would cease," he said. "Then, too, giving birth would cease," he said, "and this present number of people would continue in the same amount for all time to come. While I live on, old age will do killing and giving birth will go on in the future. As giving birth goes ahead, so deaths will go on the other way," he said. "The various birth beings, all without exception, should continue to give birth in the future, every kind of moving being, none excepted," he said. "Now, think this over, my grandchild, you can see how this thing is!" he told him. (Wyman, 1970:573)

Below are five more stories that explain the origin of death. These particular versions were gathered from individuals in the following tribes: Gros Ventre, Thompson River (Salish), Modoc, Sahaptan, and Cherokee.

1) The first story called "The Origin of Death" was told by someone who belonged to the Gros Ventre, a tribe named by the French colonists, who lived in the northern plateau region of the United States. This version, the student will note, is similar in plot to the Navajo story of Coyote.

When Earthmaker had made man and woman, and everything was finished, Earthmaker, man, woman, and the animals were all sitting around admiring how beautiful everything was and talking together. Earthmaker put the question to the humans and animals: "Now, how do you want things to run? You are going to multiply. If you die, shall you stay dead, or shall you come back to life again?" So the man and woman and animals had to decide, with Earthmaker as the judge.

The man took a buffalo chip and threw it in the water, saying: "Here's the way I want our lives to run." The chip sank and then came up to the surface. "I want life to be like that. We shall die but we shall come back to life again."

But the bear said: "No, that way won't do. Soon the earth would be full and there would be no room and not enough for everyone to eat. There will be more pleasure and happiness in life if all die. Then there will always be new generations to succeed them." So the bear took a rock and threw it in the water, saying: "Here is the way I want life to be." The rock sank and remained down.

So Earthmaker decided: "This is the way it shall be, like the rock." (Cooper, 1959:437)

2) The second story is from a Salishan tribe named the Thompson River Indians by the colonizers. When this story was collected, they lived in the Rocky Mountains of southeastern British Columbia on the Thompson River. In this version, the character who votes for death first experiences it when a member of his own family is the first to die.

The Origin of Death—From Nicola Valley

Coyote was traveling, and came to Raven, a bad, selfish chief, who wanted to make everything difficult for other people, and easy for himself. He wanted the game for himself, wanted long winters, and he did not want men to be immortal. Coyote questioned him as to why he wanted people to die. He said, "If people were immortal, there would be too many. Let them become sick and die." Coyote said, "Why should they die? Death will introduce sorrow into the world, and sorrow is very hard. If they die, what will become of them? Where will they go? Let them be sick, but not die." Raven said, "No, they must die. I do not wish our enemies to live forever. If the people should become too numerous, there would be no food, and they would be hungry. It is better for them to die." Raven's people supported their chief, and clamored for the people to die. Raven, Crow, Fly, Maggot, and many others wanted people to die, so that they might feed on corpses. Coyote said, "Let people die for a while, and then come to life again. Let death be like sleep." Raven said, "No, if they die, let them die for good, and let their bodies rot." At last Coyote agreed, and said, "Well, it is ordained that people shall die when their time has come. Their bodies shall be buried, and their souls go to the spiritland; but this will only be until the world changes again, when they will die no more."

Shortly after that, Raven's daughter became sick and died. She was the first to die. Raven tried to restore her to life, but failed. Then he wept because of his daughter. He went to Coyote and said, "Let us change what we said before. Do not let people die and remain dead forever. Let us change it!" Coyote answered, "No, it is settled now, and cannot be altered." Thus it happens that people die and are buried. (Teit, 1717:1)

3) The next story is from the Modoc people, a northern California tribe. This version includes events similar to the above story and adds another motif; that of trying to bring back someone from the Land of the Dead.

How Death Came Into the World

Kumokums was living by himself near the Sprague River, and he began to get lonesome. He called all the animals together to talk to them. "Let's build a village here," said Kumokums, "where we can all live together." The animals liked the idea of a village, but some of them didn't like the place. "It's too cold here, and the grass is stubbly," remarked the deer. "I think we should go to Yainax." "I like cold weather," Bear informed them. "That's when I can curl up and sleep as much as I want to. I'd rather stay here." So they discussed the matter, without ever really quarreling, and at last Kumokums got tired of all the talking. "Listen to me," he said. "I called this council and I am its chief. We will have two villages. In the summer we will all live in Yainax and in the winter we will live here on Sprague River. Then everybody will be satisfied." "How long is the Summer and how long is the Winter?" Porcupine asked. "We ought to divide the year," Kumokums said. "Each can be six moons long." "But there are thirteen moons in the year," Porcupine argued. "What are you going to do with

A crow tree burial. (Courtesy of the Museum of the American Indian, Heye Foundation)

the odd one?" "We can cut it up," Kumokums decided, "and use one half in Summer and one in Winter, for moving." Everybody agreed that that was a good idea, and they would go along with it. It was Summer then and the middle of the Moon When the Loon Sings, so they all packed and moved to Yainax. Kumokums and the animals lived very happily for many years, moving back and forth between their Winter and Summer villages. But they were so happy and well fed and contented that too many babies were beginning to be born. At last Porcupine took matters into his own hands, and went to talk to Kumokums about it.

"Kumokums," he said, "there are too many people around here. Our old people are dying off, and still there's too many people. We all know that when people die, they go to a land beyond, and if they have been good they are happy. Well, everybody in this village is well fed and contented, so they have been good. Why not let them go to the Land of the Dead, and they can be happy there?" Kumokums sat and thought it over for a long time. Then he said, "I believe you are right. People should leave this earth forever when they die. The chief of the Land of the Dead is a good man, and they will be happy in his village." "I'm glad you see it that way," said Porcupine, and waddled off. Five days later, Kumokums came home from fishing up Sprague River, and he heard a sound of crying in his house. He threw down his catch, and rushed to the door in the roof of his house. He climbed down the pole ladder through the smoke hole. His daughter was lying on the ground and his wives were standing around, wringing their hands and crying.

"What has happened? What is the matter with her?" Kumokums cried. He loved his daughter very dearly. "She has left us," his wives cried. "She has gone to the Land of the Dead." "No! She can't do that!" Kumokums exclaimed, and he stroked his daughter's head, and called her name. "Come back to me," Kumokums begged. "Stay with us here in our villages." Kumokums sent his wife through the village to bring in the most powerful medicine men. They sang and prayed over the girl's body, but no one could bring her back. Finally, Porcupine came waddling backward down the pole ladder through the smoke hole. "Kumokums," he said, "This is the way you said it should be. You were the one who set death in the world for everyone else:" "Is there no way to bring her back?" Kumokums pleaded. "There is a way," said Porcupine, and Bear, who is as wise as Porcupine and nodded his head. "There is a way, but it is hard and it is dangerous. You, yourself, must go to the Land of the Dead, and ask its chief, who is your friend, to give you your daughter back." "No matter how hard or how dangerous it is, I am willing to do it," Kumokums assured them. He lay down on the opposite side of the house, and sent his spirit out of his body, away to the Land of the Dead. "What do you want and whom do you come for?" the chief asked. He was a skeleton, and all the people in his village were skeletons too. "I have come to take my daughter home," Kumokums answered. "I love her dearly, and I want her with me, but I do not see her here." "She is here," replied the chief of the Land of the Dead. "I, too, love her. I have taken her into my own house to be my own daughter." He turned his head and called, "Come out, daughter," and a slim young girl's skeleton came out of the hole in the roof. "There she is," said the chief of the Land of the Dead. "Do you think you would know her now or want her in your village the way she is?" "However she is, she is my daughter and I want her," Kumokums said. "You are a brave man," observed the chief of the Land of the Dead. "Nobody else who has ever come here has been able to say that. If I give her to you, and she returns to the Land of the Living, it will not be easy. You must do exactly what I tell you." "I will do whatever you say," Kumokums vowed. "Then listen to me carefully," said the chief of the Land of the Dead. "Take your daughter by the hand and lead her behind you. Walk as straight as you can to your own place. Four times you may press her hand, and it will be warmer and rounder. When you reach your own village, she will be herself again. But whatever you do, do—not—look—back. If you do, your daughter will return to me." "I will do as you say," Kumokums promised. Kumokums held out his hand behind his back, and felt his daughter's finger bones take hold of it. Together they set out for their own village. Kumokums led the way. Once he stopped and pressed his daughter's hand. There was some flesh on it, and Kumokums' heart began to feel lighter than it had since his daughter died. Four times Kumokums stopped and pressed his daughter's hand, and each time it was warmer and firmer and more alive in his own. Their own village was ahead of them. They were coming out of the Land of the Dead and into the Land of the Living. They were so close Kumokums decided they were safe now. He looked back at his daughter. A pile of bones lay on the ground for a moment and then was gone. Kumokums opened his eyes in his own house.

"I told you it was hard and dangerous," Porcupine reminded him. "Now there will always be death in the world." (Levitas, 1924, 143-146)

4) The fourth story is from the Sahaptin people who, like the Thompson River tribes, speak a dialect of the Salishan language family. They occupied what is now southwest Idaho, southeastern Washington, and northeastern Oregon. In this story, Coyote travels to the land of the dead to bring people back so that, in the future, all people will be able to come back to life:

The Origin of Death

Coyote's married daughter was accidentally burned to death. Her husband moved away, and left Coyote alone. One night, as Coyote was sleeping, his daughter came and talked to him. "I have just come to see you," she said. "I am going on to where the dead people live. You cannot go with us, because you are alive, and we are dead." Coyote said that he would follow her.

"You can come along if you throw yourself into the fire." the girl told him. Coyote threw himself into the flames; but as soon as he felt the pain, he jumped out again. He was so badly blistered, however, that his daughter allowed him to go along. "you will never see us again," she told him, "but you will hear us later. There is nothing to eat on the trail. You must stick your hand in your mouth. That will satisfy you."

The girl led the way, and Coyote followed her voice. It often led him into rocks and trees. There was the noise of laughter ahead of him, and Coyote could see nothing. They talked only when evening came, and then Coyote would follow the sound. They traveled for five days. At the end of that time Coyote could almost see them. In five days more they would be like people to him.

When they finally arrived at the land of the dead, they feared they would have to bar him from it because he was alive. They made him sleep at some distance from the others. The land of the dead was very close to the sea. All about him Coyote saw all kinds of eggs. They gave him a bag full of holes in which to gather eggs. He filled the bag, and saw that all the eggs fell through the holes. Therefore, he did not even tie it up. When he came back to his daughter, he had nothing at all. The girl then said to him, "Next time fill up the bag; and even if it falls together, as if there were nothing in it, be sure to tie it up. Then it will be full." "That is what I thought," replied Coyote. He went back to gather more eggs. He filled the bag and tied it up. He threw it on his back, but it seemed as though there were nothing in it. Soon, however, it grew heavy, and when he reached the house, it was quite full. Henceforth it became his duty to gather eggs.

Though he heard people talk, he could not see them. He would laugh over their jokes, and they would talk about him. They said that they would put themselves into a bag, which he was to carry home. When they were ready, they told him to start. He traveled over five mountains. The girl said to him, "Father, now we are going home. Four of the mountains will be easy to climb, but the fifth one will be hard. You will hardly be able to climb it, but do not under any circumstances open your pack. When you have reached the other side of the last mountain, untie the bundle, and there will be people in it. When later others die, they too will come back in a little while." Coyote promised not to untie the bag. "I may be able to cross three mountains in two days," he said. He threw the pack on his back and started on his journey. This time he had a little food with him. He crossed three mountains, and the load began to get heavy. He heard the people laugh and talk, and he was very glad. He crossed the fourth mountain, and now there was only one more to climb. He started to climb it, and managed to get within a few feet of the top. He was very tired, still he forced himself to go about four feet more, but that was as far as he could go. Though he had only about six feet to travel, he opened his pack. Those in the pack then said to him, "Father, now we must go back, and you will have to go home. Henceforth, when people die, they will be dead forever." Then Coyote cried, and said, "I shall not be the only one to mourn a child. All people shall do the same as I. When a person dies, they shall never see him again." Thus he said, and went home. That is the end. (Farrand & Mayer, 1917: 178-179)

5) The final story is a Cherokee version from the turn of the century. The Cherokee originally lived in North Carolina until the 1800's when some were forced to move to Oklahoma during the Jackson Administration. In this version we see that a motif similar to the one used in the previous two stories is the main theme—that of trying to bring someone back from the Land of the Dead.

The Daughter of the Sun

The Sun lived on the other side of the sky vault, but her daughter lived in the middle of the sky, directly above the earth, and every day as the Sun was climbing along the sky arch to the west she used to stop at her daughter's house for dinner.

Now, the Sun hated the people on the earth, because they could never look straight at her without screwing up their faces. She said to her brother, the Moon, "My grandchildren are ugly; they grin all over their faces when they look at me." But the Moon said, "I like my younger brothers; I think they are very handsome" —because they always smiled pleasantly when they saw him in the sky at night, for his rays were milder.

The Sun was jealous and planned to kill all the people, so every day when she got near her daughter's house she sent down such sultry rays that there was a great fever and the people died by hundreds until everyone had lost some friend and there was fear that no one would be left. They went for help to the Little Men, who said the only way to save themselves was to kill the Sun. The Little Men made medicine and changed two men to snakes, the Spreading adder and the Copperhead, and sent them to watch near the door of the daughter of the Sun to bite the old Sun when she came next day. They went together and hid near the house until the Sun came. but when the Spreading-adder was about to spring, the bright light blinded him and he could only spit out yellow slime, as he does to this day when he tries to bite. She called him a nasty thing and went by into the house, and the Copperhead crawled off without trying to do anything.

So the people still died from the heat, and they went to the Little Men a second time for help. The Little Men made medicine again and changed one man into the great Uktena and another into the Rattlesnake and sent them to watch near the house and kill the old Sun when she came for dinner. They made the Uktena very large, with horns on his head, and everyone thought he would be sure to do the work, but the rattlesnake was so quick and eager that he got ahead and coiled up just outside the house. and when the Sun's daughter opened the door to look out for her mother, he sprang up and bit her and she fell dead in the doorway. He forgot to wait for the old Sun, but went back to the people, and the

Uktena was so very angry that he went back too. Since then we pray to the rattlesnake and do not kill him, because he is kind and never tries to bite if we do not disturb him.

...When the Sun found her daughter dead, she went into the house and grieved, and the people did not die anymore, but now the world was dark all the time, because the Sun would not come out. They went again to the Little Men, and the [Little Men] told them that if they wanted the Sun to come out again they must bring back her daughter from *Tsugina i*, the Ghost country, in *Usunhi yi*, the Darkening land in the west. They chose seven men to go, and gave each a sourwood rod a hand-breadth long. The Little Men told them they must take a box with them, and when they got to *Tsusgina i* they would find all the ghosts at a dance. They must stand outside the circle, and when the young woman passed in the dance they must strike her with the rods and she would fall to the ground. They must put her into the box and bring her back to her mother, but they must be very sure not to open the box, even a little way, until they were home again. They took the rods and a box and traveled seven days to the west until they came to the Darkening land. There were a great many people there, and they were having a dance just as if they were at home in the settlements. The young woman was in the outside circle, and as she swung around to where the seven men were standing, one struck her with his rod and she turned her head and saw him. As she came around the second time another touched her with his rod, and then another and another, until at the seventh round she fell out of the ring, and they put her into the box and closed the lid fast. The other ghosts seemed never to notice what had happened.

They took up the box and started home toward the east. In a little while the girl came to life again and begged to be let out of the box. They made no answer and went on. Soon she called again and said she was hungry, but still they made no answer and went on. After another while she spoke again and called for a drink and pleaded so that it was very hard to listen to her, but the men who carried the box said nothing and still went on. When at last they were very near home, she called again and begged them to raise the lid just a little because she was smothering. They were afraid she was really dying now, so they lifted the lid a little to give her air, but as they did so there was a fluttering sound inside the box. The something flew past them into the thicket and they heard a redbird cry, "Kwish! kwish! kwish!" in the bushes. They shut down the lid and went on again to the settlements, but when they got there and opened the box, it was empty.

So we know the Redbird is the daughter of the Sun, and if the men had kept the box closed, as the Little Men had told them to do, they would have brought her home safely, and we could bring back out other friends also from the Ghost country, but now when they die we can never bring them back.

The Sun had been glad when they started to the Ghost country, but when they came back without her daughter, she grieved and cried, "My daughter, my daughter," and wept until her tears made a flood upon the earth, and the people were afraid the world would be drowned. They held another council, and sent their handsomest young men and women to amuse her so that she would stop crying. They danced before the Sun and sang their best songs, but for a long time she kept her face covered and paid no attention, until at last the drummer suddenly changed the song. Then she lifted up her face, and was so pleased at the sight that she forgot her grief and smiled. (Mooney, 1900: 252-254)

In summary, the knowledge that is instilled in youngsters throughout their lives in Native American sacred tradition, is the knowledge of relationships and how they are arranged and interact with each other. Many stories tell how this harmony can be upset and what tragedies can result. And of course, experience itself is a teacher. Sacred clowns often help us understand the upside down, the opposite, and the other balances of things around us and our human ways of acting and talking. Some people, the sacred clowns for example, are individuals who take it upon themselves to become especially knowledgeable about the world and its fundamental relationships. This knowledge they can then pass on to others. Brave Buffalo, a medicine man of the Standing Rock reservation, was 73 years of age when he was interviewed in 1918. He described a dream he had which had led him to become a healer, in an incident that helps us understand how one learns the concept of interdependency and balance:

> When I was ten years of age I looked at the land and the rivers, the sky above, and the animals around me, and could not fail to realize that they were made by some great power. I was so anxious to understand this power that I questioned the trees and the bushes. It seemed as though the flowers were staring at me, and I wanted to ask them, "Who made you?" I looked at the moss-covered stones; some of them seemed to have the features of a man, but they could not answer me. Then I had a dream, and in my dream, one of these small round stones appeared to me and told me that the maker of all was *Wakan'tanka*, and that in order to honor him I must honor his works in nature. The stone said that by my search I had shown myself worthy of supernatural help. It said that if I were curing a sick person I might ask its assistance, and that all the forces of nature would help me work a cure. (Densmore, 1918:77)

3 Worship Is A Personal Commitment to the Sources of Life

A third concept basic to Native North American sacred traditions is found in the nature of personal and collective commitment, prayers, and other forms of sacred worship. There is an important and necessary link between individual worship and community well-being. And likewise, the community or special societies carry out forms of worship and ceremonials, in order to aid individuals. It is felt that each individual prayer reinforces the bond between the human being and the Great Powers. Life is made easier if you share pain. Worship makes the individual and community receptive to the blessings that are available if we are responsive to the world around us. We maintain the vitality of our bonds to one another and to the Great Powers by celebrating or worshipping in "a sacred manner."

Worship then is a way of giving thanks and centering oneself in the world. Joshua Wetsit, an Assiniboine from Montana speaks of these matters:

> ...Our Indian religion, the Great spirit; we're thankful that we're on this Mother Earth. That's the first thing when we wake up in the morning, is to be thankful to the Great Spirit for the Mother Earth: how we live, what it produces, what keeps everything alive.
> I know my old father—died about twenty years ago, almost a hundred years old—he never neglected his thanks early in the morning when he'd be out and the sun came up, shining—that's the eye of the Great Spirit...No matter what he's

doing, certain times, he looked up, just before it got into the middle of here in the sky—that's the throne of the Great Spirit. When the sun got about there, noon, he stopped, just for a few seconds, gave thanks to the Great Spirit and asked to be blessed. Then again when the sun was going down, he watched that until it got out of sight. Those are the things I always think are wonderful when we're talking about our Indian life. (Morey, 1970:48)

Before a person acted—planted corn, went to war, killed a deer—a prayer was usually given. This was done partly to prepare the individual for what was to come, to become aware of the effects this act would have on his/her self, the community, and nature. Therefore, in most aboriginal sacred traditions certain procedures are followed in order to prepare the mind and the body to be *receptive*, to be aware. At these times, because you are calling on the Great Powers for help and sympathy, you want to make yourself receptive to knowledge and divinity. Some of the procedures include: purifying, blessing, and sacrificing.

Purifying
Now you erase your thoughts. You get rid of all poisons and excesses in your body through sweatbaths, emetics, (herbal drinks to make a person vomit), bathing, smoking, and smudging (blowing smoke of cedar, sage, or sweetgrass for example, on the body). You make yourself empty.

Blessing
You pray, call or ask for power and strength. You invoke the mysteries, the unseen powers and you name the elements which are part of your memory and your knowledge. You pray for yourself, for others because when they are healthy and strong you are too.

Sacrificing
Now you take something of yourself and give it free of charge. You take a part of yourself and do so because you believe you are connected to everything else. You become aware of yourself as a

part of everything. You suffer momentarily so that someone else will not have to.

All of these procedures are usually accompanied by songs, music, and perhaps dancing. You might see examples of these procedures during the Sun Dance of the Sioux, Cheyenne, Arapahoe, and Shoshone; and the Green Corn Dance of the Seminole. In the past the solitary vision-quest,* when an individual went off alone for four to five days of fasting and lamenting to seek a vision, required help of people before and after the vigil. During these vision quests, the individual had to think about all those things that made him or her strong—relatives, happy events in his/her life, and the possibility that some spirit might come to him/her during this time. Many spirits, powers, and other elements were called upon as well. Concerning his people's sacred procedures, Antonio Garcia of San Juan Pueblo recalls:

When I was a kid I remember everything we did was religious. My parents used to get up in the morning, they'd take sacred cornmeal, they'd blow their breath on it so the Gods would know who they were and they'd feed the Gods and they'd ask for good weather, they'd ask for rain, and they'd ask for good fortune for everybody, not only people of the Pueblo, but everybody in the world. Now that is beautiful.

In the Winnebago Medicine ceremony for initiates into the Medicine Society there are many prayers given at different stages in a ritual which lasts for many days. During the night of the first preparatory day, leaders from divisions of bands seated at each of the four directions offer a greeting and prayer. The following section of one of the prayers offered by the leader of the East is a final example of the interaction between collective and personal prayer:

Our songs and prayers we must offer up seriously and sincerely, never frivo-

---

* Most common among the Plains Tribes and the Northern Woodland Tribes.

Shoshone Sun Dance scene. (Courtesy of the Museum of the American Indian, Heye Foundation)

lously. Behold! our ancestors have prepared an excellent day for us. They have connected us with the true life. It is good. What our ancestors told the members of the Rite to do they are doing. They told them to have compassion upon our poor and pitiable Indians. They were not to appeal to the spirits, but to a pitiable member of the Rite. In this way were they to show compassion. To lead a good and full life that is the surest manner of securing this compassion. Here along the Road we have been stumbling, weaklings, dependent upon others. Yet, it is a good thing. To bring the one to be initiated, He-for-whom-we-seek-life, into connection with the full life, for that the members of the Rite have assembled here. To have compassion upon him and to bless him, for that, they themselves ask compassion from the spirits. (Radin, 1945: 102)

In this prayer, the leader reminds the participants that having compassion for their fellow human beings links them with the spirit world. Each participant makes a personal commitment to the Medicine Rite and its procedure as well as the health and well-being of the initiate. Together, the participants' prayers go out into the world by means of communal worship. In this way, everyone is reminded of the interdependency between the Spirit World and the world of human beings.

4 Morals and Ethics

Native North American sacred knowledge is also responsible for teaching morals and ethics.* *Morals set the limits and boundaries of personal behavior and ethics teach social behavior or the way individuals order their behavior with one another.* We have discussed the fact that a large part of sacred tradition is devoted to maintaining a balance among the elements and forces of nature. By understanding ecological relationships and taking care to maintain them and learn from them, human beings maintain their own lives. We have also seen that Native American sacred oral traditions teach people that they are dependent on each other and on many predictable and unpredictable things in the world.

In Native communities, the moral and ethical behavior that was taught was really behavior that was necessary for survival in the natural world. The individual was taught to be responsible for his or herself but not in isolation from the rest of the community.

A Navajo man told how he learned these things from his grandfather:

> My grandfather was a great man. He said, educate yourself but we will help you. We will tell you which rattlesnake has poison, and where it is safe to walk. You will get a soreness if you walk in the poison ivy. Don't walk near a cliff for a devil might push you over. Don't throw a rock at a woman; don't be afraid of animals. They do not dislike you. Be spiritual. Don't play cards because you might lose your property. Know things in nature are like a person. Talk to tornados; talk to the thunder. They are your friends and will protect you. (Paul, 1973:110)

Traditionally The People did not rely on a concept of hell or sin to make people religious. People worshipped because they wanted to or needed to and because it was a continual part of their lives. There were figures used to frighten children and threaten them into learning to behave in certain ways—clowns, for instance. The ideals of behavior that the clowns and other Elders taught children were basic to other aspects of survival: unselfishness, awareness, patience, cleanliness, and others that we have discussed. There was an easy-going quality about morality and ethics in many communities based on the fact that life was hard enough without punishing a person more than necessary. Luther Standing Bear in his book, *Land of the Spotted Eagle*, writes:

> The Indian** loved to worship. From birth to death he revered his surroundings. He considered himself born in the luxurious lap of Mother Earth and no place was to him humble. There was nothing between him and the Big Holy. The contact was immediate and personal, and the blessings, of Wakan Tanka flowed over the Indian like rain showered from the sky. Wakan Tanka was not aloof, apart, and ever seeking to quell evil forces. He did not punish the animals and the birds, and likewise He did not punish man. He was not a punishing God. For there was never a question as to

David Kindle feeding his animals, Shiprock, New Mexico, 1975. (Photo, Nia Francisco)

---

* See Chapter Three, **Learning the Way: Traditional Education**; Chapter Eight, **The Path of Life**; and Chapter Nine, **Girls' Puberty Ceremonies.**

**In his case, Lakota.

the supremacy of an evil power over and above the power of Good. There was but one ruling power, and that was Good. (Standing Bear, 1936:256)

Stories that are told by the Elders to people of all ages teach morality and ethics. These stories are part of the oral tradition of The People. David Kindle, a Navajo, tells us a story which is basic to our understanding of morality and ethics as part of the sacred teachings of Native American people:

Monster Slayer (The Twin Brother of Born-for-Water, sons of Changing Woman and the Sun), made preparation for the inhabitants of this earth. He killed all the monsters, everything that would prey on the people. When he thought he had got rid of all the monsters that would be deadly to the people, that would devour the people, he thought he had finished his role and he was coming back to his home on that little mesa that is the cradle of our origin. Then he met someone and asked him, "I thought I killed all the enemies of the people. Are you still alive, or where did I dodge you?" Then he found out this was Poverty.

"No, grandchild, I don't want to be killed," said Poverty. "If you kill me, then it will be the end of humanity, because you will have no knowledge of the needs, the necessity of one another, and the urge to do things for yourself and others. I should be here, and it will help you to develop compassion for one another. There will be need, there will be necessity, there will be the urgency to do things for yourself and for those around you because you are a human and you have certain needs. Your moccasins will wear away and there is a necessity that you get new moccasins. It develops your mind that you have to acquire and look for those things you need and others need. If you kill me, you will be like the rest of the animal world, without compassion for your fellow man and concern for yourself. You, as a human, should retain me. But I'm not the only one. There are four of us all in this category."

The first one that he met, he didn't kill—he didn't kill Poverty. He didn't kill the need. He didn't kill the want. He saw that man needed poverty to be humble and to be concerned with the needs of others as well as himself. He met another one—as the first one stated, there were four of them. He met the second person. The Sun God boy says, "I thought I killed all the monsters that would be killing the humanity on this earth, but I notice that you're still alive." The answer came that he didn't want to be killed because "I have a definite purpose to live and to stay with you." He found it was Hunger. "Because I must have a place in your life to bother your stomach. When your stomach becomes empty, you will feel that you're hungry and you will think, develop your mind about how to get food. You will become industrious and stop being lazy. You will go out and look for game or into the fields to get the crop. I have a definite purpose to live with your people. Without me, you will be lazy and couldn't develop the qualities of mind and strength you should have for this world." So that's the second person he let go. Hunger was not killed. The Spirit of Hunger was not destroyed. It was left purposely to remain with us to make us work.

Then he went ahead and he met the third person. He asked him the same question. "I thought I had killed all the enemies of humanity. Are you still around here yet? How was it I missed you?" He found that it was Fatigue. Every night we should go to sleep. It's a must if we are not to forget the world of the spirit. We have to have the sleep to be in good health. "If you kill me," said Fatigue, "You will never rest. You have to have your sleep each night to replenish both your physical and spiritual strength. Without sleep man would forget the spirit and be aware of only the physical world. If you kill me, that will be the end. Your eyes will dry up. You won't get the necessary rest to continue your life." So he didn't kill him. He let him abide with humanity. But there is an extreme to that thing, too. If you do nothing but sleep and sleep, you'll die of poverty. You'll be lazy and die of want. It is a part of the life necessity to sleep, but if you continue to do nothing but sleep, you'll fall into the hands of hunger which forces you to work. He let Fatigue go because it was necessary that he be retained as a help to humanity.

He went on again and met the fourth person. He told him the same thing, "I thought I had killed all the enemies of humanity, and here you are. "You're still alive." He found it was Body Lice. He wanted to kill him, but the Body Lice also has a purpose.

Without lice, people wouldn't bother to keep clean. When people come together to comb each other's hair, it's kind of a leisure period for them. Those periods, they'll be talking about something that happened with the community. It serves a purpose that they have the time to visit. Body Lice forces people to make an effort to keep clean and to be sociable.

So he wasn't killed either. Body Lice he let go, to abide with humanity. Four of those, as a group, were given freedom to operate in their sphere. By viewing this legend, we know that it definitely has purpose. It is a problem—how to combat the needs in a person's life, how to think of others, what to wear, what to eat. Is he tired? Does he need that rest? Does he need that cleanliness? To my knowledge, it is those things that are an aid to humans and force us to think, to act. I think it was well that they were spared, otherwise our efforts for the needs of the human race would have dried up. (Morey, 1970:80-83)

5 Sacred Practitioners and Passing on Sacred Knowledge

In every Native American tribe in North America, there are specialists who go by various names depending on their functions or how people have tried to name them in nontribal languages—priests, medicine men, caciques, singers, and shamans.* These individuals are responsible for specialized, perhaps sacred knowledge. They help pass knowledge and sacred practices from generation to generation, storing what they know in their memories.

Among the Pueblos for instance, sacred practitioners might be individuals who have been initiated into one of several societies. Much of what they learn in these societies, which usually meet in structures called *kivas*, they cannot tell to other, uninitiated people.

Often the sacred ceremonies that people observe or participate in as dancers, are the result of secret preparations days ahead of the "public" dance. The prayers, construction of prayer sticks, and other ritual procedures are known only by these sacred practitioners who have been taught how to perform them. Among the plains tribes there are specialists who are trained to prepare, organize, and conduct the Sun Dance. Many of the procedures they attend to are secret from other people.

This secret knowledge which is the property of the sacred practitioners is not known by everyone because it is dangerous knowledge. These specialists have learned what they know by experimenting with forces in nature. In order to do so they must first prepare themselves well. First, with the technical knowledge of procedures. Second, with respect to their own bodies—they must be

---

* See Chapter Five, **Shamans and The World of Spirits: The Oldest Religion.**

27

Two-Leggings, Crow man with medicine bundle, ca. 1922. (Courtesy of the Museum of the American Indian, Heye Foundation)

ritually "purified" and consciously "emptied."

These procedures, undertaken elaborately and carefully, prepare the specialist for the task he or she must perform when called upon. Knowing little about the specialist's work and the necessary procedures connected with it, an ordinary person would not want to come in contact with these secrets because, as an individual puts it, "The power might come back at me if I exposed myself to it when I was not prepared or not ready to know about it," or, as another Pawnee woman said, "I wouldn't want to go near those medicine bundles if I didn't know how to act."

Among the Navajo there are, as in other tribes, various kinds of sacred practitioners: diagnosticians, herbalists, and *hataatli* or singers—those who know one or more healing ceremonies. The ceremonies require that the singer know the origin histories of the Navajo, the specific chants and prayers which accompany the particular ceremony, the sand paintings, the herbs, the contents of the medicine bundle and the procedures for ritual participation.

These singers or medicine men, know the *names* of the elements in their particular specialty chant. For example, the Singer of the

Mountain Chant knows the names of animals who live in the mountains (particularly the bear), and can speak their languages. The Singer of the Windway, "can call a tornado any time"—he knows the language of the winds. The Singer of the Night Chant knows the "East and the West" and the Masked Gods (Yeis). And the Singer of the Shooting Chant knows the lightning's way. (Barney Mitchell)

Sometimes sacred practitioners are self taught, like some of the *angakoq* or shamans of the Eskimo people. Many times doctors and medicine people of this kind follow a calling from the time they are young. They have a certain gift for this kind of knowledge and power. We will devote a chapter in this textbook to these specialists.

Sometimes sacred practitioners are not medicine people or officials like "priests" or caciques. Perhaps, however, they have spent their lives learning the stories and chants which tell the history and sacred knowledge of their people. Perhaps their grandfather or grandmother was a specialist—medicine person or official and they observed him/her over many years, or went with him/her to gather herbs, heal a patient, prepare a prayer stick or medicine bundle. By the time they

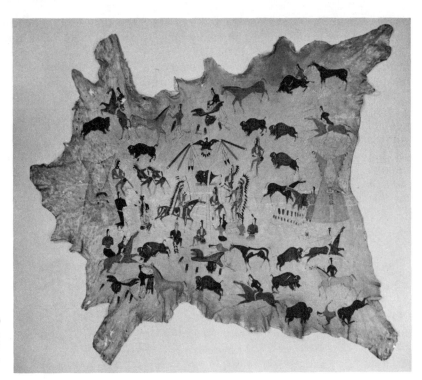

Painted elk hide of the Sun Dance by George Washakie, Shoshone. (Courtesy of the Museum of the American Indian, Heye Foundation)

were elderly they might be very knowledgeable and by knowing special or secret knowledge, important in the community.

As we said earlier, sacred practitioners and keepers of knowledge help transmit sacred forms and practices from generation to generation. There are certain aids they might have in addition to their memory for recalling certain procedures, techniques, songs, and so on. Drawings made on animal hides, on rock walls, or birchbark are sometimes used. Like a code their symbols are abbreviated forms of more complex facts that only the sacred practitioners can understand. For the most part, however, sacred practitioners store what they know in their memories. Tom Ration is a Navajo who specializes in the Male Beauty Way Chant (*Hozhonne Bikaji Hataal*) which connects to the Mountain Way Chant (*Dzil Kiji Bil'ahee*). He is also a Silversmith. He explains:

In all the ceremonies which have sand paintings, not one has the same sand painting. The figures, the lines, colors, sizes, they all differ. We who have this wonderful knowledge have long memorized all these in our minds and we know

exactly what to put into the sand painting because the picture is right in our heads. We instruct our assistants just how to make the figures, color, and sizes, as it comes into our mind how it is supposed to be made. (Translated by Dollie Tabaha)

The task of learning by memory is important for two reasons. First, people often note inconsistencies between different individuals' accounts of the same story or history. As in any oral tradition and body of sacred knowledge, there are different interpretations. Sometimes certain facts are left out. Other times more things are added. Barney Mitchell explained that a person who studies the Blessingway and all the songs, stories, and procedures that go with it, has a different way of seeing life and teaching sacred principles than a person who for instance, practices the Mountain Chant Way. The Blessingway "School" teaches a balanced, not upsetting, or "good" view of Navajo sacred principles and their culture. The emphasis is on harmony between people and ideas. Violence, quarreling, and sexual excesses are not discussed; in the Mountainway these things may appear.

Because knowledge is learned and stored by memory alone, The People can easily lose it. As we know, when in the 1800's The People died of foreign illnesses or were murdered on a large scale, much of specialized sacred knowledge was lost. Serious gaps in the sacred systems of knowledge of The People resulted and remain until this day. Memorizing knowledge is one of the most serious aspects of Native American oral sacred tradition. It requires that individuals in each generation take the responsibility for learning and passing on the sacred ways to the people. At the same time, only a handful of people together know all there is to know about their own tribe's sacred knowledge. Tom Ration summarizes this problem for us when he says:

> The stories that are told can be repeated ...to make them last. If we keep them to oursleves, in about fifteen or twenty more years we will not have them. It will all be gone. There will not be any songs or prayers because the legends go along with all this. One cannot exist without the other.

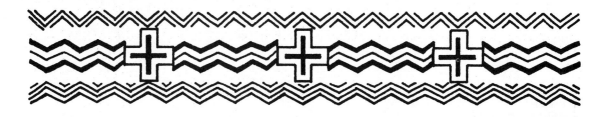

6 Humor Is A Necessary Part of the Sacred

Most Native American sacred traditions have a common belief that humor is a necessary part of the sacred and a belief that human beings are often weak—we are not gods: our weaknesses lead us to do foolish things. Therefore, clowns and similar figures are needed to show us how we act and why.*

Alfonso Ortiz, when defining religion earlier in the textbook, said it helped "make endurable" certain things: death, separation, sorrow, hunger and other times of stress. The object of a great part of the sacred traditions of The People was and is to ease the journey on the Path of Life. Too much power, too much seriousness, were to be feared for they too could "unbalance" life in the community and the environment. We are taught by the clowns, among others, not to take ourselves too seriously. This means, not to make ourselves too important. We are not *that* indispensable.

It is good to remember as we study North American Native sacred ways, that there is not a part of life without its humorous side. In many cases games and gambling had their origins in the origin histories of The People. The Ball Game (Lacrosse) of the Creek and Seminole is an integral part of the Green Corn Dance and Stomp Dance weekends.** The Moccasin Game of the Navajos is played only in the winter. The songs that are sung were given to The People by the original animal players of the game, long ago in the Chuska Mountains above Lukachukai. It was during the original Moccasin Game that the division of day and night occurred. It was also during the original Moccasin game that many animals received their special characteristics and colors.

Eskimo song festivals are ritually structured and planned, but the activities are spontaneous and full of drama, joking, and satire.

Sometimes even the seasonal or monthly calendars of certain tribes are named by the games that are played during that time, as in the traditional Cheyenne calendar:

---

* See Chapter Thirteen, **Sacred Fools and Clowns**.

See Chapter Eleven, **Sacred: Seminole Tradition in the Midst of Change.

Crow women gambling, ca. 1897-1910. (Courtesy of Smithsonian Institution, National Anthropological Archives)

Moccasin game, White Earth, Minnesota. (Courtesy of Minnesota Historical Society)

Group of Paiute men gambling. Las Vegas, Nevada. (Courtesy of the Museum of the American Indian, Heye Foundation)

San Carlos Apache men playing the hoop and pole game. (Courtesy of the Smithsonian Institution, National Anthropological Archives)

January —Hoop-and-Stick game moon
February—Big Hoop and Stick game
        moon, Big Wheel moon
April   —Spring moon, fat moon...
        When they play Wheels, when
        when high water comes
May   —May moon, shiney or bright,

ball game month...
        (Grinnell, 1972 Vol. I:71)

And as the Iglulik Eskimo proverb says, "Those who know how to play can easily leap over the adversaries of life. And one who knows how to sing and laugh never brews mischief." (Rasmussen, Vol. 7, No. 1:250)

Suggested Additional Readings

BEAN, LOWELL JOHN, and SAUBEL, K.S.
1972   *Temalpakh (From the Earth): Cahuilla Indian Knowledge and Usage of Plants*, Morongo Indian Reservation: Malki Museum Press.

CASH, J.H., and HOOVER, H.T. (eds)
1971   *To Be An Indian: An Oral History*, New York: Holt, Rinehart and Winston.

COLLINS, JUNE MCCORMICK
1974   *Valley of the Spirits: The Upper Skagit Indians of Western Washington*, Seattle: University of Washington Press.

DEWDNEY, SELWYN
1975   *The Sacred Scrolls of the Southern Ojibway*, Toronto: University of Toronto Press. (An excellent book about the birchbark scrolls of of the Ojibway, including discussion of the Origin scrolls, migration scrolls, Master scrolls, Ritual charts, Ghost Lodge and Sky Degree scrolls, Deviant scrolls and the Enigmatic scrolls which deal with philosophy and sources of the sacred. Includes a discussion of the Mide or Medicine Society and history of the Ojibway (Anishnabe) as seen through the scrolls.)

DOZIER, E.P.
1961   "Rio Grande Pueblos," in E.H. Spicer (ed.), *Perspectives in American Indian Culture*, Chicago, University of Chicago Press, pp. 94-186.

FERACA, STEPHEN E.
1963   *Wakinyan: Contemporary Teton Dakota Religion*, Studies in Plains Anthropology and History, No. 2, Browning, Montana. (Museum of the Plains Indian, Studies in Anthropology and History.)

HENRY, JEANETTE (ed.)
1970, 1971, 1972   *Index To Literature on the American Indian*, San Francisco: The Indian Historian Press. (Though this source has not been updated since 1972 it provides an excellent bibliography of books, articles, dissertations, and newspapers, devoted to materials on Native Americans. The 1972 edition does not list newspapers.)

HODGE, WILLIAM
1976   *A Bibliography of Contemporary North American Indians: Selected and Partially Annotated with Study Guide*, New York: Interland Publishing Inc. (This book is a good beginning for students wishing to do more specific research on the subjects discussed in the textbook. The author begins with a study guide to general materials organized by historical phase and region. The book, though emphasizing academic sources, covers a wide range of subject matter, from ecology, religion, and linguistics, to health care, urban life, and music. It is up to date and includes a great deal of material by Native Americans.)

INTERTRIBAL COUNCIL OF NEVADA
1972   *Numa: A Northern Paiute History*, Reno, Nevada.

——— 1976   *Nuwuvi: A Southern Paiute History*, Reno, Nevada.

——— 1974   *Personal Reflections of the Shoshone, Paiute, and Washo*, Reno, Nevada.

——— 1974   *Wa She Shu: A Washo Tribal History*, Reno, Nevada.

LONG, JAMES LARPENTEUR
1961   *The Assiniboines: From the Accounts of the Old Ones* as Told to First Boy, Edited and with Introduction by Michael Steven Kennedy, Norman: University of Okalhoma Press.

LUMMI TRIBE
1974   *Nooh WhLummi; A Brief History of the Lummi*, Marietta, Washington.

MOISES, ROSALIO
1971   *The Tall Candle: The Personal Chronical of a Yaqui Indian*, 1896-1969, Lincoln: University of Nebraska Press.

MURDOCK, GEORGE PETER
1960   *Ethnographic Bibliography of North America* 3rd edition, New Haven: Human Relations Area Files. (Organized by region and tribe, this bibliography includes sources, mostly by ethnologists and anthropologists, of material on Native Americans. The material listed was written prior to 1960 and deals with traditional subjects primarily)

NEQUATEWA, EDMUND
1967   *Truth of a Hopi: Stories Relating to the Origin, Myths, and Clan Histories of the Hopi*, Northland Press: Museum of Northern Arizona.

PHORECKY, ZENON
1970   *Saskatchewan Indian Heritage: The First Two Hundred Centuries*, Askatoon: The University of Saskatchewan Press.

PRATSON, FREDERICK JOHN
1970   *Land of the Four Directions*, Old Greenwich, Conn.: Catham Press. (A photographic book with text and dialogue by the Passamaquoddy People of Northeastern Maine.)

SLICKPOO, ALLEN P., SR. and WALKER, D.E. JR.
1973   *Noon Nee Me Poo: Culture and History of the Nez Perce People*, Vol. I, Lapwai, Idaho.

SOUTHERN UTE TRIBE
1974   *Weenoocheeyoo Peesaduehnee Yak Anup: Stories of Our Ancestors*, Ft. Duchesne, Utah.

SPECK, FRANK G.
1955   *The Iroquois*, Bloomfield Hills, Michigan: Cranbrook Institute of Science.

ZUNI TRIBE
1972   *Zuni Self-Portrayals*, Alvina Quam (tr.), Albuquerque: University of New Mexico Press.

CHAPTER TWO

Hohokam pottery design from Snaketown, Arizona, A.D. 700-900 (After Gladwin, et al. 1937)

2 Ritual Drama and Prayer

In this chapter we will seek to define in more detail the area of the sacred which is, in a sense, visible to the eye and ear—the dramatic parts of sacred tradition. We will examine or define some of the separate units or elements of ritual dramas that later, in the following chapters of the textbook, will come together as we focus on specific ceremonials in specific tribal communities. Rituals contain the elements of drama, prayer, and language within them; they are the focus for sacred knowledge and practices passed to each generation through oral tradition, pictographs, and contact with other cultures.

Rituals are a way of revitalizing (giving new life to) and putting in order, the elements in a peoples' *cosmology.** The basic concepts and elements that form a cosmology are made visible for everyone to see. The basic principles behind the cosmology—the guiding vision of

---

* A specific theory or model of the structure and dynamics of the universe. A philosophy dealing with the origin, processes, and structure of the universe. (American Heritage Dictionary, op. cit., p. 301)

the people's sacred lives—are acted out so that they can be well understood by everybody. Exactly what is going on in the ritual may not be completely understood by everyone because certain elements of the ritual itself are learned and rehearsed in secret, under the supervision of specialists. Not everyone could say exactly what the objective of the ritual is but the feeling is there. Many people help carry out this guiding vision, this sacred feeling, and so the main idea is communicated. In addition, the mood of the community changes; ideas and practices are strengthened; kin ties are renewed, and communication between The People and the Holy People is established again. Rituals allow a community to share a *mystical* experience of sacred knowledge.

Rituals mark important times of the year, like the great points of change: Winter and Summer solstices, Spring and Fall equinoxes. Rituals performed at the solstice or equinox points of the year may help make The People conscious of their economic and social responsibilities connected with planting, harvesting, and distributing food.

Tobacco planting ceremony, Crow, 1934. (Courtesy of the Smithsonian Institution, National Anthropological Archives)

Rituals may also mark the significant changing points in the life of an individual—birth, naming, renaming, puberty, marriage, and so on. Rituals performed at these times help make that individual aware of his/her particular contribution to the life of The People, and the "meaning" of life in general.

Ritual has more dimensions than other expressions of sacred worship, either individual or collective. Rituals add the *dramatic* element to worship. This means that when rituals are performed in ceremonies, or *collectively*, they appeal to the emotions, to the imagination, and to the intensity of feelings in each individual and in the group as a whole. In addition to song, ritual dramas use special dress, paint, make-up, props, musical instruments, masks, decorations, hand and facial movements, manners, and perhaps special locations.

Basically, ritual dramas provide two very necessary ingredients in the total sacred life of The People. One, they order and systematize every way human society, the natural environment, and the unseen worlds meet and come together. Two, they provide a physical expression of mystical experience for individuals and groups. This involves techniques and procedures by which The People bring themselves closer to the *mysteries*—the unseen powers of the world, the creators, the Sky Beings, the world of dreams, and ancestors.

So, in addition to their economic and specialized value ritual dramas can be mysterious, beautiful, silent, and musical; dramas which human beings perform in order to become closer to the source of the sacred. Besides marking, ordering, and systematizing, ritual dramas are also the collective or communal counterpart of the mystical and sacred experience of an individual. Alfonso Ortiz reflects on this meaning of ritual drama in San Juan Pueblo and among the Pueblo communities in general:

> ...Anyone who has followed even the summer corn dance circuit around the Pueblos—knows there are, ideally speaking, no observers, only participants. Anyone who has had the additional good fortune to follow the circuit of calendrical rituals between autumn and spring can appreciate even more fully how well the dramas mobilize a community's moods and motivations and reflect their collective identity. The larger dramas, at whatever time of the year, are carefully orchestrated performances which require sustained action at several levels of society for their success, as well as the expenditure of many resources. (Ortiz, 1972:139)

Hopi snake gatherers with eagle feather whips, sticks, and bags. Edward S. Curtis, 1906. (Smithsonian Institution, National Anthropological Archives)

Ritual dramas differ from theatre as pure entertainment because they are performed *out of necessity*. They are as necessary to The People as eating and sleeping. Because many of these ritual dramas were given to The People in their origin histories by the Holy People, they help maintain the lives of The People. Ritual dramas are dramatic highlights of the year's activities—all years since the beginning of time. Ritual dramas may be dramatic healing ceremonies which reflect all the teachings and ways of healing since the beginning of time. Whatever The People can give to their ritual dramas comes back to them.

An elder Tewa man from San Juan Pueblo once explained:

> ...the purpose of our ceremonies is not entertainment but attainment; namely, the attainment of the good life. Our dramas, our songs, and our dances

are not performed for fun as they might be in the white man's world; no, they are more than that; they are the very essence of our lives; they are sacred. (Laski, 1959:2)

Above, Xaye t'an, the Tewa man, tells us that the San Juan dramas, songs, and dances are not performed "for fun." A Lakota elder, Ben Black Bear, Sr., on the other hand, says to us concerning Lakota social dances ..."and you will use your wisdom with [these dances], there will be fun. That's the way it is and if you are not happy, then you will not come there, but if you use your wisdom, you will come and have fun. So be it." Sacred ceremonies exist in the lives of The People for more than one reason. Usually in the course of the day or week, depending on how long the ceremonials last, the drama will contain moments of great seriousness and moments of fun. What Xaye t'an means by "not performed for fun" is that the dramas he knows are performed with an *objective* in mind, within a larger context of ritualized sacred worship. Of course people enjoy themselves; drama and dance and the accompanying feasts, visiting, etc., are a break in the ordinary routine of economic survival from day to day. And it works the other way too. The Social Dances Ben Black Bear, Sr., talks about have their serious aspects as well. He goes on to say, "These are dances by which the young men, young women, and everyone else enjoy themselves. But they must first honor someone with a traditional name. Then this dance occurs."

During the time of a ceremony, a drama, a dance, the entire atmosphere of the community is charged with excitement and many special activities go on. Special foods are prepared, special decorations are made for costumes and homes, special paryer-sticks constructed, special songs composed—in short, a circle is drawn around the community and everything within that circle is sacred and taken out of the ordinary.

An example from the Plains in aboriginal times, when the various bands of the Cheyenne Tribe, for instance, came together for an Arrow Renewal or a Sun Dance, might still be witnessed today in the communities of Lame Deer (Cheyenne), Wind River (Shoshone-Arapahoe), Ignacio (Southern Ute), and Pine Ridge (Sioux), and other communities of the Northern and Southern Plains. Imagine that you have been walking for hours or driving

Shoshone Village, Wind River, Wyoming. (Courtesy of the Museum of the American Indian, Heye Foundation)

along a road with fields of grass stretched out to the horizon and suddenly as you come over a rise you see 800 teepees, below you circling a flat area by a river. 800 teepees, and as you approach closer, you hear drumming, bells, laughter, shouts, smell fires burning, meat cooking—you feel this is something out of the ordinary. When so many people come together to share a feeling, to share their goods with each other, dance in the same rhythm, sweat in the same sweatbath, a common spirit arises and brings a collective spirit to the group. The prayers that are spoken repeat the laws of ecology with respect to all creatures and elements in the universe. Ben Black Bear, Sr., shares his thoughts about these special times:

I will now tell of dancing and how many men and women among you have no interest in it. Many of you who dance (and will dance) know the beauty of it, and know that it is the highest form of enjoyment. What evil things you had planned to do, you will not do. You will keep your mind on only the dancing and your body will be well; it will not be fat. Your body will be very well. Whoever dances is never sick as long as he dances. Going to dances is good fun, and also, dancing can make your disposition good. If someone does not

do this, I do not know why he is on this earth. People use the dance to lecture those who like to strike their families. While you are alive, you give homage to the Great Spirit, and you will do favors for others, and then you will enjoy yourself. If one does not do those things, he will explode within himself. These three things are the highest in law. Realize this. These are truths. So be it.

(In Theisz manuscript n.d.)

PRAYER

One of the technical elements of ritual and ceremonials in general, is prayer. Prayers can be spoken, chanted, whispered, or sung; they can be accompanied by ritual actions, in special places with altars, or spoken alone in the woods without anything but a momentary silence. Usually prayers are directed towards something, and it is the force of the individual's will and words that make a prayer powerful. Prayers can be made by individuals alone or by groups of people together. Usually, however, one person is chosen to speak the prayer for the larger group of people. His or her words are carefully chosen and carefully listened to so that the force of the words and the images behind them travel between the speaker and the other individuals to become

Group leader in ceremonial dress, Kwakiutl, 1895. Franz Boas. (Courtesy of the Smithsonian Institution, National Anthropological Archives)

One Thought. We might call this group consciousness "collective mindfulness," because in these instances, each individual's thoughts are directed to a collective thought and collective objectives.

For example, in the Winnebago Medicine Society, which meets at certain times to cure an individual or to initiate an individual into the society as a fellow-medicine man and specialist in the Society's knowledge, the leader of the group that sits on the Eastern side of the lodge greets the attending people with a prayer. In this prayer he explains what collective prayer is for. He also explains how prayers and ceremonies should be performed:

Tonight particularly we are to take meticulous care of our manner of greeting...our heart full of thankfulness. Toward the one to be initiated, He-for-whom-we-seek-life, toward him, too, must our thoughts be directed. In singing the songs our thoughts must indeed be specifically directed toward him. That he may attain a full life, we are pleading for that. *As for myself, I know too well that I cannot attain any life by my pleading yet I can at least put my mind upon the matter and, perhaps, it may then be granted.* Ancestors, we greet you, we greet you!

You who sit around me here, my relatives, we relatives, we greet you again. Soon the dance song will start up and we will try to dance and sing as did the Indians of old in the beginning. This was always an Indian ceremony and, in the old days, everything was done with the greatest of care and circumspection. Every single seat in the lodge was occupied and all who were present had been blessed by the spirits. Every night the members gathered in the lodge to ask for life. They did everything well. When it was time to begin the dance song, all arose and danced, doing it with zest and vigor. To sing and dance in this fashion, to ask for life in this manner, we must encourage one another to do just that. This is my admonition to you.

Here, in this ceremony that the creator instituted, one can be truly invested with love and the full life. Only in this Rite that has come from above is this true. The life that we have asked and obtained from the creator, this we shall put to good use. It is ours, He has put us in control of it. Remember that Earthmaker put the means of obtaining the goods of life in control of every single spirit he created. Let us, therefore, concentrate our minds upon the creator above. Be assured that he will not take anything from us without giving something in return. That is what he himself said. So, if we pour a handful of tobacco for him who is up above, he will indeed take it; he will not reject it. (Radin, 1945:105-107)

As we said, prayers are sometimes accompanied by offerings of tobacco, as in the above example; prayer-sticks, feathers, corn meal, pollen, and other objects of life that have great importance in The Peoples' lives. Corn Pollen is one of the natural elements that is used by the Navajo People in rituals and to accompany prayers. At a healing ceremony or "Sing," the people are seated at the far end of the Hogan

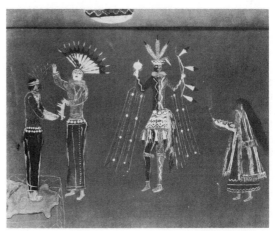

Cloth drawing made by Hostin Claw, Navajo "singer" or medicine man, about 1905-1912. Drawing shows the sick man for whom the ceremony is performed, the singer, the ceremonial dancer representing the Holy People, a woman, and a basket of blessed corn meal. (Courtesy of the Smithsonian Institution, National Anthropological Archives)

facing the door. The "Singer" (*hataatli*) or Medicine man passes his own pouch filled with blessed corn pollen, gathered in his own corn fields or given to him as a gift, to the person seated by the door which faces the East. The bag is passed from person to person going clockwise. As it is passed, starting in the East, each person takes a small pinch of the corn pollen from the bag. First he/she puts a bit on the top of his/her head, then a dab in the mouth; and, finally, he/she sprinkles it towards the chimney hole—up towards the center roof of the Hogan and offers a prayer before passing the bag on to the next person. The prayer may ask for a healthy and long life, for prosperity, for abundant crops, rain, healthy children, and so on. David Kindle, a Navajo Elder, tells us some of the reasons corn pollen is considered sacred and used in prayers and ceremonies by the Navajo People:

> This is symbolic thinking. Just imagine this corn pollen. We use this as an offering. Maybe the Great Spirit doesn't need it, but for us it's just the thing. We know we should try to offer what little we have, the pollen which is needed for all vegetation. One plant communicates with another by pollination. Even the worms, even those little ants down there, know this. Pollination is the sign of the growing of the harvest crop or anything that needs pollination; then the fruit comes following that.
>
> (Morey, 1970:62)

The expression we are using to describe this power of prayer and the concentration brought to an idea or thought by a lot of people at the same time—thinking and praying for the same thing—is "collective mindfulness." One is mindful when one is aware, respectful, careful. Group prayer, as it gives its power to something else is an example of "collective mindfulness." The following story illustrates in another way, and in other circumstances the power of collective mindfulness—how it can effect someone or something even from faraway. The story involves a young Navajo man who was fighting in New Guinea during World War II:

> One night, huddled in a New Guinea foxhole, under orders not to leave it under any circumstances because the enemy surrounded the area, the young man was trying to sleep. He did not know until later that at that very moment, his sister and grandmother (with the medicine man, relatives, and friends) were conducting a ceremony over his civilian clothes, asking the Spirit to protect him and return him to them

safely. He says that at last he fell into a sort of trance-like dream, and he heard the medicine man singing. During the ceremony such as this, it is the tradition for the one being blessed to stretch out his arms, and using a sort of "gathering in" motion, bring the fresh pure air into his "heart" four times, to make him strong. Quietly leaving his foxhole in the tropical night, this man reports,

> "I walked through the jungle and it was filled with light—like in early morning. I walked through the trees, brought the pure night air into my heart, and presented myself to God that I might be a perfect man, that I might be strong against the enemy, and that I should be returned to my people. Then I came back to the foxhole and woke up. But it had not been a dream—I had really walked, for I saw my tracks in the soft ground. After that I had no fears. I was *never* afraid again.

> "Later when the enemy bombed us as we hit the beach on Leyte Island (Phillippines) and everything was 'red, blue, and black together,' my white friend and I knew we would be safe. We fell between planks that had been unloaded from the boat, and lay there as the tracers came down—just like rain. When the raid was over and we got up and looked around us at the men who had been killed by bombs and wounded by shrapnel, we found that, even though the planks had literally been chewed by shrapnel, neither of us had gotten even a scratch. I knew then that the ceremony my family had had with the medicine man singing had protected me from all danger. I came out of the war without being touched by the enemy."
>
> (Paul, 1973:81-81)

SONG

Prayer and song are related. There are many kinds of songs; songs composed and sung as part of an annual dance as in the Turtle Dance of San Juan Pueblo; healing songs such as those that are the property of one man or woman specialist; honoring songs which are sung as part of the Social Dances Ben Black Bear, Sr., talks about; and cradle songs that are composed by mothers to sing to their children. When songs are sung with an objective in mind—as hunting prayers or healing songs—they take on a force which is as mysterious as breath and life itself. And in many North American Native communities The People equate or associate song, language, and breath—saying that human life is closely connected with breathing, and breathing with singing, singing with prayer, prayer with long life—one of the great circles of creation.

The connection of breath with life is seen in two segments of the Navajo Creation story. In the Creation story found in the Blessingway, a Navajo healing and balancing ceremony, First Man speaks to two recently formed Holy Beings, assigning to them names and functions:

> Of all these various kinds of holy ones that have been made, you the first one will be their thought, you will be called Long Life (*Sa'ah Naghai*),... And you who are the second one, of all Holy People that are put to use first, you will be their speech, and will be called Happiness (*Bik'eh Hozho*)... You will be (found), among everything (especially ceremonial affairs) without exception, exactly all will be long life by means of you two, and exactly all will be happiness by means of you two,... (Wyman, 1970:398)

And, as we have suggested before, thought (collective mindfulness, and so on), is power—it has the ability to create, transform, and vitalize. In the Navajo Creation story it is told that First Man and First Woman, with other Holy People, went into the sweat house and *thought* the word into existence. Through their thoughts, chanted in the Blessingway ceremony today, they organized and planned the world:

> I plan for it, when I plan for it, it drops nicely into position just as I wish, ni yo o. Earth's support I first lean into position. As I plan for long-life-happiness it yields to my wish as it nicely drops into position, ni yo o.
> (Wyman, 1970:115)

Later on in the Creation story, Changing Woman is ready to create the first ordinary human beings. She rubs some excess skin from her own body and when it is rolled into balls, she forms the bodies of two pairs of beings: a man and a woman in her image and a man and a woman in the Sun's image. All around at this time were the Holy People: the Talking Gods, the Sun, the Moon, the Stars, and the Wind People. They decided that the Wind People should "give them life" and so the left hand wind, the right hand wind, the spotted wind, the crystal wind and the tiny whirlwinds or gentle winds, blew in through the mouths of these four human beings and that is when they started breathing.

The connection of breath with song is made clear in the following statements of Orpingalik, a Netsilik Eskimo shaman.* Introducing a song he was about to sing, he said, "My breath—this is what I call this song. For it is just as necessary to me to sing it as it is to breathe... There are so many occasions in one's life when a joy or sorrow is felt in such a way that the desire comes to sing; and I sing as I draw breath." (Rasmussen, 1931:Vol. 8, No. 1:16) He explains further that:

> Songs are thoughts, sung out with the breath when people are moved by great forces and ordinary speech no longer suffices. Man is moved just like the ice floe sailing here and there out in the current. His thoughts are driven by a flowing force when he feels joy, when he feels sorrow. Thoughts can wash over him like a flood, making his blood come in gasps, and his heart throb. Something, like an abatement in the weather, will keep him thawed up, and then it will happen that we, who always think we are small, will feel still smaller. And we will fear to use words. But it will happen that the words we need will come of themselves. When the words we want to use shoot up of themselves—we get a new song.
> (Rasmussen, 1931:Vol. 8, No. 1:321)

Ben Black Bear, Sr., gives his reasons for singing, showing us that all the activities of life are reflected within songs:

> I want to speak about what is already known. The Lakota sing for just one

certain thing. The first thing they sing about is the sacred ways. The songs were given to the holy men. And then, through the songs, men and women, and boys, and girls, ask things for themselves and they also sing holy songs. Then they enjoy themselves. That is amusing to them and they will be happy. And than again they will be sad. These songs are like that and if someone sings, you will like him. So, that is why I'm singing from the age of twelve, love singing. That is me. So be it.

Individuals who have the skill and vision to compose songs and to sing them are special people because they, (like the individual chosen to say the prayer for a group), can create an image, a mood, a feeling, and share it with everyone else. They can sum up a whole community's experience after a tragic war; they can tease an individual who needs "taming," or who needs punishing by the community; and, as in the example below, they can sum up life itself for their people. Maria Chona, a Papago woman, tells of one of the times the Papago People came from miles around to meet for the Harvest Festival. She tells us:

We all went then, from all over our country to the Place of the Burnt Seeds. We camped together, many, many families together, and we made images of the beautiful things that make life good for the Desert People, like clouds and corn and squash and deer. The men sang about those things and my father made songs. When I was about eight years old, my father once made an image of a mountain out of cactus ribs covered with white cloth. He had dreamed about that mountain and this is the song he made:

There is a white shell mountain in the
    ocean
Rising half out of the water.
Green scum floats on the water
And the mountain turns around.

And she then comments, "The song is very short because we understand so much." (Underhill, 1936:22-23). This statement sums

A grass kitchen circle in Papago country, William Dinwiddie, 1894. (Courtesy of the Smithsonian Institution, National Anthropological Archives)

up what many Native Americans share in their simple, powerful song forms.

The simplicity and power of song comes from knowing the power of language, the origin of language. The Netsilik, Copper, and Iglulik Eskimos all have a category of language they refer to as "magic words." These are spoken to spirits or to the souls of departed humans or animals. They can heal sicknesses, keep away snow storms, or cause game animals to let themselves be killed by a hunter. Rasmussen tells us that these magic words are sung or

> spoken according to subject and purpose, either inside a house in the early morning, before anyone has trodden the floor, or outside in the open air at a place, far from the beaten track, where there are no footprints of man. It is the usual thing that ordinary speech is not used, but the special language of the shamans. Sometimes they make use of ancient words that have fallen into disuse in daily conversation.
>
> ...Magic words descend from father to son, but may also be bought for a good price of a shaman. As soon as one has given away magic words, magic prayers, or magic songs to another, they only work for the new owner, who must never speak them where others can hear them.
>
> (Rasmussen, 1931, Vol. 8, No. 1:278)

An example of magic words is given below in a Copper Eskimo's song, "Magic Words to Ensure a Safe Return." "People who are alone have this habit of saying [this magic song] when they are hunting caribou, and the sky turns dark so to their fellows-villages to come back safely":

> We rise from our bed
> The great sky's   its enormous pillars
> That keep it up,   as we overturn them,
> Down there   and up there.   They are
> Upright as pillars—we overturn them
>   Rising from our bed
>
> Big dwelling!   Rest on your arms,
>   Hold Fast!

Platform!   Rest on your arms,
  Hold Fast!
Platform! Rest on your arms,
  Hold Fast!
I hold on to it, I faithfully hold on to it,
to the island, like a gull, anxiously
screaming for its young.
(Rasmussen, 1931, Vol. 8, No. 1:284-285)

Songs are used in hunting to make animals meek and willing to be killed.* A hunter who knows these songs (the power words in the songs), will have success. One man who lived in various Eskimo communities in Alaska and Siberia once said:

> The Eskimo hunters at Indian Point said to me: "It is a mistake to think that women are weaker then men in hunting pursuits. Home incantations are essential for the success in hunting. In vain man walks around, searching, but those that sit up the lamp are really strong, for they know how to call the game to the shore..."

The true hunter, these people say, may be the person who knows the power of language in the songs—the magic words—the woman at home by the lamp in this case, not the person who finally kills the animal. For their hunting success these Eskimo people rely on teamwork or "collective mindfulness" to bring in their game. Tom Ration, the Navajo Singer and silversmith recalls a similar knowledge among the Navajo People. Songs of power, he tells us, are recorded by memory in the oral traditions of Navajo sacred knowledge:

> The Holy Divinity created the sheep and the horse and granted them to the people to use. These animals roamed the mountain ranges; they were wild. The people wanted to catch them but did not know how. Here is where the horse and sheep songs were sung to them. They came to the singer like a tame animal and became domestic thereafter. These songs are all in the Blessingway (*Hozhooji*).

SUMMARY

In summary, in this chapter we have examined certain elements basic to sacred worship: rituals, prayers, and the power of words. Later, the student will learn about other

---

* See Chapter Five, **Shamans and The World of Spirits: The Oldest Religion.**

examples of these concepts: the role of Clowns during some rituals; the mobilization of the community during the girl's puberty ceremony; and the learning of certain chants, songs, and prayers as part of the training of specialists and shamans.

In addition, we discussed the connection people make between breath and life. One concept we did not discuss was that of *silence*. Silence is also sacred, just as the origin of language and the power to speak with plants and animals is a mysterious thing, learned and known by only a few people. And also, the fact that the only way a person can learn the language of the wind, the trees, and streams is to be silent a long time, makes silence an important part of sacred language, prayer and song. We end this chapter with a part of a Zuni prayer, translated into English, spoken by Sayataca, the Bow Priest in the Night Chant:

> Through the Winter
> Through the Summer
> Throughout the cycle of the months,
> I have prayed for light for you.
> Now this day,
> I have fulfilled their thoughts.
> Perpetuating the rite of our father,
> Sayataca bow priest,
> And giving him human form
> I have passed you on your roads.
> My divine father's life-giving breath,
> His breath of old age,
> His breath of the waters,
> His breath of seeds,
> His breath of riches,
> His breath of fecundity,
> His breath of power,
> His breath of good spirit,
> His breath of all good fortune whatsoever,
> Asking for his breath,
> And into my warm body
> Drawing his breath,
> I add to your breath now.
> Let no one despise the breath of his
>   fathers.
> But into your bodies,
> Draw their breath,
> That yonder to where the road of our
> sun father comes out,
> Your roads may reach;
> That clasping hands,
> Holding one another fast,
> You may finish your roads,
> To this end, I add to your breath now.
> Verily, so long as we enjoy the light of day
> May we greet one another with love;
> Verily, so long as we enjoy the light of day
> May we pray for one another...

(Bunzel, 47th, 1932:720)

Suggested Additional Readings

BAHTI, TOM
  1970   *Southwestern Indian Ceremonialism*, Flagstaff, Arizona, K. C. Publications.
DAY, A. GROVE
  1970   *The Sky Clears: Poetry of the American Indians*, Lincoln, Nebraska, University of Nebraska Press. (Traditional songs, chants, and prayers.)
DE MEUIL, ADELAIDE, and REID, WILLIAM
  1976   *Out of the Silence*, New York, Harper and Row. (Totem pole carving in the native habitat, text by a Haida sculptor.)
KELLY, ROGER E., and LANG, R. W., and WALTERS, H.
  1972   *Navajo Figurines Called Dolls: The Remaking Rites of the Navajo: Casual Factors of Illness and Its Nature*, Santa Fe, N.M., Museum of Navajo Ceremonial Art. (Harry Walters is a Navajo artist, archeologist, and curator.)
MANGELSDORF, PAUL C.
  1974   *Corn: Its Origin, Evolution, and Improvement*, Cambridge, Mass., Harvard University Press.
NIATUM, DUANE (ed.)
  1975   *Carriers of the Dream Wheel: Contemporary Native American Poetry*, New York, Harper and Row.

POWELL, PETER J.
  1969   *Sweet Medicine*, Vols. I and II, Norman, Okla., University of Oklahoma Press. (Cheyenne sacred ways, in particular, the Renewal ceremonies of the Buffalo Hat and the Arrows.)
ROSEN, KENNETH (ed.)
  1972   *The Man To Send Rain Clouds*, New York, Viking Press. (Short stories by Native American writers.)
ROSEN, KENNETH (ed.)
  1975   *Voices of the Rainbow: Contemporary Poetry by American Indians*, New York, The Viking Press.
ROTHENBERG, JEROME
  1972   *Shaking the Pumpkin: Traditional Poetry of the Indians of North America*, New York, Doubleday.
SPINDEN, H.J. (tr)
  1976   *Songs of the Tewa*, Santa Fe, N.M., The Sunstone Press.
TOOKER, ELIZABETH
  1970   *Iroquois Ceremonial of Midwinter*, Syracuse, N.Y., University of Syracuse Press.
WRIGHT, BARTON
  1973   *Kachinas: A Hopi Artist's Documentary*, Flagstaff, Arizona, Northland Press and Heard Museum.

CHAPTER THREE

H. DENETSOSIE

3 Learning the Way: Traditional Education

One of the great mysteries and sources of inspiration for religious systems throughout the world are the questions: How did we human beings come here? Who are we? Who am I? Where will I go when I pass from this life? What is death? The attempts to answer these questions also drive human beings to search for knowledge. Knowledge includes, among other things, an understanding of human behavior and human feelings; an insight into nature's balances and relationships; an ability to create tools for survival; and methods or procedures for promoting growth and awareness in each generation of people—or *education.*

In "western civilization," the trend has been to separate knowledge from the sacred. Answers to the universal questions human beings ask are now searched for in the disciplines of science, psychology, and others that are part of western civilization's educational system. Such things as "feelings," mystical experience, and survival tools, are often left out of this education. This has come about for a number of reasons.

The societies that have dominated the world's smaller cultures and the world's natural resources for the past 200 years, have come to believe that: 1) Man can control the ways of the natural world. 2) Man can continue to exploit certain natural resources indefinitely. 3) All mysteries, all uncertainty—the unknown—can ultimately be conquered.

History has shown that only a few people have ever benefitted from this ideal and in fact many people suffer under this dominance. In societies of this kind survival means controlling all natural forces, including people by making them more *efficient* and *predictable.*

In traditional Native American communities survival means to *seek life.* Seeking life is a community matter. At the same time it can be intensely personal as the individual places his/herself in the midst of the Great Mysteries—the kiva initiate of the Pueblos; the young men fasting for a vision in the North Woods; the young girl running toward the sun at dawn of her first menstruation; the sun dancers moving back and forth from the center pole gazing into the glaring sun. The People do these things in order to be in touch with natural forces, in order to understand the forces of order, disorder, growth, and change.

Learning is unsettling, hard, funny, and different for different people. What you learn about the world though is that there are certain things that never change. These things also determine the way we live, like day and night, health and sickness, enough rain and not enough rain. If people deny that this is how the natural world is, that it has laws but it also has its mysteries, then we deny our own ability to change and grow. We deny viability, as we discussed in chapter one of this textbook.

Slowly, over the years, sacred ways, metaphysics, and nonordinary ways of learning have disappeared from daily life and the educational systems of western civilization. There are still people however, who believe this trend is ultimately dangerous and ultimately weakens the individual and the community. The exploration of Native American methods of learning sacred knowledge is one way of finding alternatives to Western dominance.

Aboriginally, basic education among Native Americans did not separate the search for knowledge from sacred learning or "religious" training. Native American sacred ways insisted on learning, on education, as an essential

Crow country; a man overlooking Black Canyon. Edward Curtis, 1905. (Courtesy of the Smithsonian Institution, National Anthropological Archives)

foundation for personal awareness. A knowledgeable human being was one who was sensitive to his/her surroundings. This sensitivity opened him/her to the Great Mysteries and to the possibility of mystical learning experiences, which were considered the only way to grasp certain intangible laws of the universe.

Learning the sacred ways of the tribe differs from community to community throughout North America. In some tribes, the Pueblos for instance, learning, for the young men in particular, may appear to be similar to the difficult, isolating often lonely training of a specialist.* The "kiva boys" of Taos for example—those young men who have reached the age where they can or must go deeper into the sacred ways and practices—study for a year in the kiva making trips to the mountains on special tasks; eating special food prepared

---

* See Chapter Five, **Shamans and The World of Spirits: The Oldest Religion.**
** See Chapter Nine, **Girls' Puberty Ceremonies,** and Chapter Eight, **The Path of Life.**

for them by their mother or another appointed woman; and not seeing anyone outside of the family except for their instructors. In other tribes a single initiation may mark the turning point in a young person's life.** After this ceremony the young man or woman is ready to receive further instruction into sacred teachings, various skills, or more personal advice. These initiations serve two purposes: to mark a point of physical growth in the individual; and to open his/her eyes to the depth and range of the Mysteries to which he/she is now exposed. Up until this time the young boy or girl is protected in playful ignorance from the power and responsibility of sacred knowledge and daily survival. Growing and initiation bring the individual—the young man or woman—into direct contact with power and responsibility.

NOT ASKING WHY

In almost all cases, learning the way for Native Americans in *classic* tribal times meant going directly to the source of the Mysteries.

The People voyaged with their entire bodies, with all their senses including language and thought, in order to find the answers to these questions, and to aid in their understanding of themselves and their world.

In order that knowledge did not get separated from experience, wisdom from divinity, the Elders stressed listening and waiting, *not asking why*. Luther Standing Bear recalls the education of Lakota children as he explains:

> Training began with children who were taught to sit still and enjoy it. They were taught to use their organs of smell, to look when there was apparently nothing to see, and to listen intently when all seemingly was quiet. A child that cannot sit still is a half-developed child. (Astrov, 1962: 39)

Larry Bird, a young Keres man, explains, "you don't ask questions when you grow up. You watch and listen and wait, and the answer will come to you. It's yours then, not like learning in school." (Tedlock, 1975: xxi) Soge Track, a young woman from Taos Pueblo says, about her learning:

Man at Taos Pueblo. Tod Powell, 1922. (Courtesy of the Smithsonian Institution, National Anthropological Archives)

All through this time I never asked of them (grandmother and grandfather) or anyone, "why?" It would have meant that I was learning nothing—that I was stupid. And in Western Society if you don't ask why they think you are stupid. So having been raised to not ask why but to listen, become aware, I take for granted that people have some knowledge of themselves and myself—that is religion. Then when we know ourselves we can put our feelings together and share this knowledge.

By not asking why, they are saying, *you might have the experience of directly confronting and learning from the Great powers of the Mysteries.* Religion and the sacred include the range of experiences we could call "non-ordinary." Learning that there is more to life than just meets the eye is a large part of *learning the way.* Orulo, a knowledgeable story teller of the Iglulik Eskimo people, describes the difference between learning sacred knowledge and the pursuit of knowledge that ignores the *intangible* experiences of human beings:

> Too much thought only leads to trouble. We Eskimos do not concern ourselves with solving all riddles. We repeat the old stories in the way they were told to us, and with the words we ourselves remember. And if there should then seem to be a lack of reason in the story as a whole, there is yet enough remaining in the way of incomprehensible happenings, which our thought cannot grasp. If it were but everyday ordinary things there would be nothing to believe in. (Rasmussen, 1930, Vol. 7 No. 2:69)

Another example of this difference in learning comes from a confrontation between the anthropologist Knud Rasmussen from Denmark and Aua, an Iglulik shaman and a man of knowledge. Rasmussen recalls this experience from the days when he was living among the Baffin Bay area Eskimo people consulting Aua on Iglulik philosophy, religion, customs, and other ways of life. He tells us:

I once went out to Aua's hunting quarters on the ice outside Lyon Inlet to spend some time with the men. For several evenings we had discussed rules of life and taboo customs without getting beyond a long and circumstantial statement of all that was permitted and all that was forbidden. Everyone knew precisely what had to be done in any given situation, but whenever I put in my query: "Why?" they could give no answers. They regarded it, and very rightly, as unreasonable that I should require not only an account, but also a justification of their religions principles.

Aua had as usual been the spokesman, and as he was still unable to answer my questions, he rose to his feet, and as if seized by a sudden impulse, invited me to go outside with him. It had been an unusually rough day, and as we had plenty of meat after the successful hunting of the past few days, I had asked my host to stay at home so that we could get some work done together. The brief daylight had given place to the half light of the afternoon, but as the moon was up, one could still see some distance. Ragged white clouds raced across the sky, and when a gust of wind came tearing over the ground, our eyes and mouths were filled with snow. Aua looked me full in the face, and pointing out over the ice, where the snow was being lashed about in waves by the wind, he said: "In order to hunt well and live happily, man must have calm weather. Why this constant succession of blizzards and all this needless hardship for men seeking food for themselves and those they care for? Why? Why?"

We had come out just at the time when the men were returning from their watching at the blowholes* on the ice; they came in little groups, bowed forward, toiling along against the wind, which actually forced them now and

again to stop, so fierce were the gusts. Not one of them had a seal in tow; their whole day of painful effort and endurance had been in vain.

I could give no answer to Aua's "Why?" but shook my head in silence. He then led me to Kublo's house, which was close beside our own. The small blubber lamp burned with but the faintest flame, giving out no heat whatever; a couple of children crouched, shivering, under a skin rug on the bench.

Aua looked at me again, and said: "Why should it be cold and comfortless in here? Kublo has been out hunting all day, and if he had got a seal, as he deserved, his wife would now be sitting laughing beside her lamp, letting it burn full, without fear of having no blubber left for tomorrow. The place would be warm and bright and cheerful, the children would come out from under their rugs and enjoy life. Why should it not be so? Why?" I made no answer, and he led me out of the house, into a little snow hut where his sister, Natseq, lived all by herself because she was ill. She looked thin and worn, and was not even interested in our coming. For several days she had suffered from a malignant cough that seemed to come from far down in the lungs, and it looked as if she had not long to live.

A third time Aua looked at me and said: "Why must people be ill and suffer pain? We are all afraid of illness. Here is this old sister of mine; as far as anyone can see, she has done no evil: she has lived through a long life and given birth to healthy children, and now she must suffer before her days end. Why? Why?"

This ended his demonstration, and we returned to our house, to resume, with the others, the interrupted discussion. *"You see"* said Aua, *"You are equally unable to give any reason when we ask you why life is as it is. And so it must be. All our customs come from life and turn towards life; we explain nothing, we believe nothing, but in what I have just shown you lies answer to all you ask. We fear the weather spirit of earth, that we must fight against to wrest our food from*

---

* Blowholes are holes in the ice the seals make where they can stick their heads out to breathe every now and then. In the winter, since the water where they swim and fish is completely covered with ice, the hunters wait at at the blowholes, hoping to spear or shoot the seal when it comes up. See Chapter Five.

land and sea. We fear Sila. We fear death and hunger in the cold snow huts. We fear Takanakapsaluk, the great woman down at the bottom of the sea, that rules over all the beasts of the sea. We fear the sickness that we meet with daily all around us: not death, but the suffering. We fear the evil spirits of life, those of the air, of the sea and the earth, that can help wicked shamans to harm their fellow men.

We fear the souls of dead human beings and of the animals we have killed. *Therefore it is that our fathers have inherited from their fathers all the old rules of life, which are based on the experience and wisdom of generations. We do not know how, we cannot say why, but we keep those rules in order that we may live untroubled.* And so ignorant are we in spite of all our shamans that we fear everything unfamiliar. We fear what we see about us, and we fear all the invisible things that are likewise about us, all that we have heard of in our forefathers' stories and myths. *Therefore, we have our customs, which are not the same as those of the white men, the white men who live in another land and have need of other ways.*" (Rasmussen, 1930, Vol. 7 No. 2:54-56)

Aua recognizes that different societies have different ways. One of the differences between the "white man's ways" and the way of learning Aua describes is that much of the dominant society's world is "man made." It is a highly technological world, invented in the form of machines, labor-saving devices, and urban systems of living. In this kind of world you learn to ask why because these inventions *do* have an origin that can be explained. But the traditional mysteries which include hunger, pain, sickness, and death, cannot be *explained.* They can only be witnessed and then dealt with through a system of knowledge and practices that let the natural world teach human society its complex, and often mysterious, ways. The natural world, as Aua has shown, determines how we live, how we will act. In turn—education or learning determines how we will use the

natural world to our benefit and how we can live harmoniously or in balance with it.

SOME WAYS OF LEARNING SACRED KNOWLEDGE

As we discussed earlier there are both general and specific types of learning about sacred ways and practices. At a certain age for instance, people in the community agree that an individual is ready to learn about more complex and sacred parts of life. Before the individual might not have been able to understand completely. Another way of looking at it however, is that training in sacred ways begins at the moment of birth, since the sacred is a part of everyday life. The way people act toward one another within the family and among kin is religious training. The way a person conducts him/herself in different situations is part of learning the way. We are told, for example that when Standing Bear "as a boy of about five killed his first bird, his father celebrated the event by giving away a horse to someone else, an old man who could never return the gift." "This was the beginning of my religious training," remarks Standing Bear. (Lee, 1959: 62)

Anishnabe man with boy drying wild rice on birch bark mat, ca. 1940. (Courtesy of the Minnesota Historical Society)

53

There are often specific people who are made responsible for the sacred training of children. In most cases the uncle, aunt, and the grandparents establish this kind of relationship with the children. Relatives, like uncles, often take the responsibility for disciplining the children of their sisters. This leaves the parents free to provide a warm, loving relationship with their children.

In other cases the extended family of kin and relatives are all "teachers", each member of the family giving something of his/her knowledge to the growing child. Since each kin member has different skills and different experiences this allows a child to come in contact with many ideas and skills without ever having to leave the community. For example, Mayer Hobson of the North Slope Borough in Alaska described traditional education of the Inupiaq People:

We Inupiaq are a nation of people occupying the circumpolar Arctic from Siberia through Alaska and Canada to Greenland. We share common values, language culture and economic system. Our culture has enabled us to survive and flourish for thousands of years in the Arctic where no other man or culture could. For thousands of years, our traditional method of socializing our youth was the responsibility of the family and community. From the first, visitors to the Arctic have universally commented on the warm disposition of our children. Corporal punishment was absolutely unknown. Boys and girls began their education with their parents and, by the time they reached their teenage years, they had mastered the skills necessary to survive on the land here. From that time forward, the youth with his family and within his community devoted his attention to his intellectual and social growth. (Tundra Times, 1976, Vol. 14, NO. 3: 1-2)

Traditionally among the Navajo, children were supposed to rise before dawn and run towards the East. In the winter, upon their return to the Hogan, they would roll in the snow. Tom Ration relates the origin of this custom and says:

It is told that they (Talking God and Hogan God) or (Calling God) were people of the dawn. It is told they came at the break of dawn with all the valued possessions. This is why we are told to rise with the dawn to meet these gods, so they can present us with worthy goods. Our parents would say to us, "Arise, wake up. What are you sleeping for? Take the ashes out. Clean around outside, we do not want trash around the hogan!" This is done so the Dawn People do not see all the trash. They will know they are welcomed to this place. "There is no wealth here, lets go in and give them some," they will say (by wealth they meant trash). Where the place is dirty and trashy, they will ignore the place and say, "too much wealth here, lets go to another place . . ."

This custom, combined with the origin history or story of it, taught children a number of important concepts and practices. The child is introduced to two important historical figures: Talking God and Hogan God (or Calling God). The child is taught to understand that an early riser opens him/herself to wealth and power. And the child is taught that respect for the surrounding environment is necessary for a good life.

As in the case of many origin histories and stories, Talking God and Calling God embody or represent sacred concepts and qualities that a child learns to recognize and admire as he/she grows older.

Soge Track recalls one of the ways in which she learned from her grandfather and grandmother at Taos Pueblo:

When I was young, my grandfather and I, almost every evening we would sit on the west side of the summer house and watch the sun set or we would sit on the east side and watch the colors cover the mountains. My grandmother would join us. Then they would tell me about the mountain, about evening sounds, my grandfather would sing a particular song and tell me "remember it." I would try. Sometimes I would ask my grandmother to help me remember. She would only tell me that that was between my grandfather and me. She would not interfere and it

Older man helping prepare younger man for ceremony, Blackfeet. (Courtesy of the Museum of the American Indian, Heye Foundation)

was the same with what my grandmother was teaching—my grandfather did not interfere. And these things they were advising me, their thoughts were the same.

Alex Saluskin, a Yakima man, explains how among his people a young person would be assigned to a tutor—an expert to be his/her teacher. These tutors were responsible for preparing a young man for his "vision quest" or spirit quest as Alex Saluskin refers to it. He tells us:

In our tribal custom, which was handed down to my grandfather...each of his children were assigned to a tutor, like he had been by his grandparents, so

that each child, each of his descendents should be trained by an expert...it was not a parent that was undertaking the teaching of the young boy or girl, it was an elder related either to grandpa, or grandma... These experts were proficient in hunting and everything for survival, as well as teaching the blessing of the Great Creator. I was assigned to my uncle... So he and his wife had undertaken to bring me under their wing for a season... (Morey, 1970: 11, 43)

He goes on to tell a story of a specific event in his early educational experience:

My grandfather came and asked my father if I would make a trip with them to the mountains where they hunt for deer, as well as mountain sheep, and gather huckleberries. They caught salmon from the spawning beds there and dried them for their provisions while they were staying in the mountains. Naturally, they depended for their livelihood on what they could catch and kill, as well as catch small fish from the streams.

When we began, first I was to learn how to control my horse, which was given to me with a complete outfit, as well as a gun. Then we came to the first camp. Early in the morning my uncle started to assume his responsibilities, got me out of bed, and he says, "Nephew, let's hurry down to the creek. It's my duty now to train you, to equip you with the wisdom and knowledge that I had acquired. First of all, we're going to go down to this swift stream and we're going to plunge in that stream and we will disturb the old lady." (We referred to the stream as an old lady.) "We'll disturb her and the old lady will rub you down and soothe up your sore muscles and give you an endurance for the rest of the day." I knew I had to do the things that I was told. We went down and we stripped off and jumped into this swift water, very cold, we stayed in the water until my body was numb. We came up and pranced around, jumped up and down to

get our circulation going. We put on our clothes and by the time we got back to the camp, the breakfast was ready.

Again, we were taught how to care for the horses and how to handle them. As we traveled, the same processes were conducted until we reached our destination. As soon as we reached our destination, I was told that the sweat house and the hot rocks which were prepared for the sweat house were blessings taught and handed down from the Great Spirit. This hot steam caused by pouring cold water on the rocks would cleanse you and purify your scent, so the wild animals wouldn't detect you. You would have the scent the same as the fir bough and reeds that grow in the mountains. So naturally I had to believe that this was the case. I followed through this system and we had to do this every morning about three o'clock while we were in the mountains. At the end of our trip, I was wiry; I could walk, probably for days and weeks if I had to. I had gone through my course of training for survival. I learned every herb, root, berries and how to take care of them. This kind uncle of mine and his wife took time to explain these things step by step. They didn't leave one thing untold and it was shown physically to me, then asked me if I could do it. (Morey, 1970: 43-45)

Acoma man and boy, ca. 1910. (Courtesy of the Museum of the American Indian, Heye Foundation)

Training like this was in preparation for the spirit quest. Saluskin discusses the significance of the quest and says that not only is it one of the most important events in the person's life who undertakes it, it is also a preparation for teaching and being someone else's tutor later on in life. So we see that this educational process of learning sacred ways involves not only many relatives of different ages, but future generations as well. Saluskin goes on to explain:

The children were taken from their parents after they became about six-seven-eight, up to thirteen years old. They were sent out for a spirit quest. They looked for the power in the wilderness and fasted for a minimum of three days and nights and a maximum of five days and nights. During the hardship, fighting for survival out in the wilderness, without anything to eat, no tools to gain energy, competing with wild animals and dark cold nights, the little fellows got down and prayed, asked the Great Spirit to help them to survive the ordeal. During the course of the training, some of these people were blessed and they carried the blessing on and handed it down to their children, and also later on they would become tutors to teach the same thing that the Indian must follow. (Morey, 1970: 11, 43)

Sometimes teaching was done during ritual ceremonies, and the teaching was given in the form of lectures or speeches designed to make an instant impression on the young man or woman being lectured. An example of such lectures comes to us from the Luiseño people of southern California. It was the traditional custom for an elder to address the boys being initiated into manhood as they gathered around a Sand Painting made for this occasion, at the conclusion of the ceremony. The student will note that, once again, the initiate is reminded that this knowledge he is learning is for him to pass on to his "sons and daughters." In other words, part of the reason for learning is to be able to pass on wisdom and knowledge to future generations so that they too will remain aware of the world around them and maintain their sacred ways.

Parts of the Luiseño boys lecture went like this:

See these, these are alive. This is bear-mountain lion; these are going to catch you if you are not good and do not respect your elder relatives and grown-up people. And, if you do not believe, these are going to kill you; but if you do believe, everybody is going to see your goodness and you then will kill bear-mountain lion. And, you will gain fame and be praised, and your name will be heard everywhere.

See this, this is the raven, who will shoot you with his bow and arrow if you do not put out your winnowing basket. Listen—do not be a liar, do not be heedless, do not eat food of overnight (i.e. do not eat secretly food left after the last meal of the day). Also, you will not get angry when you eat, nor must you be angry with your elder relatives.

The earth hears you, the sky and wood mountain see you. If you will believe this, you will grow old. And, you will see your sons and daughters, and you will counsel them in this manner, when you reach your old age. And, if when hunting you should kill a rabbit or a deer, and an old man should ask you for it, you will hand it to him at once. Do not be angry when you give it, and do not throw it to him. And, when he goes home he will praise you, and you will kill many, and you will be able to shoot straight with the bow.

And, when you die your spirit will rise to the sky and people will blow three times and make your spirit rise. And, everywhere it will be heard that you have died. And, you will drink bitter medicine, and will vomit, and your insides will be clean, and illness will pass you by, and you will grow old, if you heed this speech. This is what the people of long ago use to talk, that they used to counsel their sons and daughters. In this manner you will counsel your sons and daughters.

...Heed this speech and you will never grow old. And, they will say of you; he grew old because he heeded what he was told. And, when you die you will be spoken of as those of the sky, like the stars. Those it is said were [once] people, who went to the sky and escaped death. And, like those will rise your soul. (Kroeber, 1972: 684)

A similar kind of lecture was given to the girls at the time of their pubetry ceremony. Parts of that lecture were spoken as follows:

See, these are alive; these will think well of you if you believe; and if you do not believe these are going to kill you. If you are heedless, a dissembler, or stingy [they will kill you]. You must not look sideways, must not receive a person in your house with anger; it is not proper. You will drink hot water when you menstruate; and when you are pregnant you will drink bitter medicine.

This will cause you to have your children quickly, as your inside will be clean. And you will roast* yourself at the fire (after childbirth) and then your own son or daughter will grow up quickly, and sickness will not approach you. But, if you are heedless you will not bear your child quickly, and people will speak of your heedlessness.

Your elder relatives you must think well of; you will also welcome your daughters-in-law and your brothers-in-law when they arrive at your house. Pay heed to this speech, and at some future time you will go to their house, and they are going to welcome you politely at their house...

See these old men and women; these are those who paid attention to this counsel, which is of the grownup people, and they have already reached old age. Do not forget this that I am telling you; pay heed to this speech, and when you are old like these old people, you will counsel your sons and daughters in like manner, and you will grow old. And, your spirit will rise northwards to the sky, like the stars... (Kroeber, 1972: 685)

Of course, all of these examples do not exhaust the many different ways in which The People would teach their children sacred ways and practices. As we have seen, sometimes

teachings were presented formally, sometimes secretly, by specific individuals given this responsibility. Other times teaching was informal; in any situation during the day or night anyone might say something or point something out to a child which would become important later on in his/her life, or which would introduce the child to the guiding vision of his/her People. Learning was both a practical, physical experience for the child and an abstract or conceptual one. In the following section we shall discuss in more detail the role of stories and storytelling in the education of children.

ORAL TRADITION AND STORYTELLING

Traditionally among Native Americans the oral tradition of a tribe was its most important vehicle for teaching and passing on the sacred knowledge and practices of The People. Since there were no books, libraries, movies, film strips, tape recorders, radios, and televisions, the human voice, hand movements, and facial expressions had to serve as "mass media." They worked very well. The human memory is a great storehouse which we ordinarily fill with only a fraction of its capacity. The elders knew this and tested and trained the memory along with the other senses, so that the history and traditions of the People could be preserved and passed on. All societies want stability as well as viability for their community, just as each individual wants a long life. Oral tradition was one of the principal means The People had to maintain stability over the years in the tribal community. And traditionally, aside from some *pictographs* (rock paintings), hide paintings, or birchbark scrolls, oral tradition was the *only* means of maintaining the sacred ways and customs of the tribe.

One of the most important of the oral traditions was storytelling and the preservation of the origin histories. In these histories we are told where, as the People, we came from, how the stars were created, where we discovered fire, how light became divided from darkness, and how death originated. It is through these stories too that we are given the basic tools and ways of knowledge with which to survive in the world: healing ceremonies, prayers, dances, games, herbs, and models of behavior. The Lakota man, Luther Standing Bear told of the importance of stories to his people when he said:

---

* See Chapter Nine, **Girls' Puberty Ceremonies**—"roast" means to take a sweat bath.

Anishnabe woman reading and interpreting birch bark scroll, Minnesota, 1936. (Courtesy of the Minnesota Historical Society)

These stories were the libraries of our people. In each story, there was recorded some event of interest or importance, some happening that affected the lives of the people. There were calamities, discoveries, achievements, and victories to be kept. The seasons and the years were named for principal events that took place. There was the year of the "moving" stars" when these bright bodies left their places in the sky and seemed to fall to earth or vanished altogether; the year of the great prairie fire when the buffalo became scarce; and the year that Long Hair (Custer) was killed. But not all our stories were historical. Some taught the virtues—kindness, obedience, thrift, and the rewards of right living. Then there were stories of pure fancy in which I can

see no meaning. Maybe they are so old that their meaning has been lost in the countless years, for our people are old. But even so, a people enrich their minds who keep their history on the leaves of memory. Countless leaves in countless books have robbed a people of both history and memory. (Standing Bear, 1933: 27)

And Gerald Vizenor, in his introduction to a collection of Anishnabe stories, *Anishnabe Adisokan* tells us that among his people stories were told "during the long winter nights in the woodland when (the People) were sure *manabozho* (the compassionate trickster) was not listening in the face of an animal or flower." He goes on to say that "The tales of the Anishnabe are not an objective collection and interpretation of facts. Stories are a circle of dreams and oratorical gestures showing the meaning between the present and the past in the life of tribal people of the woodland." (Vizenor, 1970: 9-10)

A child's first memories and first learning experiences probably took place around a fire, during the winter, and in some tribes, during the other seasons as well. In the winter there was less outdoor activity, most of the family members were gathered together, and there was more of a silence surrounding the lodge, hogan, shelter, or house, in which to listen and dream. Standing Bear recalls:

> Lakota children, like all others, asked questions and were answered to the best ability of our elders. We wondered, as do all young, inquisitive minds, about the stars, moon, sky, rainbow, darkness, and all other phenomena of nature. I can recall lying on the earth and wondering what it was all about. The stars were a beautiful mystery and so was the place where the eagle went when he soared out of sight. Many of these questions were answered in story form by the older people. How we got our pipestone, where corn came from and why lightning flashed in the sky, were all answered in stories. (Standing Bear, 1933: 26)

The whole situation, the atmosphere around the fire, was dramatic—different from ordinary things like daily conversation and instruction. Maria Chona, a Papago woman explains how a child learned among her people;

> My father went on talking to me in a low voice. This is how our people always talk to their children, so low and quiet, the child thinks he is dreaming. But he never forgets. (Underhill, 1936:5)

Storytelling—the ability to tell a story, and a knowledge of stories—was and still is, one of the most admired skills an individual can have. It is a universal practice among Native American people to teach a wide variety of skills and ways of knowledge through storytelling. Persons who have this knowledge and can communicate it are specialists, as important to the People as medicine people. Tom Ration, the Navajo Silversmith, Medicine man ("singer") and storyteller, explains, "An Elder who tells stories usually prepares himself for at least two or three days and nights. This is how long it takes to tell the whole legend with the songs. These stories we value with our lives."

A good storyteller is able to communicate the universality and the timelessness of certain themes we know never change. And it follows that certain themes are employed by all storytellers because they are so universal— stories about tricky-intelligent creatures like Coyote; stories about gambling or near-escapes with death; creation stories, or stories explaining the origin of things; and love stories.

Storytelling is a very flexible method of education in the ways of sacred knowledge since the traditional forms—style, delivery, tone, and words—can be employed not only with traditional content and traditional symbols but with modern themes and content as well. For example, John Rogers, an Anishnabe man, in his autobiography, *Red World and White*, tells us about an event that happened when he was a boy. He recalls that on hunting expeditions which sometimes lasted for weeks, a storyteller would be appointed each morning; he would then have the day to prepare his stories. Rogers says that by the end of his first hunting expedition his uncle and companions felt he was ready to be able to tell a story too and so after telling of an experience his mother had had with a timber wolf he began a second story, "There was a little girl called Little Red Riding Hood"... and went on to tell that story which he had learned in boarding school the winter before. At the conclusion of the story he tells us:

> That was the story as I remember it. I knew that I had left out a lot, but my listeners thought it was good. They loved to hear stories of animals, and especially wolves. (Rogers, 1974: 125)

These teaching stories *do not just tell about physical facts with ordinary events and plots. They also teach abstract notions of behavior, cosmology, and ways of seeing or thinking about things. Sometimes the story you hear is like a code which, the more you listen to it over the years, the more it reveals.* Sometimes, if you are a specialist and the stories you know concern your special skills, you might

Navajo elder and boy. A. C. Vroman. (Courtesy of the Southwest Museum)

understand the code better than one who has not been initiated into such knowledge so deeply.

This "coding" of knowledge in stories is like not asking "why", because you have to listen more closely. Then you also have more of a chance to suddenly discover meanings, concepts, and ideas by yourself. As Larry Bird said earlier, what you learn means more to you that way. The "coding" has another advantage, the stories appeal to more people. For instance, many of the teaching stories are very funny sometimes. The humor might be "light", on one level of telling the story, for children; a little heavier, perhaps with sexual references that older children would understand. And for adults, the storyteller might add tricks of language and references to a wider range of knowledge and perhaps other sources of humor.

A way of imagining this concept of "coding" in stories is through a remark that a Navajo *hataatli* (singer or medicine man) made about the Red Ant Ceremony, one of the Navajo curing ceremonies or *sings*. A non-Navajo had a ceremony performed as part of the treatment for red ants in the system, an illness like

pneumonia which he said he had "no doubt picked up by urinating on an ant hill." Some time after the successful treatment, he asked the *hataatli* if he had really had ants in his system. The singer answered, "No, not ants, but ANTS". He went on to explain what he meant by saying, "We have to have a way of *thinking* strongly about disease."

The same thing is often true about stories, legends, and *myths* as teaching devices for sacred ways. Events that happen, creatures that are encountered, characters that appear, may be *symbolic* of something besides just what they appear to be or do. The following example of the many *dimensions* of teaching and learning that go on in these stories comes to us from the Navajo. The example concerns the Navajo man, Little Wagon, who was a good storyteller, and his family when they lived in Montezuma Canyon near Aneth, Utah. The person telling us about the particular event begins:

During a rather [hard winter], we spent most evenings sitting around the fire in Little Wagon's large hogan listening to the old man tell tales, legends, and

61

miscellaneous [stories]. A small family passing by on horseback had stopped for the night, according to the usual custom. Outside it had begun to snow lightly, and one of the traveler's children asked where snow came from. Little Wagon, in answer, began a long and involved story about an ancestor who had found a piece of beautiful burning material, had guarded it carefully for several months until some spirits (ye'i) came to claim it, and had asked then that the spirits allow him to [keep] a piece of it. This they would not allow but would see what they could do for him. In the meantime he was to perform a number of complicated and dedicated tasks to test his endurance. Finally, the spirits told him that in [reward for] his fine behavior they would throw all the ashes from their own fireplace down into Montezuma Canyon each year when they cleaned house. Sometimes they fail to keep their word, and sometimes they throw down too much; but in all, they turn their attention toward us regularly, here in Montezuma Canyon. When this long story had been completed there was a respectful silence for a moment, and then the young questioner put in: "It snows in Blanding, too. Why is that?" "I don't know," the old man replied immediately, "You'll have to make up your own story for that"...

Little Wagon commented after the travelers' departure that it was too bad the boy did not understand stories. I found that...he (Little Wagon) did not consider it a [story about origins or causes], and did not in any way believe that was the way snow originated; rather, if the story was "about" anything it was about moral values, about the [behavior] of a young [hero] whose actions showed a properly [balanced] relationship between himself and nature. In short, by seeing the story in terms of any

categories...our young visitor [had missed the point], a fact which Little Wagon at once attributed to the deadly influences of white schooling (Tolkein, 1969: 213)

This explanation holds true for stories about Coyote, Iktomi, Manabozho, the Seminole "Rabbit," and other intelligent tricksters that are the main characters in stories through North America.* At first we think of these stories as "funny stories" and of course on some levels they are, they are told partly for entertainment. The sacred aspect of these stories can be seen however, when they are told during ceremonies, in myth recitations, and chant explanations.** When asked, for example, why if Coyote was such an important mythical character (whose name cannot even be mentioned in the summer months) were such funny stories told about him, Yellowman, son of Little Wagon, answered, "they are not funny stories...They are laughing at the way Ma'i (coyote) does things, and at the way the story is told. Many things about the story are funny, but the story is not funny. If my children hear the stories, they will grow up to be good people; if they don't hear them, they will turn out to be bad...If Coyote did not do all those things, then those things would not be possible in the world." In other words, the author explains:

In one story, Coyote loses his eyes in a gambling match or gets them caught on a tree branch during a game, he replaces them with amber pitch balls, and the story ends by explaining "That's how Ma'i got his yellow eyes." But I exasperated Yellowman on one occasion by [asking] how coyotes could actually see if their eyes were made of amber balls. It turned out just as it had with Little Wagon's snow story: the essence of the tale was not on the surface at all. Yellowman explained...that the tale allows us to envision the possibility of such things as eye disease, injury, or blindness; it has nothing to do with coyotes in general; and Ma'i, himself, may or may not have amber eyes, but since he can do anything he wants to, the question is irrelevant— he has eyes and he sees, period. (Tolkein, 1969: 222)

---

* Throughout the world similar kinds of stories are told about trickster animals; for example, among the Mixe in Oaxaca, Mexico, he is an Opossum; in France, a fox; among the Zande in West Africa, a spider.
** See, for example, O'Bryan, Aileen, **The Dine: Origin Myths of the Navajo Indians**, BBAE 163.

Nampeyo, Hopi, decorating pottery. Edward Curtis, 1900. (Courtesy of the Smithsonian Institution, National Anthropological Archives)

Creative works by individuals have always been valued highly among Native American people. One of the reasons people take pride in their songs, their poetry, their bead work, their designs, and the portrayal of their visions, is because each of these works requires a fine use of the imagination. When Yellowman says that the stories are important because they allow us to envision the possibility of things not ordinarily seen or experienced, he means too that we have the ability to use our imagination—the intangible part of our thinking mind. This ability to seek for possibilities beyond the ordinary is at the root of Learning the Way. For this reason storytelling and stories are an essential part of The People's lives.

KNOWLEDGE AND RESPONSIBILITY

The People often make distinctions between learning or becoming knowledgeable, and knowing too much or being exposed to knowledge when one is not yet ready. Knowledge about one's sacred ways, about morals and ethics, and about the boundaries of one's world, are taught to the child by those who know when to teach him or her. These persons are given this responsibility through custom or dreams. After a certain point in one's life, most often puberty, one is expected to know a great deal more than one did when one was a child. One is now prepared to compare one's experience in the world with the stories one has heard. One has the opportunity to use prayers and songs for one's own needs or the needs of one's family and community. One is now a part of the ceremonial life of the tribe, with a deeper knowledge of the world of which the tribe is a part.

Most of the initiation ceremonies that are arranged at this point in a young man or woman's life teach the individual about *responsibility*. We heard the Luiseño elder lecture the young men and women about certain of their future responsibilities. At the same time the entire growing up of the child has been a learning experience, a lesson in responsibility. In the end, you are alone—that is, you have to make decisions for yourself, decisions that will effect the community and the natural world. Therefore, *personal awareness* is at the heart of responsibility: to be aware of what is going on around you and what life holds in store for you—all of life's possibilities throughout your life to Old Age. Alex Saluskin who told us of some of the events in his education, puts it this way. He says:

I'm not going to be influenced, or no one is going to influence my soul, unless

I'm the one who's going to. I'm the only one who's responsible for that soul, if I don't do the right thing here, I'm at fault, not him, not the church, not that mountain over there or the sun. This is the way they teach Indian religion. No one is going to influence you, no one is going to bring you up to your grave, but yourself. (Morey, 1970: 27)

Those who become specialists in certain categories of knowledge then have a special role in carrying on the knowledge of sacred ways for future generations. In some cases, this is a privilege handed down from father to son, especially in tribes where aboriginally, the accumulation of wealth and *aristocracy* were important. Sometimes specializing in one thing or another stays in a family from one generation to the next. Children pick up the knowledge from their parents, who themselves are specialists. We will be discussing in Chapter Five, **Shamans and the World of Spirits: The Oldest Religion**, cases where individuals *seek* knowledge—knowledge which goes beyond the ordinary. These individuals, as is often the case, have a special calling for this particular journey. They in turn, may take this added responsibility and use it to teach by example, their tribal sacred ways. Tom Ration sums up this final point when he says, "We who have the knowledge of various ceremonies give our services to the people who need us..."

SUMMARY

In this chapter we first briefly compared the differences between traditional education in Native American communities and education as it is being defined in today's modern world. Noting the differences we then suggested that, in accordance with the guiding vision of many tribal cosmologies and ways of seeing the world, tribal people chose to teach and educate their children in a particular way. These teaching methods enabled a person to both seek answers within him/herself, through tests of physical survival, as well as through conventional teaching methods that we might see today in a classroom situation. Since it was felt that sacred knowledge could not be separated from the knowledge needed for daily living, learning sacred ways was felt to be a necessary and natural preparation for life.

Among the various methods of *learning the way* we discussed were kiva initiations, lectures, vision quests, survival training, and listening, waiting, and remembering. Some individuals discussed the problem of asking "why" in relation to the kind of learning we have been talking about. And, among the various educational tools we examined, was storytelling. We observed how stories, legends, and myths have many *dimensions* of meaning to them, making them a very important teaching instrument, especially in the days before T.V.

Nowadays, people are finding that they have

Simon Ortiz, poet, writer and storyteller from Acoma Pueblo, reading from his writings in a college classroom, 1974.

to ask "why" about some phenomena of the world which seem alien, different, and often frightening. One of the creative challenges to the Native American teaching of sacred ways is to examine elements of the modern world that threaten a person's ability to *seek* life—to seek long life. After examining new philosophies, modern disciplines, and ways the world is being exploited of its resources, methods of dealing with such foreign ways can be incorporated into basic traditional foundations of teaching and learning.

Since the basic elements which make up human nature and the natural world do not change or have not changed very much since human beings found themselves in this world, basic knowledge and learning can remain unchanged. The ways people relate to one another and behave toward one another are as important today as they were in classic tribal times. Consequently even the teaching stories remain viable in today's world. Many people say that where they have been taught strong principles in the traditional way and had even a glimpse of their tribe's guiding sacred vision, they are better able to cope with and live well in today's changing world.

Suggested Additional Readings

MARRIOTT, ALICE, and RACHILIN, CAROL K.
1975   *Plains Indian Mythology*, New York, Thomas Crowell Co.

MASSON, MARCELLE
1966   *A Bag of Bones: Legends of the Wintu Indians of Northern California*, Naturegraph Press. (Told by a Wintu Indian, reveals aspects of the Wintu view of the universe and their relationship to it through legends.)

Montana Reading Publications, 225 Stapleton Building, Billings, Montana (An excellent general source of materials for elementary, high school, and college level material written by Native Peoples.)

1972   *Nu Mee Poom Tit Wah Tit (Nez Perce Legends)*, Nez Perce Tribe of Idaho, Lapwai, Idaho.

NEWCOMB, FRANC JOHNSON
1970   *Navajo Bird Tales*, told by Hosteen Clah Chee, Wheaton, Ill., Theosophical Publishing House.

ROESSEL, ROBERT (ed)
1974   *Grandfather Stories of the Navajos*, Navajo Curriculum Center, Rough Rock Demonstration School, Rough Rock, Arizona.

WHITEFORD, A.H., et al.
1972   *American Indian Art: Form and Tradition*, Minneapolis, Minn., Walker Art Center. (Color reproductions of masks, ornaments, carvings, etc. of Native Peoples, with an introduction by Gerald Vizenor, Anishnabe.)

YAKIMA TRIBE
1974   *The Way It Was (Anaku Iwacha): Yakima Legends*, Corsortium of Johnson O'Malley Committees of Region IV, State of Washington, Virginia Beavert, Project Director, Yakima Tribe.

CHAPTER FOUR

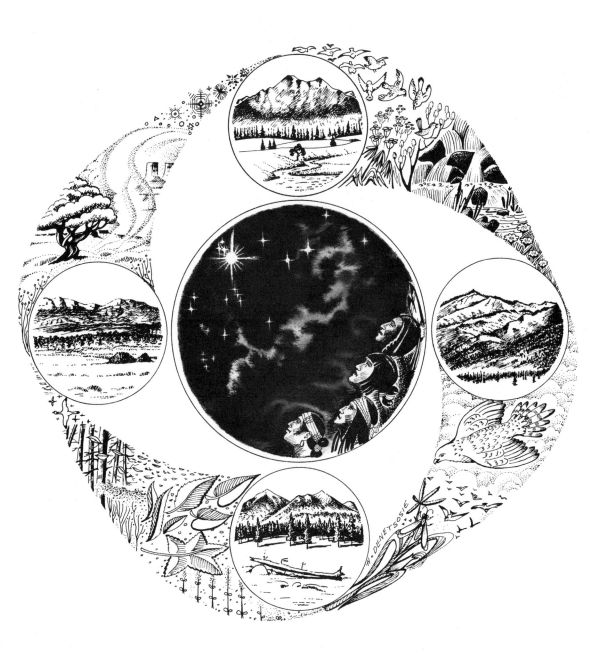

4 The Boundaries of the World: Seasons, Origins, and Other Worlds

My son, the ancient No-ho-zhi-ga have handed down to us in songs, wi-gi-e, ceremonial forms, symbols, and many things they learned of the mysteries that surround us on all sides. All these things they learned through their power of wa-thi-gtho-he, power to search with the mind! They speak of the mysteries of the light of day by which the earth and all living things that dwell thereon are influenced; of the mysteries of the darkness of night that reveals to us all the great bodies of the upper world, each of which forever travels in a circle upon its own path, unimpeded by the others. They searched for a long period of time, for the source of life and at last came to the thought that it issues from an invisible creative power to which they applied the name Wa-ko-da. (Playful Calf, Osage in: Armstrong, 1971:32)

GEOGRAPHICAL AND SACRED BOUNDARIES

As we describe geographical and sacred boundaries of a people's world in this section, it should become apparent that we are dealing with more than land. We will be discussing the natural world that all people have observed and have experienced. We will also describe how the natural environment was perceived by native people; functionally, spiritually, and symbolically. This natural environment or world has often been described with the word "nature" by native people. We will also attempt to show that it is through these kinds of perceptions that the natural world becomes symbolically valuable. That is, when its real and abstract significance is grasped or realized. Traditionally, sacred ties or relationships of native people to this natural world were deliberately and carefully maintained.

In this chapter we will be dealing with aspects of natural environment. We will briefly describe or map some land areas and locations of native people. We will discuss *"Symbolism"* and "sacred" or "holy" places. We will give examples of geographical concepts, descrip-

tions of origins held by some tribes, along with their conceptions and ways of recording time. We will also describe some physical and spiritual journeys people undertake out of necessity, into other worlds beyond the boundaries of everyday knowledge, everyday living and everyday experience.

Later on in the chapter we will give evidence of the practical or functional knowledge native people possessed of the skies and weather; *and* how they applied this knowledge to their everyday living experience and in the ceremonial side of life. One example of how this knowledge was combined and utilized is explained in the section on calendar-types of native North American people.

The objective of this chapter is to show simply how aspects of natural environment were perceived by native people *and* to show how the people put it all together (their perceptions of each) to form their own unique way of seeing the world and living in it. Yet even native people differ in their perceptions of the world and do not see the world in the same light as their neighbors.

Most tribes live within fairly circumscribed

areas. Oral tradition tells of the origins of things, places, and the people. Described in the oral tradition of a tribe are geographical areas and defined boundaries, terrestrial and supernatural.

This access (oral tradition) to a geographical area gives The People an accountable origin of arrival. Knowing it a tribe of people maintain a "sense of place" and certain rights to that place or territory. In 1915, Chief Weininock, a Yakima, was defending his People's right to their territory or homeland. He talked about those "rights" from the perspective of his tribe's oral tradition. His tribe eventually succeeded in winning support through the courts.

> When we were created, we were given our ground to live on and *from this time these were our rights*. This is all true...these were our rights as far as my memory to my grandfather... (McLuhan, 1971:10)

Though the terrain within these tribal boundaries varied, most tribes described the area each roamed or possessed as being "right" or "perfect" for that particular tribe.

> *The Crow country is a good country. The Great Spirit put it in exactly the right place; while you are in it, you fare well; whenever you are out of it, whichever way you travel, you fare worse...*
>
> The Crow country is exactly in the right place. It is good to be found there. There is no place like the Crow country. (Araphooish, Crow in: Armstrong, 1971:67)

How receptive the area was to the needs of a tribe was usually explained in the oral tradition also. The geographical area included everything attached to the earth, or associated with that part of the earth. This of course included the sky, since it could not be separated from the area a tribe knew. It was often indicated in the oral tradition that "the place" the tribe occupied was especially created to meet the needs of that tribe.

> For each tribe of men Usen created, He also made a home. In the land created for any particular tribe He placed whatever would be best for the welfare of that tribe. Thus, it was in the beginning: The Apaches and their homes each created for the other by Usen himself. When they

Crow Country, turn of the century. Little Big Horn Agency in background. Fred E. Miller. (Courtesy of the Smithsonian Institution, National Anthropological Archives)

Geronimo, his wife and children in Geronimo's melon patch. This photo taken at Ft. Sill, Oklahoma. (This was not the land Geronimo described below) (Courtesy of the Museum of the American Indian, Heye Foundation)

are taken from these homes they sicken and die. (Geronimo, Apache in: Barrett, 1970:69)

Cochise, with whom everyone is familiar, described his country, his personal and tribal relationship to it; the rootedness, the sense of belonging.

This is the country of the Chiricahua Apaches. This is where the Chiracahua Apaches belong. The mountains and the valleys, the days and the nights belong to the Chiracahua Apaches. It was so from the memory of the oldest man, and that memory comes from the oldest man ahead of him. (Armstrong, 1971:87)

Knowledge was passed on by word of mouth and through storytelling. More elaborately, knowledge was passed through ceremonials, symbols, and songs. How special places in a tribal world were created or where power was attributed in sacred or "holy" places has often been explained in storytelling too. Knowledge was confirmed over the years by specialists in sacred ways. Doctors, shamans, and medicine people returned to those places again and again to communicate with spirit powers, observe stars or gather plants. Here is a list of types of Navajo sacred places:

(1) a location mentioned in [oral tradition]

(2) a place where something supernatural has happened, in oral tradition

(3) a site from which plants, herbs, minerals and waters possessing healing powers may be taken, and

(4) where man communicates with the supernatural world by means of prayers and offerings. (Britt, 1975:92)

Following are two examples (from separate tribes) of individual explanations for special places. *The essence* of both explanations *is* that they account for the people's worlds (territories). *And* they deal with those worlds *to the people's satisfaction*; with the knowledge memorized over centuries of oral tradition and with understanding.

1) The speaker is called Sluiskin. He was a Yakima Indian. The place is Mt. Rainier, called Takhoma by the Yakima.

Takoma Wynatchie is an enchanted mountain, inhabited by an evil spirit, who lives in a fiery lake on its summit. No human can ascend it or even attempt to climb to the top and survive. At first, indeed, the way will be easy. The broad snowfields, over which often I have hunted the mountain goat, pose no obstacles, but above that there are steeps of loose rolling stones which turn beneath the climbing feet, to case any adventurer into the deep crevasses below. The upper snowslopes are so steep that not even a mountain goat, far less a man, can get over them. And he would have to pass below lofty walls and precipices where avalanches of snow and vast masses of rocks continually fall; and these would inevitably bury the intruder beneath their ruins. Moreover, a furious tempest continually sweeps the crown of the mountain, and the luckless adventurer, even if he escapes the perils below would be torn from the mountain and whirled through the air by its fearful blasts. And the awful spirit upon the summit would surely punish the sacriligious attempt to invade his sanctuary. Who could hope to escape his vengeance? Many years ago, my grandfather a great chief and warrior, ascended high up the mountain, and encountered some of the dangers, but fortunately he turned back in time to escape destruction; and no other Indian has gone so far. (Armstrong, 1971:90)

Slusken, Yakima Indian. This might have been the Sluiskin who told the story of Mt. Rainier. (Courtesy of the Museum of the American Indian, Heye Foundation)

2) The writer is a young man, Jerry Delorme, Sioux-Klamath.

Have you ever heard of Crater Lake near Klamath Falls, Oregon? It used to be a volcano, but the top caved in, or blew off. They don't really know how it happened, but its not there now. The Klamath Indians know all about it, and that is what I'd like you to hear.

Long before my grandfather's grandfather, there was once a great bird. It was a kind of eagle, I think, but this bird stood for and protected everything that was good. It watched over the Klamath lands from its high nest on the highest of our mountains. Below the Klamath lands lived our enemies, the Shastas. Their ways were different. They had no Great Being of good. Instead, when they were a small people they had a small turtle and as their people grew, so did their turtle. The turtle was really huge by then.

When the Klamath Indians' bird was away, the giant turtle would climb the Shasta Mountains and come into our land to swim in our lakes. This would turn the water to mud. The turtle would steal our food and eat our children. We told this to the giant bird and it said it would wait and kill our enemies' helper, the turtle.

When the great bird left to get food, it did not eat, but came right back to find the turtle in our lake. The turtle saw the bird and went under water, but this did not save him, for the bird grabbed his tail and flew above the mountain and dropped the turtle right on the bird's nest. Then they battled all night and into the next day. Finally, the fight became so furious the mountain caved in, so the two fought inside the mountain till the bird killed the turtle. Its blood filled the hole in the mountain and formed a lake with the turtle back above the water. The bird left the turtle there with his back forming an island, showing our enemies what had happened so it would keep them away. (Allen, 1974: 160)

Complex geographical ideas developed in a few tribes, explaining these people's world. Many times these ideas have been foreign to other people. Attempts have been made to research these ideas and their sources. One example of this research is for a concept which belongs to the Northern California Yurok. T.T. Waterman, an ethnologist, explained the Yurok world, as he perceives it to be.

The Yurok imagines himself to be living on a flat...landscape, which is roughly circular and surrounded by ocean. The Klamath River is considered in a sense to bisect the world. This whole earth mass with its forest and mountains, its rivers and sea cliffs, is regarded as slowly rising and falling with a gigantic but imperceptible rhythm... The vast size of the "earth" causes you

not to notice this quiet heaving and settling. This *earth*, therefore, *to their minds is not merely surrounded by the ocean but floats upon it*. At about the central point of this "world" lies a place which the Yurok call qe'nek, on the southern bank of the Klamath, a few miles below the point where the Trinity River comes in from the south.

...the numerous mythical tales center here, and here the culture "grew" out of nothing, back in the myth days.

At this [place] the sky was made "World-maker" fashioned the heavens after the manner and pattern of a fishnet... The story tells in detail how... he took a rope and laid it down in an enormous circle, leaving one end loose at a certain place among the hills, Traveling off in a gigantic circuit and coming around from the south to the same spot again, he joined the two ends of the rope together. Then for days he journeyed back and forth over the hills, filling in and knotting the strands across each other. *The song he sang to accompany his labors is still sung by people who work in fishnets or netted carrying bags.* When the sky net was complete, the hero took hold of it in two places and "threw it up." As it sailed aloft, it became solid, and now stretches over us as the great blue sky. Above this solid sky there is a sky country, wo'noiyik. Downstream from Qe'-nek-pul ("qe'nek-down'stream"), is an invisible ladder leading up to the sky country. *The ladder is still thought to be there.* The sky is a very definite item in the Yurok's cosmic scheme.

In their theory this sky was constructed so as to come down into the ocean, all the way around. It lies far out, away from land. The powers who decide such matters arranged that it should not be in a state of rest, but should move up and down. It continually rises and plunges down again into the sea; hence the [waves] which wash up on the world's shores. If you paddle far out where the sky comes down to the water, it is perfectly possible, by counting off the lifting and lowering, to slip through

73

underneath. This is the way to get into the regions beyond the sky. The geese have a special exit of their own, a 'sky-hole,' a round opening where they enter and leave this world. They spend part of each season in outer space beyond the sky. When flock after flock of geese sail overhead toward the northwest, they are headed for this opening...
The structure, if I may so call it, consisting of the sky dome and the flat expanse of landscape and waters which it encloses, is known to the Yurok as ki-we'sona (literally "that-which-exists"). I may repeat that the sky overhead is to the [Yurok] as real and as concrete as is the earth he treads on. This sky, then, together with its flooring of landscape, constitutes "our world." *I used to be puzzled at the Yurok confusing earth and sky, telling me, for example, that a certain gigantic redwood tree, "held up the world." Their ideas are of course perfectly logical, for the sky is as much a part of the world in their sense as the ground is.*

The Yurok believe that passing under the sky edge and voyaging still outward you come again to solid land. This is not our world, and mortals ordinarily do not go there; but it is good, solid land. Yonder lie several regions... All of these solid lands just mentioned lie on the margin, the absolute rim of things. *Beyond them the Yurok does not go even in imagination.*
Below our world is an underworld, *tso'r'ek*, a sort of cellar, of undetermined extent. This is the world of the dead, and is connected with "our" world. The dead are said to go to a lake. After going round and round and about they go down down through this water into the underworld. Two widely separate points were mentioned to me as the very spot where the souls go down... The Yurok's conception of the world he lives in may be summed up in the accompanying diagram. This was not drawn by a native; I pieced it together myself from various allusions and references. (Waterman, 1920:472-474)

Trinity River in California. Boat Dance, part of the ceremony of the White Deerskin Dance. Hupa, Karok and Yurok participated. Photo before 1898. (Courtesy of the Smithsonian Institution, National Anthropological Archives)

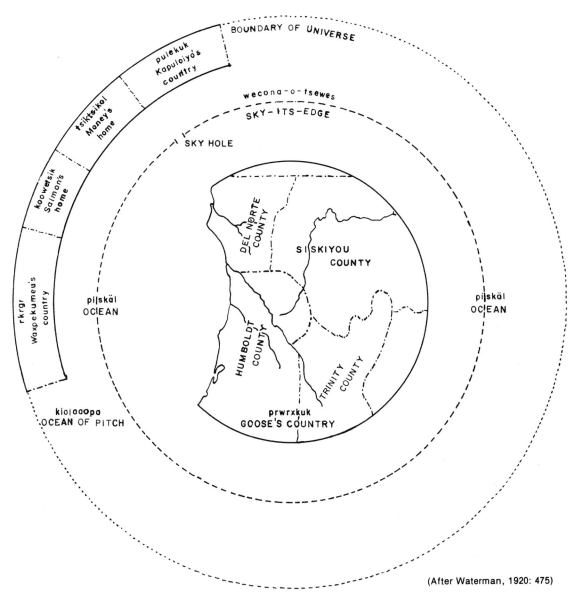

BOUNDARY OF UNIVERSE

pulekuk
Kapuloiyós
country

tsiktskol
Money's
home

koowetsik
Salmon's
home

rkrgr
Waxpekumeu's
country

wecona-o-tsewes
SKY - ITS - EDGE

SKY HOLE

DEL NORTE
COUNTY

SISKIYOU
COUNTY

pi|skäl
OCEAN

HUMBOLDT
COUNTY

TRINITY
COUNTY

pi|skäl
OCEAN

kioiaaopa
OCEAN OF PITCH

prwrxkuk
GOOSE'S COUNTRY

(After Waterman, 1920: 475)

Waterman describes how he grasped the Yurok's concept of directions. Briefly summarized, the world of the Yurok is geographically divided by a river. Consequently "up-river" and "downriver" became fundamental concepts of direction.

Aside from the directions in "this world" or the natural world where people actually lived, directions could also be symbolic.

SYMBOLISM

> ...We Indians live in a world of symbols and images where the spiritual

> and commonplace are one... (Erdoes, 1972:109)

Symbols communicate or represent those ideas, concepts and emotions which are often intangible or invisible. A symbol, which might also be called a sign, can be perceived more easily by the senses. In this way the message a symbol carries is transmitted. Without symbols, the spiritual could not be expressed or might not be perceived. *Through the use of symbolism, the intangible or invisible is made visible.*

Sandpainting of Father Sky and Mother Earth. Sandpainting is from Male Shootingway Chant, reproduced by Hostin Claw about 1905-1912. Father Sky is on left, black with white markings that represent the constellations. Zig-zag line across chest represents the Milky Way. Mother Earth is blue. The four sacred plants: squash, beans, tobacco, and corn are represented in the center of the figure. Both are surrounded by Rainbow Girl, a symbol of protection. (Courtesy of the Smithsonian Institution, National Anthropological Archives)

Certain symbols are used to represent, or stand for, or imply such-and-such. As an example: the Navajo have four colors that represent the directions; white, blue, yellow and black. This color code does not change, and if it varies, it does so only slightly. It remains consistent to carry out themes or ideas from sand-painting to sand-painting.

Nearly all aspects of the natural environment in the Navajo world are personified. There is male rain and female rain, there is Mother Earth and Father Sky. (Father Sky will be discussed in more detail later on in the chapter.) As Hoke Denetsosie explains, "All these things have inner beings. It does not matter that they are not five-fingered beings."

The sacred mountains of the Navajo will be described later. They are greatly symbolic to the Navajo and serve more purpose than defining an area of land.

Certain symbols have been used with oral traditions over long periods of time. People still use these symbols to express and orient themselves in today's world because the symbols are familiar to them and their meanings have not altered. Tradition and the natural world are both reflected and expressed in symbolism.

Dr. Alfonso Ortiz of San Juan Pueblo discusses the Pueblos as they organize their world and define themselves in relation to "boundaries."

...the Pueblos...set careful limits to the boundaries of their world and order everything within it. These boundaries are not the same, *but more important, the principles of setting boundaries* [*are the same*] *since all use phenomena in the four cardinal directions*, either mountains or bodies of water, usually both, to set them...

All the Pueblos also have a well-elaborated conception and symbolization of the middle or center of the cosmos (universe) represented by a sipapu, an earth navel, or the entire village. Among the Pueblos, the center is the point of intersection of the six directions, with a seventh being the center itself. If only four directions are given symbolic elaboration, the center will be the fifth direction.

> ...all things are defined and represented by a reference to a center... (Ortiz, 1972:142)

The Sioux have a similar idea of the center and of the directions. Through symbolism these concepts of directions can be seen or felt. With symbolism, directions both geographical and sacred, and boundaries of the world, both natural and abstract, could be dramatized in ritual and prayer. The significance and purpose of symbolism is to make the spiritual and natural world into one that can be seen and understood.

> ...everything has its place in the cosmos. All things are thought to have two aspects, essence and matter. Thus, everything in the cosmos is believed to be knowable and, being knowable, controllable. (Ortiz, 1972:143)

Sometimes oral traditions tell of people coming from much farther than the boundaries

Shrine near Zuni Pueblo, New Mexico, prior to 1898. Symbolized the Center of the World. Matilda C. Stevenson. (Courtesy of the Smithsonian Institution, National Anthropological Archives)

they presently map. Oral traditions might give accounts of supernatural origins (as explained earlier in this chapter), or make reference to the historical migration of the people. Often these histories are combined and time in the sense as we know it (broken down in hrs., minutes, etc.) becomes distorted. The histories that oral traditions relate are often without this time sense. They are timeless histories. Events that occurred in those histories might have taken place in "this world" or in other worlds which people would describe as timeless.

JOURNEYS OUTSIDE THE BOUNDARIES

Some journeys outside the boundaries therefore become very important and again, symbolic. It is like traveling back to points, places of origin and re-enacting events which occurred in histories. Those journeys could be for ceremonial purposes too.

Several tribes practiced initiation rites for young men and women. The Navajo are one of the few tribes today to practice an elaborate ceremony for the young women* A Navajo man, Barney Mitchell, gives an explanation of this puberty ceremony saying that the girl re-enacts what Changing Woman did in observation of her first menstrual period. For a brief time, the girl *becomes* Changing Woman.

Changing Woman is a prominent figure in the oral tradition of the Navajo. Changing Woman was also called White Shell Woman. There are greatly detailed stories of the two. Changing Woman or White Shell Woman is a timeless, symbolic figure. A brief, abstract way of describing Changing Woman is to say that she changes constantly as seasons do. She is young then old, and is reborn again. This theme is carried out in another description. White Shell Woman is said to live in the West (in the Pacific Ocean) in a house built for her by the Sun for whom she bore twin boys. Everyday the Sun rises, White Shell Woman is thought to be traveling to her house in the west. At dawn she is like an infant, at noon a young woman; at mid-day she starts to become old.

It is this figure or her twin boys that early Navajo people modeled themselves after.

---

* See Chapter Nine, **Girls' Puberty Ceremonies.**

Their lives set examples that are seriously conceived to be fundamental to Navajo identity today. About this idea Mr. Mitchell says, "We are imitating what the gods or holy people have done. It is a return to the beginning."

Primarily by means of dramatizing oral traditions and with the use of symbols, there is continuity that binds this natural world with other worlds. Simultaneously, there is renewal —of *awareness* toward the natural world, abstract and spiritual worlds, and awareness of origins that is necessary to native people.

Another dramatic illustration of this cycle (returning to origins) is presented, once more by Ortiz.

One summer a few years ago a man who was, like me a Tewa Pueblo Indian, and I undertook a journey... We were driving to the country of the Utes in southwestern Colorado to share in the blessings of their Sun Dance. My companion had never in his life been in that part of Colorado before. As the massive outcropping that is known today as Chimney Rock loomed larger and larger beyond the road ahead, he became very alert. Pointing to it, he said, "There is Fire Mountain! It is just as the old people spoke of it." As he recognized distinct features of the place, he proceeded to unfold tale after tale of events in the early life of our people which took place at Fire Mountain and in the surrounding country. Every prominent feature along the road began to live for him, and as he spoke of that remembered place, we, *each of us, began to realize that we were retracing a portion of the ancient journey of our people*, a journey which began beneath a lake somewhere in this southwestern corner of Colorado, who knows how many thousands of years ago, and a journey which, as long as there are Tewa to tell of it, shall always end again at this lake of emergence.

So it was that by the time we neared the town of Pagosa Springs, it was no longer July 1963, but another time, a time

in and out of time. This place is called Warm Sands in Tewa, for there are sands which are kept warm by the hot springs which gave birth to the town; sands which by themselves are said to be able to melt snow and moderate the midwinter cold; sands for the obtaining of which our religious men in other times made winter pilgrimages. My companion and I, both silent, recalled ancestors who were among those religious men. He wanted to stop, to gather some of the warm sand from the nearby springs, as did I. When we came to the sands, he knelt before the land, then he ran the sand through his fingers. And then he wept. *He had never been here, but then he had never really left*. He remembered his own grandfather and the other grandfathers who had preceded him here. He had heretofore never journeyed here, but now it was as if he had come home. (Ortiz, 1973:89-90)

Other kinds of expeditions could also be considered pilgrimages outside the boundaries. Examples of these particular expeditions might even describe seeking visions of power.

Visiions of knowledge (power) are often described as acquired in more abstract journeys; to the "Land of the Dead," prophetic trances, and in dreaming.* On occasion visions have been obtained under, or following circumstances of stress, such as illness. However, similar conditions can be created whereby these goals are sought and desired. Sacrificing through tests of endurance or self-inflicted pain is one practice that readily comes to mind. Of course, there have been instances when individuals have received power through other means.

To explain more clearly these abstract journeys, is a Hopi account of a visit to the "House of the Dead."

Once a youth sat at the edge of the mesa looking down upon the graves and wondering if those who died continued to live somewhere. At last, he took some cornmeal, sprinkled it at the edge of the mesa, and prayed to the Sun God: "If somewhere you have seen those who have died, please inform me." Having

---

* See Chapter Five, **Shamans and the World of Spirits: The Oldest Religion.**

Cheyenne medicine man, Bushy Head, after inserting skewers into young man's back. A sequence of the Sun Dance. James Mooney, 1903. (Courtesy of the Smithsonian Institution, National Anthropological Archives)

prayed to the Sun God, thus for four successive days, he sat down and observed what appeared to be a man ascending the mesa and approaching him. "Why do you want me?" he asked. "Because," said the youth, "I am always thinking about those who are buried here, whether it is true that they are living in some other life." "Yes," replied the stranger, "they are living. If you are anxious to see them, I shall give you this." Then the Sun God, for it was he in the form of a man, handed some medicine to the youth. By eating it, he could fall into a deep sleep and die. After taking this medicine, the youth actually died, visited the House of the Dead, and returned to tell others how the dead live. Since then, many people in Oraibi have had similar experiences, traveled far, and

returned to recount what they have seen.

Various people report different details, but all their stories are much the same. After dying, they set out on a path leading westward. On the way, they overtake unfortunate people traveling with great difficulty, tired and thirsty, begging for food or drink and asking to be carried at least a few steps. They pass people carrying heavy loads with burden bands consisting of a single bow string which cuts into the forehead. Cactus plants are attached to tender parts of their body to prick them afresh at every step. Some are naked and forlorn, dragging themselves along a rugged path infested with vipers that often raise their heads to hiss and strike. These sufferers are neighbors and relatives from Oraibi who are being punished for their sins.

They are the people who have not wanted it to rain, who have done something offensive to the clouds to drive them away, or who have invited bad winds and hailstorms to harass the people. They are those who have not listened to the advice of the old men, have failed to follow the straight road, have stolen private property, or have started ugly lies, causing others to worry. They are Two-Hearts, who have projected lizard tails, biting ants, snake venom, poisoned arrows, or evil thought into other people to cause their death. Theirs is a long and tortuous journey, sometimes lasting centuries before they reach the House of the Dead.

But the upright, those who have heeded the advice of the old people and have faithfully followed the Sun Trail, are permitted to take a broad, smooth highway patrolled by members of the Warrior Society (Kwanitakeas), who wear a big horn for a headdress and ring a bell to attract attention as they escort the righteous travelers over difficult passes and provide direction for the rest of the journey. Oftentimes, a good person is placed on his own kilt, lifted up by a steady breeze, and carried smoothly over the rough road as if flying.

At last, the righteous reach a place where the wicked are punished in smoldering pits, and from this horrible sight pass on into a large village of white houses where their departed relatives are living in peace and plenty. They find that those who were good on the earth hold the same ranks and positions that they had enjoyed in Oraibi. These ancestors do not eat ordinary food but only its aroma and soul, so that they are not heavy when they are transformed into clouds and float in the air. They smile at even the idea of eating solid food and say to the visitors, "You must go back again. You cannot stay with us here yet, because your flesh is strong and salty. You must work for us at home making prayer feathers (ankwakwosis) at the Royal Ceremony. As you see, these feathers are tied around our foreheads to represent falling rain. Then, we also will

work for you here. We will send you rain and good crops. You must wrap up the women in the white blanket (owa) and tie the big knotted belt around them when they die, because owas are not tightly woven and when we skeletons move along on them through the sky, thin raindrops fall from the fringes on these belts." They advised the visitors that after they have returned to Oraibi and told the people what they have seen and have assured them of life after death, it will be better for them not to think about death anymore, but to perform the ceremonies regularly, live peaceably, and keep their feet faithfully upon the Hopi Sun Trail that leads to life.

(Simmons, 1942:435-436)

MOUNTAINS

Often terrestrial boundaries are marked by mountains. This was previously mentioned by Ortiz. Mountains are important throughout the world for this reason, because they define boundaries.

Among the many people who subscribe to the belief that four mountains define tribal territory are the Navajos, all of the Pueblos, the Pima, and the Yuman tribes of the Gila River. Because these tribes are so numerous and once occupiied contiguous territories in the two-state areas of New Mexico and Arizona, we have a complex mosaic of overlapping tribal worlds defined by mountains. Variations of these beliefs extend into Central America where, some argue, they began among the great pre-Columbian civilizations which flourished there. But mountains are more, much more, than boundary markers defining the tribal space within which a people lives and carries on most of its meaningful, purposeful activities. The Pueblo people, for instance, believe that the four sacred mountains are pillars which hold up the sky and which divide the world into quarters. As such, they are imbued with a high aura of mystery and sanctity. And this sacred meaning transcends all other meanings and functions.

The Apaches, the most recent mountain dwellers among all southwestern Indians, believe that mountains are alive and the homes of supernaturals called "mountain people." They further believe that mountains are protectors from illness as well as external enemies, that they are the source of the powers of shamans as well as teachers of songs and other sacred knowledge to ordinary humans, and that, finally, mountains are defenders as well as definers of tribal territory. (Ortiz, 1973:91-92)

The Navajo identify four sacred mountains that border the Reservation today. The mountains are real... They exist. How they were formed is told now in a version of oral tradition, by the medicine man called Sandoval.

First Man and First Woman formed six sacred mountains from the soil that First Man had gathered from the mountains in the Third World and kept in his medicine bag. As before, they placed Sis na'jin in the East. Tso dzil in the South, Dook oslid in the West, and Debe'ntsa in the North. They placed a sacred mountain, which they called Choli'i'i, on the earth, and they made the mountain, Dzil na' odili, around which the people were to travel.

There were four Holy Boys. These beings First Man called to him. He told the White Bead Boy to enter the mountain of the East, Sisna'jin. The Turquoise Boy he told to go into the mountain of the South, Tso dzil. The Abalone Shell Boy entered the mountain of the West, Dook oslid. And into the mountain of the North, Debe'ntsa, went the Jet Boy.

Now the mountains to the East and South were dissatisfied. The East wanted the Turquoise Boy and the South wanted the White Bead Boy for their bodies. There was quite a lot of trouble; the mountains would tremble as though they were not satisfied. The other mountains were happy in their bodies and there was no trouble between them. First Man and First Woman called other Holy beings to them. They put the Beautiful Mixed

Stones Boy and Girl into the sacred mountain called Chol'i'. They put the Pollen Boy and Grasshopper Girl into Dzil na' odili. They asked the Rock Crystal girl to go into Sis na'jin. They put the White Corn Girl into Tso dzil; the Yellow Corn Girl into Dook Oslid; and the Darkness Girl into Debe'ntsa.

After the Holy Beings had entered the Sacred Mountains First Man and First Woman dressed them according to their positions on the earth. They fastened Sis na'jin to the earth with a bolt of white lightning. They covered the mountain with a blanket of daylight, and they decorated it with white shells, white lightning, black clouds, and male rain. They placed the white shell basket on the summit; and in this basket two eggs of the hasbi'delgai, the pigeon. They said that the pigeons were to be the mountain's feather; and that is why there are many wild pigeons in this mountain today. And, lastly they sent the bear to guard the doorway of the White Bead Boy in the East.

Tso dzil, they fastened to the earth with a stone knife. They covered this mountain of the south with a blue cloud blanket; and they decorated it with turquoise, white corn, dark mists, and the female rain. They placed a turquoise basket on the highest peak, and in it they put two eggs of the blue bird, doli. Blue birds are Tso dzil's feathers. They sent the big snake to guard the doorway of the Turquoise Boy in the South.

Dook oslid was fastened to the earth with a sunbeam. They covered the mountain of the West with a yellow cloud. They adorned it with haliotis shell, yellow corn, black clouds, and the male rain, and they called many animals to dwell upon it. They placed the abalone shell basket on the summit; and in it they placed the two eggs of the tsidiltsoi, the yellow warbler. These birds were to become its feathers. The Black Wind was told to go to the west and guard the doorway of the Abalone Shell Boy.

They fastened the mountain of the North, Debe'ntsa, to the earth with a rainbow. Over it they spread a blanket of darkness. They decorated it with bash'zhini', obsidian, black vapors, and different plants and animals. The basket they placed on its highest peak was of obsidian; and in it they put two eggs of the Chagi, the blackbird. The blackbirds are the mountain's feather. The lightning was sent to guard the Jet Boy's doorway in the North.

First Man and First Woman fastened the Sacred Mountain Chol'i'i to the earth with a streak of rain. They decorated it with the pollens, mixed chips of stone precious to them, the dark mists, and the female rain. And they fastened Dzil n'odili to the earth with the sun's rays; and they decorated it with the beautiful goods of all kinds, the dark clouds, and the male rain. They left the summits of these mountains free. But some say that Dzil na'odili was fastened to the earth with Tse'hadahonige, the mirage stone; and those people associate the Mirage Boy and the Carnelian Girl with the mountain. *All the mountains have their prayers and chants which are called Dressing the Mountains. All the corner posts have their prayers and chants, as have the stars and markings in the sky and on the earth. It is their custom to keep the sky and the earth and the day and the night beautiful. The belief is that if this is done, living among the people of the earth will be good.* (O'Bryan, 1956:23-24)

In English these mountains are: Blanca Peak, East-New Mexico (Sis naajin'i); Mt. Taylor, South-New Mexico (Tsoodzil); San Francisco Peak, West-Arizona (Dook'o'oosliid); and La Plata Mountains, North-Colorado (Debe'nitsaa). Gobernador Knob, New Mexico, (Chool'i'i) and Herfano Mountain, New Mexico (Dzil na'oodil) are two mountains within the border. They are depicted in a few sandpaintings such as the Mother Earth Sandpainting.

One of the Mountain Chants:
From the Navajo

For ages and ages the plans have been made.
For ages and ages the plans of the Hold Mountains have been made.

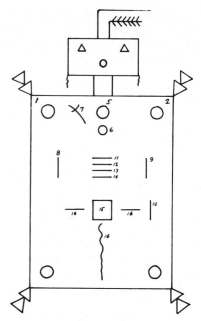

Plan of the Earth from Sam Akeah and Gerald Naile (Illustration after O'Bryan, 1956: 22)

1. Sis na jin, East Mt.
2. Tso dzil, South Mt.
3. Dook oslid, West Mt.
4. Debe'ntsa, North Mt.
5. Choli, Sacred Mt.
6. Dzil na'odili, Farmington Mesa
7. Dotso, All Wise Fly
8. Wo'neesh ch'indi dootl'izhi'gii, Cicada with Blue Eyes
9. Hasch'el't'i'i
10. Hash ch'e'wan
11. Dark World
12. Blue World
13. Yellow World
14. White World
15. Place of Emergence
16. First Growing Plants of This World

For Sis na'jin, the mountain of the East, the plan was made.
The plan was made in the home of the First Man.
The planning took place on top of the Beautiful Goods.
They planned how a strong White Bead Boy should be formed;
How the White Bead Boy should be formed, and
How the Chief of the Mountain should be made.
How he should be made like the Most-High-Power-Whose-Ways-Are-Beautiful.

For Tso'dzil, the mountain of the South, the plan was made.
The plan was made in the home of the First Man.

The planning took place on the top of the
Beautiful Goods.
They planned how a strong Turquoise
Boy should be formed;
How the Turquoise Boy should be
formed, and
How the Chief of the Mountain should be
made.
How he should be made like the Most-
High-Power-Whose-Ways-Are-
Beautiful.

For Dook oslid, the mountain of the
West, the plan was made.
The plan was made in the home of the
First Man.
The planning took place on the top of the
Beautiful Goods.
They planned how a strong Abalone Shell
Boy should be formed;
How the Abalone Shell Boy should be
formed, and
How the Chief of the Mountain should be
made.
How he should be made like the Most-
High-Power-Whose-Ways-Are-
Beautiful.

For Debe'ntsa, the mountain of the
North, the plan was made.
The plan was made in the home of the
First Man.
The planning took place on the top of the
Beautiful Goods.
They planned how a strong Jet Boy
should be formed;
How the Jet Boy should be formed, and
How the Chief of the Mountain should be
made.
How he should be made like the Most-
High-Power-Whose-Ways-Are-
Beautiful.

For Dzil na'odili, the Center Mountain,
the plan was made.
The plan was made in the home of the
First Man.
The planning took place on the top of the
Beautiful Goods.
They planned how a strong Earth's
Breath should be formed;
How the Banded Rock should be used,
and
How the Chief of the Mountain should be
made.

How he should be made like the Most-
High-Power-Whose-Ways-Are-
Beautiful.
For Chol'i'i, the Sacred Mountain, the
plan was made.
The plan was made in the home of the
First Man.
The planning took place on the top of the
Beautiful Goods.
They planned how the strong Earth's
heart should be formed;
How the Mixed Chips should be used,
and
How the Sacred Mountain should be
made.
How she should be made like the Most-
High-Power-Whose-Ways-Are-
Beautiful.
(O'Bryan, 1956:25)

Other people live near oceans and rivers and
likewise give these places special meaning
through oral tradition. But even so, there is
often a mountain somewhere in the vicinity
that is looked to by the people, as a source of
emotion; inspiration, awe, reverance, or
perhaps caution.

MYSTICAL AND SPIRITUAL BORDERS

We know through oral traditions that native
people observed the natural world or universe.
The universe with mystical and spiritual
borders existed and native people saw evidence of both. Through observation and other
means, native people experienced the natural
and mystical forces of the universe and their
laws.

A careful, detailed studied awareness of all
aspects of the universe has been demonstrated
by native people. It is significant that their
conceptions of the universe were not based
upon observation alone. These conceptions of
the universe regarded the mystical and
spiritual borders seriously and were occasionally very complex.

We will see in the following section the
astronomical observations (of prehistoric
native people) preserved in petroglyphs. The
observations of the natural and mystical world
that native people recorded in the oral
traditions were of great ceremonial significance. All knowledge was functional
knowledge, put to use in everyday life or in
ceremony.

CELESTIAL BOUNDARIES AND MARKINGS

Algonquian *"Song of the Stars"*

We are the Stars which sing.
We sing with our light;
We are the birds of fire,
We fly over the sky
Our light is a voice;
We make a road
For the spirit to pass over.
    (Gibbon, 1972:238)

Star-lore and the observation of the skies by native people has been documented as being significantly more than a past-time. Among most people it formed a complex which served as (1) *seasonal markings* and (2) described in figurative terms aspects of oral tradition (sacred teachings, history, etc.).

Documentation (of how tribes marked seasons) was undertaken after the turn of the century and produced this information:

The recurrence of the moon's phases—a phenomenon which all...tribes observe divides the year into "months" to each of which the term "moon" is applied. Seasonal events, however, usually give name to the "moon."

Among some of the Eskimo, seasonal occurrences form the only basis of reckoning for the summer. The Ungava Eskimo seem to have disregarded [moons] altogether. Their periods are named from terrestrial events, such as the breaking up of the ice; ripening of salmon berries, and the time of reindeer crossing the river; there are also references to the sun, its return and position in the sky. Several periods may overlap, but there is a specific name for each. Since more events happen in the summer, there are more summer divisions. The Point Barrow Eskimo, according to one account, have only nine moons, and for the remainder of the year "there was no moon, only the sun." The Greenland Eskimo also have difficulty with their summer months; they depend on the growth of the elder duck, the size and appearance of the seals, and the like, for the regulation of their calendar when the moon is invisible. A seasonal event furnished the starting point of the year among the Indians of the Mackenzie, Plains, Plateau, Northeast and Southeast Woodland areas, and sometimes elsewhere. *The selection of this initial event varies greatly; agriculturists seem to prefer the spring-determined by the drying of the earth or the time for planting or the harvest time or their chief crop; hunting people often choose the rutting season of some animal, but some prefer the beginning of winter, and others spring—marked by the sprouting of the grass, sea-going tribes sometimes take spring, but more often the beginning of winter. Only among several maritime and agricultural tribes of the Northwest and Southwest is the year determined solstitially rather than seasonally.* (Cope, 1919:124)

This means simply that while native groups watched the moon change in the sky, they also were keenly aware of the changes that took place in the physical environment around them, while "moons" came and went. Some tribes assigned a moon to what we call January or December, a month. The changes that took place in a people's environment, the seasons and constant state of change, were where the names of "moons" came from. Cope used the Eskimo as an example because of the great visible change that occurred in their world with the *seasons*. Where some tribes marked seasons by "moons" or lunations, which is the amount of time that elapses between two successive new moons (averaging 29 days, 12 hours, 44 minutes and 2.8 seconds), the Eskimo depended upon sequential seasonal events. Tribes which did not use this method of determining seasons depended upon their observance of the *sun*. For instance, the position of the sun was constantly noted by these tribes and the seasons were figured, based upon the sun's position. Solstices are the two points of the year in which the path the sun follows marks the beginning of summer and of winter in the northern hemisphere. This happens about June 22 (the summer solstice) and December 22 (the winter solstice). Later we will discuss those people that recorded time in this manner and why.

Tribes often used the stars as visible evidence of their oral traditions. This is shown

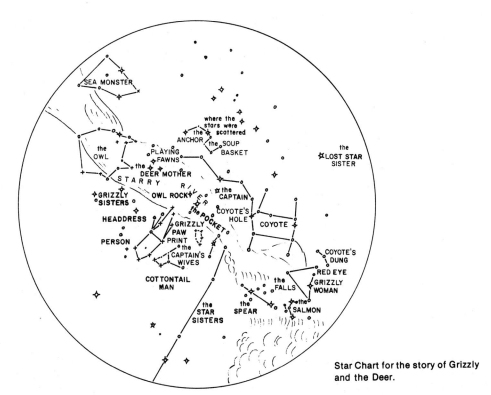

Star Chart for the story of Grizzly and the Deer.

in the following Maidu story told by Tom Epperson. Preceding it is a chart that accompanies the story.

Grizzly and the Deer

While Mother Grizzly and Mother Deer picked greens down at the lower end of This Place Meadow, their girls took turns crawling into a cave and smoking each other out, fanning smoke into the hole. (That cave, its entrance black with soot, lies on the north side of Sandy Creek Canyon). The girls in the cave could stand just so much smoke, then they hollered,

        K u m K a s
                but
                    but
                        but

and were let out. That was their sport. Every day the four of them, two Grizzly Sisters and two Deer Sisters, went to the cave and played while their mothers picked greens.

Grizzly Bear got the idea she would kill Deer Woman. She told her cubs, "I'll get the mother first—don't kill those Deer girls. We'll let them grow before we eat them."

Deer Lady told her girls, "Watch out. Grizzly wants to kill me. She'll try to kill you later. You two girls go to your grandfather, Crane." And Deer told her girls just what to do.

Mother Grizzly got ready to kill Mother Deer that day. When the two mothers went to pick food, Mother Grizzly brought along a little basket filled with sand. They picked and picked weeds. Along in the afternoon, Grizzly said, "Let's sit down and rest." And they both sat and started talking. "You have lots of lice on your head," Mother Grizzly said. "let me go over the back of your head." Deer Woman—she could do nothing—said, "All right," and she bent her head so Grizzly could louse her. Mother Grizzly said, "...You have so many lice in one place...why, I'll bite them—mash them with my teeth." Mother Deer just bowed her head. Mother Grizzly sprinkled sand on the back of Mother Deer's head. Grizzly began chewing. "Oh, just listen to the lice pop," she said. "I'm mashing a lot of them between my teeth." Suddenly, she grabbed a hold of Deer's neck and bit it in two. She killed Deer and hung her spleen high in the willows where it would light up in the early evening sun. Then, she went back to camp.

"Your mother's sick. She has the belly ache and is going to stay down below tonight. See that fire...see that fire down there? Your mother's there." Grizzly pointed at Mother Deer's spleen. The Deer girls knew all about Grizzly.

The next morning, Grizzly thought, "I'll leave my babies home today," and went down to eat on Deer. The Deer sisters went up the Canyon to play with the young Bear Sisters. The little deer said, "we'll go in first." The two young grizzlies began packing pine needles to plug the cave. They set fire to the needles, blew on them and waved branches to pile smoke into the cave. And the Deer Girls hollered,
                    K u m K a s
                              but
                                    but
                                          but
"All right." the Grizzly Girls dragged the pine needles away, and the Deer Sisters jumped out of the hole. Then it was the little grizzlies' turn to crawl into the cave. Those Deer Sisters got pine needles to plug the hole, a little more pine needles than should be. The Deer Girls did not plan to let those young bears out. They started fanning smoke into the hole. Pretty soon Grizzly Girls hollered,
                    K u m K a s
                              but
                                    but
                                          but
The Deer Girls just kept rolling in the smoke. The oldest sister sang,

Little sister put some more needles on the fire

They crowded the smoke into the cave,
                    K u m K a s
                              but
                                    but
                                          but
again. Then they heard no more noise.

The young grizzly bears had died.

The Deer Girls pulled the fire and hauled out two little grizzly cubs. Dead all right. They carted the bodies back to camp. They skinned them, cut them up some way and stuffed the best part of the meat into the belly of one bear. And the other belly, they filled with the heads, the little paws, all the worst parts of the meat. They dumped the body with the worst meat in the bottom of the fire pit, threw the one with the good meat on top. They covered the meat with coals and dirt. Then they ran about the camp and told all the pine trees, the brush, the weeds, all the sticks—everything—around "Don't tell where we're going. Don't tell where we're going." But Deer Girls missed one little pine needle wedged between two rocks: they did not tell it. (That must mean they left a sign.)

When they thought they told everything to keep still, they ran to a big rock where their mother always pounded acorns. They yanked up their mother's pounding rock, jumped into the hole it fit into. And the pounding rock rolled back into place. Those two little deer travelled under the mountain, coming out somewhere near a round house called Snowline.

The mean, old grizzly bear came home early that evening. It sounded like somebody laughing and playing near the camp. (The Deer Girls caused that). Mother Bear thought she heard her two grizzly bear girls playing over there. She looked around. Dirt covered the fire pit. She opened the fire pit, uncovered the meat. She dug out the meat and sat there, eating it. "I told my babies not to kill those two. They should have let them grow a little more and we would have had more meat." Talking like that and eating away, eating her own daughters, she finished the first batch. She shoved the backbone over to one side and started to open the second batch...her daughter's paws and all flew out. A a a a k, A a a a K. She puked. HURMP! Old Grizzly Bear questioned all of the things around the camp: the ground, weeds, trees, brush, everything else. Nobody knew anything.

Finally, she found the one little pine needle, the one wedged between two rocks, and asked about the deer girls. And that little pine needle told her. "They yanked up their mother's pounding rock and jumped under it."

HURMP: Grizzly yanked up the pounding rock and threw it down the hill. HURMP: She squeezed into the same hole and followed the Deer girls under the mountain, toward Snowline.

Those girls ran along a trail that goes between Snowline and Big Meadows. Just on top of the ridge they felt the ground tremble and heard the limbs breaking. (If a mad grizzly catches a human scent trail, the human may hear a grizzly breaking trees and limbs from half mile away as she comes after him.) They heard Old Grizzly snapping and popping the timbers as she ran after them. The girls jumped on a big flat rock and said, "Rock, twist up."

The rock twisted right up out of the ground, about twelve feet. Mother Grizzly came to the bottom of the rock. "Your mother is tired and told me to get you girls," she said sweetly. "How did you get up on top of the rock? ...I only want to get up there and talk with you.

"How did you girls get up there?"

"We climbed on our apron strings," the Deer Girls said. "First you have to shut your eyes tight and open your mouth, just as wide as you can.

"Then we can pull you up with our
  apron strings."

"I'll do that. I'll do that."

One of the girls dropped the end of her apron string as the other sister dropped a hot stone right into Mother Grizzly's mouth. Old Grizzly flopped down the rock. She rolled down the hill; grunting, rolling. It must have burnt up her insides. One Deer girl said "Rock, come down," and the rock came down, flat. (That rock still lies in Haun's Meadows.) The girls jumped off and ran to Big Meadows, where their grandfather, old Blue Crane, lived. He stood on the other side of the Big River and got ready. Blue Crane was bawling and singing because Grizzly Bear killed one of his relatives. After a while, here came old Mother Grizzly, tearing down the country.

"Where are they? where are they? where are they?" Grizzly said.

"Oh, they're on the other side of the river," said Blue Crane.

"I came to get the girls," Grizzly sweetly said. "Their mother's not feeling well and she sent me after them. How did they cross the river?"

"Those girls crossed on my leg."

"Let me get over there."

"All right. I'll stretch my leg across the river. Turn your claws up or you'll cut my leg. Don't punch my leg."

"I'll turn them up," Grizzly said. Grandfather Crane stuck his leg across Big River. When Grizzly got just about to the middle of the river, why, Crane dumped her into the water. "You punched my leg. I told you to turn up your claws," said he.

As soon as Grizzly hit the water, the Water Bug Women, who had followed her, ate her all up. The path over which the Deer Sisters ran afterwards became deer trails. Trails, the mountains, the lakes and rivers of every land now show in the stars above the land. Animals read these stars and use them to find their way. As the Starry Trail (the milky way) moves north and south across the sky, blacktail deer follow under it. The Starry Deer Trail is also Grandfather Crane's leg, stretched across Big River. At the same time it is Big River, with its falls and the jumping salmon that a salmon spear aims toward. Grizzly Woman waits in the sky at one end of Crane's leg, toward them. Safely across Crane's leg, two stars, called the Playing Deer, dance behind Deer Mother. Near the Playing Deer, the Grizzly Cubs play, one above the other. Behind them, the big horned owl in the sky always looks down the river toward his rock, Owl Rock, that pokes out of the Starry River.

The brightest star in the sky, straight up above, is the Captain. (Vega, possibly the pole star about 14,000 years ago). He never moves, he controls the movement of all the other stars. The Captain was also the first man. Across the River of

Stars stand his three wives, who came from his ribs. That's why human's lowest three ribs are so short today. Near the Captain, the Starry River has a black pocket. Here, the first man once held a pouch filled with stars. When he tried to catch his wives, they ran across the river, knocking his pouch (the big dipper) out of his hand, scattering stars across the sky. The Anchor (the present pole star) makes the pouch tip over.

A line of Star Girls near Cottontail man now run away with something that Coyote badly wants. But he looks for it on the other side of the Starry River. One Star Girl, one of Bat's wives, got lost (Arcturus). Once she sees a person she will always be with him. Seven little stars gathered about each other (the Pleiades) are trying to get warm at a big get-together when the stars get too close to each other, they get hot and sparks fly out, making falling stars. Just as sparks disappear, setting stars disappear over the ridges as they leave the sky to get some supper. (Coyote Man, 1973:89-100)

STAR PATTERNS AND STAR LORE

How one tribe, a California people, saw their world, through focusing on their skies, is shown in part by the preceding story and star chart. No matter how simple or complex, turning points of the year were marked in some manner by American Indians. Recently it has been learned that these turning points were recorded in astronomical markings.

In the Great Basin area are pictographs and petroglyphs which appear to have some connection to the star patterns visible in that area. In correlating these pictographs with the stars, the pictographs had very definite likeness to the constellations. These illustrations were definitely not drawn at random, as the student can see in the following illustration which shows these pictographs. These illustrations should be used in conjunction with a Star Atlas.

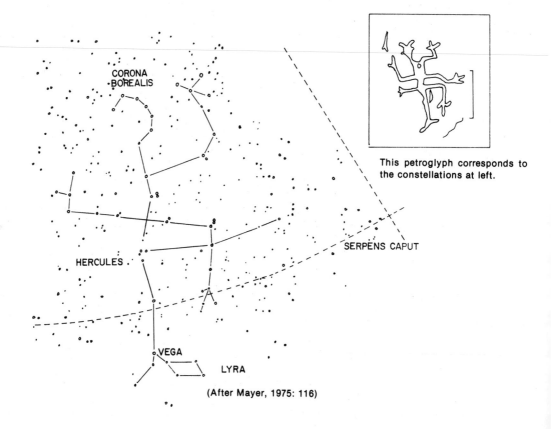

This petroglyph corresponds to the constellations at left.

(After Mayer, 1975: 116)

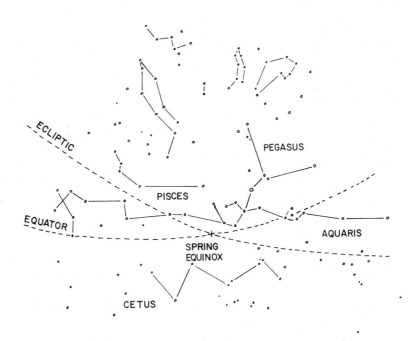

The glyph, at left, corresponds to star patterns around great square of Pegasus, Cetus and Aquarius. (After Mayer, 1975: 122)

A study of Navajo star lore similar to the production of the Great Basin star maps, was undertaken in the Canyon De Chelly area, Arizona. The canyon "apparently has the largest concentration of Navajo star paintings in the southwestern United States."

Star lore is prevalent in Navajo mythology and crosses depicting stars occur on some ceremonial equipment. The Pleiades star group occurs on some Navajo rattles used in various curing of-the-ill ceremonies.

The sandpainting of Father Sky depicts stars in the forms of crosses. The Father Sky sandpainting includes several constellations which are currently recognized by astronomers. (Britt, 1975:96-97)

The heart of all Navajo star lore is in the creation story. According to the legend, after the Navajo people emerged from underground onto the surface of the present world, certain beings began putting stars into the sky. Some references refer to these beings as First Man and First Woman (Yazzie, 1971, p. 21), or Fire Man and First Woman (Newcomb, 1967, p. 88), or Black God (Haile, 1947, pp. 23-28). These beings planned to arrange all stars in constellations representing every animal on earth. Before they were finished, Coyote came along. Seeing how slowly the work was progressing, Coyote picked up the blanket on which the remaining stars were lying and flipped them into the sky. He thus created the Milky Way and myriads of stars that are scattered among the constellations. Coyote's own star is one of these and most likely corresponds to what we know as Canopus.

According to Newcomb (1967, p. 88), First Woman, after all the stars were placed in the sky, said "now all the laws our people will need are printed in the sky where everyone can see them... The commands written in the stars must be obeyed forever." According to Navajo informant C, each constellation represents a law which all the Navajo people must obey. He further states that when the Navajo stop obeying the laws which are written in the sky, the Navajo Tribe will come to an end. In 1946, few medicine men knew the constellations, as noted by Haile (1947, p. 6), when he states, "...and while there are not many constellations, and some appear in the winter, others in the summer, some early in the night, others late towards dawn, few Navajo know anything about it at all, because it is too difficult to learn." The Navajo recognize approximately 37 constellations.

The planetarium sites in Canyon de Chelly are highly sacred places to the Navajo people and there can be little doubt that these star paintings date from approximately A.D. 1700 to A.D. 1864. (Britt, 1975: 100-101)

Most people had origin stories for the Sun and Moon, stories of the Milky Way (in some cases called the path of souls), and origins of prominent stars.

Peter Paul, from the Malecite of Maine, discusses the Malecite word for moon. This is an excerpt from a taped interview recorded in 1975.

MOON is Paguas. Analyzed, this word means he borrows or begs light from the sun and this proved too that the Indians knew about astronomy a long, long time ago. And the Indians since then have forgotten, only the name of the moon remains. And that is what Paguas really means. It means reflection of the sunlight onto the moon which goes back to the earth.

Madeline (Paul) Dedham, Malecite Indian. Mother-in-law of Dr. P. Paul, ca. 1901. (Photo courtesy of Dr. P. Paul, Woodstock, New Brunswick.)

The belief that the Milky Way was a "path of souls" or where people went upon death is a belief shared by numerous tribes. Below we give two explanations of this belief, one from the Luiseño tribe of California and one from the Eskimo. The Luiseño believed that the stars "were those of the First People who went up into the sky in the attempt to escape from death when it became known that the death of Ouiot had brought death to all upon earth." Ouiot was a person who died, but returned as the moon.

In the old times, much more was known about the stars than at present. Songs remain containing the names of stars which cannot now be identified. Only the most important stars have names. They were the chiefs among the First People, and they took their parties of adherents or relatives with them which are now the stars grouped about the chief star, but without individual names.

The Luiseños regard the Milky Way as the spirit, home of our spirits, to which they are sent when leaving earth. (DuBois, 1908:162)

The Eskimo discussion of the "soul" and its journey is a more personal description. It is based upon the information acquired by people who visited "the land of heaven."

"What happens to the soul when it leaves the body?" Ikinilik shifted in his place, and the wrinkles round his eyes deepened a little; of all the ridiculous questions. "When people die," he began, in his slow, rich voice, "they are carried by the moon up to the land of heaven and live there in the eternal hunting grounds. We can see their windows from on earth, as the stars, but beyond this, we know very little of the ways of the dead. ... [shamans] in former times made journeys to the heaven, and told what they saw. They visited the moon, and in every case were they shown into a house with two rooms. Here they were invited to eat of most delicate food, the entrails of caribou; but at the moment the visitor reaches out his hand to take it, his helping spirit strikes it away. For if he should eat of anything in the land of the dead, he will never return. The dead live happily; those who have visited their land have seen them laughing and playing happily together. (Rasmussen, 1927: 196-197)

CALENDARS, THE SEASONS

The systems for reckoning time are called calendars. The calendar as we know it today was derived from several ancient civilizations, but basically it comes from the Romans. These civilizations used the calendar for religious observances and religious activities. This was also one of the purposes of "calendar systems" of native people.

Native people correlated certain events and certain figures with the cycles of natural phenomena. Natural forces of the universe were taken into account. They were foreseen, anticipated, and marked by ceremonial events. These observances could only be done at those times. At the conclusion of this chapter we will see how figures or deities were associated with a particular season or with a particular event. The example we will use will be the Hopi ceremonial calendar.

The present modern calendar uses "artificial time intervals" such as hours and weeks to regulate or arrange time. Both the present calendar and the calendar systems of native people were based upon the movements of the moon and sun. However, the "calendar systems" of native people differed in many respects.

The methods of time-reckoning which are used by the Indians north of Mexico are remarkable for their simplicity and for the absence of uniformity, the influence of local and economic conditions being very prominent. In no case are these methods worthy of the name calendar system in its usually accepted sense...

Another interesting fact of note about these calendars *is that they were not used to record the passage of time*; that is, the "calendar" was not designed for recording the number of years or months or days since a given event took place, or between two given events. Since their occupations, food, and manner of life in general varied according to the changes of nature, it is not strange that they carefully observed the atmospheric and celestial phenomena, or had acquired a practical knowledge of the instincts and habits of animals, birds, and fishes. (Cope, 1919:120)

All North American Native people utilized three classes of "calendars." The first of these is the *Descriptive Type* of calendar. Of this calendar it is written, "It would be difficult to find a more simple form of time-reckoning than this type." This type of calendar consisted of descriptive names or designations which came from the changing patterns of nature.*

In simple calendars such as these, there is no uniformity in the choice of terrestrial events for names; they refer to the customs of man, the habits of wild animals or birds, climatic conditions, or the ripening of various fruits and berries. The beginning of the year [among tribes] varies also. (Cope, 1919:140)

---

* See Chapter Five, *The Baffin Bay Eskimos: Environmental Bodyland.*

These are some tribes that use the descriptive type of calendar:

Arikara
Bannock
Blackfoot
Carrier
Cree (Eastern and Plains)
Dakota (including Teton, Siseton, Eastern)
Delaware
Haida
Iroquois
Kansas
Kiowa
Lenape
Lower Yukon Eskimo (and those south of the Yukon delta)
Maidu
Malecite
Mandan
Micmac
Navajo
Ojibwa
Omaha
Onondaga
Osage
Oto
Iowa
Pawnee
Pima
Point Barrow Eskimo
Sauk and Fox
Seminole
Tlingit
Ute
Winnebago
Yuchi   (Cope, 1919:155)

Sometimes some tribes might have used this descriptive kind of calendar with the second type. The second kind of calendar is the *Astronomical Type*. This type of calendar is regulated by the people's observance of the sun or moon. The solstices might mark the division of the months into summer and winter, "or one or both solstices may be non-lunar periods for the purpose of regulating the year..."

Month designations referring to the *solstitial ceremonials* often replace the descriptive names. This ritualistic nomenclature has its fullest development among the Hopi, who name each of their moons from the chief ceremony of each period. On the Northwest Coast, one or more months are sometimes named from ceremonials, or ceremonial implications... (Cope, 1919:142)

These tribes use the astronomical type of calendar:

Bella Coola
Diegueno
Haida (Masset and Skidegate)
Hano
Hopi
Jemez
Kwakint (Koskimo, Nakwartok, Nimkish, and Mamelelekala)
Luiseno
Makah
Nootka
Salish
Tewa
Tusayon
Yurok
Zuni   (Cope, 1919:149)

The *Numeral Type* is the third kind of calendar. This kind of calendar's list of months is arranged numerically.

This type of calendar comprises those counts in which numeral designations have partly or wholly replaced the descriptive terms. It occurs only among the Northwest tribes and closely connected peoples—the northern Plateau and northern California tribes, and the Eskimo of southern Alaska. The Yurok alone use the numeral designations with a definite astronomical basis. (Cope, 1919:142)

These are three of the few tribes who use the numerical types of calendar:

Aleut
Modoc
Yurok   (Cope, 1919:153)

Seasons create changes in environment. Seasons control tribal activity by placing certain restrictions on a tribe, such as bad weather. In the past, the immobility of a tribe dependent upon game for survival would be greatly influenced by bad weather. Therefore, certain events had to occur with the changing seasons and some events became more celebrated than others.

The essence of seasons is the great circle of growth; life, birth to death. This naturally includes all forms of life from plant life to that of the human beings. When seasons reflect change, this change of seasons might be seen in the ritual and spiritual life of a tribe.

ACORN TIME AT CUPA is a remembrance of a festive event that occurred among the Cupeño of California when they went to gather acorns. Rosinda Nolasquez is the narrator.

Long ago the people went from Cupa to gather acorns. They went out in October, they went gathering. And they always gathered in those places: to Kut'ava, Ali'ma, Rabbit's House they went, in order to gather there. And there on the flat ground they built their shelters with this gathered-up grass, and there was a big rock, a wide one. And there were holes. There they spread out their harvest, their cracked acorns were dry. And there they pounded them. They were going to eat new acorn mush. And then those men hunted rabbits. And they brought them there then, and they cleaned them. And they cooked them. And then they ate those with acorn mush, they ate acorn mush. And then they slept. And in the morning they went, they gathered. Not a little, but ten sacks, they said, they gathered for the winter. And then this, "Candle Lighter" arrived in November, for two days. And then from there the people came down on horseback, on foot they went to Cupa. And then they arrived there at Cupa. And there then the people donated food, this coffee, sugar, flour, beans. They hunted rabbits. And the people ate for three days, they danced, they did the war dance for three days. And then it was over. And then they lit the candle. And then it burned down. And again they did the war dance, they danced, they ate. And then they went away again, they went climbing up again, they went gathering again, there, then they gathered this. Not little (they had) when they came home from there, they said. Christmas Eve time they were going to eat, this "Christmas," it is called, "Christmas." And then from there they came down. And they arrived in Cupa. And then there they made this meal, it is called a "meal," it is called a "big meal," American style. And there then they ate those rabbits, those chickens. Some had turkey. They made bread. And then there the big meal happened. And there they danced, they did the war dance, they sang enemy songs, they did the women's dance, they sang the men's songs, they stayed up til morning. And then again they ate, again they hunted. They made acorn mash a whole lot. They poured it into ollas (pots) and then they ate. (Hill and Nolasquez, 1962:29a-30a)

In the selection below, taken from *A Thousand Years of the Pueblo Sun-Moon-Star Calendar*, the author discusses the celestial events that occur with the changing of seasons and the Pueblo symbols and ceremonies pertaining to those events.

Of. . .immediate concern to the Pueblo people was Father Sun and Mother Earth who provided fertility, food, and warmth. Sun's apparent movement from the north to the south was understood to create the seasons. Since it appeared that Sun hesitated a few days in his southern "house," the Pueblos seemed it wise to put on a ceremony which would spur his decision to again take up his march northward. As part of the ritual at that time, the ceremonialists sought omens relating to the length of the growing season and hence to its success in the months ahead. The succession of horizon points over which the sun rose or set became calendar markers. The periodic reappearance of a new moon provided another reference for measuring time, and the consideration of moon and sun together was thought to strengthen chances for good omens because Moon could aid in influencing sun. Some say that Morning Star, symbol of the beloved Twin War gods and also of the Star of Sky God already mentioned, was watched because it followed Moon so closely, but this is not all of the story. Prayers were made to Sun, Moon, the Morning Star, Orion, and the Pleiades at this time and on some other occasions...(Ellis, 1975:62)

Edmund N. Nequatewa presents the Hopi Hopiwine, or the Hopi Ceremonial Calendar, (1931). It shows very clearly the importance of each ritual activity and its relationship to the next ritual in the cycle. Preparation for activities in one part of the year was done several months ahead sometimes. People were aware that each season and each half of the year—winter and summer—complemented each other. Nequatewa describes a few of those preparations.

The cycle of Hopi ceremonies begins in the winter. The dates of all the winter ceremonies are established by watching the position of the sun as it sets on the western horizon, while those of the summer ceremonies are fixed by the position of the rising sun on the eastern horizon.

WU-WU-CHE-MA: The first of the winter ceremonies is in November. When the sun sets over a particular hump on the north side of the San Francisco Peaks, the ceremony, Wu-Wu-che-ma, takes place. Four societies take part.

SOL-YA LAND-EU: After this ceremony is over, they again watch the sun on the western horizon. They just know on a certain day that it will take the sun eight days to reach its most southern point, and they announce the ceremony for eight days ahead. Thus, Sol-ya-lang-eu, the Prayer-Offering ceremony, is the Winter Solstice Ceremony, and takes place in December. This is one of the most sacred ceremonies of the Hopi. It is a day of good will, when every man wishes for prosperity and health, for his family and friends.

PA-MU-YA: In about the second week of January, when the sun has started back toward the north, the next ceremony after the new year takes place. It is called Pa-mu-ya, and lasts one day. At this time, the summer Snake or Flute ceremony is announced, and one day is spent making the pahos (prayer sticks) to be used in them.

PO-A-MU-YA: After this, in February, is the Po-a-mu-ya, the Bean Dance. When the sun goes back to the north slope of the San Francisco Peaks, and sets over the same hump mentioned in the Wu-Wu-che-ma, the ceremony is announced for the twelfth day in advance. This ceremony is held to try out

their planting luck for the coming season. In March comes the announcements of the two dances of the women, Basket Dance, which are to take place in September and October respectively.

KACHINA DANCES: During April, May and June, no long ceremonies are ever held, for all the people are too busy planting their crops. Various Kachina dances of one day's duration take place...

NIMAN KACHINA: In July when the rising sun reaches a certain place on the eastern horizon, the Niman Kachina is held. It is the time of "The Going Home of the Kachinas" to their "Olympus" on the San Francisco Peaks. All the men take part in this ceremony which is the third oldest of the Hopi, following the Wu-Wu-che-ma and the Sol-ya-lang-eu.

CHE-CHUK-TA and LA-LENT: In the month of August comes the far-famed Snake Dance, Che-shuk-ta and the less known Flute Ceremony, La-lent. These two dances come in alternate years. In even numbered years the Snake Dance takes place at Hotevilla, Shipaulovi, and Shungopovi, and in odd years at Walpi and Mishongnovi, and the Flute Dances vice-versa.

In the Snake Ceremony, the Snake Society is assigned by the Antelope Society for the following reason. An Antelope was once bitten by a Snake; the Snakes came and sucked the poison out of him and cured him. Then the Antelopes promised to sing for the Snakes every time they had a dance. In the Flute ceremony, the Flute Societies take part.

MAN-ZRAU-TU: In September, the Man-zrau-tu takes place. Only women participate in it, and it is similar to the La-la-kont, Basket Dance, which follows in October. It is one of the oldest dances of the Hopi and is still held. It lasts for eight days with a public ceremony on the eighth.

LA-LA-KONT: The La-la-kont, Basket Dance, which has been announced in March comes in October. It is named after the society of women who take part in it. The first seven days the women spend in the kiva making as many baskets as they can, and on the eighth day is the public ceremony in the plaza. In the evening after the dance, the women give the baskets away to the men and boys of the pueblo. This ceremony, like all others, is a prayer for health and prosperity; and brings an end to the year's circle of important sacred dramas.

In this chapter we have learned that native Americans were in constant awe of natural phenomena. In the past they acted accordingly. Even today many tribes elaborately recognize the changing moons and the changing seasons.

We have learned that Native Americans have watched the stars for centuries. We have learned that they then recorded what they saw, for entertainment and for more serious purposes.

In this chapter we have also seen that Native Americans, particularly in the past had intimate knowledge of their worlds. This knowledge came from observation and experience. When native people defined their worlds

it was in the abstract and physical. Oral traditions tell complex histories of native people's origins.

Most importantly we have learned that tribal people still define themselves in terms of boundaries of their worlds. People do this for several reasons; to keep collective identity (tribalism) intact; to establish order in a mysterious, complex world; and for individual psychological order or well-being. We have learned that when a people venture beyond the boundaries of their world—the limits of safety or experience—there is physical and psychological threat to the continuity of those people. With this in mind, it is easier to understand why a tribal people define themselves in terms of boundaries.

Sandoval, the Navajo medicine man, made a simple statement about order in the tribal (Navajo) world, which not only applies to the Navajo but to most tribal people in North America.

"There was a plan from the stars down . . ."

Suggested Additional Readings

BROWN, J.W.
  1975   "Native American Contributions to Science, Engineering, and Medicine," *Science*, 189: 38-40.

HAWKINS, GERALD S.
  1973   *Beyond Stonehenge*, New York, Harper and Row.

HICKS, R. D.
  1976   "Astronomy in the Ancient Americas," *Sky and Telescope*, 51:372-377 (June).

(No Author)
  1975   "Indians Record Crab Nebula," *Science Digest*, 78:19 (December).

MALMSTOM, V. H.
  1973   "Origin of the Meso American 260 Day Calendar," *Science*, 181:939-941, (Sept. 7).
MENZEL, DONALD H.
  1964   *Field Guide to the Stars and Planets*, Boston, Mass., Houghton and Mifflin.
MOMADAY, N. S.
  1967   *The Way To Rainy Mountain*, Albuquerque, N.M., University of New Mexico Press.
SMITHSON ASTROPHYSICAL OBSERVATORY
  1969   *Star Atlas of Reference Stars and Nonstellar Objects*, The Observatory.
(NO AUTHOR)
  1974   "Stonehenge, U.S.A., Wyoming's Medicine Wheel," *Newsweek*, 83:60 (June 24).

CHAPTER FIVE

5 Shamanism and the World of Spirits: The Oldest Religion

The greatest sacred thing is knowing
the order and the structure of things.
Barney Mitchell

In Chapter One, Part II, we discussed certain concepts of the sacred that many Native American tribal people share. Among these concepts were

1. A belief in or knowledge of unseen powers: The Great Mystery or The Mysteries.

2. Knowledge that all things in the universe are dependent on each other.

Reflected in many sacred systems of knowledge is the idea that the world is a mystery and yet, at the same time, the world operates according to strict, ordered relationships. Some questions can never be answered with a single answer and others can be answered simply by observing various cycles day after day, year after year; cycles like day and night, the changing seasons, and the cycles of growth in humans, plants, and animals.

In ceremonials and rituals we humans dramatize this concept. To dramatize the mysterious side of the world we offer prayers, prayer sticks, or sprinkle corn meal to communicate to the sacred powers what we cannot say in words. We do this to express feelings *symbolically* that cannot be expressed any other way. At the same time, reflecting the order of the universe, we take care to perform all our dance movements correctly, to observe certain procedures before and after the ceremony because we know that if we didn't a certain order would be upset and certain relationships would be put out of balance. How do we know these things? How do we learn about natural laws that we cannot ordinarily perceive?

In Chapter One, Part II we also pointed out another element most Native American tribal people recognize in their sacred lives. This was *that most communities and tribes recognize individuals who are responsible for specialized, perhaps secret knowledge. These individuals help pass on knowledge and sacred practices from generation to generation storing what they know in their memories.* Persons who are responsible for specialized knowledge are most often individuals *who live to understand the sacred.* Their life and their vocation is devoted to learning about the mysteries of the world and knowing and manipulating the relationships by which the world operates (by manipulating we mean "handling, working with, and using"). These individuals are born with or develop a special sensitivity to and interest in the elements that make up the sacred. Often, these persons are exposed to greater hardships than most people; personal injury, fright, anxiety, and loneliness. If they succeed in their journey or quest for knowledge and in their work as sacred practitioners, they then have greater responsibilities than most people and are respected for this.

These individuals are most often responsible for maintaining a balanced relationship between The People and the natural world and the world of the sacred powers. They spend their lives "learning the rules," exploring what Barney Mitchell refers to as "the order and the structure of things." In ancient times, it is told in the origin histories, these people were taught basic knowledge from the Holy People or from plants and animals. Today these practitioners carry on the task of learning, memorizing, teaching, and putting into practice, the ancient laws and orders of things. They know and they teach us that there are some questions that cannot be answered, some mysteries about the world that are to be wondered at, with reverence, but never explained.

In this chapter we will refer to these practitioners as *shamans* which is not a Native North American term. Rather, it is a term that has come to describe *the most obvious characteristics of those individuals who seek the sources of the sacred and who practice special ways of knowledge* in order, for example, to cure illnesses, maintain the ceremonial calendar, insure hunting success, or seek lost objects. We recognize that each community and tribe has its own linguistic term or name for these practitioners. Often there are individual names for each kind of specialized work. Sometimes a person might be an "all around" practitioner, having many talents and a wide range of knowledge. Most often however, practitioners choose a specialty or have a special vocation for one area of knowledge. Where these tribal names are available* we will use the native term along with *shaman*, keeping in mind that the term shaman merely simplifies our discussion by enabling us to use one common term throughout this chapter.

The word shaman comes from the Tungus language of the Tungus people who live in Siberia. Their word is *saman*. The shamans of Siberia have often been viewed as the *prototype* or clearest example of all the shamanistic traits we will eventually be discussing. Aboriginal Siberian shamanism also seems the best example of the kind of practice, technique, and body of knowledge that would also describe the early sacred practices of Native North American practitioners. And, like the aboriginal cultures of North America, in the tribal cultures of Central and North Asia, including Siberia, *the sacred*

life of The People centered around the shaman.

Aboriginally, because the shaman had a special vocation for searching out the *intangible*, the mysterious, and the nonordinary experiences of life, he/she was also the individual who interpreted the world for The People and who taught through stories and songs what life was all about. These individuals learned from first-hand experience the laws of natural, *ecological* relationships and the mysteries at the heart of knowledge.

In this chapter we will be discussing two ideas of shamanism: the individual shaman and his/her techniques, and the concept at the root of the sacred which shamans are aware of in their work as healers—the *concept of balance between the individual and the natural world.* First we will introduce some of the characteristics of the shaman and his/her vocation. Second, the concept of balance at the root of the sacred as seen in the tradition of hunting. And third, we will examine individual practitioners in three tribal cultures in North America: Eskimo groups from the Baffin Bay area, Pima, and Wintu.

THE CHARACTERISTICS AND VOCATION OF THE SHAMAN

Shamans are individuals who, through some inborn sensitivity or need, take as their vocation the quest for knowledge that uses a *direct* attempt at experiencing the Mysteries. Usually the most powerful shamans are individuals who are forced by illness, a compelling dream or vision, or some other need, to become shamans whether they want to or not.

A typical situation is that the shaman-to-be suddenly gets very sick, falls unconscious or begins to "act crazy." Perhaps the man or woman "hears things," complains of voices speaking at night, or perhaps he/she runs away and won't speak to anyone for a period of time. Sometimes these things keep happening to an individual on and off for a number of years. At first the individual does not understand what is happening. Later, when the individual is older and has a greater understanding of scared ways and practices he/she may see that these afflications and pains, the

---

* In ethnographic literature, native words are often spelled differently, depending on who is writing. Until recently, words and names were not verified by tribal people, especially the specialists who could help in the identification of terms. All such words then are subject to change by tribal specialists, linguists, and others.

voices and the strange dreams, are trying to tell him/her something.

At this point the shaman-to-be may seek a shaman practitioner to ask for guidance and advice and this practitioner may be able and willing to help. The shaman-to-be may be given a course of action by the practitioner that he/she has to complete in order to gain control over the forces that are making life miserable for him/her. This course of action may require a series of tasks aimed at solving specialized problems. Other sessions are spent with the teacher in which the shaman-to-be or initiate learns specialized knowledge too dangerous for other individuals to come in contact with. In addition to training the shaman-to-be receives from an experienced shaman, the shaman-to-be also seeks his/her own knowledge through tests which include vision quests, "wanderings," and other situations which force a confrontation between the shaman-to-be and the forces which give life--or the Mysteries.

The shaman-to-be may place him/herself in various physical locations that are particularly receptive to spiritual forces, such as on a mountain, near rivers, in caves, and so on. There, by means of fasting or other tests, he/she may receive a strong dream or vision. At that time the individual may be unconscious or asleep. But, because of the fasting or other physical tests, another part of the mind and the spirit takes over. A vision has been described as "when you see something with your inner eyes, that means with all your soul and spirit." In the dream or the vision, *the individual experiences all that happens in the vision as if he/she were awake.*

Since by now the shaman-to-be has received some training and help from other shamans, he/she is able to understand or interpret the dream or the vision: it is not just a crazy or frightening dream. For instance, in the vision the shaman-to-be may encounter some being, a spirit of some kind perhaps, who will advise the young shaman-to-be what to do next in order to control the pains and feelings he/she has been afflicted with. The spirit being may offer to help the shaman-to-be by teaching its own particular medicine, by offering its own particular "power." The shaman-to-be may also be taught at this time how to "call on" his/her spirit helper again in the future.

The dream or vision that the shaman-to-be receives at this time may also be the ultimate learning experience for the individual in training. After this the individual is a shaman and has acquired the tools necessary to seek knowledge on his/her own. In other words, in the dream or vision the shaman-to-be finally experiences a "clear picture" of what life is all about. Before, throughout his/her life, the shaman learned fragments of sacred knowledge and practices.

Basic knowledge about the relationships and balances in the world of humans and the natural world are taught the shaman-to-be in stories, travels, and through the ceremonials. But in setting out on a vision quest or a "wandering" test, the shaman-to-be seeks an even deeper insight into the "order and the structure of things" as Barney Mitchell described the heart of the sacred. The shaman-to-be's direct experience of sacred knowledge comes at this time. Often the shaman-to-be may not understand *all* of his/her dream or vision. But through the years, as he/she experiences other "altered states of consciousness" and has other encounters with spirit beings or other tests, the shaman comes to understand more and more. As we said earlier, shamanism is a vocation which is a quest for knowledge and most practitioners do not learn all they have to learn overnight. Sometimes it takes years to learn specialized knowledge, years to feel comfortable with the powerful spirit beings and other forces that are needed in a shaman's work.

In addition to the technical aspects of a shaman's initiation and later work as a practitioner the shaman is also an *artist* of the sacred. That is, he/she is able to experience what we have earlier referred to as *ecstasy.* The student will recall that in Chapter One, according to some Native Americans, wisdom and knowledge cannot be separated from spiritual and emotional feelings. Along with the quest for knowledge must remain a sensitivity to *experience and perceptions that cannot be explained.*

In a state of ecstasy or altered consciousness an individual may find that he/she may lose the ability to think or speak in an ordinary way. Other means of perception and communication take over then. A Shaman is an individual who can put him/herself into a trance

Lodge or "shaking tent" used by the specialists in "seeing the future, prophecy, and fortelling events. Anishnabe, Lac Courte Oreille Reservation, Wisconsin. A.E. Jenks, 1899. (Courtesy of the Smithsonian Institution, National Anthropological Archives

(one form of ecstatic consciousness) in order to perform certain tasks that would otherwise be impossible. For example, individuals who have experienced once or many times this kind of altered consciousness find that they can, without previous experience, compose songs, see into the future, foretell events, see into a body or into an illness, and even fly.*

---

* Shamans often describe one of their special techniques as "flying" because they can travel over long distances with the sensation of leaving their body behind. Sometimes they are called upon to diagnose the behavior of someone, for example, who has had a frightening experience, who is very unhappy, wanders around and won't eat. These are some of the symptoms practitioners call "soul loss." If the shaman believes that the individual has "lost his/her soul," or has had his/her soul stolen away, the shaman must then seek out the lost soul, perhaps requiring that the shaman travel by "flight" to find the soul.

** See Chapter Seven, **The World Out of Balance** and the film, *Dream Dance of the Kashia Pomo.*

It is difficult work being gifted with such abilities and powers. For example, Essie Parrish,** in her role as Bole Maru "dreamer" says that the life of a "dreamer" is a hard one because "Your dreams keep you awake." And Bryan Beavers, a Maidu man from northern California, in the film, *Bryan Beavers: A Moving Portrait,* told how he changed his mind about becoming a shaman in the middle of his spirit quest. From the spirit's home under a lake where he had swam, he decided to turn around and go back. He did, and swam up to the shore and got out of the water, leaving the spirits behind. He explained his decision by saying, "I wasn't scared, I just didn't want them hanging around all the time." Another difficulty that sometimes occurs is when shamans take a dislike to each other or are used by people to do bad works on someone else. In such cases shamans "go to war" against each other using their nonordinary powers to create dangerous situations. For example, Harold Goodsky of Nett Lake Minnesota, tells of the time someone sent a shaman in the shape of an owl to kill his uncle one night. His uncle, also a shaman, caught the owl, wrestled with it, and killed it right before Goodsky's eyes. Astonished at the power of his uncle, Goodsky exclaimed, "I couldn't even kill an owl in the daytime."

In the following account of a "wandering" a Pit River man, Robert Spring, explains to Jaime de Angulo what the difference is between an ordinary man's wandering and a shaman's-to-be. Spring tells us:

Dinihowi...that's what we Indians call luck. A man has got to have luck, no matter for what, whether its for gambling, or for hunting, for making love, for anything, unless he wants to be just a common Indian...

When a fellow is young, everybody is after him to go to the mountains and get himself a *dinihowi*. The old men say, "You'll never amount to anything if you don't go and catch a *dinihowi*." And then you hear other fellows brag about their luck at gambling, or how they got a good *dinihowi* for hunting. Well, there comes a time when a young fellow starts to feel uneasy, kind of sad, kind of worried, that's just about the time he's getting to be a man grown up. Then he starts to "Wander," that's what we call it, wandering. That's the time you go to the hills, you don't come home, you stay out all night, you get scared, you cry; two, three days you go hungry. Sometime your people get worried, come after you, but you throw rocks at them: Go away, I don't want you, leave me alone. You get pretty hungry, you get dizzy, you are afraid of grizzly bears. Maybe you fall asleep and someone come wake you up, maybe a wolf, push your head with his foot, maybe bluejay peck at your face, maybe little fly get in your ear, he say: Hey! Wake up! You better go home! I seen you wandering here, crying, hungry, I pity you, I like you. I help you. I help you. Listen, this is my song. Remember that song. When you want me, you come here and sing my song. I'll hear you. I'll hear you. I'll come...

de Angulo: But then, I don't see what is the difference between the *dinihowi* and the *damaagome*...

Spring: There is no difference. It's all the same. Only the *damaagome* that's for doctors.

de Angulo: How does the doctor get his *damaagomes?*

Spring: Just like you and me get a *dinihowi.* He goes to the mountain. He cries. Then someone comes and says, this is my song, I'll help you.

de Angulo: Well then, I don't see any difference.

Spring: I am telling you there is no difference. Only the *dinihowi* that's for plain Indians like you and me, and the *damaagome* that's for doctors... Well, I'll tell you, there is maybe some difference. The *damaagome* is kind of mean, quarrelsome, always fighting. The *dinihowi* is more peaceful.
(de Angulo, 1973:36-38)

This account is similar to others in North America. We discuss in other chapters for instance, certain times in an individual's life when he/she receives some kind of initiation into higher learning which either requires a solitary test or some kind of an organized ritual/ceremonial. Aboriginally, in some cultures like the Anishnabe for example, all young men were expected to seek a spirit helper just to aid them in hunting. But when a shaman-to-be seeks or meets a spirit being, the encounter may have stronger consequences as Robert Spring suggests; the shaman's spirits may be more difficult to control. If a shaman cannot control his/her strengths or spirit helpers, he/she will have problems carrying out his/her practice as a shaman. In the following story, Sukmit, a Pit River Shaman, relates to de Angulo an experience he had with his *damaagome* at a Hand Game:

Yes, some of them *damaagome* is mean. When I started doctoring I tried a trick. I tried bringing my poison to a hand-game. Now a doctor is not supposed to use his poison for gambling. It's against the rules. But I thought I was smart, see. I thought to hell with the rules, I do like white man, see. Well, in the middle of the game I got awful thirsty, and I get up and go to the spring, and I take a long drink of water, and I got awful dizzy and sick, I got cramps, I puke...See, my *damaagome* he do that, he mad because I bring him to hand-game, not supposed to do that. (de Angulo, 1973:39)

Through the techniques that enable the shaman to "leave" the ordinary world and to alter awareness, the shaman is able to travel beyond ordinary boundaries of experience. The shaman is able to obtain many different perspectives on the world, from seeing over great geographical distances, to seeing within a plant or the movement of the wind. In this way the shaman studies *ecological* and natural relationships and learns about the origin and the nature of things; about the migrations and changes that have occurred throughout the history of the earth and to The People living on it.

The shaman travels inward as well and learns the way human beings operate inside their minds and bodies. Aboriginally, the shaman was often an all-around sacred practitioner: a mystic, a doctor, an herbalist, a diagnostician, a hunter, a dancer, a singer, a storyteller, an artist, and a person of knowledge.

In Western terms the shaman is a philosopher, a surgeon, a priest, a magician, a botanist, and a psychologist. These are terms which only partly describe the knowledge and the vocation of the shaman. As we shall emphasize again, only recently has Western science acknowledged the skills and knowledge that are the property of the individuals we refer to as shamans. What has in the past been labeled "magic" is now studied in academic institutions as a whole complex of phenomena known as parapsychology—the study of such things as clairvoyance (seeing into the future), psychokinetics (moving objects by the mind or at will), and mental telepathy (reading thoughts).

The ethnologists who first came in contact with practitioners such as shamans, labeled their work "magic," "miracle," and "fakery." The Church, both Catholic and Protestant, termed it "the work of the devil." They used these terms because what they saw they did not understand nor could they explain it. However, today some of these attitudes are changing, for one because Western medicine has not achieved success with certain problems that native practitioners are successful at dealing with.

"Non-Western" methods of healing are practiced in cultures throughout the world. These are medical practices quite different from anything in the West and many of them are based on aboriginal shamanistic practices. In the People's Republic of China, for example, the complex system of acupuncture* and related medical systems are now being carefully studied in the West. Other techniques associated with shamanism are auric reading (or the diagnosis of disease by analyzing the color and light around or in the body, similar to the method used by the "crystal gazers" of the Navajo); massage; laying on of hands; and many forms of hypnosis. All of these techniques were or are used by tribal practitioners in North America.

We have mentioned some of the skills and non-ordinary events associated with shamans. The skills that most shamans have in common throughout North America might be summarized into the following practices:

The shaman is a composer of special healing songs.

The shaman can cause him/herself to enter into a trance or trance-like condition.

The shaman can travel after souls or to seek lost objects.

The shaman can diagnose and cure illness.

The shaman has spirit helpers whom he/she can control or with whom he/she can communicate.

The Shaman As Healer

As we said earlier, the shaman is an individual who personally seeks the sources of the sacred. One of the most important ways the shaman uses the knowledge that he/she has learned is by helping to maintain the health and well-being of his/her people. The theories and practices that are created around this vocation of healing form the core of the earliest religions and are what give shape to sacred knowledge and practices today.

Essie Parish, a Pomo, is both a shaman-type "sucking" doctor and a Mole Baru "dreamer" and dance leader.** In the course of her life she has experienced a number of non-ordinary or altered states of consciousness in which she has had a vision given to her, sometimes in dreams and other times in a trance. These visions have provided her with information concerning her role as a leader and as a doctor among her people. In Chapter Seven, *The World Out of Balance*, a dream that taught her a particular dance for the Bole Maru ceremonial is recalled. Below is another vision she had. In this vision she had to take a journey in order to find a source of strength for her people, a way of revitalizing her People's sacred ways and practices. During the course of the vision she received a clear insight into

---

* Acupuncture is a system of healing and anesthesia that utilizes, a) the theory of negative and positive balance in the body known as Ying (female) and Yang (male) and b) certain areas or "points" on the body which correspond to organs and organism relationships in the body. When activated by the insertion of special needles, the body can be anesthetisized, rebalanced, local pain alleviated, and blockages in the system removed. The student is directed to further readings in the reference section of this textbook which cover subjects related to shamanism.

**See Chapter Seven and the films, *Dream Dance of the Kashia Pomo* and *Sucking Doctor*.

the fundamental mysteries of life. In addition to receiving this sacred knowledge she learned certain techniques of healing. Essie Parrish recalls her journey below:

It is a test you have to pass. Then you can learn to heal with the finger. I went through every test on the way, that's how come I'm a shaman. "Be careful on the journey," they said, "the journey to heaven," they warned me. And so I went. Through rolling hills I walked. Mountains and valleys, and rolling hills, I walked and walked—you hear many things there in those rolling hills and valleys, and I walked and walked until I came to a footbridge, and on the right side were a whole lot of people and they were naked and crying out, "How'd you get over there, we want to get over there, too, but we're stuck here; please come over here and help us cross, the water's too deep for us." I didn't pay no attention, I just walked and walked, and then I heard an animal, sounded like a huge dog, and there was a huge dog and next to him a huge lady wearing blue clothes, and I decided I had to walk right through. I did and the dog only snarled at me. Never go back. I walked and walked and I came to only one tree, and I walked over to it and looked up at it and read the message: Go on, you're half way. From there I felt better, a little better. And I walked and walked and walked and walked and walked and I saw water, huge water— how to get through? I fear it's deep. Very blue water. But I have to go. Put out the first foot, then the left, never use the left hand, and I passed through. Went on and on and on, and I had to enter a place and there I had to look down: it was hot and there were people there and they looked tiny down there in that furnace running around crying. I had to enter. You see, these tests are to teach my people how to live. Fire didn't burn me. And I walked and walked and walked and walked. On the way you're going to suffer. And I

came to a four-way road like a cross. Which is the right way? I already knew. East is the right way to go to heaven. North, South, and West are dangerous. At this crossroad there was a place in the center. North you could see beautiful things of the Earth, hills and fields and flowers and everything beautiful and I felt like grabbing it but I turned away. South was dark, but there were sounds, monsters and huge animals. And I turned away and Eastward I walked and walked and walked and there were flowers, on both sides of the road; flowers and flowers and flowers out of this world.

And there is white light at the center, while you're walking. This is the complicated thing: my mind changes. We are the people on the Earth. We know sorrow and knowledge and faith and talent and everything. Now as I was walking there, some places I feel like crying and some places I feel like talking and some places I feel like dancing, but I am leaving these behind for the next world. Then when I entered into that place I knew: if you enter heaven you might have to work. This is what I saw in my vision. I don't have to go nowhere to see. Visions are everywhere.*

All Things Are Dependent On Each Other

One of the important concepts Native American tribal people share with respect to the sacred is that all things in the universe are dependent on each other. This concept is first introduced to a child through the stories and songs of the origin histories. Behind the ceremonials and rituals each tribe carries out throughout the year is the notion of *balance and imbalance.* Among most North American tribal people the aboriginal theories of disease include this concept of balance and imbalance. Disease is seen as a part of the total environment which includes the individual, the community, the natural world, and the world of ancestors and spirits. The shaman and other knowledgeable practitioners have developed systems of diagnosis and healing from these origin histories and from their own experimentation.

In the following section we will discuss how

---

* From a speech given by Essie Parrish on March 14, 1972. It was recorded by George Quasha and printed in *Alcherniga*, Ethnopoetics 1, 1975, pp. 27-29.

these original laws taught to the first shamans came to form the core of today's sacred ways and why we might call shamanism, "the oldest religion."

SHAMANISM: THE SOURCE OF SACRED KNOWLEDGE

The practitioners we refer to as shamans use their knowledge in three main areas:

1. They understand the laws of ecology; the balances established at the time of Creation; and the guidelines given to human beings by the creating deities, Holy People, or animals.
2. They know the order and structure of things—they know the *names* of things.
3. They are servants to The People—they maintain their power and knowledge by using it to help others.

We will discuss each of these areas in this section to enable the student to identify shamanistic concepts in the section covering individuals in three different cultures.

The Laws of Ecology Taught At The Time of Creation

Reflected in many tribal healing systems is the idea that everything is balanced in the world. An imbalance can cause illness or disease. Basic to Pima and Navajo ways of life for example, is the idea that if you "live right," live according to certain "do's" and "don't's" you will enjoy good health. Later, when we examine the Eskimo healing *seance* the student will notice the same thing: the patient becomes ill who does not pay attention to certain rules and taboos.

Often these rules were given to The People at the time of the Creation of this world. Tribal oral traditions tell of the struggles, false starts, triumphs, tragedies, and wanderings that The People and animals had to go through in order to finally arrive at the world we live in today. The guidelines of behavior that help The People survive and live a long life are given to The People in these histories. Often the oral histories have complex sub-stories, songs, chants and other accompanying tools of learning. Ceremonial practitioners and sha-

mans learn to interpret the oral histories and they learn to use the oral histories as whole systems of knowledge: a complete system of scientific knowledge, prayers, songs, and so on. *They learn to know how we must live in order to keep the balance of relationships that order the world.*

Among the Navajo there is a "chantway" which is both a healing ritual and a ritual hunting technique. One man, Claus Chee Sonny of Tsaile, Arizona, knows a body of knowledge called the Deer Huntingway. There are a number of stories and chants connected to the Deer Huntingway, as well as a system of practices and observances which go with the actual hunting of game animals, deer in particular. The stories tell of the origin of all game animals and the origin of hunting skills. They also outline what the human being's

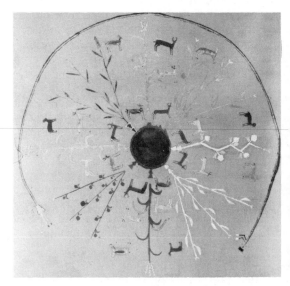

Navajo sandpainting by Hostin Claw, 1905-1912, used in the Plumeway. This sandpainting shows the Game Animals and plants—food plants and food animals. (Courtesy of the Smithsonian Institution, National Anthropological Archives)

relationship is to animal and plant life and how hunting (killing or taking a life) effects us and other balances in the natural world. Some of the teachings of the Deer Huntingway describe what our attitudes and perceptions must be to maintain the balances in the natural world. In one episode of the Deer Huntingway, as told by Claus Chee Sonny, all the game animals which had been hidden by *Hasch'ézhiini* (Black

God) were later released by a young man, the youngest brother, disguised as a puppy. The story continues:

In the ravine, where Graystreak Mountain and the Sweat Lodge hill face each other, the man who earlier had been a puppy waited in ambush. Wind had told him: "There is where the tracks are. The deer will come marching through there in single file." There were no guns yet then; only bow and arrows were used to hunt. The hunter had four arrows—one was made of sheet lightning (*hatsolaghal*), one of zigzag lightning (*atsiniltlish*), one of sunlight roots, and one of rainbow. These are the four types of arrows which also the friends of this man had.

The Large Buck

The first deer, a large buck, came with many antlers. The hunter got ready to shoot the buck. His arrow was already in place. But, just as he was ready to shoot, the deer had transformed himself into a mountain mahogany bush (*tse esdaazii*). After a while, a mature man stood up from this bush. He stood up and said, "Do not shoot! We are your neighbors. These are the things that will be in the future when human beings will have come into existence. This is the way you will eat us." And he told the hunter how to kill and to eat the deer. So the hunter let the mature Deerman go at the price of his information. And the Deer-man left.

The Doe

Then the large doe, a shiny doe, appeared behind the one who had left. The hunter was ready again, to shoot the doe in the heart. But the doe turned into a cliffrose bush. A while later a young woman stood up from the bush. The woman said, "Do not shoot! We are your neighbors. In the future, when man has been created, men will live because of us. Men will use us to live on." So then, at the price of her information, the hunter let the Doe-Woman go. And she left.

The Two Pointer

Then a young buck, a two-pointer, came along. And the hunter got ready to shoot the two-pointer. But the deer transformed himself into a dead tree (*tsin bisga*). After a while, a young man stood up from the dead tree and said, "—in the future, after man has been created, if you talk about us in the wrong way, we will cause trouble for you if you urinate, and we will trouble your eyes. We will trouble your ears if we do not approve of what you say about us." And at the price of his information, the hunter let the young Deer-Man go.

The Fawn

Then the little Fawn appeared. The hunter was ready to shoot the Fawn, but the Fawn turned into a lichen-spotted rock (*tse dlaad*). After a while, a young girl stood up from the rock and spoke: "In the future all this will happen if we approve; and whatever we shall disapprove shall all be up to me. I am in charge of all the other deer people. If you talk bad about us, and if we disapprove of what you say, I am the one who will respond with killing you. I will kill you with what I am. If you hear the cry of my voice, you will know that trouble is in store for you. If you do not make use of us properly, even in times when we are numerous, you will not see us anymore. We are the four deer who have transformed themselves into different kinds of things. Into these four kinds of things we can transform ourselves. Moreover, we can assume the form of all the different kinds of plants. Then, when you look you will not see us. In the future, only those of whom we approve shall eat the mighty deer. If, when you hunt, you come across four deer, you will not kill all of them. You may kill three and leave one. But if you kill all of us, it is not good."

This is what the little fawn said—that, what he is, is not good. "Where I go, before me travel snowstorms. All other things too, which are no good, go in front of me. This is my protection. If you are walking on an unused road and see the tracks of a doe, or if a doe catches up with you from behind, that is I. And knowing this you will not bother me.

These are the things which will bring you happiness. When you kill a deer, you will lay him with the head toward your house. You will cover the earth with plants or with branches of trees, lengthwise, with the growing tips of the plants pointing the direction of the deer's head—toward your house. So it shall be made into a thick padding, and the deer shall be laid on that. Then you will take us home to your house and eat of us. You will place our bones under any of the things whose form we can assume—mountain mahogany, cliffrose, dead tree, lichen-spotted rock, spruce, pine, or under any of the other good plants. At these places you may put our bones. You will sprinkle the place with yellow pollen. Once, Twice. Then you lay the bones. And then you sprinkle yellow pollen on top of the bones. This is for the protection of the game animals. In this manner they will live on; their bones can live again and live a lasting life."

This is what the little Fawn told the hunter. "You will be able to use the entire body of the deer, even the skin. And we belong to Talking god. We belong to Black-god. We are in his hand. And he is able to make us deaf and blind. Those among you, of whom he approves, are the good people. They will hunt with success and will be able to kill us. According to his own decisions he will surrender us to the people. The Black-god is Crow. But when you hunt you do not refer to him as Crow but as Black-god. Today, still, the game animals belong to Talking-god and Black-god."

Then, referring to what the Fawn had said, the other three deer said, "This is what will be." And this is what will be. And this is how it is. And this is how they made this story.

So these are the four who gave information. Man was created later. All these events happened among the gods, prior to the creation of man. All animals were like human beings then, they were able to talk. Thus, this story was not made up by old Navajo men. These events were brought about by the Black-god. Then, after having obtained all this information, the hunter let the four deer go. (Luckert, 1975:29-31)

Before there was agriculture and ceremonialism directed towards the growth of domestic plants, hunting was the primary means of survival—hunting and the gathering of roots (tubers), plants, nuts, and berries. In the northernmost regions of this continent the Native People did not have agriculture until the late 19th century, and today some still depend only on hunting and gathering (and, of course, nowadays, commercial food). These cultures include the Eskimo of the Baffin Bay area, the Crees in the Northeast and the Athapaskan tribal people in the northwest. The Navajo, until they encountered Pueblo people in the 16th century, were primarily a hunting and gathering people, with shamanism at the center of their religious system. The Eskimo people, until a strong campaign of Christian conversion in the 19th and 20th centuries, were a hunting society with shamanism and its realms of knowledge at the center of their sacred life and world-view. Baffin Bay area Eskimos were and still are strictly hunters since plant life for eating is very limited.

By examining the relationships that were established in the aboriginal hunting culture between animals, plants, and human beings, we can see how these principles of balance and ecology helped create sacred beliefs and procedures of human beings. And when we observe the role and function of the shaman in diagnosing and curing diseases, we see how closely related his/her work is to those of the early hunters.

One of the roles of the early hunters and shamans was to communicate directly with the animals they were hunting. Their songs and prayers were often based on the fact that they had to kill their kin, the animals, in order to survive. The *methods* they used to kill animals were also given to the hunters as we hear in the Creation and origin histories—by animals in many cases. The animals, in other words, said, "Yes, you can kill us, but to maintain the proper balance in nature, you must do it this way. And honor us before you kill one of us. You must sing the proper song or we will not hear you and we will not appear for you."

---

* For further information see, for example, A. Balikci, *The Netsilik Eskimo* (New York, Natural History Press, 1970).

Below, Claus Chee Sonny describes this relationship: the relationship of *imbalance* in the natural world to *disease*,* and the origin of guidelines created in the days before the creation of human beings, to maintain the correct balances in the natural world:

Final Hunting Instructions

All the deer gods, who lived at the beginning, went into the hole at the south side of Black Mountain; through it they returned underground to the house of their origin—to the home of Black-god which is the peak of Black Mountain. All the wild deer, which are not available, come either from the mountain mahogany bush or from the other things into which deer can transform themselves. Concerning the way in which men are expected to hunt them, the divine Deer-people gave these final instructions:

You should never point an arrow or gun at just anything. If you point your weapon unnecessarily, the deer simply turns into whatever you happen to aim at. If you walk over to it, you find plants and rocks, but not us. So you should always hold on to your weapon tightly. Because if it starts slipping away from your hand, you will only send us away. So, do not just play around.

You should not talk bad about us game animals when you hunt. We can hear you, even over a mountain. And if you find us in numbers of four, you may not kill all of us. You must leave one.

In Winter, when you think you have hunted sufficient meat to last you till spring, when you kill a male deer last you will take a whisker of the deer and throw it to the east. You call the deer by his name and pray what you wish to pray—then the hunting season is over. If you happen to kill a female deer as your last one, you do the same, except you throw the whisker to the west; pray what you have to pray, and so close the season.

You will not throw the bones away just anywhere. Everything of which we are made, such as our skin, meat, bones, is to be used. They are most useful. And this is true. Anything that we hold on to, such as the earth from the four sacred mountains, the rainbow, the jewels, the corn, all the plants we eat, will be in us. Our bodies contain all these. And because of this we are very useful. Needles can be made from the bones of the front legs and hind legs. The ends can be sharpened to a needle point. This is what we use to stitch buckskin together—and the buckskin is most useful. The usefulness of the deer is the foundation which has been laid; it serves as an example for other things. This is what is meant when we say that the deer are first in all things. We are in the gods who are mentioned, in the mountains, in the rainbows, in the roots of sunlight, in the lightnings. And so we are the most useful thing under the sun. For that reason, an unwounded buckskin— or a deer not killed by a weapon—shall be used in the sacred ceremonies. Also, we are in all the plants. In this manner, even the insects are associated with us. And so the buckskins, the white needles, and the meat are first—nowadays even the fat is hard to get. All the meat is very useful. You can put deer meat as medicine on sheep, on horses, and on other domestic animals. All livestock lives because of the deer. That is what keeps the animals moist, breathing, walking about, and altogether alive. And animals are our food. They are our thoughts.

Now this is the way in which the one who holds us in his hands, Talking-god, controls us: Talking-god is first; Black-god (Crow) is next in line; then follow Red-tailed Hawk, then Little Hawk, then Robin. So these, in that order, are the five who control us. These are the ones who put us on the earth, who still give us life. In addition there is Wind, the one who informs the deer at the tips of their ears.

...If you do everything right, if you remind your hunter companion to hunt properly, you will always have enough meat to eat. It does not matter how many people there are. You will always get

---

* *Disease, dis* = not + *ease* = "not at ease".

enough if you hunt right, if you prepare the animals correctly, if you bring them home properly, and if you dispose of the bones in the prescribed manner. And this is true today. If you follow this advice of the Deer-people, you will always get enough to eat. But if you do wrong, if against the rules you urinate on the bones or even on the hair of the deer, you will be troubled when you urinate.

The Talking-god advised you not to tamper with the head of the deer. If you do, then either a young child, or a young girl, or a young woman in the family will become blind or deaf. Both Talking-god and Black-god advise you not to think anything bad about the game animals, that you do not follow the same pattern as you do when you butcher a sheep. You will not cut the throat. If you butcher a deer like you butcher a sheep, you will become insane, you will get lost somewhere.

These rules were not made by men. They were made by the gods before the creation of human kind. These rules must be kept sacred. These rules were made so that man would be able to reach old age without losing his hearing and without losing his eyesight.

All this is information which the Deer-people have given about themselves. It is not man-made information. The gods, while taking on the form of a fully grown man, of a young woman, of a young man and a child, have told this about themselves. (Luckert, 1975:38-40)

Knowing The Order and The Structure of Things

The *spirit helpers* of shamans are often animal and bird spirits, and sometimes plant spirit helpers. Aboriginally, in many northern cultures, young men like the young men

Robert Spring talked about earlier, went on a vision quest or wandering to find a spirit helper so they would be successful hunters. The shaman, like the hunter, seeks spirit helpers but the shaman goes a step further; he/she seeks to know the ways of knowledge of all the plants and animals. He/she seeks to carry on the ancient ways of speaking with the animals and plants and knowing their "language" as Barney Mitchell said, the Singer of the Wind Way knows the language of the wind.* The shaman seeks to learn the ways of the world and his/her particular spirit helper aids the shaman in knowing its own particular style— with the eyes of an eagle, with the smell of a deer, with the quickness of a fox, for example.

When a person is not feeling well and goes to a shaman to find out the source of the problem, the shaman diagnoses the cause of the illness or the "imbalance."** In order to make the diagnosis the shaman employs the technique of *seeing* which is one of the special skills of these practitioners. Seeing may take the form of seeing the body's system as different colors, intensities of light, shadows, or other signs. The shaman is also able to see if there is anything inside the patient that is foreign to it—an *intrusion* (stone, hair, crystal, part of an animal, etc.), or if the patient has poor circulation. Often the word for this kind of practitioner in native societies is translated "one who sees."

The shaman is also able to tell where the patient has deviated or turned away from *the principles of creation*. In other words, the shaman is able to tell the patient what he/she has done, that according to the ancient guidelines should not have been done.† The shaman, using this information obtained by *seeing*, then prescribes a cure. The special abilities of the shaman mean that he/she can affect change in the patient's normal bodily functions. The shaman makes changes, rebalances or opens up some blocked area in the body so that the patient can actually cure him/herself with the assistance of the shaman. The body of the patient, in other words, responds with its own healing powers. That is why most practitioners insist on certain strict procedures before and after a healing session or ceremony: the patient is expected to do his/her part. Some of these strict rules cover what the patient can eat before and after

---

*   See Chapter One, Part II, no. 5.

** We will be discussing this in further detail in the third section of this chapter, particularly when we examine the Baffin Bay Eskimo shamans and Gregorio, the Pima shaman or *ma:kai*.

† See Chapter Twelve, **Navajo Traditional Knowledge**.

the healing session, sex habits, bathing procedures, and others. If the body responds positively to the shaman's work, then the patient is on the way to being healed. In some cases a healing session will require that the shaman merely remove an *intrusion* and also figure out where the intrusion came from if necessary. In others, the shaman must administer a healing session that will rebalance many elements that are "out of order." The longer Navajo "sings" or healing ceremonies are examples of this kind of session. The Night Chant, for example, lasts nine days and nights. On all of the nights there is dancing and on the final night masked dancers or *yeis* appear to dance. In the morning and afternoon of each day five sandpaintings are made under the supervision of the ceremonial practitioner or "singer." In addition to knowing and making five sand-paintings a day the singer also administers herbs to the patient and chants from the origin histories in between sandpaintings. Barney Mitchell explained that the language of the dawn is the knowledge that belongs to this practitioner.

What do shamans *see* when they seek to diagnose the cause of an illness or imbalance? Barney Mitchell suggests that they see the *order* and the *structure* of things. He explains that everything in the world has a structure made up of different elements grouped in a particular structure, much the same way western science talks about the structure of atoms or molecules in things. Barney Mitchell suggests that once you know the order and structure of a thing *you will know its true name*. When you know its name it is yours to use. Now you can speak with that plant, that stone, that wind, or that animal. You know what it gives its life for in the world and then you too can take its life and take that power to help cure or put that power to some other personal use. If there is an imbalance or disease in the patient as a result of the factors we discussed earlier, the order and the structure of the body is also imbalanced. One of the tasks of the shaman is to diagnose and help reorder the elements in the body and perhaps the surrounding environment to which every human is connected and related.

One of the original skills of the shaman was to aid in the hunting of animals. In Chapter Two, **Ritual Drama and Prayer**, Tom Ration reminded us that in the old days the people knew songs to catch wild animals and later, sheep. Hunters in every hunting culture had songs they would sing to "weaken" animals and to lure animals to them. Shamans, in addition to knowing these songs, specialize in songs for weakening and luring disease from the body, for making good weather, and for other purposes. What these songs and the hunting songs The People used in the old days have in common is that *the power of these songs was that the animals true name was mentioned in them*. These songs, it is told, were taught The People by the animals themselves at a time when The People could actually communicate in the same language as the animals.

James Smith, in a different version of the Navajo Deer Huntingway, told of the time The People of many years ago learned the hunting songs. They traveled to various places of the Holy People in each of the four directions. Finally, they came to the Game-Grower of Game Mountain to whom they gave jewels "of mixed colors in payment for this knowledge." "Some of your songs we want to learn, let this be in exchange for it," they told him, and he answered:

Thanks, my grandchildren, that's the way one should treat a person, then you shall learn some of my songs," he told them. The Holy Persons, too, whom he had brought, all spoke likewise.

"There are some, indeed, all of us have some." Spoke Game grower. "Hunting songs we have," he said. "Also there is its secret name. For, the various kinds of game each has its own name," said Game grower. "Now if one knows the name, only then will he kill according to his desires, he told them. "You see, if also one knows the name of all those who are in charge of it, then only it will be likewise. If one begs of them, if one prays to them, and if one sings to them and holds this sacred, then one will kill just as he desires," the Game grower told them. "Now do some learning," he told them. This they did and busied themselves with learning. (Luckert, 1975:107)

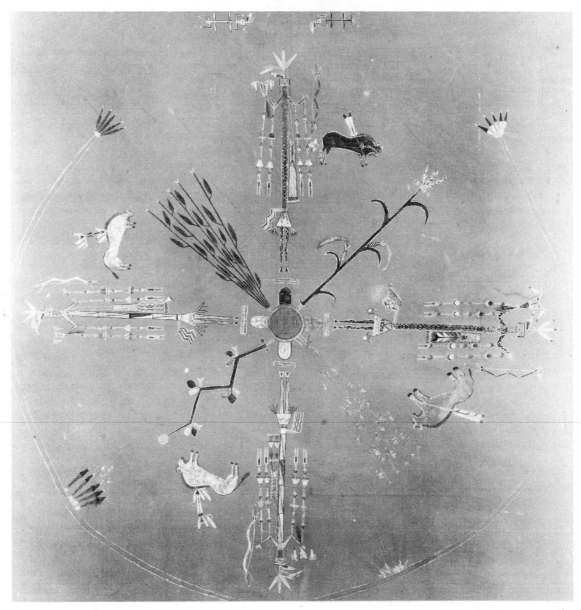

Navajo sandpainting by Hostin Claw, used in the Male Shootingway. This shows when the Holy People overcame the buffalo. (Buffalo-who-never-dies: Buffalo People at Jarring Mountain.) (Courtesy of the Smithsonian Institution, National Anthropological Archives)

Before the actual hunt, according to the procedures of the Deer Huntingway, the hunters make a circular shelter in which they sleep and erect a sweat lodge where they sweat and sing hunting songs the night before they go out after the game. Claus Chee Sonny explains:

Songs are chanted in the sweat lodge ordinarily only the evening prior to the hunt. Beginning the next morning, when the hunter is on the chase, there usually is no time available for singing songs. Prayers are then substituted. While hunting, you may stop for a moment, turn your face east, and have the point of your weapon face east also. Then you speak as many prayers as you have time for.

If there is more than one hunter, the leader who prays faces east. All others face north while glancing occasionally at the leader to imitate his movements. While the prayers are spoken, the weapons may not be loaded; an accidental discharge would disturb the solemnity of the prayer.

While you are praying, if the god on whom you call wants you to have meat, he will give it to you right then. He is standing right near you. If you believe and respect what I am telling you now, if you trust the god to whom you pray, then you will have no difficulty making your kill.

When you hunt you may not speak prayers from Blessingway. Such prayers all have special "happiness" endings which cannot be altered or omitted. Hunting prayers do not have such life-blessing endings. They are prayers to kill. Should a deer come along while you are praying, a hunting prayer can be interrupted at any time. You can stop and shoot right then.

All the prayers may be spoken right one after another. Should that be too many, you may speak only one. One prayer, spoken correctly and with the right attitude, is more effective than if you hurry through all the prayers carelessly. Now I am going to speak the prayers. (translated into English)

I

The Talking-god, my Grandfather. A Son of Early Morning, a Turquoise Prairie-dog, a Turquoise Horse, you will give me today. With the black bow in my hand, you will give me. With feathered arrows in my hand, you will give me. With an arrow in my hand which will not miss the heart, you will give me. With a notched arrow in my hand, you will give me. Before the Sun sets you will give me. Before I am tired and worn out, you will give me. My Grandfather, the Talking-god you will give me today.

II

The Black-god, my Grandfather, A son of the Setting Sun, a Whitebead Prairie-dog, A White-bead Horse, you will give me today. With a feathered bow in my hand, you will give me. With an arrow in my hand, feathered with Red-tailed Hawk feathers, you will give me. With an arrow that will not miss the heart, you will give me. Before the Sun sets, you will give me. I am the Boy-who-never-tires. You will give, my Grandfather, the Black-god, today.

III

My Grandfathers, you will give me good meat. The good meat of a buck you will give me today. The good meat of a doe you will give me today. The good meat of various deer you will give me today. Today, before the Sun sets, you will give me. My Grandfathers, Talking-god and Black-god, I have come to ask a favor of you today. You will give me meat to eat. You will do this favor today.

IV

I am the Daughter of the Setting Sun. At the top of Yellow Mountain you will give me. A buck you will give me. My Grandfather, the Talking-god, with a black bow in my hand, you will give me. With a feathered arrow in my hand, you will give me. With a notched arrow in my hand, you will give me. Before the Sun sets you will give. I am the Boy-who-never-tires, my Grandfather, the Talking-god.

V

I am the young woman of the White-one-who-blends-with-the-earth. From the top of White Mountain, you will give me a doe. With a feathered bow in my hand, you will give me. With a feathered arrow in my hand, you will give me. Before the Sun sets you will give me. I am the Boy-who-never-tires. Yeh! (Luckert, 1975:52-53)

Knowing the hunting songs, like knowing the proper names of the game animals, is part of the knowledge of knowing the order and the structure of things. As we learned earlier, it is important that the specialist know the relationships between things and the proper order given at "the time of creation." Claus Chee Sonny suggests that one must also have the *correct attitude* in order to hunt successfully. And having the correct attitude means knowing the rules and the procedures. The Deer People who gave the final hunting instructions in Claus chee Sonny's earlier narration, also tell the hunter:

> Men will have a difficult time hunting us. While they may see us, we can turn into another object. Their eyes will follow us, but we will disappear. If a man is out hunting, we can stand nearby in such a manner that he may shoot all his arrows at us. He runs out of arrows. Finally, he will go home and say, "I did not get any," or he may say, "I do not know what they were." This is because when the man started to hunt, he started with the wrong attitude. This is why he did not get any. (Luckert, 1975:40)

Billie Blackhorse of Kayenta gives us further suggestions and instructions which explain in more detail what the proper "attitude" should be. We discussed earlier how closely related the tradition of hunting and shamanism is. In the following statement of Billy Blackhorse we see that the shaman's techniques of "positive thinking" or "will power" and dreaming are also included in the instructions for hunters:

> The hunters are never permitted to walk upright or even to sleep with their legs straightened out. You walk, sit, and sleep with knees bent at all times. In that posture the hunter never tires. Hunting in that way will cause the deer to lose speed while running. The hunter can always get meat that way. And getting meat is the purpose of these hunting rules. The hunters are all encouraged to think positively about hunting and about what is to happen on the next day during the chase. There is always a "spirit of knowing" concerning the whereabouts of the deer—received either through positive thinking or while dreaming about deer during the night. If the latter happens, you go straight to the place about which you have dreamed. You will always find deer there, waiting for you to come. (Luckert, 1975:63)

Times change and nowadays another factor in the balance between the human community and the animal and plant community has entered the picture—The People are having to make compromises between the benefits of modern technology and the knowledge of old ways. The role of the shaman, as well as other sacred practices The People once learned and followed, ritual hunting for instance, has been affected by this new factor.

In the last one hundred years many fragile ecological relationships and balances between the people and the natural world have been put in danger. For example, the Eskimo people of Baffin Island have recently begun to notice with some anxiety, that trust between the animals and humans has broken down. They say that the noise of the motorboats, snowmobiles, and rifles has scared the older seals away and only the young animals can "be coaxed within shooting range." (Kemp, 1971) So the Baffin Island people have had to make some compromises in their familiar ways of life. These have resulted in new customs—new seasonal migrations for instance. Instead of hunting at certain times of the year, the men carve soapstone for selling to agencies further south. With accumulated money from outside economic sources, the Eskimo people have more time to go visiting in the coldest winter months. With their snowmobiles it is also possible to travel further in less time. When they are visiting they do not hunt. Consequently, during these periods of time the young animals have a chance to grow and mature.

In the past, due to the very fragile existence the Eskimo and other peoples led, shamans were in demand not only to help the people survive, but also to help them understand the forces of the world around them. As the people have been introduced to and begun to use new technology with which to cope with environmental conditions, or in order to compete with outsiders, the role of the shaman in the community has also changed from that of a central religious figure to a technical specialist. In some cases the shaman has been viewed with mistrust. Both governmental and missionary activity have worked to arouse people's suspicions about the worth and quality of shamans and other ceremonial practitioners' activities. But this has happened for the most part, when the young people have not had the kind of contact with practitioners they once had in the past.

One of the roles of ceremonial practitioners and shamans is to preserve sacred knowledge and to be able to pass it on to younger generations. In the past most practitioners had apprentices or students who would, in turn, seek their own vocation as practitioners. Since there have been basic changes in many traditional institutions (family life, education, language, and ceremonial life) the role of the shaman and the ceremonial practitioner has also changed. One of the central changes has been the loss of natural areas where spirit powers could, in the past, be encountered or where herbs and other medicines could be obtained. Other changes are, of course, the availability of Western medicine and doctors as well as careers in the dominant society that satisfy the intellectual curiosity of would-be-shamans.

Shamans, 'Servants To The People'

In order to keep the People's trust and maintain dignity in their work as practitioners shamans must be servants to the people. As we study examples of shamanism and practitioners in specific cultures, we will see that the individuals in these examples express

Navajo Blessingway purification ceremony, with Allie Brown as the singer. George Hight, 1964. (Courtesy of the Museum of the American Indian, Heye Foundation)

this desire: to help the people. Following is such an example. Claus Chee Sonny of Tsaile created the "advertisement" below so that more people in the Navajo Nation would become familiar with his special skills, including the Deer Huntingway. He placed this advertisement where chapter meetings are held in several areas all over the reservation. In the statement, he makes clear that the skills he has should benefit The People. The "wealth" he obtains from his work is not just money. To him wealth is the knowledge that he is living correctly, with the proper attitudes and using his skills wisely. He states:

In order to learn what I know, I presume one would need to go to school anywhere from four to six years. However I did not go to school for this. The stories and songs which I have learned are the ones which taught me the ways of living. I started my family with little livestock on a small piece of land. But because of the stories, songs, and prayers which I know, my possessions have multiplied greatly since then.

Through these stories, songs and prayers I have become attentive to the fact that the land asks me—that it be properly managed and that all the fences

Navajo singer administering herbs during healing ceremony. George Hight, 1963. (Courtesy of the Museum of the American Indian, Heye Foundation)

might be repaired. Likewise, the home speaks out on behalf of itself—to be repaired and to be cared for. The livestock does the same. Even the children let you know that they need help. So, what I know of life I have taught to my children; they understand and use it. All my children have their own place on which they make their living. All have two cars and livestock—not because I gave it to them, but they know what life is about. I know the Blessingway (*hozhooji*) and the Flintway (*beshee*). I also cooperate with the physicians at the United States Health centers. Many of the patients get well faster that way. This is the way it is with people who help: other people will come to visit them and see them, for many reasons. This is how I spend my life and make my living—by helping other people. (Luckert, 1975: 18-20)

SHAMANS IN THREE CULTURES

In this section we will examine shamans and practitioners in three cultures. First, in some detail, we will discuss shamanism in the Baffin Bay Area. This includes information about the Netsilik, Iglulik, Caribou, and Copper Eskimo. Most of the material about the Baffin Bay Eskimo shamans is from the 1920's and was collected by Knud Rasmussen, a Danish ethnographer. Second, we will examine the philosophy and practice of a contemporary Pima shaman, a man named Juan Gregorio, who was recorded in 1974. Gregorio passed away recently leaving his theories of Pima disease and curing with the ethnographer Donald Bahr, who in turn collected it into the book, *Pima Shamanism and Ka:cim Mumkidag (Staying Sickness)*. Third, we will briefly examine the practice of a Wintu shaman, Flora Jones, who is still a practitioner in California today.

In the first two cultures, Baffin Bay Eskimo and Pima, we will examine shamanism *in the context of the larger sacred order of things, i.e., cosmologies* and theories of balance and imbalance. In the last example we will focus more in terms of the shaman's techniques, i.e., sucking, seeing, and calling spirits. In this section the following topics will be covered:

1. The role and function of the shaman
2. How a person becomes a shaman
3. Theories of disease
4. Techniques of diagnosis, curing, or other tasks shamans perform
5. What aids, tools, shamans use
6. How the shaman uses spirit helpers and the shaman's relationship to the world of spirits

The Baffin Bay Eskimos: Environmental Background

To give the student some idea of the environmental and ecological context within which the Baffin Bay Eskimo shaman performs his/her tasks and within which the Eskimo people live, the following summary of the Eskimo habitat is presented. It must be remembered that all habitats affect the People's lives and color and mold their sacred ways. In the case of the Baffin Bay area Eskimos, the environment is particularly severe and demands certain things from the people. The way in which the Eskimo people have adapted their sacred lives to this severe environment has been, to a large extent, to center it around the shaman.

The Baffin Bay area is a land covered most of the year by snow and ice. It consists (see map) of inlets, islands, and large bodies of water with outlets into the Atlantic Ocean and the Arctic Ocean. During the "winter" which lasts nine months of the year, the temperature stays below zero. Great winds that create blizzards sweep over the barren land. The inland waterways freeze over and cover with snow. Because this land is very close to the *arctic circle*, or the northernmost part of the Earth, there are six weeks during the winter in which the sun never rises and it is dark over the land.

The people living in the Baffin Bay area are hunters as well as skilled tailors of clothing, carvers of soapstone and makers of fine tools and weapons. Most of the hunting centers around the seals that the people catch for meat, for fat, and for their hides which make soles for boots. The fat is a necessary part of the winter diet when the temperatures are so cold and the body needs more calories. Fat is also used to light the lamps and provides heat for cooking meat, though nowdays fuel is used.

BAFFIN BAY AREA
NATIVE GROUPS

(After Rasmussen, 1930)

GREENLAND

Smith Sound

Melville
Bay

Jones Sound

BAFFIN
BAY

Landcaster Sound

Amundsen
Gulf

DAVIS
STRAIT

COPPER

Victoria Str.

NETSILIK

Gulf of Boothia

IGLULIK

ESKIMO

Utkuhikhalingamiut

FOXE
BASIN

CARIBOU

HUDSON STRAIT

ESKIMO

Family outside of dwelling, Plover Bay, Siberia. A.K. Fisher, 1899. (Courtesy of the Smithsonian Institution, National Anthropological Archives)

The Baffin Bay Eskimos are a *migratory* people. That is, they move their camps or communities with the change of seasons in order to hunt different animals, fish, and birds. In the winter months, which last from the end of October to the middle of June, the People live on the edge of the ice, far out into the frozen-over bays and inlets. Up until a few years ago, the People made their homes out of snow blocks covered with ice, or *igloos*, during the winter. Sleds pulled by dog teams were the principle means of transportation; (Nowadays government housing and snowmobiles have become more popular.) During the winter the seals cannot be hunted by boat or kayak on the water since the water is iced over; but they can be hunted from the ice. In order for the seals to breathe, they must make holes in the ice to stick their noses through. There, by these breathing holes, the men wait with their spears and harpoons for the seals to appear. If they spear one they must then drag it over the ice to their homes. (Rifles are used by the hunters today even though there is a risk involved. When the seals are shot from far away they often sink before the men can drag them out onto the ice, whereas harpoons have ropes attached with which to hold onto the animal.)

If many men are successful on a day's hunt,

Building an igloo. (Courtesy of the Smithsonian Institution, National Anthropological Archives)

song and dance festivals are often arranged so that everyone is entertained during the dark weeks of winter and so that everyone is fed.

The ice begins to break up in June. Soon it is too dangerous to continue living out on the edge of the ice and the People pack their belongings in hides, and on sleds and on foot they begin their journey to their summer camps. Inland, with the coming warmth, birds begin arriving from the south, laying their eggs on the soft *tundra* floor. Here there is vegetation—little plants, stunted trees and millions of little flowers. The people live in hide tents and collect bird eggs and shoot the ducks or other birds. In the inland streams the men make stone-wall traps or weirs to herd the fish into. These fish are eaten there and also smoked or dried for later use. These warm weeks do not last long and soon it is time to head back on a different route to the area of their winter camp. In August the People have set up camp (hide or canvas tents) in the place where the Caribou travel through in their annual migrations. The men station themselves behind stone blinds and wait for the animals. After the hunts, Caribou meat is frozen and eaten through the beginning months of winter until the supply runs out. More important are the skins, 30 of which supply a family of four with new winter clothes which are sewn and decorated by the women. By November the People are back at their winter camps on the frozen edge of the ice preparing once more to hunt the seal.

Below is a calendar given by the Iglulik shaman, Aua. Like many of the calendars we have talked about in this textbook (see Chapter Four, **The Boundaries of the World**) the Iglulik calendar reflects the changing seasons as well as certain occupations the Eskimo people engage in during different times of the year. Aua begins the year with February because it is in that month that the people see the sun returning. He calls December and January just "winter moons" because they are "dark, cold, and hunting in them is difficult."

Division of the Year into Moons

The one of them (*the moons*) where it begins to rise (over the horizon, i.e., the sun); corresponds almost to February.

That in which births come too early (i.e., among the seals): corresponds to March, in which month many stillborn and frozen seal-cubs are found in the cubbing holes of the seals in snowdrifts among the ice hummocks.

Cubs of spotted seal; corresponds to April, when the seals normally give birth to their cubs.

The young saddlebacks; corresponds to May, when out at the edge of the shore ice young saddlebacks begin to appear in the open water.

The caribou calves; corresponds to June, when the caribou cows appear with their calves.

The eggs; corresponds to the end of June and the beginning of July, when the birds lay their eggs.

The one in which the coat becomes thin (on the caribou); corresponds to August, because during the month of July the caribou have moulted and now have the thin, stiff coat that makes the skins especially valuable for clothing.

The middlemost one (i.e., with reference to the coat of the caribou); corresponds to September, when their coats become thicker and the hair so long that they are most suitable for skin clothing for the coldest period of the year.

The one in which the skin falls off (i.e., the antlers of the caribou); corresponds to October when the thin "velvet" covering the antlers peels off.

The one in which winter begins; corresponds almost to the end of November.

The Powers of The Natural World: Eskimo Cosmology

The powers and forces of the natural world that effect the lives of the Baffin Bay Eskimos are "characters", named spirits and rulers that reflect the severe climate, the hardships, and the dangers of existence so far north. These *spirit powers* are often felt to be related to the animals that the hunters have to kill in order to survive. Earlier in this chapter we discussed the relationship between hunters and the animals and plants that are hunted. We saw how this relationship is one of the roots of a theory of disease and balance which is at the heart of sacred knowledge and shamanistic practices. Among the Baffin Bay Eskimo this relationship between animal and human *kin* and the fear of animal souls is at the center of the People's sacred knowledge and is also critical to their survival.*

A list of some of the powers in the Iglulik cosmology for example, would include the following "powers that rule Earth and mankind." The term for these powers is *ersigifavut*, "those we fear," or *mianerifavut*, "those we regard with caution." Any one of these powers is dangerous if people do not follow certain rules handed down to them through oral tradition and through the guidance of the shamans. Some of the more important powers are as follows:

Arnaluk takanaluk, "The woman down there." The spirit of the sea, the mother of marine animals living at the bottom of the sea. She is also referred to as *Takanakapsaluk*, "the bad one" or "the terrible one down there."

Sila, the spirit of the weather or of the universe.

Aningat or *Tarqeq*, the general name for the moon—the moon man or spirit. (Rasmussen, Vol. 7, No. 2:62)

The power in Igluluk cosmology that the shaman concerns him/herself with the most is *Takanakapsaluk*. When the shaman journeys to the bottom of the sea in his/her trance flight to find lost souls, he/she travels to see *Tananakapsaluk*. Rasmussen sums up the characteristics of this powerful spirit and says:

> From her come also the skins of the great seal...which are indispensable for clothes and boot soles,...But while *Takanakapsaluk* gives mankind all these good things, created out of her own finger joints, it is she also who sends nearly all the misfortunes which are [considered the most dangerous by The People on Earth.] In her anger at men's failing to live as they should, she calls up storms that prevent the men from hunting, or she keeps the animals they seek hidden away in a pool she has at the bottom of the sea, or she will steal away the souls of human beings and send

sickness among the people.... It is regarded as one of a shaman's greatest feats to visit her where she lives at the bottom of the sea,...to tame and [negotiate with] her [so] that human beings can live once more untroubled on Earth. (Rasmussen, Vol. 7 No. 1:124)

Definitions and Functions of Shamans

The Iglulik Eskimos tell the following story about how the first shamans came to be:

> In the very earliest times, men lived in the dark and had no animals to hunt. They were poor, ignorant people, far inferior to those living nowadays. They traveled about in search of food, they lived..., but in a very different way. When they halted and camped, they worked at the soil with picks of a kind we no longer know. They got their food from the earth, they lived on the soil. They knew nothing of all the game we now have, and had therefore *no need to be ever on guard against all those perils which arise from the fact that we, hunting animals as we do, lived by slaying other souls*. Therefore, they had no shamans, but they knew sickness, and it was fear of sickness and suffering that led to the coming of the first shamans. The ancients relate as follows concerning this:

> Human beings have always been afraid of sickness, and far back in the very earliest times there arose wise men who tried to find out about all the things none could understand. There were no shamans in those days, and men were ignorant of all those rules of life which have since taught them to be on their guard against danger and wickedness. The first *amulet* that ever existed was the shell portion of a sea-urchin. It has a hole through it, and is hence called [anus] and the fact of its being made the first amulet was due to its being associated with a particular power of healing. When a man fell ill, one would go and sit by him, and, pointing to the diseased part, break wind behind. Then one went outside while another held one hand hollowed over the diseased part, breathing, at the same

* See Chapter One, Part I; Chapter One, Part II, 2; and chapter Three.

time out over the palm of his other hand in a direction away from the person to be cured. It was then believed that wind and breath together combined all the power [coming] from within the human body, a power so mysterious and strong that it was able to cure disease.

In that way everyone was a physician, and there was no need of any shamans. But then it happened that a time of hardship and famine set in around Iglulik. Many died of starvation, and all were greatly worried not knowing what to do. Then one day when a number of people were assembled in a house, a man demanded to be allowed to go behind the skin hangings at the back of the sleeping place, no one knew why. He said he was going to travel down to the Mother of the Sea Beasts. No one in the house understood him, and no one believed in him. He had his way, and passed in behind the hangings. He declared that he would exercise an art which should afterwards prove of great value to mankind; but no one must look at him. It was not long, however, before the unbelieving and [curious] drew aside the hangings, and to their astonishment [saw] that he was diving down into the earth: he had already got so far down that only the soles of his feet could be seen. How the man ever hit on this idea no one knows; he himself said that it was the spirits that had helped him; spirits he had entered into contact with out in the great solitude. Thus, the first shaman appeared among men. He went down to the Mother of the Sea Beasts and brought back game to men, and the famine gave place to plenty, and all were happy and joyful once more.

Afterwards, the shamans extended their knowledge of hidden things, and helped mankind in various ways. They also developed their sacred language, which was only used for communicating with the spirits and not in everyday speech. (Vol. 7 No. 1:110-111)

The names for "shaman" among the Baffin Bay Eskimos reflect one of their most important abilities: *seeing*. When parents suspect that a newborn child will be a shaman they lift the child up to look through the afterbirth, a ceremony "which gives the child second-sight." Later, these children are called *tarak'ut inilgit* or "those who have eyes in the dark." (Rasmussen, Vol. 9:27) Among the Copper Eskimo the shaman is called *elik*, "one who has eyes" because he/she can see things that ordinary people cannot. (Vol. 9:27). The Iglulik word for shaman is *angakut* and the name comes from a spirit that "enables one to see," or *anak'ua*. The *anak'ua* consists:

of a mysterious light which the shaman suddenly feels in his body, inside his head, within the brain, an unexplainable searchlight, a luminous fire, which enables him to see in the dark...for he can now, even with closed eyes, see through darkness and perceive things and coming events which are hidden from others.

The first time a young shaman experiences this light, while sitting up on the bench [calling] his helping spirits, it is as if the house in which he is suddenly rises; he sees far ahead of him, through mountains, exactly as if the earth were one great plain, and his eyes could reach to the end of the earth. Nothing is hidden from him any longer; not only can he see things far, far away, but he can also discover souls, stolen souls, which are either kept concealed in far, strange lands, or have been taken up or down to the land of the Dead. (Rasmussen, Vol. 7, No. 1:112-113).

Besides having gifts of "second sight," prophecy, and seeing, which is a kind of "X-ray vision," shamans are also gifted with an ability to use their dreams. Upvik, a Netsilik man, tells how dreams were traditionally used to develop the shaman's abilities:

It was the spirits that came to one, especially in dreams. Now if one had the ability to retain these dreams and place them in connection with the things that happened about, it was possible— especially if one often [looked for] solitude—to develop one's thoughts so that mysteries that were [hidden] to others could be [explored]. (Vol. 8 No. 1:296)

And dreams were also used as a kind of relaxation in which to think about things in a different way than in ordinary, everyday thought. For instance, the Caribou Eskimo man Igjugarjuk explains that, during his shaman apprenticeship, when he was out alone in the cold wilderness, he "would almost doze and dream what I had come out to find and about which I had been thinking all the time."

Shamans are also individuals who can communicate with "the spirits of the earth, the air, and the sea." For the Copper Eskimo, the shamans communicate with spirits from the following places in the Copper Eskimo cosmology: *nunapqu'nanik*, the earth's surface; *nunapiluanik*, the earth's insides; *hilanik*, out from space; and *qilaplokiglinanik*, out from the borders between earth and sky. (Vol. 9:28). Through these spirit powers shamans can help their fellow human beings when they are in danger, either on their hunts; because they have become possessed by some imbalance or "evil" power; or because they have not followed the "do's" and "don't's" of daily life. Rasmussen describes one way in which the shamans get in touch with the spirits:

An ordinary *seance* is held in a snow hut or tent, preferably in a subdued light; it is said that the spirits do not care to appear in full daylight. When a shaman is going to [call] his helping spirits for some purpose or other the whole village is invited to attend the ceremony. He [calls] them by singing special spirit songs; among the Netsilingmiut these spirit songs were not necessarily about anything particular nor set to any special melody. It is simply said that there is a certain song which when sung, has the effect that the spirits like to come. Every [Shaman] has his own particular song, and it puts him into a trance. It is then believed that the spirit [that is called] moves into his body and simply speaks through his mouth. And so, as soon as he has fallen into a trance he always speaks in a voice that is not his own, often a deep, resonant *bass*, at other times in a shrill *falsetto*, and, if some animal is his helping spirit and it now dwells in him, he imitates the voice of that animal. (Vol. 8 No. 1:293)

In the Iglulik language a shaman's "helping spirit" is called an *aperfat*, or "one that exists to be questioned." As we have discussed earlier concerning shamans in general, the shaman does not choose the *aperfat*, rather they come on their own. The shaman must not be afraid of them if he/she wants to be able to use them later.

In addition to these skills the most important functions of the Baffin Bay Eskimo shamans are as follows:

They must be physicians, able to cure the sick.

They must be meteorologists, not only able to forecast the weather, but also to ensure fine weather. This is done by traveling up to *Sila*. They must be able to go down to *Takanakapsuluk* to get game animals. They must be able to visit the Land of the Dead under the sea or up in the sky in order to look for lost or stolen souls. Sometimes the dead will wish to have...a relative who is still alive brought up to them in the Land of the Dead; that relative then becomes sick and it is the business of the shaman to make the dead release such souls. (Rasmussen, Vol. 7, No. 1:109)

How A Person Becomes A Shaman

The first account of how one individual became a shaman is told by Igjugarjuk, a Caribou Eskimo shaman. Of the many ways a person can become a shaman he chose "suffering—starving and exposing himself to cold—in order to become "wise," to become an *anatkoq* which is the Caribou word for shaman. *Sila* or *Hila* in his dialect, is, as we read earlier, the power or spirit of the weather—the cold, the snow, the wind—everything that the Caribou Eskimos fear from the air and that can bring about disaster. If a man or woman knows how to approach *Hila*, he/she can help keep disaster and hardship from his/her people. Igjugarjuk learned how to do this, and what he learned then became his "way" of knowledge. This is his story:

When I was to be an *anatkoq*, I chose suffering through the two things that are most dangerous to us humans, suffering through hunger and suffering through cold. First I hungered five days and was then allowed to drink a mouthful of warm water; the old ones say that only if the water is warm will Pinga and Hila notice the [apprentice] and help him. Thereafter I went hungry for ten days, and then could begin to eat, though it only had to be the sort of food on which there is never any taboo, preferably fleshy meat, and never intestines, head, heart or other entrails, nor meat that had been touched by wolf or wolverine while it lay in a *cache*. I was to keep to this diet for five moons, and then the next five moons might eat everything; but after that I was again forced to eat the meat diet that is prescribed for all those who must do penance in order to become clean. The old ones attached great importance to the food that the would-be shamans might eat; thus [an apprentice] who wished to possess the ability to kill had never to eat the [salmon]. If they eat [salmon] they will, instead of killing others, kill themselves.

My instructor was my wife's father, Perqanaq. When I was to be presented to Pinga and Hila, he dragged me over on the other side of Hikoligjuaq. It was a very long day's journey inland to a place called Kingarjuit: the high hills, which are at Tijerarjuaq (by the southeast shore of Hikoligjuaq). It was in winter time took place at night with the new moon; one could just see the very first streak of the moon; it had just appeared in the sky. I was not fetched again until the next moon was of the same size. Perqanaq built a small snow hut at the place where I was to be, this snow hut being no bigger than that I could just get under cover and sit down. I was given no sleeping skin to protect me against the cold, only a little piece of caribou skin to sit upon. There I was shut in. The entrance was closed with a block, but no soft snow was thrown over the hut to make it warm. When I had sat there five days. Perqanaq came with water,

wrapped in caribou skin, a watertight caribou-skin bag. Not until fifteen days afterwards did he come again and hand me the [same thing], just giving himself time to hand it to me, and then he was gone again, for even the old shaman must not interrupt my solitude. As soon as I had become alone, Perqanaq told me to think of one single thing all the time I was to be there, to want only one single thing, and that was to draw Pinga's attention to the fact that there I sat and wished to be a shaman. Pinga should own me. My [apprentice-ship] took place in the middle of the coldest winter, and I, who never got anything to warm me, and must not move, was very cold, and it was so tiring to have to sit without daring to lie down, *that sometimes it was as if I died a little.* Only towards the end of the thirty days did a helping spirit come to me, a lovely and beautiful helping spirit, whom I have never thought of; it was a white woman; she came to me while I had collapsed, exhausted, and was sleeping. But still I saw her lifelike, hovering over me, and from that day I could not close my eyes or dream without seeing her. There is this remarkable thing about my helping spirit, that I have never seen her while awake, but only in dreams. She came to me from Pinga and was a sign that Pinga had now noticed me and would give me powers that would make me a shaman.

When a new moon was lighted and had the same size as the one that had shone for us when we left the village, Perqanaq came again with his little sledge and stopped a long way from the snow hut. But by this time I was not very much alive anymore and had not the strength to rise, in fact I could not stand on my feet. Perqanaq pulled me out of the hut and carried me to Kingarjuit. I was now so [thin] that the veins on my hands and body and feet had quite disappeared. For a long time I might only eat very little in order to again get my intestines extended, and later came the diet that was to help to cleanse the body.

For a whole year I was not to lie with my wife, who, however, had to make my

123

food. For a whole year I had to have my own little cooking pot and my own meat dish; no one else was allowed to eat what had been cooked for me.

Later, when I had quite become myself again, I understood that I had become the shaman of my village, and it did happen that my neighbors or people from a long distance away called me to heal a sick person or to "inspect a course" if they were going to travel. When this happened, the people of my village were called together and I told them what I had been asked to do. Then I left tent or snow house and went out into solitude; away from the dwellings of man. Now those who remained behind had to sing continuously: just to keep themselves happy and lively. If anything difficult had to be found out my solitude had to extend over three days and two nights, or three nights and two days. In all that time I had to wander about without rest and only sit down once in a while on a stone or a snow drift. When I had been out long and had become tired, I could almost doze and dream what I had come out to find and about which I had been thinking all the time. Every morning, however, I could come home and report on what I had so far found. But as soon as I had spoken I had to return again, out into the open, out to places where I could be quite alone.

These days of "seeking for knowledge" are very tiring, for one must walk all the time, no matter what the weather is like and only rest in short snatches. I am usually quite...tired, not only in body but also in head, when I have found what I sought...

True wisdom is only to be found far away from people, out in the great solitude, and it is not found in play but only through suffering. Solitude and suffering open the human mind, and therefore a shaman seeks his wisdom there. (Vol. 7 No. 2:51-55)

The second account of becoming a shaman comes to us from Aua, the Iglulik *angakut*. Though there are some basic similarities in the two accounts, the food eating taboos for example, Aua's apprenticeship was also very different from Igjugarjuk's. In the following account the student will note that Aua was destined to become a shaman before he was born—his mother and others regarded Aua's sensitivity to taboo-breaking as a sign that when he was born he would become a shaman. However, because of the circumstances of his birth and the events before he was born, Aua could never find a teacher when he came to the age in which he could apprentice himself to another shaman. Instead, one day, his first spirit helper or *aperfat* came to him unexpectedly. Later, another one spoke to him and Aua took him as a helping spirit. Aua created his own "way" of being a shaman and his own philosophy of life.

In contrast to Igjugarjuk's "suffering way," Aua's way, though requiring a certain amount of solitude and study out in the wilderness, is felt by Aua to be joyful. In fact, he says that spirits are more sympathetic to humor and singing than they are to suffering and sorrow. And the Baffin Bay Eskimos in general say that evil will stay away from a place where the people are happy.

In addition to these points, we should note the very strict rules Aua and his family, particularly his mother, followed in order that he be born and live. Aua now tells his story:

I was yet but a tiny unborn infant in my mother's womb when anxious folk began to inquire sympathetically about me; all the children my mother had had before had lain crosswise and been still born.

All were very sorry for her and a woman named Ardjuag, who was a shaman herself, called up her spirits that same evening to help my mother. And the very next morning it could be felt that I had grown but it did me no good at the time, for Ardjuag had forgotten that she must do no work the day after a spirit-calling, and had mended a hole in a mitten. This [breaking] of taboo at once had its effect upon me: my mother felt the birth-pangs coming on before the time, and I kicked and struggled as if trying to work my out through her side. A new spirit-calling then took place, and as all [rules] were observed this time, it helped both my mother and myself.

But then one day it happened that my father, who was going out on a journey to hunt, was angry and impatient, and in order to calm him, my mother went to help him harness the dogs to the sledge. She forgot that in her condition, all work was taboo. And so, hardly had she picked up the traces and lifted the dog's paw before I began again kicking and struggling and trying to get out through her navel; and again we had to have a shaman to help us.

Old people now assured my mother that my great sensitiveness to any [breaking] of taboo was a sign that I should live to become a great shaman; but at the same time, many dangers and misfortunes would pursue me before I was born.

My father had got a walrus with its unborn young one, and when he began cutting it out, without reflecting that my mother was with child I again fell to struggling within the womb, and this time in earnest.

But the moment I was born, all life left me, and I lay there dead as stone. The cord was twisted around my neck and had strangled me. Ardjuaq, who lived in another village, was at once sent for, and special hut was built for my mother. When Ardjuaq came and saw me with my eyes sticking right out of my head, she wiped my mother's blood from my body with the skin of a raven, and made a little jacket for me of the same skin.

"He is born to die, but he shall live," she said.

And so Ardjuaq stayed with mother, until I showed signs of life. Mother was put on very strict diet, and had to observe difficult rules of taboo. If she had eaten part of a walrus, for instance, then that walrus was taboo to all others; the same with seal and caribou. She had to have special pots, from which no one else was allowed to eat. No woman was allowed to visit her, but men might do so. My clothes were made in a special way; the hair of the skins must never lie pointing upwards or down, but fall across the body. Thus I lived in the birthhut, unconscious of all the care that was being taken of with me.

For a whole year my mother and I had to live entirely alone, only visited now and again by my father. He was a great hunter, and always out after game, but in spite of this he was never allowed to sharpen his own knives; as soon as he did so, his hand began to swell and he fell ill. A year after my birth, we were allowed to have another person in the house with us; it was a woman, and she had to be very careful with herself; whenever she went out she must throw her hood over her head, wear boots without stockings, and hold the tail of her fur coat lifted high on one hand.

I was already a big boy when my mother was first allowed to go visiting; all were anxious to be kind, and she was invited to all the other families. But she stayed out too long; the spirits do not like women with little children to stay too long away from their house, and they took vengeance in this [way] the skin of her head peeled off and I, who had no understanding of anything at that time, beat her about the body with my little fists as she went home, and made water down her back.

No one who is to become a skillful hunter or a good shaman must remain out too long when visiting strange houses; and the same holds good for a woman with a child in her [house].

At last I was big enough to go out with the grown up men to the blowholes after seal. The day I harpooned my first seal, my father had to lie down on the ice with the upper part of his body naked, and the seal I had caught was dragged across his back while it was still alive. Only men were allowed to eat of my first catch, and nothing must be left. The skin and the head were set out on the ice, in order that I might be able later on to catch the same seal again. For three days and nights, none of the men who had eaten of it might go out hunting or do any kind of work.

The next animal I killed was a caribou. I was strictly forbidden to use a gun, and had to kill it with bow and arrows; this animal also only men were allowed to eat; no woman might touch it.

Some time passed, and I grew up and was strong enough to go out hunting walrus. The day I harpooned my first walrus my father shouted at the top of his voice the name of the villages he knew and cried: "Now there is food for all!"

The walrus was towed into land, while it was still alive, and not until we reached the shore was it finally killed. My mother, who was to cut it up, had the harpoon line made fast to her body before the harpoon head was withdrawn. After having killed this walrus, I was allowed to eat all those [delicious things] which had formerly been forbidden, yes, even entrails, and women were now allowed to eat of my catch, as long as they were not with child or recently delivered. Only my own mother had still to observe great caution, and whenever she had any sewing to do, a special hut had to be built for her. I had been made after a little spirit, Aua, and it was said that it was in order to avoid offending this spirit that my mother had to be so particular about everything she did. It was my guardian spirit, and took great care that I should not do anything that was forbidden.

Even after I had been married a long time, my catch was still subject to strict taboo. If there lived women with infants near us, my own wife was only allowed the meat of my killing, and no other woman was allowed to satisfy her hunger with the meat of any animal of which my wife had eaten. Any walrus I killed was further subject to the rule that no woman might eat of its entrails, which are [considered especially delicious] and this prohibition was maintained until I had four children of my own. And it is really only since I have grown old that the obligation laid on me by Ardjuaq in order that I might live have ceased to be needful.

Everything was thus made ready for me beforehand, even from the time when I was yet unborn, nevertheless, I [tried] to become a shaman by the help of others; but in this I did not succeed. I visited many famous shamans, and gave them great gifts, which they at once gave away to others; for if they had kept the things for themselves, they or their children would have died. This they believed because my own life had been so threatened from birth. Then I sought solitude, and here I soon became very [sad]. I would sometimes fall to weeping, and feel unhappy without knowing why. Then for no reason, all would suddenly be changed, and I felt a great joy, a joy so powerful that I could not restrain it, but had to break into song, a mighty song, with only room for the one word: joy, joy! And I had to use the full strength of my voice. And then in the midst of such a fit of mysterious and overwhelming delight I became a shaman, not knowing myself how it came about. But I was a shaman. I could see and hear in a totally different way. I had gained my enlightenment, the shaman-light of brain and body, and this in such a manner that it was not only I who could see through the darkness of life, but the same light also shone out of me, [unseen] to human beings, visible to all the spirits of earth and sky and sea, and these now came to me and became my helping spirits.

My first helping spirit was my namesake, a little Aua. When it came to me, it was as if the passage and roof of the house were lifted up, and I felt such a power of vision, that I could see right through the house, in through the earth and up into the sky; it was the little Aua that brought me all this inward light, hovering over me as long as I was singing. Then it placed itself in a corner of the passage invisible to others, but always ready if I should call it.

An Aua is a little spirit, a woman, that lives down by the sea shore. There are many of these shore spirits, who run about with a pointed skin hood on their heads; their breeches are queerly short, and made of bearskin; they wear long boots with a black pattern, and coats of sealskin. Their feet are twisted upward, and they seem to walk only on their heels. They hold their hands in such a fashion that the thumb is always bent in over the palm; their arms are held raised up on high with the hands together, and [continuously] stroking the head. They are bright and cheerful when one calls them, and they resemble most of all sweet little live dolls; they are not taller than the length of a man's arm.

My second helping spirit was a shark. One day when I was out in my kayak, it came swimming up to me, lay alongside quite silently and whispered my name. I was greatly astonished, for I had never seen a shark before; they are very rare in these waters. Afterwards it helped me with my hunting, and was always near me when I had need of it. These two, the shore spirit and the shark, were my principal helpers, and they could aid me in everything I wished. The song I generally sang when calling them was of few words, as follows:

Joy, joy
Joy, joy
I see a little shore spirit
A little aua,
I myself am also aua
The shore spirit's namesake,
Joy, joy!

These words I would keep on repeating, until I burst into tears, overwhelmed by a great dread; then I would tremble all over, crying only: "Ah-a-a-a-a, joy joy! Now I will go home, joy, joy!"

Once I lost a son, and felt that I could never again leave the spot where I had laid his body. I was like a mountain spirit, afraid of human kind. We stayed for a long time up inland, and my helping spirits left me, for they do not like human beings to dwell upon any sorrow. But one day the song about joy came to me all of itself and quite unexpectedly. I felt once more a longing for my fellow men, my helping spirits returned to me, and I was myself once more. (Vol. 7 No. 1:116-120)

An Iglulik Group Healing Session

One of the techniques of healing among the Iglulik is the communal healing session and *seance* in which the shaman attempts to find the cause of an "imbalance" in the patient's life. In the case that we will present, the Iglulik *angakut* Angutingmarik conducts a kind of question and answer session in which the audience participates with the patient; in this case the "audience" consists of the patient's neighbors and kin.

The *angakut*, consulting with his spirit helpers, *sees* certain things that might have "unbalanced" the patient. In other words, he sees instances in which the patient did not obey the rules and the taboos of Iglulik life. The *angakut* questions himself, he questions the patient, he questions his spirit helper, and he asks the audience for help identifying what he is seeing and if they might help the patient understand what she did not do correctly.

Upon learning of the patient's mistake or wrongdoing the *angakut* does not criticize the patient and the audience is also sympathetic. In such a closely knit community it helps to have all members of the community in good health and therefore everyone encourages the patient to admit any wrongdoing. By talking about all the possible mistakes the patient might have made the patient feels better and the audience learns something besides: reminders of what rules the Iglulik people should be aware of in relation to the natural world and the community. The shaman, having the knowledge to diagnose the imbalances, the mistakes, and the discomfort of the patient, directs the process of the session until he is certain that the patient is on the way to recovery. Below is part of one Iglulik healing session, as observed and recorded by Rasmussen:

A woman named Nanoraq, the wife of Makik, lay very ill, with pains all over her body. The patient, who was so ill that she could hardly stand upright, was placed on the bench. All the inhabitants of the village were called and Angutingmarik asked his spirits the cause of the disease. The shaman walked slowly up and forwards with mittens on, talking in groans and sighs, in varying tones, sometimes breathing deeply as if under extreme pressure. He says:

"It is you are Aksharquarnilik, I ask you, my helping spirit, where the sickness comes from which this person is suffering? Is it due to something I have eaten in defiance of taboo, lately or long since? Or is it brought about by the sick woman herself? Is she herself the cause of the disease?"

The Patient answers: "The sickness is due to my own fault. I have not performed my duties well. My thoughts have been bad and my actions evil."

The shaman interrupts her, and continues:

"It looks like peat, and yet is not really peat. It is that which is behind the ear, something that looks like the cartilage of the ear? There is something that gleams white. It is the edge of a pipe, or what can it be?"

The listeners cry all at once:

"She has smoked a pipe that she ought not to have smoked. But never mind. We will not take any notice of that. Let her be forgiven."

The shaman:

"That is not all. There are yet further offenses, which brought about this disease. It is due to me, or to the sick person herself?"

The patient answers:

"It is due to myself alone. There was something the matter with my [stomach] inside."

Listeners:

"Let her be released from that. Oh, such a [little] thing let her be released!"

Shaman:

"We have not yet come to the end of her offenses, of the causes of her sickness. Here is a caribou breast come to light, a raw caribou breast."

Listeners:

"Yes, we know! Last summer, at a time when she was not allowed to eat the breast of a caribou she ate some all the same. But let her be released from that offense. Let it be taken from her!"

Shaman:

"She is not yet free. A seal comes forth, plain to be seen. It is wet. One can see how the skin has been scraped on the blubber side: it is all plain as could be."

The patient:

"I did scrape the skin of a seal which my son Qasaga had killed at a time when

I ought not to have touched seal skins."

Shaman:

"It is not yet removed. It has shifted a little way back, something very like it, something of the same sort, is visible nearby."

Listeners:

"Oh that was last summer, when her husband cut out the tusk from a walrus skull, and that was shortly after he had been ill, when he was not yet allowed to touch any kind of game. Let her be released from it!

Shaman:

"Now this evil is removed, but in its place there appears something else; hair combings and sinew thread."

The patient:

"Oh, I did comb my hair once when after giving birth to a child I ought not to have combed my hair; and I hid away the combings that none might see."

Shaman:

"She is not freed from guilt even yet. It seems now as if the earth beneath our feet were beginning to move."

Patient:

"I have picked moss at a time when I ought not to have touched earth at all, moss to melt lead with for my husband's rifle bullets."

Shaman:

"There's more yet, more forbidden work that has been done. The patient has not only melted lead for her husband when it was taboo, but she did it while still wearing clothes of old caribou skin, she did it before she had yet put on the garments made from the new autumn skins."

Listeners:

"Oh, these are such little things. A woman must not be suffered to die for these. Do let her be released."

Shaman:

"She is not yet released. There is more yet about forbidden food."

Patient:

"Can it be because I once stole some salmon and ate it a time when salmon was forbidden me?"

Shaman:

"Here you are, helping spirit, dog Pungo. Tell me what you know."

Shaman:

"She is not yet released. Ah, I fear it may not succeed. She still droops, falling forward, she is ill even yet. I see a fur garment. It looks as if it belonged to some sick person. I suppose it cannot be anyone else who has used it, who has borrowed it?"

Listeners:

"Oh, yes, it is true, she lent a fur coat to someone at a time when she was unclean."

Shaman:

"I can still see a piece of sole leather chewed through and through, a piece of sole leather being softened."

Patient:

"The spotted seal from the skin of which I removed the hair, and the meat of which I ate, though it was taboo."

Listeners:

"Let it pass. Let her be released from that. Let her get well."

Shaman:

"Return to life, I see you now returning in good health among the living and you, being yourself a shaman, have your helping spirits in attendance. Name but one more instance of forbidden food, all the men you have lain with though you were unclean, all the food you have swallowed, old and new offences, forbidden occupations, or was it a lamp that you borrowed?

Patient:

"Alas yes, I did borrow the lamp of one dead. I have used a lamp that had belonged to a dead person."

Listeners:

"Even though it be so, let it be removed. Let all evils be driven far away, that she may get well."

(Vol. 7, No. 1:132-141)

The patient in this healing session was herself a shaman. However, since she had broken many taboos and her health had failed her so badly, she was unable to cure herself and had to call upon another shaman to help her. The *angakut*, like doctors in all cultures which employ such group therapy healing sessions, helps the patient help herself. Such a healing session becomes almost a ritual in which all the members of the community participate and collectively reinforce basic sacred beliefs and practices.

Summary

We have briefly examined some aspects of the sacred life of the Baffin Bay Eskimo people. In this culture *the sacred* is directly connected to day-to-day survival. Survival in this climate and environment is dependent on hunting. Hunting means interfering with or killing other souls*—specifically those of animals. Since the women are responsible for sewing animal skins and preparing food made from animals, they too are exposed to the danger such interference can produce. Not only does the existence of animal souls create a danger to the Baffin Bay Eskimos, but the harsh environment is always a threat. Learning the ways of the environment is like getting to know a personality, a being. The natural world is therefore made up of many forces and spirits, which have names and positions of power in the Eskimo *cosmology*.

In this culture the shaman has an added responsibility. A shaman must remember all the rules of daily living and also maintain contact with the spirit world. This contact is initially made because the shaman is born with a particular sensitivity to the world and with particular abilities that only shamans possess. Those forces that daily affect the Eskimo people's lives—wind, snow, cold, food scarcity, and souls—are things the people ask the shaman to be responsible for. The shaman's responsibility is to have knowledge of the balances between the people and the natural world. Not obeying the rules handed down from the beginning of time by the ancestors can bring sickness. Therefore, the shaman cures illness as well.

The shaman, like human beings in the old days, can talk to the animals, the plants, and to the elements of the world. The Baffin Bay area sacred ways of knowledge reflect this *aboriginal* existence when human beings lived

---

* See Chapter One, Part II, 2.

close to the very roots of existence. In contrast to many other tribal cultures in North America, the Baffin Bay Eskimo cultures center their religious life around the shaman. They show us clearly the relationship between the role and functions of the shaman and Native North America Sacred Ways of Knowledge.

The Pima Shaman and *Ka:cim* (Staying) Sickness

The Pima people live on the opposite end of the continent from the Baffin Bay people. In southern Arizona where the climate is temperate, often hot, and dry, the Pima farm, keep domesticated animals, gather desert fruits and catch desert animals. The shaman, called *ma:kai*, is an individual recruited by animal spirits who is a specialist in diagnosing and curing illnesses among the Pima. He is particularly called upon by The People to diagnose cases of *ka:cim* or "staying" sickness. These are feelings of discomfort and disease found only among the Pima people, and like the disease of the Iglulik woman treated in the curing seance, they are brought about by a failure to follow the rules of Pima life set down at the time of Creation. The Pima shamans then, are specialists in the elements and relationships of the Pima *cosmos or world*. Pima healing and the concept of *ka:cim* sickness tells us something about the Pima world and Pima sacred ways. In this section, we will discuss the following points, letting the Pima shaman, Gregorio, explain in his own words* the details of Pima shamanism.

1. Recruitment of shamans, or becoming a *ma:kai*
2. The characteristics and abilities of the *ma:kai*
3. *Ka:cim* sickness as a reflection of the Pima world
4. The *dúajida* (diagnosis) and cure

Becoming a *Ma:kai*

In this section Gregorio explains how an animal spirit appears in a vision to the shaman-to-be (who can either be a man or a

---

* Recorded in the book, *Pima Shamanism and Ka:cim Mumkidag (Staying Sickness)* by Donald Bahr, Juan Gregorio, et. al. (1974). Gregorio's words, spoken in Pima, were translated by David L. Lopez and Albert Alvarez.

woman). The spirit teaches the shaman curing songs which are songs that describe the typical character of the spirit—these are mostly animal songs since spirits appear in the shape and character of animals.

There is, Gregorio says, a proper relationship maintained between the shaman-to-be and the spirit. The shaman apprentice, since he/she is just learning and acquiring skill and powers, should not "go too far" into the world of the spirits but remain, for the most part, in the world of human beings. The *ma:kai* should be careful and avoid letting his/her soul slip away into the world of spirits. If this happened Gregorio says, the *ma:kai* would no longer be of any use in the world of humans. The *ma:kai's* body would be in the world of humans but it couldn't function because the soul would be somewhere far away unable to get back in its body.

Gregorio also emphasizes a point we made earlier in this chapter which is that the shaman's power comes partly from the people themselves. In order to maintain his/her power, the *ma:kai* must help the people. If the shaman-to-be does not "begin his shamanizing" as soon as he has learned what he is supposed to know, he will "be damaged," Gregorio says.

Gregorio:
What are the animals or whatever they are which appear in visions, and teach something to a person? Yes, it seems to be true, many things are like that, it's true about it whatever kind of animal it may be...it will be caused to teach a person and somehow he will do it and the person will easily acquire it whatever teaching it will be whatever the way of the animal will be...

Well, and during that teaching it will have to be done some kind of animal's way. Sometimes it happens this way, look...whatever animal, such as those which are runners on the earth, and the animal sometimes will meet one, and it will tell him something and it will take him just so far, and show him how something is. Well, and perhaps it will be the case that it will teach songs to him. And that animal will be the source of it, it will be the musical characteristics of it, it will be intended for ritual curing, or it will be intended for the *dúajida*, however it may be.

Look, just any [animal] is like that, it can be any kind of animal whatever kind it may be, and will meet the person. Well, and during that teaching the person has to get knowledge [and] understand it, well, and the animal will give it to him. Look, that's how it is.

What is the reason why an animal or spirit teacher will quit a person? ...the decision to cut off instruction is up to the teachers if they don't intend to continue teaching, well, then they won't have to continue with it whatever it will be... The student himself may cause the [instruction to stop] if he won't take proper care of himself as I have already explained that there is a thing, menstruation, dangerous, well, that is not liked by those kinds of persons who will be leading him or her through that instruction, they will have to drop him or her... It is said that the thing [spirit or animal] which teaches a person may bother his heart, the person just damages himself, and who is responsible for it? The man who enjoys instruction although he cannot endure it? Or perhaps it is the animal's responsibility, because it got bothered about it? Yes, it really is like that... if he is inclined toward something whatever he will learn. Well, and it ought to be the case that later on it will become apparent that the instruction should stop at a certain point, well, then he should start working on shamanism. And then sometimes it happens to one of the students, because of that instruction, he get damaged...

Well, and then damage will happen to the students, yet, it should be understood, the spirit teacher just appears to be something, but it isn't something like we are around here, namely, people. Sometimes we real people meet one another, and we talk with each other, well, this spirit teacher is not like that. It is made in the darkness, but yet it is real... It really happens that somehow that spirit something gets observed, well, and it should be like that [that only

people and not spirits are proper companions.] Then otherwise it will happen that the student will already have passed it if there is a limit to what has been permitted if there is a limit to what the student will know. He shouldn't exceed it, it won't be right. Well, and that's what it is, which is the reason why the person is damaged, it just sickens him...if he does not begin to work at shamanism soon enough... (Bahr, et. al., 1974:307-317)

In his account of how one becomes a *ma:kai* Gregorio describes the spirits who "teach" the *ma:kai* student. He says that the spirit teacher "appears to be something" but its not like people. It is "made in the darkness," and yet "it is not real." Spirits have their proper place as teachers, and the student, though taking instruction from them, should remember that only human beings make "proper companions." Becoming a doctor as soon as possible helps keep the *ma:kai* in the world of humans. Gregorio also mentions that a menstruating woman cannot take instruction but must wait or else she will be damaged.

The Characteristics and Abilities of the *Ma:kai*

Gregorio defines the characteristics of the *ma:kai* in two ways: the *ma:kai's* "heart" and his "tools." The *ma:kai's* heart is that special gift of knowledge, sensitivity and power that, in addition to training, make a person a *ma:kai* and not just an ordinary Pima individual. The tools a *ma:kai* uses include an eagle feather for "pushing the smoke" which is blown (in the form of cigarette smoke) over the patient's body during the preliminary diagnosis session; a rattle which accompanies the shaman's songs; and crystals that help the shaman *see* the "strengths" or sickness within the patient's body. Spirits are called "tools" as well.

However, tools and spirits cannot be used successfully by just anybody. It is the *ma:kai's* heart of special powers that work *through* the tools and make them effective. Also, depending on the number of helping spirits the *ma:kai* has, the *ma:kai* will have a greater range of knowledge.

Gregorio:

Well, there are always many kinds of things that the shaman has with which he can do the *dúajida*, by means of which he understands. Well, truly, he will use his whatever-kind-of-crystal. Well, there are diverse other things if he will understand several things. Well, and yet one of his various possessions will be present which is the means by which he will learn, perhaps he will take it out, and he will use it. It just might happen, that then the strength will clearly emerge, "Ah, yes, look, you sickness are doing it," he will think. And truly, they, the public, call them *ma:kai*. Of course, his heart appears to be somehow special, but is is not true that he only uses his heart, there is something else with it whatever thing he will know, whatever thing he will use, and it is his gift. It means that the gift is the means by which he figures out or it's the means to help the patient if he will try to do away with the sickness. Look, that's what it means and how he does it. It's not true that he does it by his heart alone.

How is the *ma:kai*'s heart which gives him the right to suck or to blow? Yes, it is this kind of person which we call *ma:kai*, it's true that he seems to be something special, because he understands something, and it is his own right, and none of us ever sees inside his heart how the several things are by means of which he understands. Well, and we call them *ma:kai*, yet, they are not the same, one of them will understand several things, two, three, four, if he is rather superior, well, it is from that number of things that he knows. And none of us know what the thing is which he understands. One tool or several more if there are several, nobody knows. And it is only up to him how he will observe something, he will illuminate it, and figure it out, or learn how it will be. Well, it may be the case if it will be up to him if he can do it if he will take some of the strength away. Well, and necessarily he will suck it, and he will do away with it, or he will put something into the patient by means of which the strength will get

done away with. Look, that's how it is, they are not the same.

Well we don't know, in what manner he understands, and we may ask one of them. It is only up to him. He may want to tell it to the public, and he may tell, "I have several of them." Perhaps it will never be told, because some things may be thought about it by him, and it is only up to him... (Bahr et. al., 1974:207-215)

In this discussion Gregorio indicates what the powers of the *ma:kai* are, but he says that one never really knows what it is that aids the *ma:kai* in curing. This is because the *ma:kai* often keeps secret the kinds of spirit helpers he/she has. Or perhaps different *ma:kais* use their power differently—their "hearts" are never the same, just as their characters are never the same. He also says that *ma:kais* have specialties—some suck away illness, some "put something in" the patient.

Ka:cim (Staying) Sickness As A Reflection of The Pima's World

The Pima place sickness in two categories: Staying Sickness (*ka:cim mumkidag*), and Wandering Sickness. Staying Sickness is "caused by dangerous objects which have ways and strengths" or parts of dangerous objects which have ways and strengths (Bahr, et. al., 1974:22). Wandering Sickenss is caused "by various noxious substances such as germs, heat, or pus." Such things as sorcery, bites, infant deformities, retardation and constipation are not considered sickness. Of all the above categories, only Staying Sickness is the property of the Pimans alone. They are, in other words, the only people in the world who can suffer from Staying Sickness. Gregorio explains in the next text that a special relationship exists between the Pimans, the rules given to the Pimans at the time of Creation, and their sicknesses or diseases. Sicknesses or diseases, Gregorio says, were "given to" the Pimans during their early history. The Piman people must accept these sicknesses as part of the balance of Creation and life, even though they are unpleasant and dangerous. The student will also recall David

Kindle's story about the four enemies,* poverty, hunger, fatigue, and body lice. The twins agreed that though each of these remaining enemies to the People were unpleasant, they were also necessary to *remind* people of the right way to live a long life.

Pimans get *ka:cim* sicknesses because they have *behaved improperly* toward a "dangerous object" which was given "dignity" at the time of creation. *Ka:cim* sicknesses are cured by rituals which "appeal to the dignity of the offended object." Problems such as retardation and deformities cannot be cured because their source is different from *ka:cim* sicknesses. These problems come from having made fun of such afflicted people—people or objects that *were not given dignity* at the time of Creation.

In summary, *Gregorio sees Ka:cim sickness in sacred, moral terms rather than in terms such as Western medicine uses, like bacteria or germs. He sees sickness in terms of balance and relationships. By considering sickness in terms of the sickness's relationship to the environment, to the laws of Creation, and to the community, the Pimans accordingly place disease in the context of all that is sacred.* Those laws and rules which govern the Piman's health also tell how one should not act toward certain animals, plants, or other objects. Unlike the Western medical practitioner, the Pima *ma:kai* must understand these laws and be able to rebalance any situation which threatens the balanced relationships within the Pima individual and in the natural world.

Gregorio:
   Ka:cim sickness never wanders, it only goes around here, because it is established here by whatever thing or god gave it or commanded the order of all things, including sicknesses to us; whatever made us and whatever he gave to us. And even though the commanded order seems wrong, still it has its source in [the proper way] which is the origin of that kind of sickness, *Ka:cim* sickness originates from that given order and it is

only here, it only exists right here, and truly it only goes around here, it only applies to us [Pimas.] (Bahr, 1974:38-39)

Below are some examples of "dangerous objects" and how, when they are treated "improperly," cause *ka:cim* sickness. The causes are also listed:

   Cow—Parent of unborn child looking at a dying cow during slaughter of the animal for a fiesta; anyone slaughtering a cow for a fiesta and failing to pray properly; parent of unborn child tormenting (teasing) a cow.

   Coyote—Anyone eating melon which a coyote has bitten into; anyone killing a coyote.

   Deer—Anyone choking while eating deer meat; anyone killing deer in a cruel manner; parent of unborn child killing deer; anyone eating too much deer fat.

   Eagle—Anyone killing an eagle; picking up feathers.

   Lightning—Anyone using firewood from a tree which has been struck by lightning.

   Quail—Failure to wash hands after eating quail eggs.

   Turtle—Thoughtless killing; anyone failing to be polite.

   Rabbit—Anyone killing a rabbit and picking it up before it is dead; parent of unborn child killing a rabbit or looking at one while it is dying.

   (Bahr et. al., 1974:284-298)

A person becomes ill with *ka:cim* sickness from the moment he/she acts in an improper way. But the sickness many not show itself for a long time, or the person who has the symptoms may ignore them or not think anything of them. So it may happen that a person over a period of years, becomes ill with more than one *ka:cim* sickness. The sicknesses become "layered" inside the patient and are referred to later by the shaman as "strengths." A person may become sick before birth as a result of his/her parents' actions. A person may become sick during childhood, in which case the sickness might reach the person when he/she is an adult, or a person may get sick with *ka:cim* sickness as an adult or in Old Age. *Ka:cim* sickness is complete when it reaches the patient's heart and kills him/her. It is the shaman's task, in the case of several "strengths" of sickness inside the patient, to diagnose each one of them, separate them, and remove them as far as it is possible.

Gregorio:

How does it happen that a sickness reaches people? Yes, it is quite clear because the victim is aware during his life of how he normally feels. He never has any different kind of stimulation. Well, and then when it happens that something (strength) comes to him, and reaches him. And already something (an earlier strength) may have stimulated him a little bit, but especially when all of them will get to him, then he will really know there is something wrong. (148-250)

Look, that's what I mean by saying that something is a "beneath sickness." It is whatever sickness that arrived there first, and got something on top of it. Well, and only it will be observed, because it is on top. Look, and the lower one, he won't observe it if it gets covered by something. It will be worked on and then it will emerge. (Bahr et. al., 1974:149-150)

The *Dúajida* (Diagnosis and Cure)

The *ma:kai* is called upon by a person who feels or notices the symptoms of a *ka:cim* sickness. Gregorio tells us:

...he will really know there is something wrong. Well, then it happens that he will decide to find out, "what is it, and it stimulates me?" Because many different things sicken us, but the things differ, it is never just one thing that in some manner stimulates them, and that will be all there is to it. It happens differently, so that sometimes some things (a few strengths) seem to be similar, but yet they are different. Look, it is up to the patient that he will look around and see whether one of those *ma:kai* will be sitting someplace who could tell him what the thing is that is

stimulating him. Well, and then the patient will tell the *ma:kai* and then the *ma:kai* will observe the patient. Perhaps the *ma:kai* will say, "that one kind of strength seems to have caught up with you. That's the one that reached you and sickened you. Look, it will get done to you, and you will get cured. You will be all right..." (Bahr, et. al., 1974:149-153)

When the *ma:kai* comes to see the patient, he/she can do one of two things: a *kúlanmada* or a *dúajida*. The *kúlanmada* is a shortened, day-time version of the *dúajida*. The *kúlanmada* involves blowing smoke, some singing, and sucking out the strength or sickness. The word is translated to mean "to apply something" or "to mix with something." (Bahr, et. al., 1974:122)

Dúajida means "vitalization" or "to cause to be healthy" and it involves blowing, sucking, and singing songs directed at spirit helpers. In the *dúajida* the shaman "figures out" the sickness and actual cure might take place sometime afterwards and can be done by a non-shaman in a singing ritual ceremony called *wúsota*.

The *dúajida* takes all night. After the end of the night-long diagnosis session the shaman may "name" the sickness. At this time the patient must then try to remember when he/she acted improperly towards a dangerous object, as we discussed earlier. The *dúajida* is a diagnosis session performed to discover the "strengths" of the *ka:cim* sickness within the patient. The patient lies on a bed with the shaman at his/her side. There may be others present in the room, but the only interaction or, if necessary, conversation, is between the patient and the shaman. The shaman may do the following things during the course of the night-long *dúajida*. He may suck out "strengths," put something in the patient to counteract the "strength;" put something in the patient in order to separate several strengths; or gather them together. Bahr goes on to say:

Each of these actions takes place at the end of a *dúajida* or at the ends of subparts within it, for example, sucking out one strength to clear the path for later actions toward deeper strengths. These actions occupy only a small portion of

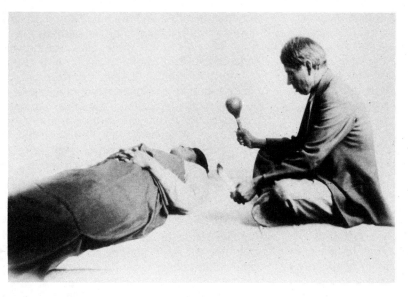

Jose Panco, Papago medicine specialist treating a sick man with rattle and deer tail. San Xavier Reservation, Arizona, ca. 1920. (Courtesy of the Smithsonian Institution, National Anthropological Archives)

the total time spent in performing a *dúajida*, perhaps ten minutes [out of the] ten hours. (Bahr, et. al., 1974:170)

The rest of the *dúajida* consists of identifying strengths by singing, illuminating with crystals, fanning with an eagle feather, and blowing smoke. These actions are all directed to another "place" outside of the room or within the patient's body and to non-human beings, or spirit helpers. When Gregorio speaks of the "tools" or the "spirits" he used in the *dúajida*, he often calls them both "somethings." One reason is because his divining feather and his rattle are also powerful tools since only he has the gift of shamanizing with them; and he received this gift from training with his spirit helpers who first appeared in a vision.

Gregorio:
Well, and anytime it is all right for *kúlanmada*, in the day or the evening well, he will go and observe it and if the sickness is very bad, well, he will just observe a little bit of it. That's what is called "*kúlanmada*." And on the other hand, that *dúajida* takes place when the *ma:kai* really works, and he will figure it out how it is, whatever the thing is that is doing it. Well, in the night he will concentrate on it whenever he sits down, and from there he will figure things out. And the sickness may be a certain kind of thing. And he will try to change it he will concentrate on the patient's complex sickness. And he will do still another different thing, he will go on and on doing different things to discover the various strengths in the patient, and then the night is finished—at dawn, well, and whatever kind of strength will have shown up. Look, this is what it is called *dúajida* . . .

Well, and whatever the diagnosed sickness may be, whatever thing is making him sick, well, and some things can be cured anytime, in the day, whatever it may be, and some things of course have to be cured at night. As I have already explained, '*dúajida*,' is the thing from which the *ma:kai* will try to figure it out, or change the sickness. (Bahr, et. al., 1974:126-129)

I guess it's always true about the kulanmada that there is something else along with the *ma:kai*; it [whatever is along with him] is not only from his own heart, however it may be that the *ma:kai* will observe something in the sick person. Well, and necessarily the *ma:kai* owns something which he will use, and he will try to change it whatever kind of sickness it is. . . . And, however, there is another situation, if the *dúajida* should go on all night, definitely he will get his rattle going, he will fan the patient with

135

his equipment for finding things [*i.e.*, feather].

Whatever thing he will find, well o.k., it is all set that he has something whatever will stand against that kind of sickness, well, and by means of it he will try to change the sickness. But whenever he finishes his work, then he will tell him, look, that's what happens in the night.

How do they do it, those who *duajid* them?...there is "something" which gets with the *ma:kai*, and because of that "something" the *ma:kai* figures it out if there are many things he is acquainted with which he will use. Look, suppose it would be that he first tried to use "something." And it didn't stand against the sickness, the following one also, he will keep on, however many tools he has. Well, and he will find all of it if it falls clear eventually whatever thing he used, he will really follow whatever spirits. The cause of sickness gets followed all night long, and it really gets studied if something happens to exist and tries to hide. But when it is worked on and bothered, then it will have to emerge, look, that's how this *dúajida* happens... (Bahr, et. al., 1974:173-180)

In the first part of Gregorio's explanation he describes what the objective of the *dúajida* is without going into specific detail. Every sickness, of course, requires a different approach. As Gregorio says, the *ma:kai* will try many different things to try both to figure out the source of the sickness and also to rid the patient of the sickness. "Figuring out" the sickness requires that the *ma:kai* employ his/her techniques of seeing and his/her powers of concentration. During the course of this diagnosis, the *ma:kai* may be able to cure the patient, because to really "figure out" the sickness the *ma:kai* must breathe it up, separate it, and draw it out of the patient.

In the second part of the statement Gregorio goes into more detail describing what methods the *ma:kai* employs if the sickness is very strong in the patient. Not only will the *ma:kai* use the power of his "heart," but he must use, in addition, something that "will stand against that kind of sickness." He will use his "heart,"

perhaps his rattle, and his fan. Then there is a "something"—a spirit helper perhaps—with which he will "follow" the sickness until it "falls clear." Spirit helpers are tools that can go into the patient and search out the causes and strengths of the sickness. Since originally the sickness is caused by the patient's improper behavior toward a dangerous object (most often an animal), then the spirit helper (who is also the spirit of an animal) is more likely to be able to find the sickness and "stand against it."

The *Ma:kai*'s Curing Songs

In the following section, Gregorio tells us about the *ma:kai's* songs. These are curing songs which appeal to both his spirit helpers and to the animal or object that has been offended by the patient who did not show respect; who acted improperly. The songs, like the appeals made by the Iglulik shaman, Aua, are "funny." Gregorio explains that the animals like funny songs and listen to them better that way. He explains that this works much the same way a clown teases a person—the clown points out something about us and by doing so in a funny way, teaches us more easily then if we were lectured about it. The words and message of the shaman's song pick out some special characteristic of the animal and sing about it in one or two lines, for example:

Over there, Coyote
as the sun sets in the mountains
runs with the taste of
Rabbit on his snout.

Gregorio:
Well, if the things about the animal's way are clearly told by singing then the animal will feel very pleasantly, it hears its song which is true, how the way it is sung, and pronounced, as it vocalizes. Well, and perhaps the sickness is some kind of stimulating thing, the [animal or spirits] will quickly do away with the *strength* because the song has been accurately pronounced how the animal's way is.

It is true that the curing songs about the animals are funny? How are those songs funny? Yes, because the songs are of the sort about how a thing will be, and be in the animal's way if it does things in some notable manner. Sometimes the song is stated in some manner that something interesting get done to the animal, or whatever kind of dangerous object it may be, and that event which happens to the animal is what is funny, so for that reason one will speak about the reason why songs are funny if it should be like that. If I, for example should happen to go someplace. And some people at a distance will be watching in some manner. Then I just might do something, then I might almost fall, then they will really laugh at me, watching me through the corners of their eyes. Look, this is similar to the songs, and that is what is meant, funny songs. Look, that's how it is. (Bahr, et. al., 1974:245-249)

Summary

In summary, we have shown how one Pima shaman, Juan Gregorio, describes the connection the Pimas make between a sacred system of natural (ecological) and social relationships and the role of the shaman. Like the Baffin Bay Eskimo people, at least one category of disease among the Pima is associated with Piman oral tradition or history. The source of disease, as well as the source of curing goes back to the aboriginal times when the world and the Piman people were created.

We were also shown how a special relationship exists between the shaman and animals or plants. The student will recall Barney Mitchell's comment that the greatest sacred thing is knowing the order and the structure of a thing—this also applies to the shaman's relationship to plants, animals, and the spirits of these objects. In his/her training, the Pima shaman is allowed to enter the very center of sacred knowledge: he is taught the order and structure of Ka:cim sickness, and taught songs that will help cure these sicknesses.

Finally, we also heard that it was important for the shaman to do his/her work, his/her shamanizing, as soon as possible after the completion of his training. As Essie Parrish said in the description of her vision earlier in this chapter, "if you enter heaven, you might have to work." The shaman's powers and gifts remain healthy and useful as long as he/she puts them to work for the people who need them.

The Wintu Shaman, Flora Jones

Flora Jones is a practicing shaman in northern California; a Wintu woman who combines modern and traditional elements in her curing techniques and in her philosophy of the Wintu universe. In an article about Flora Jones, in *Natural History*, the following details about her life were given by her to the author of the article:

Flora, an adolsecent at the time, was attending a federal school in San Francisco when she first experienced the vivid dreams that eventually led her home to become a shaman. These dreams confused and terrified her but they also challenged her to [learn how to live both in the world of the "White man" and the world of the Wintu.]

Born in 1909 of racially mixed parentage (her great-grandfather was the last great chief of the McCloud River Wintu), she was baptized a Methodist, yet also accepted childhood encounters with tribal animal spirits. Although formally educated in government schools, she was reared by a mother who spoke Wintu and often relied upon Wintu Shamans to maintain her daughter's health. As a young girl, Flora was lured by fantasies of a career as a Hollywood actress, yet she shot her first deer at the age of ten and following tribal tradition [did not] eat this first flesh.

At the age of seventeen came the [special] event of her calling—her first trance. She was [concentrating] on a card game with friends when, without warning, her ears were filled with a ringing sound and a burning pain.

"It was like a hot bullet going through my ear," she recalled. "The pain went through me and I passed out for four days." Years later she viewed this [frightening] experience as her first ecstatic encounter with a helping spirit—*the star spirit.*

137

She awoke from her long period of unconsciousness singing. With her were four older Wintu shamans, who as in the traditional initiation ceremony, sang and cared for her administering medicine and later taking her to sacred places to pray. In the days that followed her helping spirit taught her doctoring songs and tutored her in the healing arts of the shaman.

Finding her acceptable in their own trances, the elder shamans established her as a shaman in her own right, although she did not begin doctoring until years later. By singing songs, visiting sacred places, and entering trances, Flora found that a new calm had settled over her. No longer, as in years past was she bothered by mental turmoil and sickness, by the contradictions of her upbringing and by self-doubt; no longer were the spirits taking her to the mountain. (Knudtson, 1975:8)

Flora has a number of helping spirits, each of which has a special character and usefulness. Her helping spirits are representative of the Wintu world, just as the Baffin Bay Area Eskimo and Pima spirit powers reflect their particular *ecosystem* and worlds. She explains that the spirits take many forms. They may be "spiritual forces that live in sacred places or in the sky, the spirits of animals, or the souls of departed relatives" among others. Speaking of her own spirit helpers:

She describes the suckerfisher spirit as a trickster, a mischievous [being who talks in many languages] not to be trusted during a trance. Another, the black wolf spirit [appears] as a hostile character and [comes] most often during times of deep distress. Others—a star spirit, a moon spirit, a mountain spirit, the soul of an ancestral shaman—may appear to her during a seance as well. When several spirits enter [at the same time, carrying on an] animated discussion during a trance, the mountain spirit acts as a leader and spokesman.

Flora explains, "the spirits use me for just a tool—something to get into to tell the people what is going to happen and what they can do." (Knudtson, 1975:6-7)

Among the other tools Flora uses during her shamanizing are a staff, Yellow Hammer* feathers, which can be used to "pull evil dreams" from a person, and a wooden pipe which has special power and can be consulted for advice.

As we have discussed before, among the Wintu, as in other Native American cultures, there are different types of shamans and ceremonial practitioners. Among the Wintu there were five types:

The first two, the dreamers and the singers, are shamans possessing powers of [second sight] not associated with curing. Tracer doctors were [good] at locating lost objects or souls. And sucking and healing doctors were specialists in healing... Each of the five types [did their work in a trance state, although] the sucking doctors were traditionally the most powerful and highly [respected] by [The People]. They cured by [taking out very small, diseased] spirit missiles, or "pains." They removed the pains by sucking while in a trance—a procedure which... affected the local blood flow as well.

Flora considers herself a healing doctor, diagnosing illnesses with her hands during an ecstatic healing seance. But like many shamans, she has [shown an ability] in more than one specialty. For example, as a healing shaman, she has sucked pains from certain patients, but like a tracer doctor, she predicted the location of a missing corpse on a nearby river. (Knudtson, 1975:8)

A typical healing seance, in which Flora Jones summons her helping spirits in a trance, is presented below:

Flora's seances usually take place in the company of a traditional assistant or "interpreter," the patient, and various friends and family members. [An interpreter is needed to tell Flora what she has said during her trance state, since, after such trances one loses all memory of the event. Nowdays Flora may

---

* A type of bird.

also use a tape recorder. She said that at first her spirit helpers were critical of this, but soon got used to it.]

Once assembled, the participants in a seance join the shaman in summoning the helping spirits by singing the appropriate Wintu songs. (One such song, according to Flora, describes a shaman's search for a path taken by the souls of the dead to heaven and his conversations with trees and flowers along the way.) Periodically, the shaman (Flora) accepts a pipe of tobacco from the interpreter, inhales deeply, then resumes singing. Traditionally, shamans used a species of wild tobacco to enter a trance: today commercial tobacco [is used].

The arrival of the spirit-helpers is marked by the shaman's sharp inhalation; the group falls silent as the spirits begin to speak through the shaman's voice, offering advice or prophecies and sometimes quarreling or joking among themselves.

The shaman drinks clear water, than a solution of acorn water from a small container—an offering to the helping spirits. With the diagnostic powers of the spirit-helpers acting through her hands, she begins to move her fingers carefully across the patient's body sensing unseen, internal injuries or abnormalities. Flora explains, "I feel for the sores, the aches, and the pains. When I put my hand over the body I can feel every little muscle and every little vein. I can feel the soreness. It hurts me. If they have heart trouble, my heart just beats. Any place they are hurting I hurt. I become a part of their body."

If the spirits [find] the source of the sickness, they prescribe for the patient's care, speaking through the shaman. Remedies may be offered for both physical and psychological ills and often include traditional herbal medicines, which Flora collects and stores.

Upon awakening from the trance, the shaman learns of the spiritual diagnosis from the interpreter and proceeds to treat the patient accordingly. In the past, a patient's family would present the shaman with a tiny, hand-made basket of characteristic striped design following a successful treatment. Now the transaction usually involves money and takes place regardless of the outcome of the therapy.

Only in the most dire cases, when a patient is unconscious and death eminent, does Flora perform the Soul Dance—a final attempt to recapture the victim's wandering soul. This ritual is performed at midnight. As the shaman dances to the rhythmic beating of sticks she waves a staff wearing a miniature basket in which to catch the lost soul. If the shaman's search is successful, the soul is brought back to its owner and placed over his heart, its natural resting place. (Knudtson, 1975:12)

For Flora Jones, shamanism and doctoring are very important sources of Wintu traditional sacred knowledge. She feels that they are at the heart of Wintu life. Shamanizing and curing, collecting the herbs and the feathers and other things that are needed for the healing session; walking to the special places of power in the forest and in the mountains—these things keep the Wintu sacred ways alive. For Flora Jones, this path is also one which keeps people healthy and sane. She tells us:

> This is what the spirit tells me—get my people together. Get them to believe because if you don't they are going to go wild. They are going to kill one another. Whoever has sacred places must wake them up, the same as I am doing here—to keep my old world within my heart and with the spiritual. For them to help me and for me to help my people. (Knudtson, 1975:14)

CHAPTER SUMMARY

In this chapter we have discussed one element of religion that most Native American cultures have in common—*shamanism*. We have discussed the possibility that shamanism is a very ancient tradition and forms one of the main roots of aboriginal sacred ways and religions in general.

As we look at the ceremonial life of Native peoples throughout North America, we see that the sacred systems of each culture are different from one another, and that each one is very complex. No one single person knows everything there is to know about the sacred knowledge of his/her culture. But beneath this rich complexity and variety of sacred practices are fundamental traditions rooted in a hidden world—*the world of the order and the structure of things*. This is the world we see reflected in the oral tradition of The People—the Emergence histories, the Migration histories, the Creation.

In these histories, the original inhabitants on the Earth learned from the animals and other beings. As we saw in the lesson of the Navajo Deer Hunting Way as told by Claus Chee Sonny, Billie Blackhorse, and James Smith, some of the first "laws of survival" and ways of worship the people learned had to do with hunting animals for food and taking plants for curing. Later, we saw how these same laws and communications with animals and plants came to be the special knowledge and practice of shamans. As we saw in Chapter Two, *Ritual Drama and Prayer*, many people besides the shaman learn songs and prayers in order to strengthen their occupations, for example in farming, sheep herding, and hunting. But the shaman goes a step further. He/she learns a greater amount of knowledge, studying hard, exposing him/herself to dangers, in order to doctor people and maintain balances between the people and the natural environment; within the community; and with respect to each individual's health.

We have seen how shamanism is often a very personal or private profession and at the same time it affects a great many people. The shaman practitioners in this chapter are specialists in healing and they are also responsible for passing on the teachings of The People and knowledge about the mysteries in the world. Because the shaman is in touch with great, often mysteirous powers in the world, he/she may bring that world closer to The People, either in healing ceremonies, or in the case of many Pueblo communities, by fulfilling certain annual ceremonial duties. (In the Pueblos curing specialists are organized in societies for the most part, not as separate individuals as we saw among the Baffin Bay Eskimos, the Pima, and the Wintu.)

In almost all cases, whether or not the shaman is a solitary person like the *angakut* Igjugarjuk, a shaman like Essie Parrish who is both a "dreamer" and a Mole Baru leader, or a Pueblo practitioner who works in a group, the shaman has certain characteristics that define his/her work.

The shaman is a composer of special healing songs.

The shaman can cause him/herself to enter into a trance.

The shaman can travel after lost souls or to seek lost objects.

The shaman can diagnose and cure illnesses.

The shaman has spirit helpers with whom he or she communicate and whom he/she can control.

Nowadays the role of the shaman is changing, just as many elements in Native North American sacred systems are changing. But, as we have seen in some of the examples in this chapter, the shamans themselves are trying to carry on their work to fit the changing times. Claus Chee Sonny works with the United States Health Centers, Flora Jones uses a tape recorder in place of an interpreter, and in many places throughout the country Native American practitioners are being acknowledged as important sources of medicinal knowledge and medical techniques.

One of the problems that confronts shamans nowadays, as Flora Jones pointed out, is that the "sacred places"—areas in the mountains, by lakes, in caves, and so on—where spirits dwell or where sources of power are, are being threatened by logging and mining operations, Forest Service regulations, urban housing, highways, and other dangers. Therefore, one of the new roles of the sacred practitioners in Native American communities today is to figure out how to maintain this source of sacred knowledge in the midst of modern life.

Suggested Additional Readings

BALIKCI, ASEN
"Shamanistic Behavior Among the Netsilik Eskimos," *Southwest Journal of Anthropology*, 19:380-396.

BOGORAZ, VLADIMIR G.
1969   *The Chuckchee*, New York, Johnson reprint (Reprint of the 1909 edition).

CHADWICK, NORA K.
1942   *Poetry and Prophecy*, Cambridge, Mass., Cambridge University Press.

ELMORE, FRANCIS H.
1943   *Ethnology of the Navajo*, The University of New Mexico Bulletin, Monograph Series, Vol. 1, No. 17, pp. 1-136.

HANDELMAN, DON
1967   "The Development of a Washo Shaman," *Ethnology*, 6 (Oct.), pp. 444-464.

JONES, DAVID EARLE
1972   *Sanapia: Comanche Medicine Woman*, New York, Holt, Rinehart and Winston.

Journal of the American Society for Physical Research, 5 West 73rd St., New York, New York 10023.

LANTIS, MARGARET
1966   *Alaska Eskimo Ceremonialism*, Seattle, Wash., University of Washington Press. (For aspects of shamans' procedures.)

KIEV, ARI (ed.)
1974   *Magic, Faith, and Healing: Studies in Primitive Psychology Today*, New York, Free Press.

KOESTLER, ARTHUR
1972   *The Roots of Coincidence*, New York, Random House. (Discussion of non-ordinary experience.)

LOMMEL, ANDREAS
1966   *Shamanism: The Beginning of Art*, New York, McGraw Hill.

_____
1967   *The World of the Early Hunter*, London, England, Evelyn, Adams, and Mackay.

MANN, FELIX, M.D.
1973   *Acupuncture: The Ancient Art of Healing And How It Works Scientifically*, New York, Vintage.

"Stones, Bones, and Skin: Ritual and Shamanic Art," *ARTSCANADA*, 30th Anniversary Issue, 129 Adelaide St., West, Toronto, Ontario, M5H 1R6, Canada.

TART, CHARLES
1972   *Altered States of Consciousness: A Book of Readings*, New York, Doubleday.

CHAPTER SIX

6 The Changeable Earth:
The Colonizers and Genocide

The White Man excused his presence here by saying that he had been guided by the will of his God; and in so saying absolved himself of all responsibility for his appearance in a land occupied by other men.*

In this chapter we will be focusing on historical events which have led up to the present-day situation which confronts Native American traditional cultures and sacred ways. We will examine historical events, attitudes, and policies which have greatly affected aboriginal tribal sacred ways in North America. In order to study Native Americans in the context of today's world we have to understand what forces of change are at work altering the concepts and procedures of these ways of life. As we have talked about "the sacred" in the worlds of Native American people, we must see how "religion" has been defined from the dominant society's point of view.

In this chapter we will specifically examine the historical roots of government policy and missionary attitudes towards Native American sacred teachings and practices. By government policy we mean the main currents of thought regarding the ways in which the Federal Government (1) defined its attitude towards Native Americans, (2) the plans it devised for the containment, extermination, or assimilation of Native Americans, and (3) the

methods the Federal Government (through the war department, territorial agents, department of interior, missionaries, and Bureau of Indian Affairs Commissioners) carried out these plans. By missionary attitudes we mean partly the specific attitudes certain Christian *denominations* had of Native American people, cultures, sacred teaching and practices, and similar attitudes held by (mainly) Christian colonists in the first waves of settlement in North America. Since we feel that these missionary attitudes created an atmosphere in which the Native peoples and colonists met and grew to know each other, it is important to know what these attitudes were.

The colonizers came to this continent from Europe and met many cultures they did not understand nor often tried to understand. Native Americans, too, had a hard time understanding the colonizers' attitudes towards Native people. If we can make some sense out of the tense situation created by misunderstandings and prejudices, we might be able to imagine a different history. What, for example, would history have been like if the colonizers had simply accepted the differences among the cultures they met and themselves, and not criticized native customs and teachings. And second, what might have happened if the colonizers had respected geographical and ecological boundaries of various tribal societies and had not tried to take over all the native lands?

We will also examine Native peoples'

---

* The quotation is from Luther Standing Bear (1933:249). The title of this Chapter comes from one of the names given to the Fifth World according to Navajo History. In this case, Sandoval (Hastin Tlo'tsihee) has provided the name which is translated, the Changeable Earth. Other names for this world are the Glittering World and the White World.

responses to these attitudes and policies. The first shock of colonization has never completely disappeared, and the deeper sadness at witnessing the destruction of a People and the land is still with us. In relation to the extensive history covering these historical events our discussion will be brief. Additional reading material has been cited for the student wishing to do further research on this subject.

There were a number of factors which brought about change in native tribal sacred practices over the past 200 years. The two most important were the *economic exploitation* of the land by the colonizers and the too often *insensitive* or disrespectful attitudes of missionaries and many colonists towards the native cultures they confronted in the "New World." These factors united in a common cause within the agencies of the Federal Government assigned to "Indian Affairs." These agencies were not well defined in the early years of the colonies. At first, the war department carried out general policies, centering its efforts in the fort-system which spread from east to west over the continent. Later these forts became the centers of "Indian Agencies" when government policy began switching from extermination, wars, and containment to assimilation and reservation policy. Basically, however, the common cause of all federal government policy was to protect the economic interests of the settlers, gold-seekers, trappers, traders, and other colonists who came from Europe to this continent. This cause was combined with the other factor we mentioned; a strongly rooted feeling that the religion and values the colonists had brought with them from Europe were superior to the values and religions among the native cultures living on this continent. Since the colonists felt superior from the beginning and felt they were destined by "God" to come to this continent, it was not difficult to rationalize any government policy that would further their cause and their values.

Fuchs and Havighurst, in their book, *To Live on This Earth* summarize the federal government's early policies towards Native Americans:

> ...The Constitution of the new United States of America also [gave] the Federal Government the right to regulate commerce with the Indian tribes, make treaties, and to control the public land Indians occupied. Indian peoples continued to be dealt with as foreign nations with whom the new United States fought and concluded treaties. In addition, admission of new states to the Union could be regulated. This latter provision set the stage for requiring new states to give up any claim to jurisdiction over Indian lands—a right the original states retained. These were to remain under federal jurisdiction, creating the legal framework for the later reservation system and direct relationships between Indian tribes and the federal government.
>
> The Continental Congress concluded a treaty with the Delaware in 1778, the first of 389 treaties made or remade with the Indian tribes between 1778 and 1871, when Congressional action halted treaty making with the Indian tribes. By 1871, the Cherokee and other eastern tribes had been relocated across the Mississippi, countless battles had been fought, the Indian population severely depleted. Indians increasingly became easy targets for hostility and abuse as their territories gradually were touched by westward expansion of settlers, mining prospectors and ranchers.
>
> The various treaties ceded over a billion acres of land in exchange for which the federal government, with some variation from treaty to treaty, promised to allow Indians to keep certain lands as inalienable and tax exempt. In addition, the treaties usually included promises of federal services in such matters as education, health, technical, and agricultural learning.
>
> The Indian tribes, however, remained an embarrassing impediment to *manifest destiny*.* (Fuchs and Havighurst, 1973:4)

Basically, the settlers who came to this continent wanted something from the land and so government policy was devoted to serving

---

* A term used throughout the colonists' history in the United States meaning that *the settlement and continuous acquisition of Land by the United States Government was destined to be,* either by circumstances, by God, or by virtue of superiority.

the individual and corporate exploiters of this land's natural resources. From the beginning the colonizers *saw the land in terms of political boundaries*—not ecological regions within which tribes shared certain lands and the rights to other lands through oral tradition and economic custom. (See Chapter Four, *The Boundaries of the World*.) Foreign countries and their colonists fought against each other over these arbitrary political boundaries, carving up the land and dividing it up among themselves. They divided the land for the resources it would provide, not with respect to the ecological relationships that were balanced within connected regions. When the wars were over, the colonists demanded the land they had won, and demanded that the government protect them. So the Native Peoples' lands were separated, closed in by treaty, or taken away completely. This was a pattern. Wherever there was a new discovery of a natural resource—gold in the Black Hills of South Dakota and Northern California, silver and copper in the Southwest, lumber and pelts in the Upper Midwest, oil in Oklahoma, and rich farm land in many places—Native lands were colonized, divided, and taken away. At first, the choice The People had was to move from areas where settlement was taking place. Soon, however, this became increasingly difficult to do as more and more areas were blocked off by the westward moving settlers and subsequent armed government protection. Having to move and retreat, move again and eventually to take up war against the colonists, was very disrupting for the native people. The attitude of the colonists toward the land was something totally alien to The People as well. Vine Deloria explains how these events affected native Peoples:

Almost every tribal religion was based on land in the sense that the tribe felt that its lands were specifically given to it to use. The proceedings of treaty councils are filled with protests and declarations by Indians to the effect that lands cannot be sold since no human has the power or right to own them. Some of the old chiefs felt that, because generations of their ancestors had been buried on the lands and because the sacred events of their religion had taken place on the lands, they were obligated to maintain the tribal lands against new kinds of exploitation. The famous Nez Perce war began because white settlers invaded the Wallowa Valley in eastern Oregon and because Chief Joseph's father had made the young chief promise never to sell the lands in which his ancestors lay buried. (Deloria, 1974:252)

Since for Native American people sacred traditions were based on cosmologies which included certain lands, the waters upon them, the sky above them, and all the creatures inhabiting these places, *taking and destroying the land meant destroying what was sacred.*

At the root of these events were certain attitudes the colonists held that were very different from attitudes and values found among the different tribal communities inhabiting this continent. And these attitudes affected the way the colonists viewed native ceremonialism and ways of life.

One great difference between the native Peoples and the colonizers was the concept of wealth and power as opposed to greed and exploitation. For most Native American cultures, to be wealthy meant one had lived well—carefully, with knowledge which had enabled the individual to hunt well, sew well, bring up children well, and if necessary, fight well, depending on one's responsibilities. To be wealthy meant one had many goods, enough to give them away, to gain respect as a generous person in the eyes of one's family, kin, and tribe. To have knowledge, wisdom, and skill meant one had the power, both to acquire these skills and to use them to guide one's people, perhaps cure illnesses if one had that special power, or to teach younger people one's skills. Most important, to have wealth and power meant that one knew where wealth and power had come from. One was aware of the equal balances of power and wealth in the things of the universe and that wealth and power were a gift one might acquire in one's lifetime—a lifetime that is very short compared with the lifetime of the world, of a tree, of a river. And wealth and power did not only include goods, but it included songs, skills, and dances, things that were created through the human spirit.

Greed and exploitation are forms of wealth

and power without the awareness of *balance* and without the tempering of spirit. Greed *wants* and exploitation *takes without giving back*. There is no sharing, there is no humility, and most important, this concept of wealth is based on the acquisition of *material goods* only. Greed makes one blind to the needs of others and the needs of the ecological balances in nature. With some exceptions the first explorers and colonizers were not "seekers of life" nor did they see their role as the simple human one of journeying on the Path of Life: they were seeking wealth of the kind we have just mentioned.

The second great difference between the colonizers and the native Peoples inhabiting this continent was in their concepts of *religious respect* and the freedom to worship as they chose. We read in our history books that some colonizers came to this world to worship the way they chose. However, the actual act of religious freedom and cultural freedom was not practiced by the colonists, partly explainable by their own history of religious oppression in Europe before they migrated to this continent. The first explorers and colonists were, in fact, ignorant of the complex religious systems belonging to the native Peoples.

The *Middle Ages** were a time of great political and religious change in Europe. In the centuries before, Roman invaders had traveled north, east, west, and south, conquering native tribal peoples living in Gaul (France), England, Ireland, and other lands. When they conquered them, they left their Catholic priests with the people to convert them. Conversion to Catholicism spread over all of Europe so that by the Middle Ages entire communities of country people were dom-inated by the Catholic church, its institutions, schools, and political rulers. Wars were fought in faraway lands of the Middle East and young people were forced to join in the "crusades"** to fight for the Catholic church against non-Catholic peoples. During these years, native religions, native curing systems, and folk knowledge passed by oral tradition were discouraged or banned by the Church. When the Protestant denomination broke away from the Catholic Church, they too condemned folk and tribal peoples' religions. Medicine people, people of knowledge within the country villages or in the countryside were often punished or killed for practicing "supersti-tions," "evil," and non-Christian ways. Women mid-wives and curers were called "witches,"† and they too were punished and killed.

Consequently, both church missionaries and colonists, having lived under many years of influence by Church doctrine, came to this continent with preconceived ideas about how one should worship and how one should live. Below are some brief examples of how the Spanish Catholic missionaries in the early 1800's in California viewed the native peoples there.

From the Mission of Santa Cruz, the authorities wrote:

> At this place they ordinarily live on salmon and lampreys, of which there are many in the river which flows at the mission.
>
> Their dances are most *insipid*. They gather in a circle and without moving from the spot bend their bodies. They move their feet and make many contor-tions to the sound of their disagreeable voices, with which they do not form articulate words. (Kroeber, 1908:24)

And from the missionaries among the Luisueño came the report:

> They have an idea of a rational soul, which they call *hamson*, and believe that when they die this goes below to *tolmar*, where all come together and live forever in much happiness. With this they have, however, no idea of reward or punish-ment. (Kroeber, 1908:10)

---

* The middle-ages are considered the years between 476 A.D. to 1453 A.D.

** The Crusades were wars undertaken in the 11th, 12th, and 13th centuries, to try and take the Holy Land, claimed by the Christians, from the Moslems.

† *Witch* comes from the tribal language, Anglo-Saxon. In Anglo-Saxon the word was *wicca* and meant, "wise one."

As we have said, colonists arriving to this world from Europe came indoctrinated with a special vocabulary which prevented them from accepting or even perceiving the rich cultures and complex sacred ways of the native people living here. It is useful therefore, to examine some of the words that made up the vocabularies of these colonists, words that have since dominated the textbooks, history books, and movies on Native Americans.

When the explorers, conquistadores, and other colonists came to this land, they labeled the religions of the native Peoples as *pagan*. They called The People *savages* and said they were *primitive heathens*. All these words are apparently negative or *derogatory* words. In order *to change the Native American people, to make them give up their land*, the missionaries had to make The People feel *pitiful*, at the mercy of evil forces, make The People feel backwards and their powers shameful. These words were used to describe The People so that throughout the years their way of life would lose respect in the eyes of the young people and they would begin to deny all those concepts and ceremonials that were a part of their religious system, philosophies, and paths of life. But if you look at the original definitions of these words, in any dictionary, you will find that they are not negative at all. They really only describe a different way of life, a way of life that apparently frightened the church and threatened its powers in Europe. So over the years, under the domination of the church, these words took on a meaning very different from their original definitions. *Pagan*, for example, comes from the Latin word that means "country dweller," from the word *pagus*, which means "village." In other words, a pagan is someone who lives in a country village. *Savage* comes from the Latin word *sylvanus* which means "woods," "forest," or "untouched by man." Savages then were people who lived in the woods before they were "discovered" by people who told them they were savages. *Heathen* was an Old-English word for a person who lived on the heaths or moors of northern England and Scotland. Heather, a purple-flowered plant, grows on the desolate moors in Scotland where the people were and still are, sheep-herders. From the plant heather, the heath got its name and the sheerherders living there were

called heathens—as someone in New York would be called a New Yorker.

Primitive actually means early, earliest, or simple. Primitive people certainly lived on this continent earlier than the colonists who came and called them primitive. The primitive people knew how to live in the places they chose better than those settlers who came and had to ask to be shown by The People how to survive. The People had tools to serve them and these tools were simple tools, made without metal for the most part. The tools, pots, baskets, and arms were artfully made however, and served their purposes as well as many of the implements the settlers brought later. The People's shelters were perhaps simple from the point of view of modern materials and construction, but as we can see today, they served in their particular environments as well or better than the prefab dwellings and trailers of today. The word "primitive" in this context, then, does not mean "bad" or "worse" or as the word often has come to mean today, ignorant. Primitive, in this case, merely indicates that there were people living on this continent at the time of the colonists' arrival and the People's technology did not include the advances made in tools and arms in Europe.

However, often the technological "advances" that were introduced to this continent, or have been used in place of more primitive implements or designs, have proven to be disastrous to the ecological balances both in human and biological communities. Guns, we know, without proper awareness, killed too many animals too rapidly. The use of fossil fuels has polluted the atmosphere and destroyed the land in many areas of this continent. Improper shelters have caused respiratory diseases. Reliance on sophisticated technology (cars, trucks, snowmobiles) have completely altered primitive economics, forcing people to work for and rely on the dominant economic system. We mention all of these things in order to point out to the student the implications of particular words and so that we can examine more clearly the implications of language on people and society in general. Even though these words originally were not meant to be derogatory, many peoples still choose to use these words in a derogatory manner.

GOVERNMENT POLICY AND EDUCATION

Both the attitudes brought to this continent by the colonizers and the economic needs of capitalism helped to mold government policy with regard to the education of Native American children and youth. Government policy itself was not actually formulated until late in the 1800's, but the general view of education mirrored the attitudes towards Native cultures and ways of life that we have been examining. From the beginning the basic feeling was that the native cultures were inferior and The People should be brought in contact with European cultural values and ultimately live by them. The authors of *To Live on This Earth* write:

Education policy for Indians parallels the troubled history of European conquest and colonization of The New World. When the Europeans first gave a false name to the native peoples of this continent, there were several hundred societies speaking more than two hundred languages. Though they came to be known as "Indians" they differed widely in their economic, social, and religious life. However, they did share similarities in that communities tended to be kinship oriented, united by residence and constant person-to-person interaction, and by common understanding of their uniqueness as separate peoples.

During the colonial period,* the various European nations exerted differing approaches to and influences upon the native Americans.

Western education and formal schooling were introduced to the Indians by Roman Catholic priests who were the earliest missionaries to America. The Jesuits, mainly French, were active in the St. Lawrence River area, Great Lakes region, and the Mississippi between 1611-1700. Their goals were to teach Christianity and French culture, following the order of Louis XIV to "educate the children of the Indians in the French manner." To accomplish this, the Jesuits removed children from their families and

---

* The 1600's and 1700's.

This photo was taken in 1879 or 1880 at Kingsclear, New Brunswick (Canada), on Corpus Christi Day. The canoes are made of birchbark; the men, other than the priest, are dressed in traditional style dress except that the clothes are made of cloth. The woman is in cloth traditional style dress with beadwork typical of the style which reached its peak in the early 1800's. (Photo courtesy of Andrea Bear Nicholas)

tribes. They taught French language and customs and emphasized the traditional academic subjects. Singing, agriculture, carpentry, and handicrafts were also included.

The Franciscans, mainly of Spanish origin, entered the south with Coronado, influencing the peoples of Arizona, New Mexico, Texas, and California. The policy of the Franciscans was to gather the native peoples into villages around missions. Families were kept intact. The schools, while teaching Spanish, did not emphasize the academic subjects, placing greater stress upon agriculture, carpentry, blacksmith work, masonry, spinning and weaving.

The Protestants also established schools, primarily in the East. King James on March 24, 1617, issued a call for the education of the Indians, and clergymen such as John Eliot took up the call. Dartmouth was founded for the education of "youth of Indian tribes... and also of English youth and others." Harvard was established for the education of English and Indian youth, and the campus of William and Mary included a special house for Indian students in 1723.

On the whole, education in the colonial period in all but the Spanish dominated colonies, offered a curriculum to Indian youth that was the same as that offered non-Indian youth with major emphasis upon the area of academic study. Significantly, the school was established as an agent for spreading Christianity and the transmittal of Western culture and civilization. No consistent attempts to incorporate Indian languages, culture, or history were made in the curriculum offered. (Fuchs and Havighurst, 1973:2)

It was not altogether clear, however, that the tribal people at the time were in complete agreement that their youth should go to these schools. There was some criticism of the new type of education on the part of some tribal leaders. When, for example, Benjamin

Franklin offered tribal leaders* the opportunity to send their youth to these colleges, he was given the following reply:

But you, who are wise, must know that different Nations have different conceptions of things; and you will therefore not take it amiss, if our ideas of this kind of education happen not to be the same with yours. We have had some experience of it; several of our young people were formerly brought up at the Colleges of the Northern Provinces; they were instructed in all your Sciences; but, when they came back to us, they were bad runners, ignorant of every means of living in the Woods, unable to bear either Cold or Hunger, knew neither how to build a cabin, take a deer, or kill an enemy, spoke our language imperfectly, were therefore neither fit for hunters, warriors, nor counsellors; they were totally good for nothing. We are, however, not the less obligated by your kind offer, though we decline accepting it; and, to show our grateful sense of it, if the gentlemen of Virginia will send us a dozen of their sons, we will take great care of their education, instruct them in all we know, and make men of them. (Fuchs and Havighurst, 1973:3)

The schools of this period "touched few persons." The reasons given are, 1) hostilities increased as the amounts of territory taken by settlers grew, 2) intertribal hostilities increased as the colonial powers took sides—took different native tribes as allies, and 3) the People resisted giving up their religions and "styles of life."

As soon as the United States Government was established in 1789, these initial attitudes grew into actual policy—educational policy which changed its course at different points along the way but which basically followed one basic concept: *civilize* the native people. This policy grew out of two factors: 1) the territorial demands of westward colonial expansion and the need for raw materials the capitalist economic system demanded; 2) the insensitive attitude toward native sacred teachings and practices by the colonists and missionaries.

When the War Department controlled

---

* The particular tribe is not documented by the authors.

Pupils in front of school buildings, Paiute, Panguitch School, Utah, 1907. (Courtesy of Museum of American Indian, Heye Foundation)

"Indian Policy" their policy usually meant war. Forts were established throughout the westward-moving country. Educational policy followed the trend from extermination of native peoples, or genocide, to a policy of *assimilation*. The authors, Fuchs and Havighurst tell us that gradually the federal government came to the conclusion that:

> Reservation confinement—to make Indians models of small farmers requiring little land—and education for assimilation, were more human and less costly than military control and extermination of those native Americans standing in the way of uncontrolled westward expansion. Extinction by force or extinction by assimilation were the alternatives presented The People whose language and cultures were ignored except as subjects for romance, entertainment, or contempt. (Fuchs, et al., 1973:4 and 224)

We have mentioned some of the economic factors behind the emerging educational policy. The other factors were the attitudes we discussed earlier, based on different cultural and religious values. The authors above summarize the history of missionary involvement in the educational policy of the federal government toward Native Americans in the 1800's and the creation of the boarding school system:

Indian education was influenced by the great religious awakening which took place in the new nation in the early 1800's. Many of the churches were evangelistic and supported widespread missionary activity. This had the effect of encouraging proselyting and education among the Indians as opposed to a policy of extermination. The Bible was the primer, and the hoe and plow the weapons of those who sought to "civilize" the Indians rather than physically eliminate them.

In conjunction with the mood in 1802, Congress approved an appropriation not to exceed $15,000 annually to "promote civilization among the savages."

In 1819, Congress, at the request of President Monroe, passed an act which apportioned funds among those societies and individuals that had been prominent in the effort to "civilize" the Indians. In this way, education was turned over to the missionary societies. The annual appropriation was not repealed until 1973.

The Bureau of Indian Affairs had been established first in 1836 as part of the War Department, but in 1849 it was shifted to the newly established Department of Interior. But not until 1892 were teachers and physicians placed under civil service.

The decimation of Indian peoples, the enforced reservation status as wards of the government, and the frequent breaking of the treaties as westward expansion proceeded characterized relations with the Indian tribes through much of the nineteenth century.

In 1871, Congressional action prohibited further treaties with Indian tribes. Indians were now confined to reservations. They were to be fed, housed, clothed, and protected until such time as Congress considered they were able to care for themselves; and a state of enforced welfare dependency ensued. The government reports in the years following called for humanizing, Christianizing, and educating the Indians.

From the beginning the federal government was uneasy about running schools itself and sought to turn over responsibility to other agencies. Continuing into the late nineteenth century, funds were distributed to various religious denominations to maintain mission schools. But public protest against federal aid to sectarian schools and the unconstitutional nature of the practice led the government to discontinue the practice. As a result, a system of federally operated schools was developed under the jurisdiction of the Bureau of Indian Affairs.

Paying little attention to the many linquistic and other cultural differences among Indian peoples, and ignoring the varied traditions of child rearing in preparation for adulthood in the tribal communities, the government entered the school business in the late nineteenth century with a vigor that caused consternation among the Indians. The package deal that accompanied literacy included continuing efforts to "civilize the natives." Old abandoned army forts were converted into boarding schools, children were removed—sometimes forcibly—long distances from their homes, the use of Indian languages by children was forbidden under threat of corporal punishment, students were boarded out to white families during vacation times, and native religions were suppressed. These practices were rationalized by the notion that the removal from the influence of home and tribe was the most effective means of preparing the Indian child to become an American. (Fuchs, et. al., 1973:4-6)

And those tribes that had developed their own schools were forced to close their schools and could no longer have control over their children's education.

Pupils entering school (Courtesy of Southwest Museum, Los Angeles)

Several of the tribes maintained extensive school systems operated and financed by themselves. Among these were the more than two hundred schools and academies of the Choctaw Nation in Mississippi and Oklahoma which sent numerous graduates to eastern colleges, and which flourished until the 1890's.

The Cherokee Republic also developed an extensive school system, and estimates of literacy for the nineteenth century Cherokee run as high as 90 percent. Cherokee had a higher percentage of better educated persons than the white settler population of Texas or Arkansas. The Cherokee schools taught not only English, but Cherokee as well, using the alphabet invented by Sequoyah. The Creeks, Chickawas, and Seminoles also maintained schools.

But by the late 1890's, these schools were closed by the federal government and the education of Indians came under the control of a paternalistic government. Cherokee education, for example, came under control of a federal superintendent in 1903, and in 1906 when Oklahoma became a state, the whole system was abolished. It was not until the late 1960's that the Indian tribe once again would be in a position to direct the formal education of its children in a school. (Fuchs, et. al., 1973:6-7)

All over the country children were sent to boarding schools where they were not allowed to speak their own language, where they were disciplined in a totally new and strange way. This was not a discipline for survival in the natural environment. It was one that would enable children and succeeding generations, to step more easily into the new mold being created for them by the government and various missionary groups. In terms of the cultural attitudes we have examined, these schools, like the words used to name The People, were designed to *break the spirit* of The People. Listen to how Caroline Nolasquez remembers the time just before they built the first school for Cupeño children in California:

We use to get up in the morning, after that we went to bathe. And then we use to go outside, and we went to our houses and we would eat something. And then we would go to play, we use to jump, we use to play the kuliat bird game. And we played hop scotch, and we played jacks on rocks, and we played dolls. And then they built the school, and we never played anymore. (Hill and Nolasquez, 1973:46a)

Salvadora Valenzuela also remembers those days. She, too, was a Cupeño. She tells us below, that when she was a child she didn't "know how to do anything." Games, she says, were "the only thing I knew." But were these just games? As we suggest in the Chapter, *Learning The Way: Traditional Education*, games were often valuable learning experiences for children. Games were ways they imitated their parents and relatives; in this way they learned the fundamental skills of living. As we point out in that chapter, *morals* and *ethics* were often learned during these years, coming from the direct experience of how to get along in a closely-knit community. In the following transcription we see that Salvadora Valenzuela's games were important to her learning and, for her, they made more sense than the school she eventually had to go to:

When I was a child I didn't know how to do anything. I was just the only child of my mother, and games were the only thing I knew about. And many children and I would go all far away to look for something, for milkweed to squeeze, for yucca flowers to eat, for manzanita berries to eat. The boys were all together with us, but nothing bad ever happened among us, and our mothers never worried about us. In the evening we came home by ourselves. We bathed in the water whenever we wanted, there was hot water at our homes, water naturally hot.* In the morning again we went to the wood, and sometimes we followed the grownup girls when they went with the young men. Sometimes they threw stones at us, but we didn't care, and they would return. We would come back with them, and they would send us away, so

---

* From hot springs.

we heard nothing. And then they would come back, and then they built a school for us, and then we didn't go out every day. On Saturday and Sunday we played, we sang with the rattle, we danced the pina'xwil, and we played whatever we wanted to. And at school some children were good, and some were bad, and the teachers used to whip us a lot. They punished us because of our naughtiness. It must have been good, however, for us to learn, but we didn't care. All we wanted was to play, and because of that I did not learn much. And then I became a young lady. (Hill and Nolasquez, 1973: 46a)

And a Tewa man from San Juan talks about his schooling experience, how it affected his traditional culture and how he thinks educational policy has not changed too much from when he went to school:

We're dying because of acculturation ...no one wants to do all these [ceremonials]. Things are dying because we're becoming acculturated. We go to school and even now, they don't come right out and say "that's paganism," they don't like when I went to school that's what they told me, you know. "You're a pagan and you shouldn't do these things, you should become a Christian and a good white man. You're going to hell." So most of the people my age are the product of all this somewhere because I had a little schooling: I look back and I say, "Hey, its not all that bad...its good to be an Indian, these are good beautiful things."

THE SUPPRESSION OF TRIBAL CUSTOMS AND SACRED TRADITIONS

The Eskimo asked the local missionary priest, "If I did not know about God and sin, would I go to hell?" "No," said the priest, "not if you did not know." "Then why," asked the Eskimo earnestly, "did you tell me?"*

Educational and other assimilation policies on the part of government agencies were designed to change or destroy the sacred teachings and practices of The People. And as it has been noted, missionaries from the different Christian denominations played a major role in carrying out this task. There are many reasons why it was such a simple matter for the missionaries to get government backing in their efforts to enter tribal communities and try and convert the people. One reason is that from the first exploratory voyage to the "New World" by the Spaniards, a voyage that brought back to their government tales of "golden cities," "fountains of youth," and other reports, colonists from Europe felt that they were "destined" to come here and establish themselves.

The explorations began at a time of religious *fanaticism* in Europe. All non-Christians feared for their lives, and political warfare between countries was based as much upon religion as upon economic objectives. But the two went together. The Catholic country of Spain was competing for markets with the Protestant country of England. Both of these countries sent explorers and colonists to this continent and both arrived with strong religious prejudices. So from the beginning, the colonization of North America and the exploitation of its resources were tied to religious doctrine. When groups are competing for land and resources and feel they are doing so in the name of their God, the strategies are often ruthless and ignore the human beings and the natural environment in the midst of that competition.

Below is an example of the kind of argument that many missionaries use to explain their "presence in a land occupied by other men," as Standing Bear put it. The article was written in answer to the question, "Did White Men Have a Manifest Destiny?" As the student will note, the argument has no basis in actual experience on the land, nor does it include many other historical facts that could tell us a completely different story, for example, other people's histories and legends,

---

* From (Dillard, 1974:122).

and records of other influential migrations of people and tribes over the centuries.*

Did God really give this land to Anglo-Saxons "to reward their brave spirits?" To answer this question, we must look into a historical section of the book of the White Man's religion, the Bible. Anciently, the God of the Bible spoke to a powerful and wealthy patriarch named Abraham. This story is recounted in Genesis, beginning in Chapter 12. God promised to give material and spiritual blessings to Abraham and to many generations of his descendants because of Abraham's loyalty and faithfulness. God also promised Abraham that he would be the father of many nations. The covenant relationship between Abraham and God was to have a great effect on the world even in modern times. The covenant did not end with Abraham's death, but was transmitted through his son Isaac and his grandson, Jacob, who was renamed Israel. From Jacob was to come a nation and a "company of nations." (Genesis 35:11)

As time progressed, the newly formed nation, composed of descendants of Jacob's twelve sons, forgot their covenant relationship with God. They repudiated His laws and customs. They took on the ways of the peoples around them. The historical record in the Bible explains how they went through a series of invasions and finally national captivity as punishment for the individual and national sins. Ten of the twelve tribes disappeared from their homeland in the Middle East long before the Roman Empire emerged as the dominating force on the world scene. Millennia later, they emerged again from obscurity to continue receiving the very promises given to Abraham.

Though white Americans today know little of their origins, no one can deny the coincidence that the peoples of the United States and the British Commonwealth have. In fact, inherited the wealth, and power promised in the birthright to Abraham and his descendants. No other nationalities have become the single greatest "nation" and the most expansive "company of nations" respectively, in all of earth's history. These are facts of history. (Akwesasne Notes, Early Winter, 197:28)

The attitudes that prejudiced the missionaries against the Native Peoples led them to call native traditional practices "evil." The following article which recently appeared in a mission newspaper in Mesa, Arizona, is a typical example of the more *fanatic* attitude towards Native religious practices:

Hopi Bible School: Polacca Community Hall was the location, from the song, the joy of the Lord filled every heart. Many decisions were made for Jesus, and hearts were truly blessed.

Pray for Mishongnovi, a Hopi village steeped in Witchcraft. Many people feel the Indian dances are for show and entertainment. However, this year, all visitors have been banned from the snake dance.

If you are ever near one of these dances, you can feel the very presence of evil forces as they actually worship the devil. This is in the United States!

Will you help us pray? A few weeks ago, a grandpa in this village over 100 years old who had given his heart and life to Jesus died. The part of the family that were Christians stopped by the trailer and asked us to come and have a Christian burial. When Virgil Ochoa and I arrived in the village, the non-Christian side of the family and traditionals had banned us from helping. They told us to leave and that they were going to bury him according to traditional ways. We then went to the grave site and were met there by a group of traditional men and were told that we had better get out.

They buried him in a sitting position facing the west in their traditional way. Even though we could not give him a Christian burial, his decision before

---

* Cultures that have records of their migrations include, for example, the Irish, the Hebrews (Jewish People), Hopi, Mayan, to name a few.

death is what counted, not the way he was buried.

These people need Jesus. PRAY! PRAY! PRAY!

There are a few Christians in this village and oh what persecution they suffer. Pray for them. If enough Christian people would ban (sic)* together and pray, we could bind the forces of evil and claim this village for Jesus. We have seen this happen in other Hopi villages. (Akwesasne Notes, Early Winter, 1975: 29)

This extreme form of prejudice sometimes led to brutal actions against Native Peoples. For example, in California where the Catholic Mission system was widespread and particularly severe, a Castanoan man born in the Santa Cruz mission in 1819, named Lorenzo, was interviewed in an early historical record on what life in the mission was like. He said:

The Indians at the mission were very severely treated by the padres, often punished by fifty lashes on the bare back. Any disobedience or infraction of the rules, and then came the lash without mercy, the women same as the men. If any of us entered the Church with a dirty blanket, he was punished with fifty lashes, men and women alike. We were always trembling with fear of the lash. (Harrison, 1892)

And from the San Francisco Mission there is recorded historical testimony from fugitives who ran away from the mission in 1797 and were recaptured, brought back and questioned as to why they ran off. Here are some of the reasons that were given. "He" refers to each fugitive:

1. He had been flogged for leaving without permission.
2. He ran away because he was beaten and also was hungry.
3. He was hungry. When he returned voluntarily he was given twenty-five lashes.

4. He was frightened at seeing how his friends were always flogged. When he wept over the death of his wife and children, he was ordered whipped five times by Father Danti.
5. He was put in the stocks while sick.
6. His wife and son had run away to the country and at the mission he was beaten a good deal.
7. Because of a blow with a club.
8. His mother, two brothers and three nephews all died of hunger, and he ran away so he also would not die.
9. His wife sinned with a rancher and the priest beat him for not taking care of her.
10. They made him work all day without giving him or his family anything to eat. Then, when he went out one day to find food Father Danti had him flogged.
11. After going one day to the presidio to find food, when he returned Father Danti refused him his ration, saying to go to the hills and eat hay.
12. When his son was sick, they would give the boy no food, and he died of hunger.

(Cook, 1943)

In most cases, however, the main point of government policy toward native sacred traditions and practices was to try to prevent them from having an effect on future generations through means supposedly "acceptable" to native peoples. The way this was done was to finally *ban sacred practices*, considering them "offenses" under certain federal regulations; the government supposed this would be acceptable. Banning sacred practices was combined with an attempt to convert The People to Christianity with a policy of sending children to boarding schools, and a policy of forcing The People to give up their land through the Allotment Act intended to make The People farmers. These policies, plus attempts by "Indian Agents" to persuade The People to surrender their sacred practices, were supposed to result in the complete assimilation of native peoples into the dominant society. It was assumed that The People would ultimately comply.

---

* "Sic" indicates that a word was misspelled in the original text. In this case, sic indicates that the word "ban" is misspelled. It should read "band."

Altar boys asleep, St. Mary's Mission, Red Lake, Minnesota, 1956. (Courtesy of Minnesota Historical Society)

In the National Archives in Washington, D.C., the communications between the Bureau of Indian Affairs commissioners and regional agents is documented for the years in which these policies (aimed at native sacred teaching and practices) were enforced and publicized. In the following pages three of these documents are presented as examples of the attitudes we have been discussing, as well as examples of cases in which basic civil rights were denied to Native Americans—the freedom of speech, the freedom of worship, and the freedom to publicly congregate.

The first document, dated April 26, 1921, (Circular No. 1665) was distributed to the Area Superintendents of the Bureau of Indian Affairs and was issued by the Department of the Interior Office of Indian Affairs, Washington, D.C. The document is titled *Indian Dancing*. The text is printed below:

Dear Superintendents:

An examination of the latest reports to Superintendents on the subject of Indian dances reveals encouraging conditions, indicating that they are growing less frequent, are of shorter duration, interfere less with the Indian's farming and domestic affairs, and have fewer barbaric features; that they are also generally more orderly because better supervised than formerly. On a number of reservations, however, the native dance still has enough evil tendencies to furnish a retarding influence and at times a troublesome situation which calls for careful consideration and right-minded efforts.

It is not the policy of the Indian Office to denounce all forms of Indian dancing. It is rather its purpose to be somewhat tolerant of pleasure and relaxation sought in this way or of ritualism and traditional sentiment thus expressed. The dance per se is not condemned. It is recognized as a manifestation of something inherent in human nature, through which elevated minds may happily unite art, refinement, and healthful exercise. It is not inconsistent with civilization. *The dance, however, under most primitive and pagan conditions is apt to be harmful, and when found to be so among the Indians we should control it by educational processes as far as possible, but if necessary, by punitive measures when its degrading tendencies persist.*

*The sun-dance and all similar dances and so called religious ceremonies are considered "Indian Offenses" under existing regulations and corrective penalties are provided.** I regard such restriction as applicable to any dance

---

* The italics are ours.

which involves acts of self torture, immoral relations between the sexes, the sacrificial destruction of clothing or useful articles, the reckless giving away of property, the use of injurious drugs or intoxicants and frequent or prolonged periods of celebration which bring the Indians together from remote points to the neglect of their crops, livestock and home interests; in fact, any disorderly or plainly excessive performance that promotes superstitious cruelty, licentiousness, idleness, danger to health, and shiftless indifference to family welfare. In all such instances the regulations should be enforced, but only through the exercise of thoughtful discretion and mature judgment, after patient advisory methods have been exhausted. Among these methods should be the efforts of the superintendent to reach an understanding and agreement with the Indians to confine their dances and like ceremonials within such bounds as he may with reasonable concession approve; an arrangement for careful supervision at such gatherings, and provisions as far as possible for sanitary dance places with decent surroundings, and something in the way of wholesome, educational entertainment that will tend to divert interest from objectionable native customs. The moral influence of our schools must, of course, go far towards fixing the standards of individual virtue and social purity that should be able to strengthen participation in missionary activities in the attraction of the Indian to a higher conception of home and family life, and to the dignity and satisfaction of his personal labor and attainments. It seems to me quite necessary to Indian progress that there should be no perversion of those industrial and economic essentials which underlie all civilization, and that therefore meetings or convocations for any purpose, including pleasurable and even religious occasions, should be directed with due regard to the everyday work of the Indian which he must learn to do well and not weary in the doing, *if he is to become the right kind of a citizen and equal to the tests that await him.*

These suggestions are offered with a view to drawing the attention and efforts of our service towards a better control of Indian dancing so far as it retains elements of savagery or demoralizing practices. I feel that it is within our power to accomplish more than we are doing for the Indian's social and moral elevation, not by offending his communal longings or robbing his nature of its rhythm, but by encouraging those instincts to serve his higher powers and by directing his desires and purposes towards the things he needs to make him strong and capable and fit to survive in the midst of all races.

I shall hope that Superintendents will give some special thought to this subject with a view to developing a line of action that will in the next few years reduce to the minimal all objectionable conditions attending Indian dances or ceremonial gatherings.

Respectfully,
CHAS. H. BURKE
Commissioner
(American Indian Historian, Vol. 8, No. 3:43-44)

This documented governmental policy covered a wide range of activities which, from what we know about native aboriginal sacred teachings and practices in North America, amounted to supression of an entire way of life. Some of our parents and grandparents can probably remember during these years when they had to travel hundreds of miles to hold secret pow wows, as they did in Minnesota, or when the necessary seasonal rituals in agricultural communities had to be carefully concealed, within kivas or by ingenious methods The People invented to continue their special procedures, prayers, and dances.

In 1873, sweatbaths were forbidden the Native American people. In the San Carlos Mission near Monterrey, California sweatbaths were forbidden the people earlier in the 1800's. It is reported by one perceptive Spaniard in the Mission reports of 1811 what the purposes of the sweatbaths (*temascal*) were for the Costanoan people and what happened when they were denied access to them:

There is a custom among the men of entering daily a subterranean oven which is called temescal. Into this they bring fire. When it is sufficiently heated, they go in undressed. Then they sweat profusely, so that when they come out they look as if they had been bathing. It is known that this is very beneficial to them. For some time the [sweathouses] were forbidden, and many itches, tumors, and other epidemics were found among the men. *On the [sweathouses] being given back to them, hardly a man with the itch could be discovered, and this is a disease common among the women and children, who do not use such sweatbaths.* The women who have recently given birth employ another method of sweating. They make a hole inside of the house, put wood into it, light this, and put many heavy stones upon it. When the stones are hot, they cover them with much green verdure which makes a sort of a mattress. The woman who has given birth lies down on this with the baby. The mother sweats much and the child is kept warm. They do this for six or seven days, and then are as agile as if they had not given birth. (A. Kroeber, 1908:21-22)

The next document, dated February 14, 1923, is titled *Indian Dancing: Supplement to Circular No. 1665* and is also addressed to the Superintendents. The text follows:

At a conference in October 1922 of the missionaries of the several religious denominations represented in the Sioux country, the following recommendations were adopted and have been courteously submitted to this office:

1. That the Indian form of gambling and lottery known as the 'ituranpi' (translated 'give away') be prohibited.
2. That the Indian dances be limited to one each month in the daylight hours of one day in the midweek, and at one center in each district; the months of March and April, June, July and August be excepted.
3. That none take part in the dances or be present who are under 50 years of age.
4. *That a careful propaganda be undertaken to educate public opinion against the dance and to provide a healthy substitute.*
5. *That a determined effort be made by the Government employees in cooperation with the missionaries* to persuade the management of fairs and 'round-ups' in the town adjoining the reservations not to commercialize the Indian by soliciting his attendance in large numbers for show purposes.
6. *That there be close cooperation between the Government employees and the missionaries in those matters which affect the moral welfare of the Indians.* *

These recommendations, I am sure, were the result of sincere thought and discussion, and in view of their helpful spirit, are worthy of our careful consideration. They agree in the main with my attitude outlined in Circular No. 1665 on Indian dancing.

Probably the purpose of paragraph 2 can be better fulfilled by some deviation from its specific terms according as circumstances or conditions vary in different reservations. Likewise, the restrictions in paragraph 3 may reasonably depend upon the character of the dance, its surroundings and supervision. I would not exclude those under 50 if the occasion were properly controlled and unattended by immoral or degrading influence.

The main features of the recommendation may be heartily endorsed, because they seek lawful and decent performances free from excess as to their length, conduct, and interference with self-supporting duties; because they urge cooperation towards something better to take the place of the vicious dance, and because they suggest the need of civilizing public sentiment in those white communities where little interest is taken in the Indians beyond

---

* Italics are ours.

the exhibition for commercial ends of ancient and barbarous customs.

After a conscientious study of the dance situation in his jurisdiction, *the efforts of every superintendent must persistently encourage and emphasize the Indians' attention to these political, useful, thrifty, and orderly activities that are indispensable to his well-being and that underlie the preservation of his race in the midst of complex and highly competitive conditions. The instinct of individual enterprise* and devotion to the prosperity and elevation of family life should in some way be made paramount in every Indian household to the exclusion of idleness, waste of time at frequent gatherings of whatever nature, and the neglect of physical resources upon which depend food, clothing, shelter, and the very beginnings of progress.

Of course, we must give tact, persuasion, and appeal to the Indian's good sense, a chance to win ahead of preemptory orders, because our success must often follow a change of honest conviction and surrender of traditions held sacred, and we should, therefore, especially gain the support of the more enlightened and progressive element among the Indians as a means of showing how the things we would correct or abolish are handicaps to these who practice them. *We must go about this work with some patience and charity and do it in a way that will convince the Indian of our fidelity to his best welfare, and in such a spirit we may welcome cooperation apart from our service, especially from those whose splendid labors and sacrifices are devoted to moral and social uplift everywhere.*

The conditions in different reservations or sections of the Indian country are so unlike in important respects that I hesitate to attempt improvement by an administrative order uniformly applicable, so am, therefore, sending with this an appeal to the Indians of all our jurisdictions to abandon certain general features of their gatherings, as indicated, and to agree with you as to the general rules that shall govern them.

I feel that it will be much better to accomplish something in this way than by more arbitrary methods, if it can be done* and therefore desire you after one year's faithful trial to submit a special report upon the results with your recommendations.

The accompanying letter should be given the widest publicity possible among the Indians, and if necessary additional copies can be supplied for that purpose.

Please acknowledge the receipt hereof.

Sincerely yours,
CHAS. H. BURKE
Commissioner

(American Indian Historian, Vol. 8, No. 3:44-45)

The student will note that the attitudes and objectives behind government policy toward Native American cultures is stated very clearly: to foster a competitive, individualistic economic mentality and a Christian faith, using missionaries as aides in this effort. For example, note in paragraph four the commissioner's reference to the "highly competitive conditions." In this case he means the conditions of the dominant society in which the various tribes were and are colonized. In that paragraph he compares what he thinks are the characteristics of both societies. His description is representative of the attitude in the government at that time towards Native American cultures later discarded during the Collier tenure of the Roosevelt administration.**

In numbers 5 and 6 of the "denominations recommendations" the relationship between the federal government and the missionaries is actually put down on paper. It is important to note, that written into the United States Constitution, is *the concept of the separation of church and state*, which means the non-interference by the church in government affairs. By federal decree then, we can see that

---

* Italics are ours.

See quote from speech of Senator Dawes in Chapter Ten, **Sacred and Secular: Seminole Tradition in the Midst of Change.

native peoples were not protected from interference in government policy by the church. Vine Deloria tells us:

> Christianity has made gigantic inroads into many tribes because of the nearly 60 years, from the 1880's to the 1940's, when the native religions were prohibited by the government. During this time, Christian denominations were given a free hand in gathering converts on the reservations; at one time the churches merely divided up the various reservations among those groups that desired to proselytize tribal members. Such allocations are no longer made and today competition among various missionary societies on reservations is accompanied by peripheral conflict of a religious nature that intrudes into the social, political and economic life of the tribes. (Deloria, 1974: 251)

In aboriginal Native American societies there was no need to make laws outlining the separation between a church and a state. In fact, as we see in many examples throughout this textbook, the concept of such a separation did not exist in aboriginal societies. One reason is because there were no "denominations"—different groups that wanted to dictate the moral guidelines of government policies and other laws. The sacred was not broken down into a once-a-week worship in specific locations owned by specific denominations. Certainly there were often *factions* in tribal societies, often one clan was considered especially powerful or particular families maintained special status through many generations due to the skills and wealth of their offspring. These groups often had greater influence in public meetings than others, but they did not dictate the sacred teachings of the tribe. Not until the tribes were divided into factions by the different denominations, as

Deloria suggests, did tribal in-fighting begin *based on religious preference.* *

The last document is the letter referred to in the previous document (last paragraph) that "should be given the widest publicity possible among the Indians."

To All Indians:

Not long ago I held a meeting of Superintendents, Missionaries and Indians, at which the feeling of those present was strong against Indian dances, as they are usually given, and against so much time as is often spent by the Indians in a display of their old customs at public gatherings held by the whites. From the view of this meeting and from other information I feel that something must be done to stop the neglect of stock, crops, gardens, and home interests caused by these dances or by celebrations, pow wows, and gatherings of any kind that take the time of the Indians for many days.

Now what I want you to think about very seriously is that you must first of all try to make your own living which you cannot do unless you work faithfully and take care of what comes from your labor, and go to dances or other meetings only when your home work will not suffer by it. I do not want to deprive you of decent amusements or occasional feast days, but you should not do evil or foolish things or take so much time for these occasions. No good comes from your "give away" custom at dances and it should be stopped. It is not right to torture your bodies or to handle poisonous snakes in your ceremonies. All such extreme things are wrong and should be put aside and forgotten. You do yourselves and your families great injustice when at dances you give away money or other property, perhaps clothing, a cow, a horse or a team and wagon, and then after an absence of several days go home to find everything going to waste and yourselves with less to work with than you had before.

I could issue an order against these useless and harmful performances, but I would much rather have you give them up

---

* Examples of this might be seen among the Florida Seminole and Creek where leaders in the newly formed tribal governments are Christians and the traditionalists do not acknowledge the tribal organization; or among the Navajo when, in the 1974 Tribal Chairman election, members of the Native American Church tended to favor one candidate who was sympathetic to the Peyote group.

of your own free will and, therefore, I ask you now in this letter to do so. I urge you to come to an understanding and an agreement with your Superintendent to hold no gatherings in the months when the seed-time cultivation of crops and the harvest need your attention, and at other times to meet for only a short period and to have no drugs, intoxicants, or gambling, and no dancing that the Superintendent does not approve.

If at the end of one year the reports which I receive show that you are doing as requested, I shall be very glad for I will know that you are making progress in other and more important ways, but if the reports show that you reject this plea, then some other course will have to be taken.

With best wishes for your happiness and success, I am

Sincerely yours,
(s) CHAS. H. BURKE
Commissioner

(American Indian Historian, Vol. 8, No. 3:45-46)

The "give-aways" certainly were a threat to the economic objectives of capitalism which the federal government was trying at this time to foster and protect. For in give-aways were symbolized one of the values basic to most Native American communities in aboriginal times: sharing and community responsibility towards its individual and kin members. Give-aways were one method of distributing wealth among members of the community. They were also a way of acknowledging that the tribe was composed of related members, like a family, all of whom were dependent on each other. Give-aways demonstrated a person or family's wealth—they were wealthy because they could afford to give away—they did not worry about the loss of their possessions they gave away because they knew they too would some day be the recipients of others' gifts and besides, a person was respected for his or her ability to give gifts of food and other material goods. Give-aways were and are mostly a phenomena of the "plains" tribes, but other communities, the Pueblo communities for instance, have many occasions in which food and other goods are distributed in some way to chosen people, families, friends, or the community in general.

A further commentary on all three of the documents comes from the *American Indian Historian*, which notes:

Aside from the presumptuous, paternalistic, and dictatorial contents of these

Doctor from the National Department of Health, barbering Rita, a Caribou Eskimo, 1947. (Courtesy of the Smithsonian Institution, National Anthropological Archives)

documents, is the fact that they cannot be understood merely as a denial of Indian rights, rights to which all human beings are entitled. Conditions of those times will reveal that the Native Americans had little or no livestock, that those who did always made arrangements to have their stock cared for during their absence, that farming implements were not available and indeed most of the land was not suited to farming; hence there was widespread "idleness" due to indescribable poverty. (American Indian Historian, Vol. 8, No. 3:46)

RESPONSES TO GOVERNMENT POLICY BY NATIVE AMERICANS

Tribal communities and individuals responded in different ways to these policies. Some of the effects of these policies were, of course, pan-tribal. Children sent away to boarding schools, ceremonials banned; these things strained the very heart of all native communities and demoralized The People. In other chapters of this textbook we examine more specific examples of ways in which The People came to terms with the changes brought about by government policies. In the Chapter, *The World Out of Balance* we briefly discuss some of the *millenium* movements that spread through communities in northern California and in Chapter Eleven, *Sacred and Secular: Seminole Tradition in the Midst of Change*, we will see how Christianity, in this case, was brought to the Florida communities by native peoples, not by non-native missionaries and has perhaps served to help people make the transition from their undisturbed traditional environment to a life today of encroaching urban developments and technological change.

Basically, The People had to make some compromises in order to exist the way they wanted to or in order to fit into the growing domination of the colonial society. Sometimes these compromises were destructive and other times individuals and communities managed to retain much of their traditional core values. In Chapter Fourteen, *The Wandering Ground*, we will examine the contradictions and problems native people in North America face today with respect to their spiritual lives and

day-to-day survival. Below is a transcription of a speech made by the government-appointed constable, Domingo Moro at a fiesta among the Cupeño people of southern California, January 5, 1920. It is interesting to note Domingo's attitude towards the new law prohibiting dances and ceremonials. He, like many others of his time, believed in the good "intentions" of the government and other colonists. He believed that it was possible for his people to change from a hunting and gathering people (small game, roots, berries, and acorns) to a farming people. He believed that the dominant society's education would serve his people. And yet, there is a hint that he recognized the value of the disappearing values in the traditional life of his community still carried on by the "old people," as he refers to them. He is not sure what the "future" is going to bring—at this stage it is but promises and money. The old people on the other hand, he says at the end of his speech: "They know what they have."

Women and men, hear me a little. These words are passing to you at the request of the Agent. This is the last night that this fiesta is permitted to us. And tomorrow it ends in the morning. And you have to go to work, to look around. I am not the only one who says, women and men, that we have wanted to have a good day, to pass the time just as the first people passed the time. This is the way they used to do. Today, when we dance this dance our bodies are all covered. We do not dare to have half our fingernails sticking out. The ancestors used to do it, they were not like us. They covered their bodies with some tiny thing. And this is how we danced today. They asked just that they should make some crops. This occasion we take part in today, we take part in it as if we were in church, because at the time there were no priests to say mass. And today we merely imitate what they used to do. And now the customs that they used to have are going. A few of the old people still remain here and there. And when they are gone, then no one will remember how it used to be. It will be finished, because you young people like me, my friends, you know that a government school is established where they can teach us to know how to take care of ourselves. And the government is doing a lot, it is spending a lot of money for us with which we can learn, because if there were no school, you would not know how to take care of yourselves. These old people, I do not speak to you. There is much need, however, that you young adults not look behind you, but look ahead, as the ancestors used to do, just as long ago the old people would store something away which they had found just as today we do from now on. You young adults, let us take care of your money, because you will always be young. And that is why you should take care of your money. When you grow old or lie sick, with it you take care of yourself. And for that reason look after your homes, cultivate your land, your gardens, clean them, plough them, because even a little is worth something when you have made it, or when you work it. But you, women, do not go visiting around from house to house, you should look after your work. You should not be dependent on a man. There is much work to do to help your husband. And do not lose a single day, because a lost day is not worth anything. It is not like long ago, when the first people used to take care of themselves. They had nothing to work for, when they rose in the morning they thought only to go hunting. Then that was all the work they had. Anyway you are all educated, and you want to see yourselves living according to the old ways. Now we all imitate the ways of the white men. And we must keep on looking ahead, because the government says that these ways, the customs of the whites, we are to imitate. They spend much money on us to give us the white man's language and his customs. We should give thanks, we young adults, because upon us there is much money spent, so that we learn the customs, the customs of the white men. I say nothing more to these old ones, because they have passed on too far. And anyway, more than enough, they know what they have.

That is all. (Hill and Nolasquez, 1973: 27a-28a)

The People resisted attempts to change their ways of life and their ways of sacred worship. Politically, tribal communities had a more difficult time resisting than they did silently, inwardly, and with their spirit and prayers. Throughout the ordeals of two centuries, some people remained certain of the strength in their traditional sacred values. A Hopi man of knowledge some years ago was recorded in a conversation with a missionary, by an ethnographer. The missionary was trying to convert the Hopi man and was telling him how foolish the Hopi sacred beliefs were, when the Hopi man answered:

We may be foolish in the eyes of the white men, for we are a very simple people. We live close to our great mother, the Earth. We believe in our God as you believe in your God, but we believe that our God is best for us. Our God talks to us and tells us what to do. Our God gives us the rain cloud and the sunshine, the corn and all things to sustain life, and our God gave us all these things before we ever heard of your God. If your God is so great, let him speak to me as my God speaks to me, in my heart and not from a white man's mouth. Your God is a cruel God and not all-powerful, for you always talk about a devil and a hell where people go after they die. Our God is all-powerful and all-good, and there is no devil and there is no hell in our Underworld where we go after we die. No, I would rather stick to my God and my religion than to change to yours, for there is more happiness in my religion than there is in yours. (Monsen, 1907, 270-271)

Harold Goodsky, an Anishnabe man from Minnesota, tells us that his grandmother was the one who counseled him to resist the policies of acculturation. He says, "One thing that scared me is when I was young my grandmother told me never to speak English, never to go to church. Because, she said, "if you do, you'll become half animal, half snake, and half man, and you'll be swimming in water all your life."

And Joe Littlecoyote of the Northern Cheyenne people has written:

...there are many aspects to the religious ways of the American Indian. First of all, the religious ways of the American Indian have not been institutionalized. The Cheyenne's approach to religion is purely a spiritual approach (i.e., a way of life). For religion to be institutionalized means that it is *dogma* oriented, at which time the religion either becomes stagnant or defunct.

In recent times past, our people were prohibited by the United States Government from practicing their religious ways; also, the many different Christian denominations condemned and persecuted our people for their traditional beliefs in their Creator and their way or worshipping Him.

Many of these lamentable facts could be cited to illustrate the pressure under which the practice of our traditional religious ways had to exist. This oppressive outside condemnation of our ways of worship forced our traditional people to go underground in the practice of their traditional beliefs. Only in recent times has a tolerant atmosphere allowed our traditional people to practice their beliefs in a more open and public manner. These ways or worship are still not freely practiced in that even now they are merely tolerated which means that we practice our religion with fear. (*Wassaja*, October, 1973)

As we pointed out in the preface of this book, aboriginal sacred ways, too, have passed through changes over the centuries as tribal people have met one another and exchanged ideas, songs, dances, stories, and medicine. But very rarely if at all, did one tribe ever go to war against another in order to change its sacred oral tradition, the way the people worshipped, or their children's education. Red Jacket, a Seneca leader summed up this basic difference between the colonists' attitudes and the philosophy of religious freedom among native peoples, when he told a Boston missionary:

...You have now become a great people, and we have scarcely a place left to spread our blankets. You have got our country but are not satisfied; you want to force your religion upon us. Brother; we do not wish to destroy your religion, or take it away from you. We only want to enjoy our own.

Suggested Additional Readings

BROWN, DEE
1971   *Bury My Heart At Wounded Knee,* New York, Holt, Rinehart and Winston.

CAHN, EDGAR S.
1969   *Our Brother's Keeper: The Indian in White America,* New York, World Publishers.

GORDON, SUZANNE
1973   *Black Mesa: The Angel of Death,* New York, The John Day Co., (About the coal stripmining of Black Mesa, Arizona)

HOLDEN, MADONNA
1976   "Making All Crooked Ways Straight: The Satirical Portrait of Whites in Coast Salish Folklore," *Journal of American Folklore,* Vol. 89, July-Sept., no. 353.

HOWARD, JAMES H.
1976   "Yanktonai Ethnohistory and the John K. Bear Winter Count," *Plains Anthropologist,* Memoir II, Vol. 21, No. 73, part 2. (Includes a large appendix of published and unpublished Winter Counts.)

JACOBS, PAUL AND SAUL LANDAU, WITH EVE PELL
1971   *To Serve The Devil: A Documentary Analysis of America's Racial History and Why It Has Been Kept Hidden,* Vol. I, New York, Random House.

KAROL, JOSEPH S., S.J.A.B.M.A. (eds.)
        Red Horse Owner's Winter Count (The Oglala Sioux, 1786-1968), Martin, South Dakota, The Booster Publishing Co.

LEACOCK, ELEANOR & N.O. LURIE, (eds.)
1971   *The North American Indian in Historical Perspective,* New York, Random House.

MCNICKLE, D'ARCY
1975   *They Came Here First,* rev. ed. New York, Octagon Books.

MEYER, WILLIAM
1971   *Native Americans: The New Resistance,* New York, International Publishers.

OSWALT, WENDELL H.
1973   *This Land Was Theirs,* 2nd Ed., New York, John Wiley and Sons.

SANDOZ, MARI
1964   *The Beaver Men: Spearheads of Empire,* Hastings House.

VAN EVERY, DALE
1966   *Disinherited: The Lost Birthright of the American Indian,* New York, Morrow.

WASHBURN, WILCOMB
1971   *Red Man's Land—White Man's Law,* New York, Scribner, 1971.

————————, (ed.)
1964   *The Indian and The White Man* (Documents in American Civilization Series), New York, Anchor Books.

WORCHESTER, DONALD E.
1975   *Forked Tongues and Broken Treaties,* Caldwell, Idaho, The Caxton Printers Ltd.

CHAPTER SEVEN

7 The World Out of Balance

Friends, what is hard in life comes in fours, you say. Also, there are many last times.*

In this chapter we are going to examine the reactions of some northern California tribes to government policies, and historical events of the late 1800's and early 1900's. There were many different kinds of reactions among the tribal groups of northern California. The reactions on the whole, however, were sudden and dramatic. They led to a forming and reforming of new religious *movements*** and altered religious *cosmologies*. Some of the movements were brought to communities by powerful, vocal, and dramatic leaders.

In the late 1800's, a number of cults† and movements, starting with the Ghost Dance, created a large following in various tribal communities. Some of the movements were the result of what we might call a "millenium crisis." Millenium is defined as a "hoped for period of joy, serenity, prosperity, and justice." It was a word that originally described the millenium cults of the early Christians in Europe who conceived of it as "the one thousand years during which Christ was supposed to rule on earth."‡ *Millenium movements generally spring up when social, political, and environmental changes happen suddenly and people are left without the means to affect what is going on about them.* Their most basic structures of belief and their concepts of the universe (or cosmologies) are shaken and thrown out of balance. *Something must then be constructed quickly to put the world back in balance—a religion or spiritual element that will fit the new context* and the unfamiliar events. During this crisis period of the late 1800's, some people were led to convert to Christianity. Most of the new

religious cults borrowed symbols and images from the Pentecostal Church and incorporated them into their traditional, aboriginal religions. In Chapter Ten, *The Peyote Spirit*, we can see some instances of this same thing happening.

Before we introduce the historical events, the religious movements, and the people involved, we will review a concept of how a world could become unbalanced.

In the first chapter of this textbook we defined *religion* and world-view. The student might review that chapter and those definitions.

In a balanced tribal culture world-view and sacred practices go hand in hand. The world is made conceptually or intellectually *and* emotionally in a well-ordered system of symbols, ceremonials, education, and daily chores. Alfonso Ortiz suggests what happens when religion or, in this case, sacred traditions

---

* The quotation is a Lakota "At Home Song" or *Sunka Olowan, Tiyata Olowan*. These songs, "are very old and have not been heard since ca. 1930. A man would sing these in the morning or evening when he was away from home." (Theisz, ms.)

**A movement may be defined as the activities of a group of people to achieve a specific goal; or a tendency or trend which includes a number of people. (Adapted from the American Heritage Dictionary).

† A cult may be defined as (a) obsessive devotion for a principle or ideal, or (b) an exclusive group of persons sharing an esoteric, special or secret interest. (Adapted from the American Heritage Dictionary)

‡ The American Heritage Dictionary.

are taken away and the people's world-view can no longer *express* the people's emotional feelings and symbols:

> When there is no longer this fit (between world-view and religion, between reality as it is defined and as it is lived) we have reactions ranging from millenial dreams to violent revolution, all designed to reestablish a reasonable integrated life.
>
> (Ortiz, 1972: 136)

Ortiz mentions above some of the forms "unbalancing" can take. Among the various "cults" that appeared in northern California we find such examples as visions of the end of the world, the coming of a time of peace and prosperity, the death of the enemy, and the gift of super-human powers.

In these cases "balancing" meant that the people involved in the cults had to test their aboriginal beliefs in the new context of a foreign society's ideals and prejudices. In addition, the new cults were often introduced to people in strange or unfamiliar environmental contexts, for example, in the migrant worker camps of the northern California hop fields, or within the new reservation lands. Not only were non-native concepts introduced to The People, but different tribes were suddenly in much closer contact than they had been aboriginally, exchanging ideas and observing each others' ways from within common boundaries.

One other point should be emphasized here, because it is a question that will come up again. That is—it is impossible to really know exactly what the factors are which make a person suddenly convert to a different system of beliefs or new ways of behaving. As we proceed in this chapter, we will look at the most obvious historical events of those years and give general examples or descriptions of people's responses to these events. We must remember that, as in every society, there were those who did not participate, there were those that resisted change, and there were those that just could not see anything of value in a movement that seemed to be converting everybody else.

On the other hand, there were those who felt that without the new movement everything would be destroyed, their lives would

disappear. That is exactly what appeared to be happening in those years. Foreign settlers began settling native lands by the hundreds: their preachers were bringing "the word of god" in dramatic, song and shaking tent meetings. And, at the same time, there were destructive earthquakes, floods, and later the Great Fire of San Francisco. The student should perhaps try to remember once in his/her life when one small rumor caused two or three days of unsettling confusion in a school or community he/she lived in. Multiply this by ten or twenty rumors concerning the very survival of yourself and your family, and you may have a better idea of what it was like to live in northern California during the years of the new religious movements. In the light of this discussion we will now examine some instances of the unbalancing of world-view and sacred ways in Native American communities of the 19th Century.

BACKGROUND OF THE RELIGIOUS MOVEMENTS

The tribes that were effected by the Ghost Dance, Earth Lodge, and Bole Maru movements lived in four geographical areas in Northern California. Sometimes tribes of the same language group lived in different ecological areas. (See Map.) The Wintu, for example, lived both near the Pacific coast and inland as far as the mountains of the Sierras. Separate groups of the same tribe had language and oral histories in common even though they might live far apart. The Miwok, like the Wintu were a tribe that had groups living in more than one geographical region.

The Karok and the Yurok were coastal tribes and lived for the most part, on foods the Pacific ocean and coastal rivers privided. All the tribes mentioned in this chapter gathered the basic foods in their diets from the rivers, swamps, and forests that were abundant in Northern California. These foods included such things as berries, roots, small animals, and acorns which were a staple in the diet. Traditional houses were made pit-style beneath the ground; out of wood; or out of reeds.

Among the tribes there were great differences in world view and patterns of sacred life. These differences were reflected in the ways in which The People accepted or

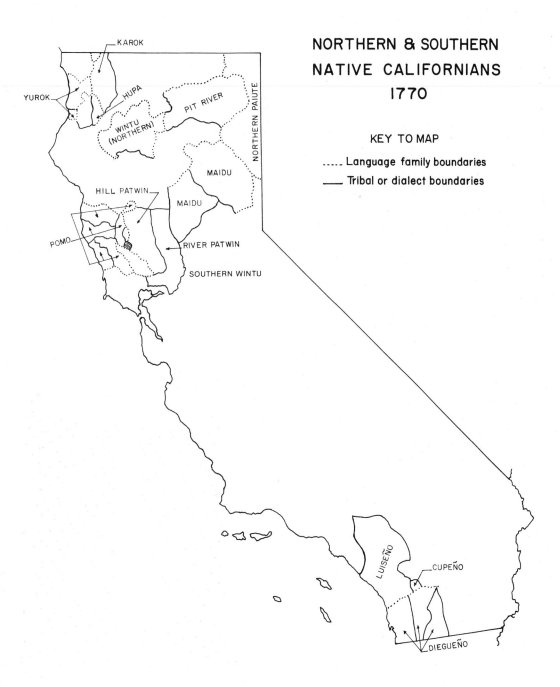

NORTHERN & SOUTHERN
NATIVE CALIFORNIANS
1770

KEY TO MAP

..... Language family boundaries
——— Tribal or dialect boundaries

KAROK

YUROK

HUPA

WINTU
(NORTHERN)

PIT RIVER

NORTHERN PAIUTE

MAIDU

HILL PATWIN

MAIDU

POMO

RIVER PATWIN

SOUTHERN WINTU

LUISEÑO

CUPEÑO

DIEGUEÑO

CRESCENT
CITY

KLAMATH RIVER

BIG BEND R

ROARING CREEK R

HOOPA
VALLEY IR

SULPHUR BANK R

ROUND
VALLEY IR

STEWARTS
POINT R

**Present location of some of the California
tribes mentioned in this Chapter.**

Pomo man Clear Lake, California, in tule reed boat, 1908. (Courtesy of Museum of American Indian, Heye Foundation)

rejected the religious cults that swept through Northern California from the west and south.

In 1849, in North Central California, gold was discovered. From that year on, massive groups of settlers traveled across the continent or came around South America on ships, to colonize California. Even before this Spaniards had set up a mission system that covered an area from the very southern regions of California to San Francisco. In the late 1800's there was an addition of settlers into the river valleys of the north—the Trinity River System in particular.

Logging operations and other exploitation of resources brought the settlers and soon there was mounting pressure on the tribes that occupied that territory, for the rivers and the forests were basic to their survival. The settlers, in turn, called upon the United States Government to consolidate their new land holdings and other claims. At one point, Federal Laws were passed prohibiting the native people from chopping down trees or using forest materials, forcing the people to buy lumber to build their lodges.

The Government soon began removing various tribal communities from their territories to lands set aside as reservations (see map on contemporary tribal lands). In many cases, the people went without a struggle though sometimes there were skirmishes against the government authorities. Since many different tribal groups were thrown together during these moves to reservation lands there were difficulties within and among the tribes as well.

At the same time, different and foreign cultures were meeting each other, communities were being uprooted, and natural resources were becoming scarce. Protestant (Pentecostal) missionaries entered the new settlements and traditional communities preaching a new gospel of christianity.* In 1873, the Federal Government banned sweatlodges, one of the many policies aimed at supressing traditional sacred activities. From 1871 to the 1920's, these changes and events, along with the accompanying responses among the native people, created a great deal of turmoil in and among the various tribal communities. To attempt to understand the foreign cultures' ways and to deal with new customs individuals spontaneously created ceremonial procedures by which the people could come together and re-balance their lives.

---

* Pentecost is a festival of the Christian Church occuring on the seventh Sunday after Easter to celebrate the descent of the Holy Ghost upon the disciples. (The ghost of Jesus was said to have returned to visit his disciples in order to give them a message and teaching.) *Pentecostal* designates any of various Christian religious denominations or congregations that seek to be filled with the Holy Ghost, imitating the disciples on that first Pentecost. (American Heritage Dictionary)

As we discuss in Chapter Two, *Ritual, Drama and Prayer*, ceremonial procedures are necessary elements in tribal societies where religion and life are one and the same. Ceremonials "mobilize a community" (Ortiz). They bring people together in one spirit to dedicate themselves to one common task—whether it be to Renew the Power of the Sacred Arrows; Bring Rain to the Growing Crops; to Honor an Army Veteran Returning from Combat; to Celebrate a Young Woman's Womanhood; or to mark the Change of Seasons. The individual at these times has special responsibilities: the one who pledges himself in the Sun Dance, the Midewin initiate, the young people who are "scratched" in the Green Corn Dance. An individual who is dancing, for instance, knows that his/her perfect steps make the entire dance a perfect one—and consequently make it successful and the community strong.

A summary of the religious movements and the tribal responses follows.

Ghost Dance is a general term that has been used to cover a series of related religious movements that developed between 1869 and 1872. The original doctrine of the cult said that the dead would return, and that the end of the world was near. With the end of the world, White People would be eliminated. The cult originated among the Paviotso of Pyramid Lake and various groups of the Modoc, Klamath, Shasta, and Karok tribes. Another strand of the cult spread to the Wintun and Hill Patwin. Among these two tribes another cult developed which is known as the *Earth Lodge Cult*. The Ghost Dance had stressed the return of the dead and the Earth Lodge Cult (which got its name because the people built special ceremonial lodges underground) stressed the end of the world. The people in this religious movement were to be protected from the catastrophe by these underground lodges.*

Soon after the Earth Lodge cult was introduced to the Wintun, Hill Patwin and the Pomo, a third religious movement began. This

Buckskin Ghost Dance leggings, Arapahoe. (Courtesy of Museum of the American Indian, Heye Foundation)

was called the *Bole Maru*, the Patwin and Pomo words for "dreaming" ("dreamers" or prophets introduced ceremonial procedures and the religious doctrines). The Bole Maru stressed the ideas of an "afterlife" and of a supreme being, like the Christian "God." Each tribal group had its own cult leaders or "dreamers" and therefore the ceremonial procedures varied slightly from community to community.

These lcoal dreamers, prophets, and interpreters were the local authorities behind the new religious "movements," though the cults themselves originally came from outside the community. California tribes were concentrated in local communities who took their authority from specialists in the sacred traditions and practices, legends, and customs specific to the community. Therefore, when religious cults came from the outside they soon found their way, if they were accepted, into the local legends and into the hands of specialists and authorities on the sacred practices. For instance, we are told that in most tribes for short periods during the Ghost Dance and Earth Lodge cults, dreaming

---

* At the (beginning) prophets of the Ghost Dance emphasized the giving up of white man's culture completely, so that the earliest dance houses were built in an entirely aboriginal way without nails or other material derived from whites. (Barrett, in Meigham & Riddell, 1972)

was "epidemic"—many individuals were "dreaming" devising new procedures for the dances and new rules of behavior in daily life. Eventually this slowed down and dreaming concentrated in the hands of a few particular dreamers or "preachers" as they were sometimes called in the early days of Christian influence in tribal communities.

The influence of these leaders depended, of course, upon the local community, but basically the leaders were important in two areas: they paved the way for further *acculturation* and Christianization, and they reshaped the aboriginal practices of doctoring and *shamanism*.

At the onset of the religious cults, the leaders emerged in communities in the form of "prophets" bringing with them the new concepts of the Ghost Dance and Earth Lodge cults. They played a major role in introducing The People to the many marginal Christian *sects* of Pentecostalism (Four Square Gospel, Shaker, Assembly of God, Holy Rollers) and incorporating Christian ideas into aboriginal oral traditions and sacred practices.

Under the leadership of more conservative individuals, prophets provided The People with procedures and concepts that helped make the transition from old ways to new ways—the ways of closer identification with the dominant society, *without sacrificing their entire aboriginal system of beliefs and ceremonials*.

As we examine these religious movements and The People's responses to them, we will look closely at the following factors which may have influenced the creation of the new cults:

1. Historical factors such as government policies, economics, and environmental changes;
2. The role of Christian (Pentecostal) doctrine on the new movements;
3. The reasons behind traditional resistance to the movements;
4. The role of aboriginal concepts and procedures in the new religious movements.

The tribal people of northern California had been fairly isolated from the rapid growth of the colonies in the eastern United States. Suddenly, in the 1850's, California became the new frontier for colonizing settlers. Throughout the country railroads were being built, mining and lumber were becoming big business, and religious evangelism brought by government-sponsored missionaries was spreading its influence to Native communities across the continent. Tribal people in northern California began to seek money-making work in the dominant society's economic system.

Pomo woman making basket, with man and boy in front of house, Ukiah, California. H. W. Hensaw. (Courtesy of the Smithsonian Institution, National Anthropological Archives)

These individuals began to bring back reports of what was happening "out there."

The People's history up until this point had been carried down from generation to generation through the oral traditions of story-telling, specialized teaching, and ceremonial orations. The People, through certain specialists, also had their prophecies about the future. In the 1870's, these prophecies began coming true. Rumors about the settlers; stories about what was happening in the rest of the United States; together with aboriginal prophecies noted in the oral traditions, led to rumors which circulated among The People. The new doctrines spread by prophets and "dreamers" and the cults which sprang up during these years, reflected the rumors and stories which passed from community to community. One aspect of the Ghost Dance doctrine was that the dead would come back to life. Jennie Clifton, a Modoc, gave an account of the opposition which grew up toward the new doctrine among traditional doctors or shamans:

All the doctors said this was the wrong way to worship. They said it was bad for the dead to come back. They told the people that there was no such thing. One man who was part Modoc and part Klamath came and told them it wasn't true. His name was John Smilie (*Psim-dadamnui*, i.e., night traveler). He was not a doctor but he went all around the reservation talking to the Indians. He had traveled all around the United States four or five times in a boat. He said this country was a big island and there was another one far to the south. He said the dead were not coming back. He interpreted the message as meaning that the whites were coming from the east. He told all about the whites, their churches and houses; how they were coming like beavers mowing down the timber, like badgers and moles in turning up the earth for their mining, like grasshoppers in cutting down the grass. He said the whites were all around us and we were a little island of Indians, but the whites would come and we should see the truth of what he said. It was the whites and not the dead who were coming from the east.

He didn't know how to describe the whites. He said they had eyes like panthers, necks like cranes, and were white like pelicans. He traveled to all the Modoc and Klamath and helped to put an end to that idea (i.e., return of the dead). (du Bois, 1939: 11-12)

Another man, a Pomo, said that all "dreamers" believed that the end of the world was close at hand. He, himself, believed this also because he said:

All the old-time prophecies about the whites coming to this country and about guns, have come true, so the end of the world is probably true too. All the dreamers preach that if you don't believe you will turn into an animal or a bird. When I was a young man I didn't believe. Then a maru man, called Oregon Charlie, came to Round Valley to preach. They didn't dare give dances but they preached in secret. He didn't know me but he could see right away that I didn't believe. That night he preached. When he was through, everyone raised his hand to show that he believed. He told everyone to shut his eyes. Then he made the whole house shake. After that I believed. Our dreamers never did things like that. (Note: The Pomo dreamers did not perform miracles to convince converts as did the Wintun and Paviotso.) (du Bois, 1939: 90)

Rumors and interpretations about the behavior of the new settlers, combined with actual physical events helped lead to the creation of the Earth Lodge cult. A northern Pomo man remembers:

They said the world was to end. Our grandfathers and grandmothers who were already dead were glad when they heard this. The world ending must mean that the people are dying away and that the world ends with the people. Maybe the world will get angry. The Big Man made the world and takes care of it. He doesn't want the world abused. He puts people there for his own purpose. The whites upset everything. They put tunnels through the earth. Maybe the Big Man was angry at this.

The world was to end and all were to build an earth house to die in. When they died they didn't want to lie around on the earth, I guess, so they built a house to lie dead in. They didn't say exactly how the world was to end. They say that all which is in the world are people—brush, wind, rocks, trees, valleys. They all had a meeting, like a trial in a court house. They wanted the world to end in fire, but then they thought that looked bad. Then they said water might be pretty good, it would wash bodies away down toward the south. Maybe they thought the ground would get soft and the bodies would sink down in. The wind was to blow over the people and blow them off.

We were told not to fight or rob, to keep our hearts free. We must all have a good time. Everyone was to believe this word. Charlie [the Maru "dreamer"] said, "I am not talking for myself but for you people. We all have to die when this world ends. We can't stop it. We can't escape it." Everyone stopped working and started to build a house. The whites were angry because the Indians stopped working so they sent them to Round Valley before the dance house was finished. They were building special houses at Upper Lake, Sulphur Bank, in the Sacramento Valley, everywhere. When we went up to Round Valley, the Yuki had already heard the word. Someone from the Sacramento Valley had brought the message to them.

The new houses were different. They were deeper and bigger. They were called *le* (death) *tca* (houses). When they built the one at Potter Valley no one but the captain was allowed to talk; no one could eat or drink unless all stopped and ate together. That was usually only at the beginning of the day. Maybe that is what happened up there among the dead. (du Bois, 1939: 90)

Another example of traditional or aboriginal concepts and history mixing together with the confusing events of the late 1800's and early 1900's is seen in the Wintun *Hesi* ceremonies performed during these years. The Hesi ceremony was traditionally a ceremonial given around harvest time in the fall. During the ceremonial, the director or main leader, delivered a series of speeches. These speeches, given in a special style and with special emphasis had several objectives. The leader would recount the history of the world and would outline the reasons for its present condition; he would also tell of its future and the ultimate destiny of mankind. The speeches were a summary for the people of the community, of their cosmology and beliefs. Consequently, the speeches began to reflect the events of the late 1800's and early 1900's. These events were difficult to explain and often happened very suddenly with great implications for the Wintu people and their sense of history, their sense of cosmology. Summarized below are some of the ideas expressed in the Hesi speeches of the 1900's:

The world originally had a different form, but in those days there were comparatively few people. Later, as its population increased, the earth was stretched to accommodate the people and for a time all things went satisfactorily. Again the population grew, the world became crowded, and the earth was stretched; thus, it has up to the present time been enlarged four times. The last time its form was materially changed and the present mountains were created. There is to be a fifth and final upheaval and stretching, which will bring these mountains down and make the world a level plain as is the Wintu home of the dead. To be sure, the Wintun population has since the coming of the whites, greatly decreased, but the influx of Americans has greatly increased the population of the region, so that the country is very crowded at present, and it is expected that this final great world change may come at any time. When the earthquake of April 18, 1906, was felt, it was considered part of this final upheaval, and especially was the belief confirmed when the Wintun saw the effect on upper Cache Creek, which drains Clear Lake. Here a body of earth, large enough to block the passage of the stream, slid into the canyon, backing the water up into the lake itself. After a time the pressure broke through the dam and

179

carried the debris down in a great flood through Capay and the other valleys along the lower course of Cache Creek.

Another feature which had recently inspired astonishment and fear among the Wintun people of the region was the immense mass of smoke which was visible to them from the San Francisco fire. Some said that at night even the glare of the fire could be seen. By many it was feared that this was the final great world fire, which, in common with the other Indians of this part of California, they anticipated. (Barrett, 1919: 463)

THE GHOST DANCE MOVEMENT: A COMPARISON OF TRIBAL RESPONSES

He said it was crowded up above and God was going to turn them loose. The dead might come back any day. When they come back the people would be so thick that you had to have everything you valued with you or it would be lost. For that reason men who left the sweat house to bathe carried their beads with them and women wore their good shell dresses everyday. Charlie cried when he told the people these things. He never spoke of the world ending. All who lost relatives believed in him. At first they danced every night for ten nights because the dead were coming. For the first year they danced all the time. Then it began to cool off and they danced only when a person was sick.*

In this section we will briefly examine the effects of the Ghost Dance movement on three different tribes: the Shasta, the Yurok, and the Hupa. Each of these tribes accepted or rejected the Ghost Dance in varying degrees and for different reasons. One of the main factors affecting the acceptance or rejection was, it has been suggested, *the degree of stability within the tribal community*.

The greater the stability of the group, the less likely it will be to accept ideas and behavior that are radically different from its own. And if there is any acceptance, the more

likely it will be that a stable group will take the new ideas, concepts, and procedures, and weave them into its traditional cosmology and sacred ways. By stable we mean that the environmental, ceremonial, and social context of the group is fairly constant and balanced with regard to daily life and history. Among three tribes whose territories were next to each other, there were three different amounts of "stability"—ceremonial, social, and environmental. The Shasta "enthusiastically" followed and took in the new cult, without patterning it after their traditional sacred practices. The Shasta were badly disintegrated at the time they received the Ghost Dance and accepted all three waves of the modern cults—the Ghost Dance, the Earth Lodge cult, and the Bole-Maru. The Yurok, at first accepted parts of the Ghost Dance on their own terms, and in the end rejected it. The Hupa resisted the Ghost Dance and other cults completely. (du Bois, 1939)

The Yurok accepted the cult, but reluctantly. They adapted some of the features to the aboriginal beliefs and procedures but other features of the Ghost Dance were revolting to the people, especially to the elders and specialists in Yurok knowledge and ceremonialism. The Yurok and Hupa people had a very strong sense of the connection between *daily life and the teachings of oral tradition*. Their social structure was a conservative one, with wealthy families making a sort of "aristocracy" at the top, setting the examples for sacred behavior and ethics in the community. The older people and the aristocrats with "vested interests" in the established order formed the backbone of the resistance to the new cults. Before we examine exactly what these people rejected and what they wove into their traditional sacred procedures, we will present a case that happened from 1872 to 1873, in which the Ghost Dance was introduced to the Yurok and Hupa people by a man named Naigelthomelo. We will see what was required of The People and why, in the end, they rejected these requirements. The man telling the story is Robert Spott, a Yurok:

Early in the next morning, Nalgelthomelo and his wife left Crescent City and reached Requa late that night. He told the people there that the dead were

* Tolowa woman speaking in (du Bois, 1939:18)

coming back and that he wanted to give a dance, but they wouldn't let him. They made him angry because they said no such thing was possible. Most of the Requa people were up-river at Wohkero where the White Deer Skin dance* was being held. They left early the next morning in a canoe. His wife was afraid they would kill him if he tried to give a dance at Kootep (near Wohkero). He said he would give it in his own house so no one could say anything. They went on to Kootep where they lived. He took down the sides of his house and told his family to move out everything because he was going to give a dance. Then he went to Wohkero where the White Deer Skin dance was being held. There were people there from Hupa, Orleans and the Coast. He got the people together and told them of his visit to Burnt Ranch, of his dreaming and of the dead coming back. He said, "At one time Deer Skin was a good dance, a religious dance, but now let us put it away. Now we are going to

have a new dance, and all must join in. How glad we shall be to see our mother, daughters, brothers. We shall be happier." Most of the people yelled, "No, you just upset the earth. There is no such thing." The old people said, "Creator made all, and it has been handed down from generation to generation that a dead person is buried and dead. Everyone puts lots of rocks on him to hold him down. If a dead person ever comes back, he is going to kill all the live ones. That isn't our word, but the word of the Creator that our old people have told us." Naigelthomelo said, "We eat white people's food and wear their clothes now, so we must believe in the whites." Someone else said, "A white man looks at paper and talks to it and laughs. His skin is lighter. They are better than us. We can't set ourselves up with them." Naigelthomelo and his sister, who was a doctor, began dancing in their own house. People began drifting in. Soon the place was full. First the young people started dancing then the older ones. His sister went crazy first. She said, "I see my relatives and ancestors and all the dead. They are not in the cemetery, but above

* A traditional ceremonial dance.

Karok Deer dance scene, 1908. (Courtesy of Museum of American Indian, Heye Foundation)

there." Some believed her, but some didn't. The house floor was so crowded they couldn't dance.

No one might hide his property. He had to wear it or give it to someone to wear. All the property which had been hidden away would turn to rock, when the dead came. So the next day everyone brought all the riches they had and piled them up on the floor. All the property in the village was there except that which belonged to some of the people who didn't believe and stayed away.

In the morning all the men and women bathed together without clothes. It was breaking the command of the Creator, who said men and women should bathe separately. When they came from their bath, they all dipped their hands into a large basket of water into which Naigel-thomelo's wife had stirred ashes. They dipped in their right hands, rubbed them across their left ones and then passed both hands from the chin upward over the face to the hair, leaving streaks of ashes on their faces. At first they danced only at night, but when the older ones joined in, they began dancing during the day, too. They danced in rings, the men outside circling to the right, the women and children inside circling to the left. Some of the songs came from Siletz, others were dreamed by the people when they were in a trance. All the songs were wordless. The dancers wore the old-time dress. Most of them went crazy and then they could see the dead. Some saw the dead, others saw only light, others saw nothing. Older people began to get the power, too.

They took the boards from graves in cemeteries to help the dead come back. If a person tried to come to life and the grave boards were still there, he would turn to stone instead. All the graves in Kootep and Wohtek were uncovered. Everyone killed his dog because the dead don't like dogs and would turn to a stone or tree if they saw dogs. They tied stones around their necks and threw them in the river. People put baskets of acorn soup at a distance from the dancing place to feed the dead. They thought the dead were all

around and were hungry. Captain Spott (informant's father) went to look at those baskets for two days and saw nobody had touched them, so he gave up dancing and said it wasn't true. The Klamath River people were against this dance from the beginning. It is the law of the Klamath that if you bury a man and hear him moving, you must pile rocks on him to keep him down. If the dead get up, they will kill the whole village. The Creator said not to let anyone out of the grave after burying him. But, Naigelthomelo wanted to get them up, that is why the old people were against him. All the dead were to arise from the grave, not return from another world.

The dancing lasted eight or nine months on the Klamath (i.e., from fall of 1872, since the White Deer Skin is held in the autumn, to the spring of 1873). In the spring they went to Orleans (Karok). Orleans had gotten the word from Oregon some place (actually from Shasta) because the Weitchpec (Yurok) people had heard of it from the Orleans people before the news was brought to Kootep. The Orleans people sent a man to Kootep in the Spring to get the people there because the dead were to appear first at Orleans. All those who believed went up there. Even people from Requa went to Orleans. It was to be five days before the dead came and talked. The Klamath River was [turbulent] and black, so that even those who didn't believe began to think there might be something to it. They thought the upstream dead getting out of their graves [made] the river [turbulent]. A man at Orleans had prophesized about the five days. Everybody waited there for those five days. Then they kept on waiting from one day to another. They stayed ten days in all, then they lost faith. Those at Orleans who didn't believe wanted to kill the dreamer there.

After this dance, people began to get all kinds of sickness. Four or five people would be buried in a day, even in midsummer when people didn't usually get sick. The people around Kootep called a council and decided this dance had caused the summer sickness and all the thunder storms of that summer. So, they wanted to kill Naigelthomelo just the way the Burnt Ranch people killed his brother-in-law and had sent his wife and children back to Siletz after the five days of mourning. Naigelthomelo didn't live very long after that. One day some men insulted his wife by saying her mother was about to rise (from the dead). It was an insult to mention her dead mother's name. Naigelthomelo wanted to collect payment for that insult, but everyone hated him and told him he had better be careful or he would be killed. The Kootep people said if any one dreamed or tried to make that dance again it would mean death. (Robert Spott in du Bois, 1939: 22-23)

First, what were the features of the Ghost Dance the Yurok could see in their own traditions? In many Yurok ceremonies it was very important to put on a display of wealth—striving for wealth being very important in this aristocratic-oriented culture. Therefore, the demand that all wealth be displayed or it would turn to rock was something the people identified with in the beginning. Other features that had a similarity to elements in the traditional Yurok beliefs were the prohibition against eating before dancing and the separate house in which medicine was made by the prophet (dreamer) while the dance was in progress. The Yurok, unlike the Pomo for instance, who cremated their dead, buried their dead in cemeteries. Therefore only the Yurok could remove the grave boards to allow the dead to arise. (du Bois, 1939:23)

What features of the Ghost Dance did the Yurok resist? As Robert Spott told us, many of the people were shocked at the idea of mixed bathing in the sweat lodge. And a fear of ghosts prevented an easy acceptance of resurrection, i.e. the dead arising from their graves. Also, the names of the dead were not supposed to be spoken, and since dead relatives were the main topic of conversation, this must have also angered the elders. And, as we mentioned earlier, sacred procedures among the Yurok were governed by strict formulas and knowledge handed down in oral history. Aboriginal sacred ways among the

Yurok were not the invention or creation of one individual. They were an entire cosmology, parts of which were reflected in the oral histories in various formulas of procedure, and in a code of ethics based on many factors in the social structure and the environment. It is said that during the Ghost Dance, the poor and the young people, not yet knowledgeable in the more complex aspects of Yurok sacred ways were the ones who accepted the Ghost Dance most quickly and easily. As we will see in Chapter Eleven, *Sacred and Secular: Seminole Tradition in the Midst of Change*, certain elements of Pentecostal Christianity appeal to those who are outside the realities of the "American Dream"—or the wealth, goods, easy life, advertised on television and on the radio. "The poor will enter the kingdom of God" says Christian doctrine, and this statement was also echoed in the Ghost Dance and later in the Earth Lodge cults as well. Among the Yurok, this factor was compounded since the "Yurok Dream," (in this case a sacred ideal) was to accumulate wealth. The poor were doubly tempted by the doctrine of the Ghost Dance and the Christian elements within the new cults.

As for the Hupa's response to the Ghost Dance—they rejected it completely. Sam Brown, a Hupa, tells us:

The dance never reached Hupa, although we heard about it. The Hupa said it was against their religion, that there was nothing like that in their old belief, and they they didn't have anything to do with it. In the dances the women let their hair hang loose all over their faces. In the old dances it should be parted in the middle and wrapped. Hair hanging loose was just for mourning. (du Bois, 1939:24)

James Marshall was a Hupa man who probably did not think much of the Ghost Dance from the beginning. He thought it was making his people behave in ways that were against their traditional ethics and morals:

James Marshall commented unfavorably on "how all the Indians went crazy." Then he told with strong disapproval, a story in which a mother from Orleans left three small children to care for them-

Pomo woman gathering tule reeds, 1924. (Courtesy of Smithsonian Institution, National Anthropological Archives)

selves while she attended the dances. The children burned down the house in her absence. This so angered their uncle...that he armed himself with a gun and broke up the dancing. (du Bois, 1939:24)

And, finally, another reason that led the Hupa to reject the Ghost Dance was one of the rumors that went along with the Ghost Dance during the course of the movement; this was that half-bloods would be turned into frogs. To the Hupa, many of whom had some "white" blood, the concept seemed ridiculous—it just was not taken seriously in other words. One man who had "white" blood said that after they had heard this he was teased in a good-natured way and "urged to practice jumping."

In the next section we will discuss how the Pomo took the Earth Lodge cult and later, the Bole Maru, and were able to combine new concepts with aboriginal ones during these years. In doing so, they strengthened their community in its traditional sacred ways and in addition, introduced modern ideas and beliefs.

THE BOLE MARU AND CHRISTIANITY

From the beginning of colonization in california, Christianity in the form of Catholicism was the dominant religion of the colonizers and missionaries. In the later part of the 1800's, however, *Pentecostal* religious sects and missionaries appeared in California and established missions. The Catholic missionaries in northern California did not condemn the traditional and sacred practices of the native people. But, the Pentecostal church did. And as in many other regions of the United States, they would not allow an individual to participate in both traditional ceremonies and the church. Preachers called for the burning of all costumes, feathers, and ornaments that accompanied traditional sacred procedures. And Pentecostalism was an *evangelical* religion—it used militant and zealous preaching to spread its gospel. At the same time that the evangelist preachers were preaching about the righteous Christian path, the return of Jesus, the sins of *paganism*, and the rewards of the hereafter, tribal people were finding it increasingly difficult to practice their own traditional sacred ways. Their communities were also being upset by environmental, economic, and conceptual intrusions.

Religious movements developed at this time in response to these influences and often depressing conditions. "Dreaming" for example, was originally a way that the prophet or dreamer communicated with the dead. As dreaming developed the dreamers (or preachers, as The People were beginning to call them) talked "about heaven" and what "a nice country it was up there." Everyone was to be resurrected and join their dead relatives in heaven. For this, they must be "good" and lead the right kind of life. The traditional figures of Coyote or Fox were supposed to pass judgement on the people who were to be ressurected. Some preachers said that the "judgement day," or the end of The Peoples' lives, would come with a great fire or flood.

These changes in doctrines of the new religious movements reflect both the influence of Christianity and the despair the tribal people felt as they saw their traditional ways of life being suppressed and destroyed. The concept of resurrection and meeting dead relatives in "heaven;" the ending of life by fire or flood; and the association of the Christian "God" with Coyote or Fox, show the growing influence of Christianity. Christianity itself, developed hundreds of years ago in the Middle East, under similar conditions. The peoples' living conditions had become intolerable, changes in daily life and politics came rapidly. The concepts and ceremonials of Christianity originally offered an escape from that reality.

The Bole Maru religious movement which still flourishes today, especially among the Pomo, is one example of where Christian and traditional elements mixed together to form a new sacred way, a way considered more "traditional" than Christianity by young people and more "new" and innovative by the older people.

The traditional ceremonials like the Kuksu and Hesi dances were very difficult to perform and direct. Those who participated needed rigorous training. By 1870, there were only a few men capable directing the ceremonies. This, combined with the government policies aimed at suppressing traditional religious ceremonies, turned the California native people to other ceremonial forms, like the Bole Maru.

The Bole Maru was an outgrowth of the Earth Lodge Cult:

Followers of the Earth Lodge [Cult] constructed large subterranean Dance Houses designed as places of refuge against the predicted destruction of the world. By 1872, the Earth Lodge Cult had reached Pomo territory, where it underwent still further modification to become the Maru Cult. It is characterized by a Maru, or "Dreamer," who serves as the chief religious functionary and who leads the people by means of dreamed rules of ceremonial behavior.

The center of Maru activity at any one time is the [local community or] rancheria which has active Maru, or Dreamers. Although the dances have community backing, they are initiated by individuals. One or more persons in the group "dream" the rules of the dance and pass them on to the rest of the people. Lacking these dreams, there seem to be no rules to guide ceremonial activity, and

if, for some reason or other, there is no Dreamer at a rancheria, the people will visit the dances of other groups but will not hold ceremonies of their own. Thus, the influence of the individual is of marked importance, and lack of the proper individual will largely stop or slow down the ceremonial activities of the group. (Barrett in Meighan & Riddell, 1972:9-11)

The influence of Christian ideas and terminology on traditional concepts is seen in the use of the terms "God" and "Heaven and Hell."

Traditionally, the Pomo, for example, did not have a concept of a "supreme being," like the "God" in Christianity. As we have discussed in earlier chapters of this textbook, there were very few Native American aboriginal sacred systems that had one supreme "God" at the center. However, as the dreaming cult developed in northern California, the concept of "power," the unseen, the mysterious, or the "Great Spirit," became translated into the terms "heavenly father" or "God," as in Christianity:

Some unknown person or possibly someone who has recently died appears in the dream as a messenger from Marumba [a creator figure] and teaches the dreamer. On the coast, Coyote was supposed to have been the . . . creator in former days. The modern Maru dreams, however, do not come from Coyote, but from the "Father in Heaven." The person who tells about the dreams says that he saw God in the form of a mist, and that he talked by means of the wind.

Some dreamers did make the association between "our father" and Coyote, but it cannot be generalized. It is probable that with the growing influence of Christianity the concept of "our father" is being divorced more and more from the Marumba or Coyote concept of older days. (Loeb, 1936: 395 and footnote)

Additional comments on the power behind dreaming were made by Pomo individuals familiar with the Bole Maru:

Charlie Gunter, Eastern Pomo:
Maru men were prophets for "father

above." Marumba was Coyote. He was different from "father above."

George Patch, Southeastern Pomo:

Dreaming is just like the Bible. It isn't plain sleep dreaming. Dreamers get sick, faint, do terrible things, before they get their dreams. They preach not to steal, not to drink, not to kill. "Do good and we shall go to the dance house above." Our father tells the dreamers these things. He is just like the white people's God.

Susie Shoemaker, Coast Central Pomo:

Dreamers work with power gotten from *yakibaea* (our father). Old-time curers also got power from *yakibaea*, but in the old days he was Coyote. He isn't Coyote anymore. He is like a man. Dreamers see things as in a looking glass. They see right through people and their thoughts. Common people don't know about these things.

John Smith, Northern Pomo:

Maru means to dream something. Indians always dreamed, but this Maru is new. God gives the dreams to the Maru dreamers. (du Bois, 1939:102)

In the aboriginal sacred systems there had been no concept of "good" or "evil," "heaven" or hell." Morality and ethics, as we said in Chapter One, part 4, were something a person learned in order to survive and to get along in a closely knit community. However, as Christian missionaries entered the tribal communities and other settlers were observed worshipping in their Pentecostal churches or tent meetings, the concepts of good and evil, heaven and hell, became incorporated into the religious movements of The People. This, along with the new idea of "God," is discussed by Clifford Salvador, a Southeastern Pomo man:

Dreamers all say they dream from God. If they don't do what their dreams say they will be punished. Marumba (Coyote) is just a story. It isn't true. Dreamers are like the angels coming from heaven to Abraham. The whites put that in the

Bible, but the Indians just carry that in their heads. In the beginning there was a story about Coyote and his brother, Kuksu, making this world because there was no place to rest. That creation is just a story. It is different from dreaming. Coyote stories are different everywhere, but the Maru God is the same everywhere. No one ever saw God; they just hear him. The Maru say dead people are in a different place. All who die go there. When the world ends we shall meet with the dead. If you believe in Maru, you go to the dead land when you die. If you don't believe, you will go to another place which is bad. The world has to end and be cleaned out before the dead can come back. (du Bois, 1939: 102)

And finally, Billy Gilbert, an Eastern Pomo man explains from his point of view:

The word for God in our language is Maru. In this Maru religion, the three dreamers from Upper Lake all preached the same thing as Lame Bill. The world was to end some day. Everybody must believe to go to the best place. If you don't believe, you will go to the fire. Good Indians must believe in their preachers just like the whites. A good person, one who doesn't kill, steal, or lie, goes up to heaven like a bird flying up. The bad go to fire. There are two roads forking. The left one goes west, the right one goes north. The right one is a fine smooth road with flowers along the way and all kinds of good food, like meat, pie, bread, and cake. One man (fire person, i.e., devil) stands at the divide and tries to make people take the smooth road. That fire road leads to the bad place, where there is gambling and whiskey. Chairs and tables are upset. There is fire all around. The other road is just a common road. It looks untraveled because there is grass growing on it. That is the way to heaven. In heaven everyone is young and wears good black clothes. They don't have any worries. There are no bad men. All is clean, and everybody is friends. (du Bois, 1939: 102)

THE BOLE MARU AND DOCTORING: NEW VERSUS OLD

We saw how the Christian elements of a supreme being and good/evil entered the vocabulary of native sacred knowledge and practices. We can assume that certain other types of behavior also changed at this time. For instance, the institution of gambling with its songs, its traditional legends, and its relationship to "power," was criticized by the new christian-type morality. Other ways changed, too. One of the most important and obvious changes was the emphasis, in the new Maru Cult, on the *dreamer*, or preacher as he was sometimes called. The dreamer dreamed the rules of the dance and dreamed what kind of costumes should be made. The dreamer organized the dancers and the singers and saw that all went according to the rules. In one way the individual dreamer was a new development.

Before, tribal sacred practices and knowledge covered all areas of daily life as well as the particular ceremonial events that required special sacred knowledge. However, there was also a tradition among the tribes that accepted the Bole Maru Cult, of *doctors*, specialists who received their "power" and knowledge through dreams and who doctored or healed in a state of trance. These individuals were outside the system or organized sacred procedures, histories, formulas, and rituals. Their original dream was their own, their spirit helpers (if they had them) were their own, the songs they used during curing were their own, and the procedures they used to doctor were their own. The doctors could also participate in the sacred traditions of their communities, but in addition they were known to have special powers. When the Bole Maru Cult developed, the *dreamer* followed two models, the pentecostal preacher and the aboriginal doctor.

In the beginning of the Bole Maru there were many "Dreamers" in the Ghost Dance movement. Many people participated in dances, chanting, and other means which produced trances and visions. But, this gradually died down and the inspiration and dreaming concentrated itself among a few "preachers:"

One leader drew to himself a following similar to a church group. In fact, [The People] compare these "preachers" to the recent Pentecostal missionaries who have built churches in the area. [The People] term these leaders "preachers" and "doctors" synonomously... Yet, they are not confused with the older shamans in their minds. (du Bois, 1939:48)

Henry Joseph, a Karok, tells us:

Old-time doctors worked hard. They dreamed of God [Ikhareya: "an ancient spirit" in Karok. An original word for those beings that came before human beings]. They would sing four or five nights to cure a person and all the people came to help them sing. They sucked wherever you are sick, and then they opened their mouths and picked the poison out with their fingers. When I first began doctoring, I dreamed of small firs 3 or 4 feet high. They were singing and talking among themselves and they said, "These firs are good for sick people." When people asked me to cure I took fir tips and sang the song I heard in my dream and brushed the sick person with the fir tips until the sickness came out. This was just a dream. God (Ikhareya) did not give me this. Later, God did give me power and I got two sets of feathers. Ikhareya looks like a man. He does good to everybody. You dream and he talks and sings to you and tells you what to do, then you have to do it. An Indian doctor has to fix himself up every year, then everthing goes fine. I don't suck, I just catch the poison with my hands and pull it out. (du Bois, 1939:18)

Mr. Joseph, a doctor, indicates to us that he himself is caught between the old doctoring methods and the new way which consists of visions of a supreme being and "brushing away" or "catching" the poison instead of sucking it out. Below Jack Fulsom explains how doctoring changed, referring probably to the influence of the Pentecostal church where the preacher "lays on his hands" to cure ailing people:

Now doctors cure by preaching. They don't suck anymore, they just brush the sickness off with their hands and the power catches the pain. God told the doctors not to suck. It is old fashioned. They preach by God now. We don't have a word in our language for God. We talk about the white man's God, not about Coyote or Fox. Some doctor dreamers say Coyote is there sitting alongside of God. (du Bois, 1939:50)

The Christian missionaries condemned aboriginal medicine ways, just as they condemned gambling and the dancing and costumes of ceremonials. However, what is strong and effective usually persists in any culture, even if the participants have to go "underground" to continue their traditional practices. In the case of the Pomo, for example, many of the dreamers-turned-preachers or "doctors" took over the role of the aboriginal curing specialists. For the time that the people were making the transition to a new way of life, these dreamers/preachers served the people as doctors. However, as the Bole Maru Cult grew more established in the various communities, a new development was seen. Women, who aboriginally had been excluded from "leader" roles in sacred ceremonials, emerged *in their traditional role of curing specialists or aboriginal doctors*, to take over the leadership positions in the Bole Maru dances. Davis Mike, an Achomawi (Pit River) comments on doctoring during this transition period:

This new-time singing and preaching doctoring isn't very strong. They just put their hands on the patient. The old-time doctors sucked them. Old-time doctoring was awfully hard. There are no women preaching doctors, but there were old-time women doctors. We use the same word for the old-time doctors and the preaching doctors (*tsigiualo* for men, *tsigita* for women). Old-time doctors had *damakome** (Pains or poisons). They were their power and they could kill persons with them. The new preachers cure by "above power," by a man who is above, who never lies, who tells about the sick. Preaching doctors sing about

daylight coming and flowers... (du Bois, 1939:50)

One woman, Essie Parrish, a Kashia Pomo from Stewart's Point Rancheria, has been a Maru leader for many years; she is also a sucking doctor. There is a story about Essie Parrish, and how she became a prophet or Maru dance leader:

When Essie Parrish was about seven years of age she saw a man wearing a feather cloak sitting beside the trail as she was on her way home through the woods. This was a magic garment, and to see such a person could produce sickness or even death. She was badly frightened and ran home. Upon arrival she went right to bed. Almost immediately she lost consciousness, and despite all efforts could not be aroused during that day or the following night.

Finally, a man who was thought to possess one of these magic garments was called in. He restored her to normal health... Very soon after this experience Essie Parrish began to dream and have the revelations which have been so important to her and the religious activities at Kashia. The men possessing the magic garments are believed to make a peculiar sound, which Essie Parris heard as a child and still hears upon certain occasions. (Barrett, in Meighan & Riddell, 1972:119-120)

THE KASHIA BOLE MARU

At Kashia, some aboriginal features of the ceremonials now dominated by the Maru dances are still seen today. Others have been modified. Two of these modifications are that women now wear articles of clothing, or costumes, formerly only worn by the men. Another is that women now play the major dancing roles and the leadership is entirely in the hands of the prophet or leader, Essie Parrish. She gives the instructions for the presentation and details of the Maru ceremonials. In other words, she dreams the dances that her helpers will perform. Helpers consist of the male singers and clapstick players, male feather dancers, and women dancers, singers, and orators who play the major role in the dances and the feasts. When

---

* See Chapter Five, **Shamans and The World of Spirits: The Oldest Religion**

Essie Parrish, Bole Maru leader with assistant outside of dance lodge. (From Plate VIII, *The Maru Dance Cult of the Pomo Indian*, Clement W. Meighan and Francis A. Riddell, Southwest Museum, Los Angeles, 1972)

Essie Parrish dreams of a dance it must be performed. In addition to dreaming the movements and details of the dance, she dreams the design of the costumes and other paraphernalia, such as the designs for the flags that fly outside the dance house or the other decorated cloths or hoops the dancers might hold while they are dancing certain dances. After she has had a dance dream, the women who are to perform sew the designs and the costumes. The Maru dances all follow a basic pattern, but each dance is different since it comes from the leader's dream, and is affected by the needs of the community that she might anticipate. Essie Parrish says the life of a dreamer/doctor is not an easy one because, "your dreams keep you awake."

Below is a brief summary of some of the dances and events one might see if one attended a Maru ceremonial among the Kashia

Pomo. As we said earlier, the basic patterns stay the same—such as the counter-clockwise direction the dancers move in—but dances with new names and new costume designs may be introduced. One such dance, for example, was a dance Essie Parrish introduced for protecting men overseas in the armed services, which was very successful in its objective. Aside from the Big Head Dance, which is a special dance requiring large feather-and-rushes ornate headresses, most of the dances are performed (by the women) in long dresses with long sleeves, styled after the dresses the women settlers wore in the 1800's. The men wear decorated vests at times and the women decorated dresses or vests with the designs of stars, crosses, and other geometrical patterns appliqued on. Ribbons are tied to the women's fingers and when they move about the dance floor moving their arms up and down, swaying with the rhythm of the songs and clap-sticks, the ribbons arch and flutter in the air.

The Maru dances that Essie Parrish leads are held in a dance house, a round house made of lumber with a steep, shake-covered conical roof. The house is about 45 feet in diameter and the rafters are held up by a large center pole about 12 feet high. The floor is hard packed earth and there are benches against the wall for the audience which sometimes consist of a hundred people. A summarized report on a 1958 ceremonial follows:

Entrance to the Dance House is through a tunnel about ten feet in length facing toward the southwest. A few feet directly in front of the inner end of the tunnel is the fire, with a smoke hole in the roof directly above it. The fire is, as of old, presided over by the usual official Fire-Tender. Both men and women performers were barefooted. The Singers took their places on a bench just behind the center pole and began the first song. This was led by the prophet, Essie Parrish, as were all other songs except those of the feather, or "forty-niner" cycle... Several preliminary songs were sung, accompanied by four men as... singers. The prophet and two of the men used clapper rattles... Later... the prophet then took her place before the center pole and made a stirring exhortation to all present. This was followed by more singing, this time with several... singers. [In the Flower Dance] ...one feature reminiscent of aboriginal patterns was the use of the hands. Dancers, especially women dancers, formerly carried in their hands certain objects, such as tassel-like pendants of tules or rushes, which they brought alternately up and down in time to the rhythm of the music... The end of [the Flower Dance] concluded with the dancers dividing into two lines on either side of the Dance House, facing toward the audience. After a short interval, the dancers quickly faced inward toward each other, where they danced in place for a short time. The lines then advanced, each dancer passing through the opposite line and coming to a position facing the audience. Immediately the dancers whirled so that the two lines again faced each other. This action was repeated four times. Finally, the dancers passed in single file, in a counter-clockwise direction, four times around the center pole and fire, and out through the tunnel entrance, thus concluding this first cycle of dances. As they passed through the tunnel they left their floral ornaments on some shelves on either side of the tunnel.

[In the Feather Dance] the male dancers wore aboriginal regalia over his everyday clothing each man wore a feather skirt tied about his waist and hanging down nearly to the floor. About his head was bound a head-net and on his forehead was a flickerfeather hand-band. From either side of the head projected a forked feather dart.

To the music of the "old-time songs... these dancers executed a series of the older Pomo dances such as were to be seen before the Ghost Dance of 1870... [In the Table or Mesa Dance] following still further singing at the center pole, eleven women came into the Dance House, each carrying a piece of white cloth about three feet square. Each cloth was embroidered with a distinctive design, no two of which were alike. All embroidery was in black except that on two cloths, each of which had a fraction of its design in a pinkish tone, the remainder in black. The designs were in all kinds of geometric patterns.

It was said that the original of this dance was the result of a vision of a former Dreamer many years ago, and that upon her death her paraphernalia (including her clothes) were burned. Essie Parrish reportedly revived this dance and dreamed the designs now used... During the Mesa Dance each dancer grasped the upper corners of her cloth, holding it so that the design faced outward and moving her hands alternately up and down giving a gentle waving to the cloth.

In this dance the traditional counter-clockwise movements, repetitions in fours, and other movements described above for the Flower Dance, were duplicated.

[In the Shell Dance] ...After a short recess for refreshments three men and four women appeared [dressed] in costumes for the Shell Dance, or the Abalone Shell Ornament Dance, as it is sometimes called. Each man wore over his [clothes] a special vest on the front of which were two vertical rows of abalone ornaments. On the back of the vest were two similar lines of ornaments, there being a total of eight ornaments on each vest. Each woman wore a complete dress over her other [clothes], each having similar ornaments except that the lines ran down to the hem of the long skirt. Two of the shell ornaments were worn above the waist (as in the men's vests) in each vertical line of ornaments; six more were worn below the waist as the line continued down to the hem of the skirt. Each woman's costume therefore bore 32.

The individual shell ornaments were identical, made of a three inch disc of abalone shell to which was attached three narrow pendants of the same shell. The pendants, about three or four inches long and less than an inch wide, were suspended from perforations—one perforation in the center of the disc and the other two at the lower edge of it. These brilliantly irridescent ornaments glinted beautifully in the fire light as they moved in the rhythm of the dance. No less pleasing were the tinkling and clinking sounds made as the pendants swayed back and forth. Such ornaments are said to signify "righteousness." The Shell Dance is said to have been originated by Annie Jarvis, the immediate predecessor of the present prophet.

The dance procedures were the same as for the other dances. At the end the dancers merely [took off] their special costumes and placed these with the other paraphernalia on the table back of the center pole.

Essie Parrish then announced that the end of the ceremony was at hand. Next followed a very brief interval of singing, and again a woman (not the same one who opened the proceedings) appeared before the center pole, where she spoke in a low voice for some minutes while everyone either sat or stood with bowed head. The ending of her discourse was the same, word for word, as that of the opening invocation. This was a benediction, and with it the crowd dispersed, to gather again for the "barbecue."

The Barbecue—In ancient times every ceremony called for a feast, or for repeated feasts on successive days, and many days in advance were occupied in preparations. The women ground acorns and prepared various vegetable foods. The men were occupied with hunting and fishing. Much of the cooking was done in the underground oven, a preheated pit two feet across and about as deep, in which foods wrapped in leaves were placed between layers of hot stones, the whole oven being covered with a layer of earth surmounted by a lively fire.

A modified version of the earth oven was used for the Kashia occasion. A pit about eight feet in diameter and four to five feet deep had been previously excavated. At about 3:00 p.m. on July 3rd, the day preceeding the feast, a heavy bonfire of large logs was started in this pit. After three hours of burning the fire, coals, and ashes were removed and 22 packages of meat were placed in the pit, covered with more earth for a few inches, and then the fire was rebuilt and kept going until the next day. The pieces of meat, weighing about ten pounds each, were wrapped in aluminum foil or heavy brown wrapping paper, then covered with a wrapping of burlap and tied with bailing wire. No stones were used in the fire pit.

When the pit was opened and the fire scraped out a man retrieved the packages of meat with a garden rake, hooking the wires with which they were bound. The packages were then put into a wheelbarrow and retrieved as needed. The first package of meat was not taken directly to the serving table but to detour into the Dance House.

With it went the prophet who, with her clapper rattle, performed a short ceremony to consecrate the food before it was served. A similar consecration ritual was performed with a token portion of each kind of food. Two young men took into the Dance House two large beautifully frosted cakes, each covered with a multitude of little candles. Others took in some loaves of bread, packages of cookies, a watermelon, a bowl of potato salad, etc. Each kind of food had its own separate short consecration ceremony.

Other than the meat, all foods were the donations of individuals. When all was [ready] the donors formed a procession carrying their own contributions and following the prophet and her husband. All marched in a counter-clockwise direction slowly around the two dining tables under an arbor. Four rounds were completed and then all the food offerings were placed on the tables. Following this the procession continued, empty-handed for four more rounds, after which all foods were removed to the serving tables and the feast began. All foods were free to everyone, except the roasted meat, for which a charge was made.

Throughout the ceremony and the following barbecue the taboo on drinking was strictly enforced and no one was seen drinking. (Barrett, in Meighan & Riddell, 1972:111-117)

The leader of the Kashia Maru dance, Essie Parrish, is also a doctor. In her curing ceremonies, in which she enters a trance in order to "see" the sickness, locate it, and suck it out of the patient's body, she also employs helpers. In this case her helpers, men and women, sing to the rhythm of the clap-sticks. For curing, she dances alone. In both curing and leading the Maru, her objective is the same—to help people, to keep the community well. The object of the Maru dance and Maru religion is to practice unselfishness, friendliness, and careful living. *Essie Parrish* feels strongly about the importance of the Maru religion, because for one, it has been able to blend non-native concepts with native or traditional ones to create a new way of life for the people of the community. In this way, through the constant maintenance of dance performances and the spirit behind the leader's dreams, a certain balance in the spiritual and physical life of The People is established; one that can change with the changing times.

SUMMARY

In summary, we examined some of the historical and environmental causes of the "unbalancing" that took place among the northern California tribal communities. We observed some of the people's responses to the changes in their lives, changes brought from outside their local communities by both the colonizers and people from other tribes. We saw how many elements of the Pentecostal Church lent themselves to borrowing by individuals no longer able to maintain their traditional sacred systems in the face of confusing events and other political or economic pressures beyond their control. *

Finally, we also observed how some tribes, given different circumstances and social structures; different precedents in their oral traditions, and different sacred procedures, rejected the new movements in favor of aboriginal concepts and customs. And, as in the case of the Bole Maru, we saw how it is possible to combine the new and the old in the rapidly changing world of today, so that young and old people can find ways of balancing their lives with respect to physical, social and economic conditions and their spiritual needs.

---

* See also Chapter Eleven, **Sacred and Secular: Seminole Tradition in the Midst of Change.**

Suggested Additional Readings

1970   *The Autobiography of Delfina Cuero: A Diegueno Woman*, as told to Florence Shipek, Morongo Indian Reservation, Malki Museum Press.

COLSON, ELIZABETH (ed.)
1974   *Autobiographies of Three Pomo Women*, Berkeley, Ca., Archeological Research Facility, Dept. of Anthropology, University of California.

KROEBER, ALFRED
1976   *Yurok Myths*, Berkeley, Ca., University of California Press.

MOONEY, JAMES
1965   *The Ghost Dance Religion*, Chicago, Ill., University of Chicago Press. (The Plains version of the Ghost Dance)

WALLACE, ANTHONY F. C.
1972   *The Death and Rebirth of the Seneca*, New York, Random House. (Revitalization movements among the Seneca)

CHAPTER EIGHT

8 The Path of Life

The place from which you had started at the beginning seemingly a long time ago, will now appear very close as if you had started but recently.

(Radin, 1945:262)

Within several religions around the world is the philosophy or idea that life is envisioned as a path or road. The terrain through which it winds and goes is representative of the pitfalls, or turns of life one must encounter as one travels the "road of life." This is made explicit in the ceremony, like the Mide of the Winnebago. The above quote comes from this ceremony.

At the root of Native American aboriginal concepts is the belief that the road conveys an eternal return. There is no end. At death one returns in some way to the beginning. On the path of life, when one has reached old age, one knows what one knew when one was born, but only *realizes* and *acknowledges* it for the first time. The concept is at the root of aboriginal beliefs because like the road, the "sacred" had no beginning or end. This road is continuous and never ending.

This is how an Arapaho describes the Arapaho road.

The road of the Arapaho was an old and good one, and we believed it had been traveled since the beginning of the world.

Since long before the white man came, the Cheyenne and the Arapaho had followed much the same road. We had joined together against our common enemies and so had made war together; our religion, our stories, our way of doing things in camp and on the hunt and the warpath were much alike... (Sweezy, 1966:2-3)

In Peyotism, the Peyote "road" is also discussed. An explanation, metaphorically, is given about the altar of a crescent moon.

At the west corner, horns to the east, is the crescent altar with a groove or "path" along it from horn to horn, interrupted by a flat space in the center where the "father peyote" is later to rest on springs of sage. The "path" symbolizes man's path from birth (southern tip) to the crest of maturity and knowledge (at the place of the peyote) and thence downward again to the ground through old age to death (northern tip). (La Barre, 1969:46-47)

The priest swung a pointing finger along a narrow groove running the crest of the altar moon. "You follow life's road," he explained to me, "then you meet peyote, and your life changes. It has for everyone in here. We meet peyote and then we continue in that Way." (Nabokov, 1969)

Through these roads or paths life is given more meaning, purpose, and responsibility. We also find that these roads provide means or procedures by which the people may attain or achieve certain desired goals. This is the role of religions. The path of life is analogous to this role.

Some of the phases each individual must pass through, major details of landscape along the path, would be birthing, naming, childhood, adolescence, family, old age, death and,

197

of course, those relationships that pertain to each phase.

When a child is born, he/she is seen by others as having a direction to go. Patterns have been established in order for a person to live well and long. Of course, these patterns or hopes for a child are not obvious to that child at the beginning of his/her life, during infancy. However, his/her parents may immediately, after the birth of the child, begin the child in the established pattern. Because the child is loved, and respected as a human being, those close to the child wish him/her a good life and a long life. Therefore, aboriginally, numerous tribes had major ceremonies for each individual at every stage of life, including ceremonies for the newborn.

CHILDHOOD CEREMONIES

This is the Zuni presentation of an infant to the Sun.

> On the eighth day of life an infant's head is washed by his "aunts"—that is, women of his father's clan, his most important ceremonial relatives. Corn meal is placed in his hand and he is taken outdoors, facing the east, at the moment of sunrise. Corn meal is sprinkled to the rising sun with the following prayer, spoken by the paternal grandmother:

> Now this is the day
> Our child,
> Into the daylight
> You will go out standing.
> Preparing for your days,
> When all your days were at an end,
> When eight days were past,
> Our sun father
> Went in to sit down at his sacred place.
> And our night fathers
> Having come out standing to their
>   sacred place,
> Passing a blessed night
> We came to day.
> Now this day
> Our fathers,
> Dawn priests,
> Have come out standing to their sacred
>   place.

> Our sun father
> Having come out standing to his
>   sacred place,
> Our child

Woman and child. Spokane Indians. Colville Reservation, Washington State, 1900. (Courtesy of Museum of American Indian, Heye Foundation)

> It is your day.
> This day,
> The flesh of the white corn,
> Prayer meal,
> To our sun father
> This prayer meal we offer.
> May your road be fulfilled
> Reaching to the road of your sun
>   father.
> When your road is fulfilled
> In your thoughts (may we live)
> May we be the ones whom your
>   thoughts will embrace,
> For this, on this day
> To our sun father

We offer prayer meal
To this end
May you help us all to finish our roads.
(Bunzel, 1932:635-636)

In the past of the American Indian, a child was lavishly protected in order for that child to reach old age. Of course, this instinct to protect the young is still with us, but the manner of doing so may have changed with the people and time. As we can see by the Zuni ceremony, the child beginning his road generally held a special place in the tribal world. A Lakota man, Ben Black Bear, Sr., expresses the affection of the Lakota for their children.

I will tell some truths now. What we consider the most important thing on this earth is our children. The small baby boys and girls. What we call babies, we love, we cherish, and we want to raise them. Those children are those people who are living today. Once you were all children. They are put to sleep and are fed (from the breasts). They are looked after carefully. We want to raise them. So be it. (Theisz, Mss., N.D.)

The Omaha people also performed a ceremony for their newborn. Like the Zuni, it also took place on the infant's eighth day after being born. The right to perform the ceremony was inherited. As an example of change in tribal ceremonial life, it was particularly noted by the recorder (of the ceremony) that, "Unfortunately the full details of the ceremony had been lost through death of [those] who had charge of it." The ceremony may serve to show the Omaha's relationship to the universe; a relationship that extended to, and included the Omaha newborn.

When a child was born it was ...simply...a living being coming forth into the universe, whose advent must be ceremonially announced in order to assure it an accepted place among the already existing forms.

On the appointed day the priest was sent for. When he arrived he took his place at the door of the tent in which the child lay and raising his right hand to the sky, palm outward, he intoned the following in a loud, ringing voice:

Ho! Sun, Moon, Stars, all that move in the heavens, I bid you hear me!
Into your midst has come a new life.
Consent ye, I implore!
Make its path smooth, that it may reach the brow of the first hill!

Ho! Ye Winds, Clouds, Rain, Mist, all ye that move in the air,
I bid you hear me!
Into your midst has come a new life.
Consent ye, I implore!
Make its path smooth, that it may reach the brow of the second hill!

Ho! Ye Hills, Valleys, Rivers, Lakes, Trees, Grasses, all ye of the earth.
I bid you hear me!
Into your midst has come a new life.
Consent ye, I implore!
Make its path smooth, that it may reach the brow of the third hill!

Ho! Ye Birds, great and small, that fly in the air,
Ho! Ye animals, great and small, that dwell in the forest,
Ho! Ye insects that creep among the grasses and burrows in the ground.
I bid you hear me!
Into your midst has come a new life.
Consent ye, I implore!
Make its path smooth, that it may reach the brow of the fourth hill!

Ho! All ye of the heavens, all ye of the air, all ye of the earth,
I bid you all to hear me!
Into your midst has come a new life.
Consent ye, consent ye all, I implore!
Make its path smooth—then shall it travel beyond the four hills!

This ritual was a supplication to the powers of the heavens, the air, and the earth for the safety of the child from birth to old age. In it the life of the infant is pictured as about to travel a rugged road stretching over four hills, marking the stages of infancy, youth, manhood, and old age. (Fletcher & LaFlesche, 1911: 115-116)

This ceremony expresses the belief of the Omaha that everything in the universe was related and interdependent. Therefore, the Omaha made the announcement to the universe that another human being was taking its place among the other existing life-forms. The Omaha followed this ceremony with another when the child was ready to walk. At this point, a child was introduced to the tribe and took its place in the tribe. This ceremony has been translated to mean "Turning the Child." It took place in the spring, "after the first thunders had been heard." This ceremony was for all children. When they could walk alone, through this ceremony, they were symbolically "sent into the midst of the winds." A child needed a new pair of moccasins for this ceremony. After the ceremony, a child's baby name was thrown away. Its new name was announced to all of nature and to the crowd of people who had gathered to see the ceremony.

The significance of the new moccasins put on the child will appear more clearly by the light of the following custom, still observed in families which all the old traditions of the tribe are conserved. When moccasins are made for a little baby, a small hole is cut in the sole of one. This is done in order that "if a messenger from the spirit world should come and say to the child, 'I have come for you,' he could answer, 'I can not go on a journey—my moccasins are worn out!' " A similar custom pertains to the Oto tribe. A little hole is cut in the first pair of moccasins made for a child. When the relatives come to see the little one they examine the moccasins, and, seeing the hole they say: "Why, he (or she) has worn out his moccasins; he (she) has traveled over the earth!" *This is an indirect prayer that the child may live long.* (Fletcher & LaFlesche, 1911:117)

In the tent where the ceremony was held, a fire burned in the center. To the east was a stone, upon which the child's feet would be placed. This stone was symbolic of "long life upon the earth and of the wisdom derived from age." It was the mother who brought the child to the tent where she approached the man, or "priest" who represented the Thunder. He acted in the role of the Thunder.

At the door she paused, and addressed the priest within, saying: "Venerable man, I desire my child to wear moccasins." Then she dropped the hand of the child, and the little one, carrying his new "moccasins," entered the tent alone.

. . .she again addressed him, saying: "I desire my child to walk long upon the earth; I desire him protection, we hold to you for strength."

The priest replied, addressing the child: "You shall reach the fourth hill sighing; you shall be bowed over; you shall have wrinkles; your staff shall bend under your weight. I speak to you that you may be strong." (Fletcher and LaFlesche, 1911:118)

The priest then continued by singing an invocation, a prayer that was directed to the winds. After this song the child was "turned" upon the stone. Another ritual song was sung.

Free translation

Turned by the winds goes the one I send yonder;
Yonder he goes who is whirled by the winds;
Goes, where the four hills of life and the four winds are standing;
There in the midst of the winds do I send him,
Into the midst of the winds, standing there.

(The Thunder rolls.)
(Fletcher & LaFlesche, 1911:119)

New moccasins were then put on a child's feet, as another song was sung. A child was then "made to take four steps typical of its entrance into a long life."

The Zuni presentation of an infant to the Sun and the Omaha introduction of a child to the universe are not very far apart in function and ceremony. Both speak of a road or path an infant must take and follow.

In the Jicarilla Apache ceremony for the newborn child, it is stated that it "is a long-life ceremony." The name of the ceremony is "water has been put on top of his head."

The gods gave the people this ceremony in the beginning. It is handed down from old times through the tribe. This ceremony was given to the people when they were already on this earth, before Monster Slayer came, however, and before the monsters were killed. It was not needed for life in the underworld before the emergence, for down there, there was no sickness, no death, no need for a "long-life" ceremony like this. But the earth is dangerous...this takes the children to the puberty ceremony safely. (Opler, 1946:14)

The functions of each of these ceremonies was to direct children to long life. This direction was consistent and at intervals on the path of life this goal was reinforced by participation in other ceremonies which might help one attain long life.

Another significant time in a person's life is during naming. The customs of naming were different among tribes. Occasionally at the end of one's life, he/she might have had accumulated several names. In the ceremony of the Omaha, a child discarded its baby name after "the turning of the child," when the new name of the child was announced aloud to the assembled crowd and also to the universe.

"The hills, the grass, the trees,
the creeping things both great and small,
I bid you hear! This child has thrown

Jicarilla Apache man called Vicentito, holding two babies. Ca. 1925. (Courtesy of the Smithsonian Institution, National Anthropological Archives)

away its baby name. Ho! (a call to take notice.)"
(Fletcher & LaFlesche, 1911:121)

Among the Mandan, "until the child received a name, it was not considered a part of the...village but of the 'baby home' from whence it had come." When the child received a name his status in the tribe was recognized.

The Mandan believed that there was a Baby Hill...like an earth lodge, in which an old man cared for them. If a child died before being named, it returned to the Baby Hill. People claimed to have seen baby tracks on the tops and sides of these hills. It was believed that the spirits in the hill near the Heart River came north when the Mandan came north. If a woman had been married a number of years and was childless, desiring a child, she would go to one of these hills to pray for one. Those wanting a daughter brought girl's clothing and a ball; for a son she brought a small bow and arrow. The Mandan believed in rebirth.

A girl usually keeps her first name as long as she lives. If she was sick or unlucky, her parents frequently put up a feast to get a new name for her. If she had grown up, her brothers and sisters helped her prepare a renaming feast. (Bowers, 1950:60)

The ceremonies children underwent were also in preparation for the special roles they would play later in life. There were certain desirable traits a boy should have, and other traits were desirable for girls. Of course, these traits were determined, in part, by the lifestyle of particular tribe. A Kwakiutl mother desired that her infant girl become an industrious woman. Therefore, the infant was prepared for this later role, though the child was yet an infant.

When a girl is born by her mother it is washed by the midwife who takes care of the woman who has given birth. After she has washed her, she wraps her in warm covers. Now the mother of the child takes a little mountain goat wool and she takes a narrow strip of cotton cloth. Then she prays to it...

201

As soon as she stops praying she wraps the narrow strip of cotton cloth around the four strips of wool...She puts them into a small basket in which the clothes of her child are. Now she waits for the naval cord of her child to come off. As soon as it is off she ties it around the right hand of her child. Now it stays on her hand, and until the time when the child is nine months old it will not be taken off. As soon as the child is nine months old her mother takes the remains of the wool and she takes the four strings and wraps around them the cotton cloth that has been washed, around the four strings of wool. Then she ties it around the right hand of her child and she also takes one piece of wool and cuts it up so that it is like flour. She puts a little water with it so that it becomes pasty. Then she prays to the finely cut wool and says, "O, supernatural power of the Supernatural-One-of-the-Rocks, go on, look at what I am doing to you, for I pray you to take mercy on my child and, please, let her be successful in getting property and let nothing evil happen to her when she goes up the mountain picking all kinds of berries; and, please, protect her, Supernatural One," says she as she puts her first finger into what is like milk, the wool mixed with water, and she puts it on the tongue of the child. Four times she does so. When she has finished she suckles her child. Now for four days she does this in the morning, then she stops after this.

Now this woman who has been treated grows up and she really gets much when she picks all kinds of berries on the berry picking places on the mountains of Knights Inlet and therefore she has many berry cakes and crabapples and Viburnum. She is rich in property, for the woman is industrious. That is the end. (Boas, 1969:283-284)

As an example of a rite for a young boy, we will use the Omaha ceremony of the "Consecration of the Boy to Thunder." This ceremony is the follow up to the "Turning of the Child," if the child is a boy. In this ceremony the boy's hair was cut "from the crown of the boy's head."

The severing of the lock was an act that implied the consecration of the life of the

Woman and child, Havasupai, 1897, G. Wharton James. (Courtesy of Museum of American Indian, Heye Foundation)

boy to Thunder, the symbol of the power that controlled the life and death of the warrior—for the power that controlled the life and death of the warrior—*for every man had to be a warrior* in order to defend the home and the tribe. (Fletcher & LaFlesche, 1911:122)

This states very simply the role and status of the warrior in the tribe.

INSTRUCTION AND THE FAMILY

As children grew physically and ceremonially, their places as men and women were clearly defined by tradition and observation. Instruction often came in the form of "lecturing." Of this system of teaching, "traditional education," a Winnebago describes his experience as a teacher.

I still keep up the old system of teaching my children at the camp fire. In the morning I wake them up early and start to teach them as follows:

My children, as you travel along life's road never harm anyone, nor cause anyone to feel sad. On the contrary, if at any time you can make a person happy, do. If at any time you meet a woman in the wilderness (i.e., away from your village), and if you are alone and no one can see, do not scare her or harm her, but turn off to the right and let her pass. Then you will be less tempted to molest her.

My children, if you meet anyone on the road, even though it is only a child, speak a cheering word before you pass on. Fast as much as you can, so that when you grow up you can benefit your fellowmen. If you ever get married you must not sit around your lodge near your wife, but try and get game for your wife's people. So fast that you may be prepared for your life.

My daughters, if at any time you get married, never let your husband ask for a thing twice. Do it as soon as he asks you. If your husband's folks ever ask their children for something when you are present, assume that they had asked it of you. If there is anything to be done, do not wait till you are asked to do it, but do it immediately. If you act this way, then

they will say that your parents taught you well.

My son, if you find nothing else to do, take an ax and chop down a tree. It will become useful some day. Then take a gun and go out hunting and try to get game for your family.

As soon as I see that the children are showing signs of restlessness then I stop immediately. (Radin, 1970:132)

Among all tribes this method of instructing the young was used. It taught rights of individuals, morals, and standards of behavior. It also indicated what would result if any of the above were violated.

So continued this lecturing or counseling until young people reached adolescence, which was considered a time of maturity. In childhood awareness of life usually comes through inevitable contact or experience with death. Of this state in life it was eloquently described by the Omaha in the expression, "old enough to know sorrow." It pertained to the "period when the youth is at the verge of his conscious individual life...[and] should enter into personal relations with the mysterious power that permeates and controls nature as well as his own existence." These kinds of personal relationships, when people began to make sacred commitments, usually occurred in adolescence.

Following adolescence and initiation of young people into manhood and womanhood, marriage was the next major step in life's path; marriage and the family relationship. Young men and women began to seriously consider the responsibility for perpetuating human life by making a family (among other things). The family relationship was the center and core of the tribe. Below is a Pomo interpretation of "family."

What is a man? A man is nothing. Without his family he is of less importance than that bug crossing the trail... A man must be with his family to amount to anything with us. If he had nobody else to help him, the first trouble he got into he would be killed by his enemies because there would be no relatives to help him fight the poison of the other group. No woman would marry him because her family would not let her marry a man with no family. He would be poorer than a newborn child; he would be poorer than a worm, and the family would not consider him worth anything. He would not bring renown or glory with him. He would not bring support of other relatives either. The family is important. If a man has a large family and a profession and upbringing by a family that is known to produce good children, then he is somebody and every family is willing to have him marry a woman of their group. It is the family that is important.

"Without the family we are nothing, and in the old days before the white people came the family was given the first consideration by anyone who was about to do anything at all. That is why we got along. We had no courts, judges, schools, and the other things you have, but we got along better than you. We had poison, but if we minded our own business and restrained ourselves, we lived well. We were taught to leave people alone. We were taught to consider that other people had to live. We were taught that we would suffer from the devil, spirits, ghosts, or other people if we did not support one another. The family was everything, and no man ever forgot that. Each person was nothing, but as a group joined by blood the individual knew that he would get the support of all his relatives if anything happened. He also knew that if he was a bad person, the head man of his family would pay another tribe to kill him so that there would be no trouble afterward and so that he would not get the family into trouble all of the time.

"That is why we were good people and why we were friends with the white people when they came. But the white people were different from us. They wanted to take the world for themselves. My grandfather told me that the white people were homeless and had no families. They came by themselves and settled on our property. They had no manners. They did not know how to get along with other people. They were strangers who were rough and common and did not know how to behave.

We would not bury our dead with no show. We would kill another person by poisoning him if he was an enemy, but we would not treat a stranger the way they treat their own brothers and sisters.

"With us the family was everything. Now it is nothing. We are getting like the white people, and it is bad for the old people. We had no old peoples' homes like you. The old people were important. They were wise. Your old people must be fools." (Aginsky, 1944:43-44)

STATUS OF THE AGED

Historically, the status of the aged in North American Indian tribes was one of honor and respect because having lived long entitled both men and women to certain privileges not extended to other members of the tribe. Among the Gros Ventres, now located in Montana, "It was believed that a person who had lived to a ripe old age had been privileged to do so by the Supreme Being." It was from these elderly people that young people

Pomo man carrying basket of wood with burden strap, ca. 1890. H. W. Henshaw. (Courtesy of the Smithsonian Institution, National Anthropological Archives)

requested names and blessings. This was done because these elderly people were thought to be favored people.

Therefore...if you are good to old people, these in turn will pray to the Supreme Being for your health, long life, and success. Children were instructed explicitly to be good to the aged, to feed them, to clothe and to help them in difficulties, as well as to seek out those so blessed and ask for their prayers. (Cooper, 1957: 195)

Among all tribes, elderly people had certain rights. They could give advice, lecture and counsel younger people. Whether the advice or counseling was heeded or not was another matter. But it was the right of elderly people to make their opinions known. Often elderly people held positions of authority in the household. Older people often spoke of their age and what it meant in terms of life's cycle.

...men can better their existence and soften the harshness of fate. Now I no longer feel alone, and my old age is a restful time. But when I chance to think of my childhood and recall all the memories from those days, then youth seems a time when all meat was juicy and tender, and no game to swift for a hunter. When I was young, every day was as a beginning of some new thing, and every evening ended with the glow of the next day's dawn. Now, I have only the old stories and songs that I sang myself in the days when I delighted to challenge my comrades to a song-contest in the feasting house. (Rasmussen, 1930:17)

The preceding speaker was an Iglulik Eskimo man called Ivaluarjuk. The second speaker is Maria Chona, a Papago woman.

It has been a long time since my children were married. My old husband and I lived with them, and then we lived with our grandchildren. Thirty years my husband and I were together. He grew blind. He lay on his mattress all day long, and I had to pull it round the house to keep it in the shade. All the time he sang. He knew every song in the world, and he lay there singing in a low voice. Sometimes he slept in the day when it was warm and he sang in the night. We would wake up in the night and hear him singing.

Seven years ago he died. He said, "Now I'm going to rest and you shall rest, too." He meant I need not work for him any more, pulling that mattress around the house.

"But I won't come when I am dead to frighten you," he said. "Only when it's time for you to go. Then I'll come to call you. But not yet, I will not call you yet. First you'll hear some man say: 'I want to marry you.' "

The next year I did. I had great grandchildren then, but still a man came and asked me to go to his house. But I was tired, I said: "No, I am too old. I cannot cook for you."

So I stay now with my grandchildren. Don't you think my baskets are good? I make them all day—all day long, and the young women do the cooking.

While I work I hear voices: "Put a turtle there! Put a Gila monster here! Here put a zigzag." Then I seem to see a woman holding up the finished basket and I know how it will be.

I like to work at my daughter's house, at the Burnt Seeds. She has corn meal there and cactus seeds. I can eat when I live there, and every year I go with her to the drinking ceremony. They want me, for I can sing. But when I go to someone's house I have to stay a long time before I can walk back. It is not good to be old. Not beautiful. When you come again, I will not be here. (Maria Chona, in Underhill, 1936:63-64)

Perhaps the most controversial privilege extended to many elderly native people, in the last century, by family and by the tribe, was the right to determine when and where his own death might come about. This custom has been documented in written histories of native peoples. Abandoning an elderly person was practiced by some groups on occasion, such as during war times. However, these were voluntary acts on the part of elderly people, and on behalf of the entire tribe. In order to

Three generations, Leech Lake Reservation, ca. 1929. (Courtesy of Minnesota Historical Society)

help understand this custom, one must remember that in most tribes, with very few exceptions, death was not looked upon as a fearful thing. Neither was it conceived to be the *end* of anything. This belief does not contradict the role one has on the path of life where one strives to live well, in order to attain a full life and reach old age. The concepts of life and death are related and similar.

DEATH AND THE PATH

On the path of life, one is continually prepared for his/her life *and* death. Death is greatly respected because it is inevitable. Death was conceived to be more-or-less a state or time of transition. Chief Seattle said of this, "There is no death. Only a change of worlds." The path of life could then be said to extend into death. Many tribes incorporated this idea in their rituals of burial, and other major ceremonies. There was a specific place one's self, or soul must journey to in the afterlife. Harold Goodsky (Anishnabe) volunteers more information, concerning the path one must take up, after death.

I buried my dad too long ago and it was one of the hardest things I have ever done. Buried him in a traditional Indian

ceremony. One of the things I really got out of that [was] I could never go through this whole concept of Indian burial. It has a lot to do with people that were here, your own relatives, your relations that passed on before you (and animals) that are going to help you. One of the various things that caught me in there is along side the way, on the way, by the happy hunting ground—there's going to be a big dog waiting there for you. In some instances it pertains to cats, or whatever, a bear. The things that you've done in your life will get back at you and it'll take you longer to get to the happy hunting ground, or it might be their way of saying you might spend your life [death] in limbo.

The sins that you've committed here against animals or your own people will be waiting for you when you go to the happy hunting ground and that would stop your entrance...cause there will be a big dog waiting for you when you reach the fork in the path to where you are going.

The medicine man said this dog would be standing there, but don't worry about him. You have nothing to fear if you've been or done all right to animals and etc. You have nothing to fear.

...You know I was telling you before about the dog, and how it relates to my dad's death—when you meet the dog, or when you meet some other type of animal, who'll threaten him [father] and if my dad has no guilt or any conscience whatsoever, or no guilt of what this thing represented or who it represented, he'll get to the happy hunting ground, was my interpretation of it.

ANISHNABE PATH

Some will be trying to entice you, to stop you from going the right way, but the person whose with you will lead you through it, and the journey is supposed to take five days or seven. That is a brief

discussion of it. It is really a beautiful ceremony. (H. Goodsky, 1975)

Several other tribes describe their roads and the encounters. A Winnebago gives this description.

I will tell you about this road, and what I tell you, that is how you shall go, that is what I am going to speak about to you. Now the very first thing you will encounter will be this. You will come upon a ravine. It will be quite unpassable. It will extend to both ends of the earth right into the water; that kind of a ravine it will be. You will look about from one end to the other but it will be found to be impossible to circumvent it. "But what did my grandfather say when I asked, 'How will I get through?'" Did you not think that he said "Plunge right through?" And thus you will do; go right through it, go through it completely. The footprints of the members of the Medicine Rite will be plainly visible and in these you must step. You will be walking along quite nicely and then you will come to quite a number of

Chippewa burials and mourners. (Courtesy of Minnesota Historical Society)

sticks (brushwood), sharp-criss-crossing-tangled. It will be impossible to get through this tangle for at no point will it seem possible to penetrate it; everything will stop right there. But, nevertheless, you must try to go right through. Indeed as you look from end to end it will not seem possible to circumvent it. "My grandfather said that I was to go right through," so he said to me. Thus you should act. Nothing will happen to you. Continue on right along and you will come upon evil little birds and the din they create will fill your ears. However he told me, "You should simply listen." Then, go on. Evil-and-foul phlegm will fall upon you and endeavor to adhere to you. Do not attempt to brush it off, do not pay any attention to it. Now you might forget yourself and brush it off. But that is not the proper way to behave, and if you act correctly-and-properly here, it will mean life to you afterwards, it is said.

And then, after a while, you will come to where half of the earth is burning. It will not be possible to pass through this half, it will not be possible to circumvent it. This will be scorching-you-and-impeding-you, but you will go through it. Remember, "My grandfather said I would be able to pass through it anyway." Plunge through it and then you will go on. You will go through the other side and nothing will happen to you. Very safely you will have gone through it. Never be discouraged. This it is that constitutes life.

Then go on. The fourth obstacle you will encounter will be perpendicular cliffs. It will not seem possible to pass through them. At each end they will appear uncircumventable, at each end it will seem as if you would be stepping into the ocean. "My grandfather said I was to go right on." Remember this. Then plunge right through and pass through it. Nothing will happen to you. You will pass through it quite safely. Thus will you obtain life. This life is what they the Medicine Rite members are trying to obtain. Then go right on. Soon a hill will come in view. Go towards it.

Then you will come to the foot of the hill. There you will find what you are to eat, dried bear-ribs, mixed with sacred-spirit food and permeated with life-and-light. When you are finished eating you are to climb this hill and there you should look about you. Indeed you are to look ahead of you, you must look ahead. Ahead of you the road will be full of hazel. Brushwood. The people ahead will take-hold-of-you-and-lead-you. Behind you, if you look, you will not see anything or anybody; you will be the last one walking along. After a while you will see another hill. Towards it you must go, for it is the place of their destination, that of the Medicine Rite members a most beautiful country, the place of red rock; there you will be going. Right to the very foot of the hill you should go and when you get there you will find food, you will find a greasy kettle. There you must eat and, when you are finished eating you are to climb the hill. When you get to the top of the hill you are to look ahead of you. There will be less people than you saw before. When you look behind you, as you go along, some will now be following you. And then you should go on. A third hill will now come in view and towards this you are to go. When you get to the foot of this hill you will find clusters of red willows and reeds; towards these you will have been going. At the foot of the hill there will be food piled up for you to eat and presents of the most pleasing kind. There you are to eat. Now when you have climbed to the middle of this hill you should take a rest. From there, where you are resting, you will notice a reddish smoke. Then you will continue your steps to the top of the hill and stand still and there you should look ahead of you. You will notice not so many people ahead of you as before. If you look behind you, on the contrary, where before you had been the very last one, now there will be many following you and in back of you. They will take hold of you and lead you. Then you should go right on. Ahead of you a fourth hill will now come into view. Towards it you should go and in that direction you will come to a most pleasant country of white poplars. Again you will come to the foot of the hill. There you will come upon something to eat; most pleasing food and presents will be there. There you should eat. When you have finished eating then you should climb, directing your steps to the top of this hill and stand there. If you look in front of you, not anyone will be there; but if you look behind you, the place from which you started will seem only a short distance. Behind you, from the place where you started, this will be full of people following you. Then you should go on. You will not have gone very far before you get to a large, oval lodge and this you should enter. "Greetings, grandson, how have you been behaving?" "Grandfather, I do not know." Then he will tell you. He will say to you, "However, grandson, I know; you have behaved well. But now, grandson, eat." Thus he will speak to you. Right in front of you, there a dish will be placed containing the meat of a horned, white-haired animal, the horns scorched in different places; this will be mixed with sacred-spirit food. This you should eat; four times you should put it in your mouth. Then, again, a second plate will be given you and again you must eat four mouthfuls; then there will be a third plate and again you must eat four mouthfuls; then there will be a fourth plate and again you must eat four mouthfuls. Then you will be starting out to go on, your body having the appearance of a dog, your body looking like a fly. You will not lose consciousness right away, however. The ladder which is the possession of the Medicine Rite members will be there. Now the right end side of this ladder is like a frog's leg, twisted, and dappled with light-and-life. The other end is like a red cedar, blackened-from-frequent-usage and very smooth-and-shiny. You must grab hold of this ladder by both ends. Then you will come to where earthmaker sits and when you get there those who dearly love you, your relatives, will recognize-and-receive you. This is a place over which evil winds never burst upon man, where no one is ever in want

of food, food of any animal, where no one has to work and where everything is most pleasant-and-delectable.

Earthmaker's servants will come after you to conduct you to him. Then earthmaker will address you and say: "You have done well and if you wish to return to life again, you may, to whatever tribe of people you desire. Whenever you wish to be born again and live you may do it. Indeed you can, if you wish, come to life again in the form of an animal." Thus he will speak to you. (Radin, 1969:69-71)

In some funeral customs of North American Indians, the spirit of the deceased is addressed, directed, and encouraged on its journey. The first example, of preparation for the journey by the family of the deceased is described by William W. Warren, Ojibway.

When an Ojibway dies his body is placed in a grave, generally in a sitting posture, facing the west. With the body are buried all the articles needed in life for a journey. If a man, his gun, blanket, kettle, fire steel, flint and moccasins; if a woman, her moccasins, axe, portage collar, blanket and kettle. The soul is supposed to start immediately after the death of the body, on a deep beaten path, which leads westward; the first object he comes to, in following this path, is the great Ode-e-min (Heart berry), or strawberry, which stands on the roadside like a huge rock, and from which he takes a handful and eats on his way. He travels until he reaches a deep, rapid stream of water, over which lies the much dreaded Ko-go-gaup-o-gun, or rolling and sinking bridge; once safely over this as the traveler looks back it assumes the shape of a huge serpent swimming, twisting and untwisting its folds across the stream.

After camping out four nights, and traveling each day through a prairie country, the soul arrives in the land of spirits, where he finds his relatives accumulated since mankind was first created; all is rejoicing, singing and dancing; they live in a beautiful country

Tamarac Lake, Chippewa burials, 1941. (Courtesy of Minnesota Historical Society)

interspersed with clear lakes and streams, forests and prairies, and abounding in all that the red man most covets in this life, and which conduces most to his happiness. It is that kind of paradise which he only by his manner of life on this earth, is fitted to enjoy. (McLuhan, 1972:33)

The next description is representative of the Winnebago burial custom, and is the speech of the chief mourner. He first addresses the mourners and then the deceased is addressed by another mourner.

I greet you all. I know that I am not performing any great action in greeting you, but I was in trouble, and all my relatives have come to comfort me. I feel strengthened by their actions. You all have asked me to live (not to sucumb to my sorrows), and I shall try to overcome my grief and sorrow. I will not forget all the good you have done for me. You have been a comfort to me and you have helped me in many things. Now this is the last night and I am glad that it is a good night for the warriors to relate their experiences. If they should say anything funny, I hope that you will not hold back your laughter. I, too, will laugh with you. You are free to make all the noise you care to, for I will feel all the better if you do it. This is what I want you to remember. I greet you all who are present here.

Then the one who is to address the spirit speaks:

I greet you all. We have come to this (wake) for a purpose, much as we would wish that the occasion for it had never happened. Now I will tell the spirit of the departed the route he is to take, nor will I, by my words, cause him to go astray. On an occasion like this not everyone can talk to spirits (spirits of departed people); not everyone can do it. My grandfather obtained the right to speak to them and handed it down to my father, and he in turn gave it to me. Now I will tell the spirit of the departed the right road to take and I will not cause him to stumble. I shall breathe upon the spirit of the departed, and I wish all those present to do the same. It is said that for those who do not make this sound it is a sign that they will die soon. Now all of you say it.

Then he says "ha-a" and "ha-a," and all join with him in repeating it.

Then he speaks again (addressing the spirit of the departed):

I suppose you are not far away, that indeed you are right behind me. Here is the tobacco and here is the pipe which you must keep in front of you as you go along. Here also is the fire and the food which your relatives have prepared for your journey. In the morning when the sun rises you are to start. You will not have gone very far before you come to a wide road. That is the road you must take. As you go along you will notice something on your road. Take your war club and strike it and throw it behind you. Then go on without looking back. As you go farther you will again come across

[some obstacle]. Strike it and throw it behind you and do not look back. The object you throw behind you will come to those relatives whom you have left behind you on earth. They will represent victory in war, riches, and animals for food. When you have gone but a short distance from the last place where you threw objects behind, you will come to a round lodge and there you will find an old woman. She is the one who is to give you further information. She will ask you, "Grandson, what is your name?" This you must tell her. Then (you must say), "Grandmother, when I was about to start from the earth I was given the following objects with which I was to act as mediator between you and the human beings (i.e., the pipe, tobacco, and food)." Then you must put the stem of the pipe in the old woman's mouth and say, "Grandmother, I have made all my relatives lonesome, my parents, my brothers, and all the others. I would therefore like to have them obtain victory in war and honors. That was my desire as I left them downhearted upon the earth. I would that they could have all that life which I left behind me on earth. This is what they asked. This likewise they asked me, that they should not have to travel on this road for some time to come. They also asked to be blessed with those things that people are accustomed to have on earth. All this they wanted me to ask of you when I started from the earth.

"They told me to follow the four steps that would be imprinted with blue marks, grandmother." "Well, grandson, you are young but you are wise. It is good. I will now boil some food for you."

Thus she will speak to you and then put a kettle on the fire and boil some rice for you. If you eat it, you will have a headache. Then she will say, "Grandson, you have a headache, let me cup it for you." Then she will break open your skull and take out your brains and you will forget all about your people on earth and where you came from. You will not worry about your relatives. You will become like a holy spirit. Your thoughts will not go as far as the earth, as there will be nothing carnal about you.

Now the rice that the old woman will boil will really be lice. For that reason you will be finished with everything evil. Then you will go on stepping in the four footsteps mentioned before and that were printed with blue earth. You are to take the four steps because the road will fork there. All your relatives (who died before you) will be there. As you journey on you will come to a fire running across the earth from one end to the other. There will be a bridge across it but it will be difficult to cross because it is continually swinging. However, you will be able to cross it safely, for you have all the guides about whom the warriors spoke to you. They will take care of you.

Well, we have told you a good road (to take). If anyone tells a falsehood in speaking of the spirit road, you will fall off the bridge and be burned. However, (you need not worry) for you will pass over safely. As you proceed from that place the spirits will come to meet you and take you to the village where the chief lives. There you will give him the tobacco and ask for those objects of which we spoke to you, the same you asked of the old woman. There you will meet all the relatives that died before you. They will be living in a large lodge. This you must enter. Ho-o-o, Ha-a-a. (Radin, 1970:94-96)

We have seen that the Road of Life has been spoken of frequently with blessings such as in the ceremonies and prayers shared here. There are countless other tribal ceremonies and prayers...which could not be used here, but if they could have they would serve the same purpose to show how the people, in the past, traveled the road of life. For instance, in many Navajo chants, prayers, and songs, the "Pollen Path" is mentioned and of course other tribes have similar descriptions for familiar roads they have been compelled to follow.

We find that through the sacred means of ceremonies, song and prayer the Road of Life and Death has been given a great deal of power by the people. This is done because at specific points in a man or woman's life (path), he or

Crow woman and child. (Courtesy of Museum of American Indian, Heye Foundation)

she may not want to continue (living). The confrontations one has during life (the path) have been powerfully and emotionally felt. These confrontations might be representative of love, pain, or separation. Ultimately, people realize that eventually he/she must meet death. As a result of these confrontations, people sometimes ask themselves, "Well, if we know we are going to die, or if we must die eventually, then why is life so hard?" Through these roads or paths people choose to follow, life is given meaning, purpose, and responsibility. And as stated at the beginning of the chapter, the path of life has a means of procedure to make life worthwhile and rewarding. We have seen that on the path, long life is considered the pinnacle of achievement for a human being despite, or perhaps because of the encounters along the way.

Another part to the Road, is the philosophy that the path will be the same for everyone, no matter how he travels it. In addition to this, it is important to note that it is said to be believed that in the end, one's own road shall meet and merge with that of his people. In conjunction with this idea, Dr. Ortiz closes this chapter with his reflections.

A wise elder among my people, the Tewa, frequently used the phrase Pin pe obi, "look to the mountaintop," while he was alive. I first heard it 25 years ago when I was seven years old, as I was practicing for the first time to participate in relay races we run in the Pueblo country to give strength to the sun father as he journeys across the sky. I was at one end of the earth track which ran east to west, like the path of the sun. The old man, who was blind, called me to him and said: "Young one, as you run look to the mountaintop," and he pointed to Tsikomo, the western sacred mountain of the Tewa world, which loomed off in the distance. "Keep your gaze fixed on that mountain, and you will feel the miles melt beneath your feet. Do this and in time you will feel as if you can leap over bushes, trees, and even the river." I tried to understand what this last statement meant, but I was too young.

On another occasion a few days later, I asked him if I really could learn to leap over treetops. He smiled and said, "Whatever life's challenges you may face, remember always look to the mountaintop, for in so doing you look to greatness. Remember this, and let no problem, however great it may seem, discourage you nor let anything less than the mountaintop distract you. This is the one thought I want to leave with you. And in that dim coming time when we shall meet again, it shall be on the mountaintop." Again I wondered why he was telling me these words and what they meant. I did not have long to wonder why, for the following month, when the cornstalks were sturdy on the land, he died quietly in his sleep having seen eighty seven summers.

Although he knew I was too young to understand, he also knew there was not much time left to impart his message to me and, perhaps, to others like me. In accordance with our beliefs, the ancestors were waiting for him at the edge of the village that day he died, waiting to take him on a final four-day journey to the four sacred mountains of the Tewa world. A Tewa must either be a medicine man in a state of purity or he must be dead before he can safely ascend the *sacred mountain*. This final journey always ends when the ancestral spirits and the one who has returned enter a lake near the top of any of the sacred mountains, for these lakes are the homes of the gods.

In the most basic, trancendental sense, then, life for a Tewa consists of trying to fathom the meaning of these words, "look to the mountaintop," for they contain a guiding vision of life, a vision evolved through untold millenia of living on this land. Only in recent years have I come fully to realize that this was a priceless gift, for it sums up a people's knowledge of what it means to be of a time and of a place, also beyond time and place. Yet I also know that I shall never fully understand all that is meant by these words, for if ever I or anyone living should do so, it would be time to rejoin the ancestors, to make the last journey to the mountaintop. (Ortiz, 1973:95-97)

Crow woman and child. (Courtesy of the Museum of the American Indian, Heye Foundation)

Suggested Additional Reading

DYKE, WALTER (ed.)
1967 *Son of Old Man Hat: A Navajo Autobiography.* Lincoln: University of Nebraska.

FANSHEL, DAVID
1973 *Far From the Reservation; The Transracial Adoption of American Indian Children.* Metuchen, N.J.: Scarecrow Press.

INTERTRIBAL COUNCIL OF NEVADA
1974 *Etok: A Story of Eskimo Power.* New York: G.P. Putnam.

PELLETIER, WILFRED
 Two Articles. Toronto: Newin Publishing Co., n.d.

SPRADLEY, JAMES P. (ed.)
1969 *Guests Never Leave Hungry: Autobiography of James Sewid, a Kwakiutl Indian.* New Haven: Yale University Press.

WEBB, GEORGE
1959 *A Pima Remembers.* Tucson: University of Arizona.

CHAPTER NINE

HOKE DENETSOSIE

9 Girls' Puberty Ceremonies

Maria Chona, a Papago woman, begins this chapter by telling us the story of her participation in the Papago girls' puberty ceremony and the story of the ceremony's origin.

When I was nearly as tall as my mother, that thing happened to me which happens to all our women though I do not know if it does to the Whites; I never saw any signs. It is called menses.

Girls are very dangerous at that time. If they touch a man's bow, or even look at it, that bow will not shoot any more. If they drink out of a man's bowl, it will make him sick. If they touch the man himself, he might fall down dead. My mother had told us this long ago and we knew what had happened in our village.

There was a girl once who became dangerous and she did not tell. They were having a good time that day. All the village was planting in her father's field, and he had given them a meal of succotash. They were eating out in the field, her mother was cooking over a campfire. My mother was there and she said this girl was standing with a bowl in the crook of her arm, laughing and eating. It began to rain. The girl and her sisters ran home to take in the bedding, because we sleep out of doors in the summer and it was on the ground.

There was a crash of thunder. All the eating people stood still and then, from the house of that girl they heard a long sigh. They ran there. All the family were lying stunned on the floor, one sister was blind, and that girl was dead. The men dragged the people out into the rain and the house began to burn. "See," said those people, "what has happened to us." Her relatives buried that girl all alone and no one would go near.

Then there was a girl who was going to build a fire, and it seemed that it reached out, and took her, and burned her up. And there was another whose mother was struck by lightning. For it is not always you who are hurt if you commit this sacrilege; it may be anyone in your family.

That is why, when the lightning strikes a village, they send for the medicine man to see what woman was dangerous. He summons all the girls and looks at his crystals to see who did it. They do not punish that woman. It is enough to know that she has killed her friends.

Our mothers watch us, and so mine knew when it came to me. We always had the Little House ready, over behind our own house. It was made of some branches stuck in the ground and tied together at the top, with greasewood thrown over them to make it shady. There was no rain then, for it was winter, but it was cold in that little house. The door was just big enough to crawl through, like our house door, and there was room for you to lie down inside, but not to stand up. My mother made me a new bowl and drinking cup out of clay, and put them in that house. When my mother cooked food at the big house, she would come over and pour some in my bowl, but no meat and nothing with salt in it. My father sharpened a little stick for me to scratch my hair with, because if I touched it, it would fall out. I was so afraid to lose my nice long hair that I kept that stick in my mouth all the time. Even when I was asleep, I had it there.

It is a hard time for us girls, such as the men have when they are being purified. Only they give us more to eat, because we are women. And they do not let us sit still and wait for dreams. That is because we are women, too. *Women must work.*

They chose my father's cousin to take care of me. She was the most industrious woman we had, always running with the carrying basket. That old woman would come for me in the dark when morning-stands-up. "Come," she said, "Let's go for water over across the mountain. Let's go for firewood." So, we would run, far far across the flat land and up the mountain and bring the water back before daylight. I would leave it outside my father's house and not go in. Then that old woman would talk to me.

"Work hard. If you do not work hard now, you will be lazy all your life. Then no one will want to marry you. You will have to take some good for nothing man for a husband. But if you are industrious, we shall find you a good old man."

That is what we call our husbands—old man. But this woman did it out of modesty, too, so that I should not have young men in my mind. "When you have an old man," she said, "you will grind the corn for him and you will always have water there for him to drink. Never let him go without food. He will go to the houses of someone else to eat and you will be disgraced."

I listened to her. Do you say that some girls might think of other things and not listen? But I wanted to be a good woman! And I have been. Ask anyone in our village if they ever saw me with idle hands. Or legs, either, when I was younger.

All the girls came around the Little House while that woman talked. They did not come near, because that would not be safe, and she would call to them: "Go away." But they sat and listened and when she was tired of talking, they laughed and sang with me. And we played a game with the little stones and a ball. We pick up the stones in different ways with one hand while we catch the ball in the other. Oh, we have good times at the Little House, especially when that first month is over. But other women who were dangerous did not come; that would be too much.

I had to stay four days and then I was not dangerous anymore. Everything goes by fours with our people and Elder Brother arranged it that even this thing should be the same. No woman has trouble for more than four days. Then they gave me a bath just as they did to my father. Oh, it was cold in the winter time! I tell the girls who come of age in the summer they do not know what hardship is. The water even feels nice in summer.

My mother came in the dark of the morning with the water in a big new jar. The women had to run all day to get that water ready for me. I tried to get away, but my mother caught me and made me kneel down. Then she dipped a gourd in the jar and poured that cold water down over my forehead.

Hail!
I shall pour this over you.
You will be one who endures cold.
You will think nothing of it.

It is true, I have never felt cold. Then my mother washed my hair with soap-weed fibres. That is the way women should always wash their hair and it will never grow gray. She cut it so it came just to my shoulders, for we women cannot have hair so long as the men; it would get in our way when we work. But we like to have it thick and shiny, and we know that everybody is noticing. There was quite a lapful that my mother cut off, and she saved it to make hair ropes for our carrying baskets. She had new clothes for me; two pieces of unbleached muslin, tied around my waist with a string. We did not know how to sew in those days. We pinned them together over our hips with bought pins, but it was very modest.

Then I could go back to our house, only still I had to use the stick for four days and I could not eat salt. And then they danced me. All that month they danced me, until the moon got back to the place where it had been at first. *It is a big time when a girl comes of age; a happy time.* All the people in the village knew that I had been to the Little House for the first time, so they come to our

Papago woman mending a coiled basket outside brush house. San Xavier Reservation, Arizona, 1894. William Dinwiddie.
(Courtesy of the Smithsonian Institution, National Anthropological Archives)

house and the singer for the maidens came first of all.

That singer was the Chief's Leg, the man I told you about. He knew all the songs, the ones that Elder Brother first sang when he used to go over the country, dancing all the maidens. That Leg was the man who danced every maiden in our village when she came of age. His wife danced opposite him. She was the one who was to get the hair that my mother had cut off. He had another wife, too, but not such a good dancer.

"Come out," said my father on that first night. "Now you must dance or the Leg will drag you out. He's mean."

I did not want to dance; I was sleepy and I had run so far. Always when I had heard the others singing those maiden songs, from far away, I had been wild to

go. But now it was my turn and all I wanted to do was sleep. But Luis, the Leg, came into the house and took me by the arm. He always danced next to the maiden, with his arm over her shoulders and the rattle in his other hand. He and I were at one end of a long line of people and his wife at the end of a line opposite. There was first a boy and than a girl, all down the line, with their arms over each other's shoulders and the blankets held along at the back. I told you the boys always liked that dance.

The lines went to and from, toward each other, and they kept wheeling a little, till at last they had made a circle.

On top of Baboquiviri Peak
There is a fire burning.
So near I came.
I saw it blow all over the ground

219

Shining.

On the flat land
There is a house of clouds
There stand white butterfly wings (of
   clouds).
It pleased me. That was what I saw.

There were the songs they sang, with the rattle going in the night. We had no fire; we kept warm dancing. After every four songs Luis stopped, because his voice was hoarse. Then he let me go, and we girls went and sat together while the men smoked. How dark and cold it was then, with only one ember to light their cigarettes!

There were girls who did not come to sit with us and boys who did not sit with the men. How dark it was! Some mothers went looking for their girls in the night and some did not.

At midnight my mother brought jars of succotash. She had been cooking all day for this dance, and every day after that she cooked and ground corn and baked bread in the ashes. Every morning we gave gifts to Luis and his wife. My cut-off hair and dried beans and cooked food and the hand woven cotton that I wore for a dress. And to the girl friends who danced beside me, I gave my beads and my baskets because these people had suffered and endured sleeplessness with us.

We stopped dancing in the dark of the morning and then my mother said: "Come and get firewood. Do you want to grow up a lazy woman?" So then I went out in the dark to pick up the dead branches and bring them back before I slept. It seemed I slept only an hour before they were saying "get up! Get water. Get wood. Grind the corn. If you sleep at this time, you will be sleepy all your life."

Oh, I got thin in that time. We girls are like strips of yucca fibre after our coming of age is over. Always running, and mostly gruel and ash bread to eat, with no salt. And dancing every night from the time the sun sets until morning-stands-up. I used to go to sleep on Luis' arm and he pinched my nose to wake me.

Every night they came, the people who were not too sleepy from the night before. And always the young people came. Even Luis did not know songs enough for all that month and other men sang, too. It is a nice thing for a man to know maidens' songs. Every man likes to dance next to the maiden and to hold her on his arm. But Luis was an old man and his wife danced opposite. The wife always does.

At last the moon had come around again and they gave me a bath. It was over. I looked like half of myself. All my clothes were gone. All our dried corn and beans were eaten up. But I was grown up. Now the medicine man could cleanse me and give me a name.

You have to be cleansed as soon as the month is over; you must not wait. A cousin of mine did that once. She meant to be cleansed but she just waited. I think, perhaps, she did not have anything to pay the medicine man. But while she waited, one of her brothers was chopping wood. Something fell on him like a hot coal and killed him. So I went the day after my bath.

My mother and I went to the house of the medicine man early in the morning, with a big basket my mother had made, to pay him. He drew a circle on the ground and made me sit in it, cross-legged, with my back to the rising sun. In front of me he put a little dish. Then he walked away where we could not see him and took something out of a little deerskin bag. It was the clay that he carries to charm the evil away from women. No one ever sees the medicine man dig up the clay and no one knows how he mixes it. But I know, because my brother was a medicine man and because I myself have seen things.

He put that clay in a tiny bowl before me, mixed with a little water. Then he walked up and down four times, facing the sun that was behind me. Everytime he came up to me he blew over my head and dusted me off with his eagle feathers to brush away the evil. And every time he turned he made a noise like an owl. The fifth time he took up the bowl of clay and stirred it around with a little owl feather that was standing in the center of it. Then he put the clay to my mouth. "Drink this up!" So I drank it all. Then he marked me, the sacred marks that are put on the men who have got salt from the magic ocean; the marks that take away bad luck and bring you a good life. On my breast, on my shoulders, my back, and my belly.

"Your name shall be Cha-vella." I did not know before what name he was going to give me, neither did my parents. The medicine man names one from his dreams. Some of my friends had names that could be understood like Leaf Buds, Rusting Leaves, Windy Rainbow, Dawn Murmur. But I have never understood my name and he did not tell me.

After all that work, I did not menstruate again for a year! (In Underhill and Chona, 1936:31-36)

MENSTRUATION: PRACTICES AND BELIEFS

The beginning of menstruation was an important time in a young woman's life. *It signified womanhood.* In many tribes, she was welcomed into womanhood elaborately. It was the time girls were (and still are) taught what they should know about their future, about the role of the woman in the tribe. Instruction is sought for such a girl. It is given by their grandmothers, or through some other relationship.

The kind of instruction given at this time was usually in preparation for marriage, and her role thereafter. The initiation ceremony varied from tribe to tribe, but all the ceremonies had some common features. This is also true regarding the beliefs concerning menstruation.

(1) The menstruating women of the tribe, and the young women being initiated, were usually isolated from their families and remainder of the tribe for *four days*. (2) The patterns of behavior prescribed for menstruating women and pubescent girls were similar in their reasoning and objectives. (3) Menstruation was equated with power which could be utilized for healing or curing. The power had to be recognized by a woman and others around her. When she adhered to the prescribed rules of behavior, this power was acknowledged.

(4) A girl's puberty ceremony was usually a festive time for the people, though it might have been a test of endurance for a young woman.

When women were menstruating they separated themselves from other members of the family and the tribe. They did this because they believed that the power attributed to them might affect themselves or another in a negative way if they did not separate themselves.

Among the Cheyenne, the customs concerning women were recorded about the turn of the century by G. B. Grinnell. He obtained his information from the older women of the tribe. Here he presents, in his words, the Cheyenne custom concerning the power a woman possessed during the menstrual time. His interpretation, however, deals only with the negative aspects in regard to this power.

Young men will not eat from the dish nor drink from the pot used by her; one who did so would expect to be wounded in his next fight. She may not handle or even touch a shield or any other war

Cheyenne girl. (Courtesy of Museum of American Indian, Heye Foundation)

implement, nor may she touch any sacred bundle or object. If the camp moves, she may not ride a horse, but is obliged to ride a mare. Women in this condition are careful to avoid entering a lodge where there is a medicine bundle or bag. To do this is supposed to cause an increased flow.

A married woman during this time does not sleep at home, but goes out and sleeps in one of the menstrual lodges. Men believe that if they lie beside their wives at this time, they are likely to be wounded in their next battle. (Grinnell, 1904:14)

While in isolation the women took and ate their meals separately. They prepared the meals themselves or another woman who was attending to the needs of the women who were confined prepared them. There were definite food taboos within tribes. Some tribes such as the Winnebago, now located in Nebraska, the Washo of California and Nevada, and the Puyallup tribe, practiced fasting. Therefore, during the time they were secluded the women were not allowed to have anything to eat or drink, except water occasionally.

How a young woman behaved during her puberty ceremony was believed to give shape to her disposition and attitudes, influence her mental and physical health and well-being, and give meaning and understanding to her life.

...the Chiricahua believe that the disposition a girl shows at this time of the ceremony will be here all through life. If she gets angry, she is going to be mean the rest of her life. They say, too, that if a girl doesn't mind at this time, bad weather comes. If she is pleasant and goes through the ceremony well, she will always be that way.

And, it seems to me that it turns out this way. There's my wife. She went through the ceremony very well, obeyed, and was good. You take C., she was mean and balky... Today she's very mean. And now she's cross, has a bad mouth and a high temper. But she's a goodlooking woman all right! (Opler, 1965:93)

In the course of the ceremony, certain demands were made upon a young woman. How she reacted to those demands was to give evidence of her behavior in later life. The Washo people expected a young woman to "be active and not be lazy" during her "girl's dance" which is what they called the girl's ceremony.

If she behaved properly during the dance and the four days preceding it, she would be hard working, energetic, self-effacing, able to withstand hunger, generous, and able to endure discomfort all her life.

The view that at the time of her first menses a girl was malleable and that her entire life would be shaped by the way she behaved at this time was widespread. (Downs, 1966:24)

Another desired trait was modesty. Often it was called something else such as "being shy." Young women were encouraged to be modest. This modesty might be displayed with silence, or either by looking at the ground, and not looking at people in the face or eyes. To attain certain long-range goals of the ceremony such as long-life, a young woman was urged to fulfill the temporary demands of the ceremony which were ritually placed upon her.

That menstruation was associated with power, or was power in itself was an idea held once by most people of the world. Though it has been recorded that there were beliefs based upon fear of menstruating women, who might affect others (including male animals) who came in contact with her, it has also always been recorded that among Native Americans, there were beliefs that these women and pubescent girls could cure and heal as well.

My nojishe [grandchild], you cannot properly understand, without an illustration, how strong the mino manito [good spirit] and matchi manito [evil or bad spirit] are during this period.

When I was a young man I had many warts on my hands...I was almost covered by them. An old woman of my tribe [Anishnabe tribe] advised me to go to a girl who had built a bakan ishkotawe [refers to making a fire elsewhere, away

Havasupai woman weaving basket. (Courtesy of Museum of American Indian, Heye Foundation)

from own lodge] at some distance away from our odena [village], and who was undergoing the giigwishimowin [fasting] period, and have her cure me. I disliked the warts very much, and being ashamed of my ugly looking hands, I reluctantly concluded to follow her advice. I was warned about crossing her tracks and to approach the lodge from the side very carefully, and if I reached it safely, to pass my hands in the front and say, I have come to you to cure my hands.

I approached the lodge, passed my hands in, and repeated the words as directed. She wet her fingers with her saliva and touched all the warts on my hands, and when she had completed this, I retraced my steps and returned to the village. In five days, all the warts on my hands had disappeared. (Vizenor, 1970:30-31)

As a further example of these descriptions of power, a Cibeque Apache explains how a pubescent girl "is just like a medicine man, only with that power she is holy."

She can make you well if you are sick even with no songs. Anyone who doesn't feel good can come to her. It doesn't matter who it is. Sometimes, if there has

been no rain, they put that cane in the ground inside (a wickiup or shade) and ask her to sprinkle water on it. That way she can make it rain. I've seen it. (Basso, 1970:68)

The benefits received for undergoing a puberty ceremony are many for a young woman. She receives practical advice or instruction from an older woman on how to behave throughout her life. (Symbolically, this is done in the ceremony.) As stated earlier, the purpose of the ceremony is for the attainment of certain goals. Besides those specific goals already mentioned (modesty, endurance, etc.), there were general goals which included everything else. Old Age is probably the most familiar goal. It was and is believed that a young woman who had the ceremony was more likely to attain old age than a young woman who did not have the ritual performed for her. Then, during the ceremony, other aspects of womanhood were emphasized. She should be a worker, a "gatherer," modest, etc.

The puberty ceremony may be interpreted as isolating symbolically four critical life-objectives towards which all Apache girls on the threshold of adulthood should aspire. These are physical strength, an even temperament, pros-

223

perity, and a sound, healthy old-age. To understand why these particular life-objectives are emphasized, ...consider their relation to other aspects of Western Apache culture, powers, the role of women in native economy, the conduct of interpersonal relationships, and the natural environment.

...the puberty ceremonial not only defines longevity as a life-objective but also helps the girl attain it. (Basso, 1970:68)

The puberty ceremony in many tribes was usually an event that everyone could share through contribution and participation. The majority of tribes no longer perform the puberty ceremony for their young women for several reasons. Tribal groups are scattered and related families are often separated by great distances. This is important because it was often through these relationships in the tribe and family that a puberty ceremonial was possible. It required a good deal of energy from everybody involved if it were to be successful. The intent of the ceremony and the demands placed upon a young woman in the ceremony (demands which were once considered an absolute necessity for a long and fruitful life) have often been misunderstood. Consequently today, a young woman might have some misgivings about undergoing such a ceremony as this one described by the Cupeño. The Cupeño Indians are from California, related to the Cahuilla and the Luiseño Indians. The girl's custom is no longer practiced by the Cupeño.

They use to initiate the girls, *in order that they would not die*, for them to grow up beautiful. *A girl who had not been initiated was raw, she had not finished growing, she was sick.* And so the firetender called the people who did not live there, he named them, "Come here with your voices," and then they make the girls from outside stand up. And then the man calls over her three times, (her relatives) give him a basket. And then the girls' relatives take out things to throw, either money, clothes, or grain. They do the same to another girl. They call another person. Doing the same to that one, then they finish and they make them drink tobacco with water, they sprinkle water on them. And then they dig a hole in the ground, and when they finish they put down pachivat and wikut. And then

Luiseño women at Cabrillo celebration, California, 1892. (Courtesy of the Smithsonian Institution, National Anthropological Archives)

they covered them with that same grass. And then the women danced the feather dance. And now there they were, and then they sang, they made them sleep, they danced over them, they sang enemy songs. At night they sang to the rattle, there was much food, it went on many days. I saw them a few times initiating the girls, with the finest expensive things, many of their relatives would have spent a great deal in food, clothing, and money. From here and there they would arrive by parties, bringing their treasures to pick them up in that place, upon making exchange. They would pick them up before they would put down money. And they would arrive, they would come into the wamkish, the girls who were menstruating, the women would come doing the feather dance, they would sing the enemy songs, and at night the men would sing to the rattle, and then in the morning they would leave, others arriving in their place while many greetings were made. And they would come singing to the rattle, they would come singing enemy songs, and then the menstruating ones were on the fire, the ones they were going to roast. No matter how many, either two or three or four that each chief had children related to him who are living, those they closed up in the house, they secreted them. And then they would bring them out, all wrapped up with goods, they make them sit down, they sing over them, they throw things like tobacco, they make them drink. The men sang to the rattle at night, there was much food, it ran for many days. They would come from here and there in parties, bringing their treasure to pick up things in return. They would finish then, if the chief sees the food soon, then they do the same; one night they sing and in the morning they come, they do the same, they scatter things over them. And then they show them that sand painting which they made. And it is said there are three holes. And then first the people from outside go around with her, they put a little piece of meat in her mouth, they go around the sand painting with her, they showed the

ones who kill people when you are bad, when you steal, when you do bad things, so that you would not finish growing up. In the last place she would spit the meat out of her mouth to down in there, and if it just went straight into the hole, then her relatives would shout their enemy songs. And if the meat should come out slimy with her saliva, then they would be angry at the girl, for that showed that she is not going to do well. In that way they finish with all of them. After that then they would paint them with charcoal and white clay, and the wife of the firetender would paint them with black and white clay, and there are wreaths of pachivet. Then they would bring them the wreaths of pachivet, they put them away, they go with the girls and the boys and stand in a row. From there from the house the firetender shouts three times, then they run, the fastest runner arrives at the house first, and they do the same, the relatives meet them with their things to throw, then the mothers take the girls by the hand. They do not eat salt or meat; nothing but tasteless stuff do they eat; they drink warm water and then they make headpieces with hair; they put beads on them; they tie up their wrists with hair; they wrap nets around them. They paint their faces with red powder; they make straight lines on top with black; every morning one person who is related some way or other paints them and combs their hair. And then they eat; she comes to know some way or other that her painting is coming. And they say that those who are patient finish their paintings; they would repeat again, but the ones who were not patient would eat something in the middle. Those who have finished, their mothers sympathize with them, then they make them eat meat or something with salt in it, and then they would vomit. And it is said that long ago the ones who were initiated would get married, but I never saw that; this is the end of what I know. (Told by S. Valenzuela in Hill & Nolasquez, 1973: 33-35a)

There are other versions of this ceremony described by the Luiseño and Diegueño. In

225

Model of sandpainting for girls' ceremony. Luiseño. This sandpainting is supposed to represent the world or universe. (From Plate 17, Fig. 2, *Religions of the Luiseño Indians*, Constance Goddard DuBois, University of California Publications in American Archeology and Ethnology, Vol. 8, No. 3. Published in 1908 by the Regents of the University of California.)

some versions of the ceremony, young women might be tattooed on the face. They all make references to a sand painting made for the girl's ceremony. This ceremony was called "the roasting of girls."

The Diegueño, whenever questioned, say that the purpose of the ceremony is to make the girls live long. (Waterman, 1910:293)

ORIGINS OF MENSTRUATION

These people, the Diegueño, believed that the moon was responsible for women having their menses.

The moon was sent up into the sky to watch the people and regulate everything, and all goes according to the moon. Especially is this so in regard to women who have their menses, but men are also affected by it, and become strong or weak as the moon waxes and wanes. (du Bois, 1908:164)

The origin of menstruation, according to oral tradition, also explains the origin of taboos identified with menstruation.

Havasupai Origin of Menstruation

Squirrel and his daughter and Coyote lived together. The squirrel was a little older than the coyote; he was coyote's uncle. The squirrel went hunting and brought in a deer. While coyote was skinning it he put his finger in the blood and flipped it on the inside of the girl's thigh. Coyote said to her, "Sister, you are menstruating. You can't eat the meat for four days." When he said that, the girl didn't believe him. Finally she grew angry; coyote knew about menstruation, the girl didn't. . .(Smithson, 1971:36-37)

Catamenia, Omaha Origin of Menstruation

This...was considered as "Wakan'da a'cica," pertaining to Wakanda (sacred). In the myth of the Rabbit and the Black Bear, Mactcinge, the Rabbit threw a piece of the Black Bear chief against his grandmother, who had offended him, thereby causing her to have the catamenia. From that time women have been so affected. (Dorsey, 1970:267)

The Apache and Navajo, related groups, still perform the puberty rite. The Apachean groups credit White Painted Woman "with establishment of the puberty rite. Often associated with her in this undertaking is her son." Navajos identify Changing Woman as the figure who set the precedent for the *Kinaalda*, which is what the Navajo calls the girl's ceremony. The accurate or acceptable translation of *Kinaalda* is disputed by several people, including medicine men and scholars.

Apache version

It was not until Child of the Water (Son of White Painted Woman) was rid of all the monsters and evil things, until there were many people and the different tribes began to be seen, that the big tepee (girl's puberty rite) was known.

There was a woman who had a daughter who was almost grown. It was time for her to have her first flow. The Child of the Water and White Painted Woman showed them what to do; this good time was given to the people. (Opler, 1965:89)

Another Apache version

White Painted Woman said, "From here on we will have the girl's puberty rite. When the girls first menstruate, you shall have a feast. There shall be songs for these girls. During this feast the masked dancers shall dance in front. After that there shall be round dancing and face-to-face dancing. (Opler, 1965:89)

Navajo version by Frank Mitchell

I am going to tell the story I know about the beginning of the Kinaalda ceremony, its purpose, and why such thing were laid down for the people.

Kinaalda of Changing Woman

It was a long time ago the Changing Woman had her Kinaalda. She made herself become Kinaalda. She naturally became one. This happened after the creation of the Earth People. The ceremony was started so women would

Chippewa women weaving mat in shade of bark house. (Courtesy of Minnesota Historical Society)

Apache women and children. Fort Apache Reservation, Arizona, 1923. (Courtesy of the Smithsonian Institution, National Anthropological Archives)

be able to have children and the human race would be able to multiply. To do this, women had to have relations with men. *The Kinaalda was created to make it holy and effective, as the Holy People wanted it to be.* They called many meetings to discuss how they should do this ceremony.

In the beginning, there was fog at the top of Blanca Peak. After four days, the fog covered everything down to the base. Coyote, of course, went there to find out what was happening. When he went running over there, he saw a baby floating on the lake which was at the top of Blanca Peak. He wanted to pick up the baby and bring it back, but he was not able to. So he came back and reported it to Hashch'ehooghan (Hogan God). Hashch'ehooghan went over there and could not get it either. Then Talking God went there, got the baby out of the lake and brought it to the top of Gobernador Knob.

The one who was picked up as a new baby was Esdzaanadleehe (Changing Woman). She was taken home to be raised. In four days she grew up and became Kinaalda. When this happened, they decided to have a ceremony for her.

At this time, the Holy People were living on the earth. They came to her ceremony, and many of them sang songs for her. They did this so that she would be holy and so she could have children who would be human beings with enough sense to think of themselves and a language with which to understand each other.

The first Kinaalda took place at the rim of the Emergence Place in the First Woman's home. All kinds of Holy People were there. The first time that Changing Woman had it, they used the original Chief Hogan Songs. The second time, they used the Hogan Songs which belonged to Talking God.

The first ceremony took place at

Ch'ool'i'i (Gobernador Knob); this is a place that is now on the Jicarilla Apache Reservation. When Changing Woman became Kinaalda, Salt Woman, who was the First White Shell Woman, gave her her own name, "White Shell Woman." She dressed her in white shell clothes. Changing Woman was also painted with white shell; that is why she was called "White Shell Woman."

The Kinaalda started when White Shell Woman first menstruated. *It is still done the same way today.* At her first ceremony, White Shell Woman ran around the turquoise that was in the east. That is why the Kinaalda today wears turquoise. During her second ceremony, she started from the west, where there was white shell. The second menstruation was connected with white shell.

Nine days after that, Changing Woman gave birth to Naaghee' neezghani (Monster Slayer) and ToBajishchini' (Born for Water) twin boys. These two were put on earth so that all the monsters which were eating the human beings would be killed. They rid the earth of all these monsters; that is why they were called Holy People. As soon as they had done this, their mother, Changing Woman, who was then living at Gobernador Knob, left and went to her home in the west, where she lives today.

After she moved to her home in the west, she created the Navajo People. When she had done this, she told these human beings to go to their original home, which was the Navajo country. Before they left she said, *"After this, all the girls born to you will have periods at certain times when they become women. When the time comes you must set a day and fix the girl up to be Kinaalda*; you must have these songs sung and do whatever else needs to be done at that time. After this period, a girl is a woman and will start having children."* (Frisbie, 1967:11-12)

With most tribes, an important prerequisite to the rite is that the young woman undergoing the ceremony should be pure. She should not have experienced sexual relations. This is what most tribes preferred. However, in the past, a few tribes, such as the Gros Ventre, gave the girls in marriage before puberty.

It was a common belief among the Gros Ventre that for conception to occur, sex relations must continue over a period of time, conception could not occur as the result of one copulation. The fact that a girl would be given in marriage before she reached physiological maturity tended to confirm this belief, which is also linked with another one, namely, that a girl would not menstruate unless and until she had experienced sex relations. (Cooper, 1957: 127)

Today, with both the Navajo and Apache, the rite continues for four days. There is socializing, feasting and participation in events of the ceremony. For the girl there is instruction; her body is pressed and molded that she might be beautiful and healthy, in the likeness of Changing Woman or White Painted Woman.

There are inconsistencies in the rite itself, including story-telling, relating to the origin of the puberty ceremony in both Navajo and Apache. It has been noted that, "Ten versions of the story of the first Kinaalda, Changing Woman's Puberty Ceremony, have been published." These, however, are minor differences that have not stopped the Navajo and Apache from performing them.

Today the Navajo womenfolk teach their girls to observe the same instruction and teaching which was handed down to them by Holy People, so they might grow up into a wholesome, normal, mature maid (womanhood). Each girl when she becomes of age, in every family, is supposed to have this ceremony done. If it is not done, the girl may not know the value of womanhood and take the role lightly. (H. Denetsosie Interview, 1976)

Comparatively speaking, the Indians of North America have some basic religious concepts in common. There are certain similarities in their rites and their beliefs. The girl's puberty rite is an example of those similarities.

Among a very few tribes, the Kinaalda or the equivalent of the Kinaalda, was and is still generally looked upon with the reverent attitude expressed here by a Navajo.

According to our legend, when Changing Woman had her first period they prepared her by using the dews of various plants. They put that into her body to enable her to produce offspring for the human race. On that account, today we believe that when a girl has her first period there is nothing wrong with that. It is something sacred to us. (McAllester in Frisbie, 1967: 399)

Suggested Additional Readings

BASSO, KEITH H.
1970   "Cibeque Apaches," *Girl's Puberty Ceremony.* New York: Holt, Rinehart & Winston, pp. 53-72.

DU BOIS, CONSTANCE GODDARD
1908   "Religion of the Luiseno Indians," *Wukunish Girl's Adolescence Ceremony.* University of California Publications in American Archaeology and Ethnology, Vol. 8, No. 3, pp. 69-186, PL 16-19.

FRISBIE, C. J.
1967   *Kinaalda, A Study of the Puberty Ceremony,* Middletown, Conn: Wesleyan Univ. Press.

OPLER, MORRIS EDWARD
1965   "Apache Life-Ways: The Economic, Social and Religious Institutions of the Chiricahua Indians," *Girl's Puberty Ceremony.* New York, Cooper Press, pp. 82-83.

WATERMAN, T. T.
1910   "Religious Practices of the Diegueno Indians," *Atanuk, Girl's Adolescence Ceremony of Diegueno.* University of California Publications in American Archaeology and Ethnology, Vol. 8, No. 6, pp. 271-358, PL 21-28.

CHAPTER TEN

10 The Peyote Spirit

We have been taught that all men have the right to worship God in the manner and form most satisfactory to their own conscience.

(Osage Peyotists, 1912 in Slotkin, 1975:133)

PEYOTE

The definitions of Peyote are multi-faceted and varying. It depends, of course, on whom one asks and their knowledge, or experience with Peyote. Obviously many interpretations will range from the abstract, personal, and emotional to an objective concrete, scientific explanation.

Examples of the abstract are:

Peyote is a power. There is a power in there. That power, he has many names. You don't know how much power is there. It will take all your lifetime and you will know only a small part of the power. This is what I was told.

This description comes from a young Navajo man, Ron Barton, who was introduced to Peyote as a small child and has since made a commitment to it. Larry Etsitty, also a Navajo and Vice-President of the Navajoland Native American Church (1975) defines Peyote in this way,

The Peyote to me, is my bible. I know what I should be doing and shouldn't be doing. To me, when I take that Peyote, I feel humble (respectful) all the time.

Peyote has always been a religion. It is used mainly to gain power. (Manuel Watchman, Navajo)

Peyote is a plant or an herb, of the cactus species called *Lophophora Williamsii Lemaire*. Peyote is a plant foreign to most North American tribes. It grows along the Rio Grande, in Texas and southward.

Peyote is a spineless cactus with a nearly flat grey green top that protrudes about an inch above the ground and with one or more long carrot like roots. The surface is broken by furrows that divide it into numerous nodules and from the center of each of these emerges a tuft of white hair. The nodules are smaller and more numerous toward the center areole, about half an inch in diameter, and densely filled with hairs that enclose the reproductive organs. In the growth of a plant the nodules evolve outward from this center. Arising within the center are small rose-tinted whitish flowers that, after blooming briefly, degenerate into the small brushes of hair. With the continuing growth of the plant these become the centers of nodules that expand radially outward over the surface and eventually pass down the side and onto the root, which is covered with tough bark formed of modified epidermis. When fertilized a nodule gradually develops into a new plant. As it does so, it extends roots within the parent plant and as the nodule passes to the side and is about level with the ground the new plants, grown to about half an inch in diameter and complete with areola and furrows, thrust dendritic roots into the adjacent ground and gradually separates itself. Peyote is consequently usually found in small clusters with some degree of connection among the roots of the individual plants. (Flattery & Pierce, 1965:18-19)

The word, Peyote, comes from the Aztec, *Peyotl*. The historical use of Peyote in Mexico has been documented by the Aztecs in pre-columbian times.

According to the four surviving Aztec codices, or papyrus books of religions and tributes, peyote was one of the offerings made to the Gods in Aztec temples, where the plant was ritually consumed by the priests. In other parts of Mexico peyote was ceremonially eaten by any men who wished to partake of it, but was seldom eaten by Mexican women. (Marriott, 1971:16)

In contemporary Mexico, the Huichol Indians (men, women, and children) retrace annually a traditional hunt for Peyote and allude to it the phrase, "to find our life."

The first documented consumption of the plant in the Southwest is mentioned in a 1631 inquisition brief, describing one Francisca, a Santa Fe medicine woman, who urged a "bewitched" lady to eat Peyote so she might "see" the person who laid the spell and thus recover. (Nabokov, 1969)

PEYOTISM AND DIFFUSION

Peyote has migrated from the tribes in Mexico and along the Rio Grande, into the great plains area and into a few embracing tribes of Canada. Other names applied to Peyote by present day tribes of North America include Medicine, Healer, Power, Father Peyote, and the Peyote Spirit.

When Peyote is used ceremonially or in a ritual, this use of Peyote is called *Peyotism*.

In North America, Peyotism has been identified in two major forms. In the earlier form:

...Peyote is used by individuals primarily as a medicine, to obtain visions for purposes of supernatural revelation. When used by a group, as an element in dancing rites, the Peyote evidently being used to induce a trance state during the dance... (Slotkin, 1975:28)

Setting up the tipi for the ceremony, 1891. James Mooney (Courtesy of the Smithsonian Institution, National Anthropological Archives)

234

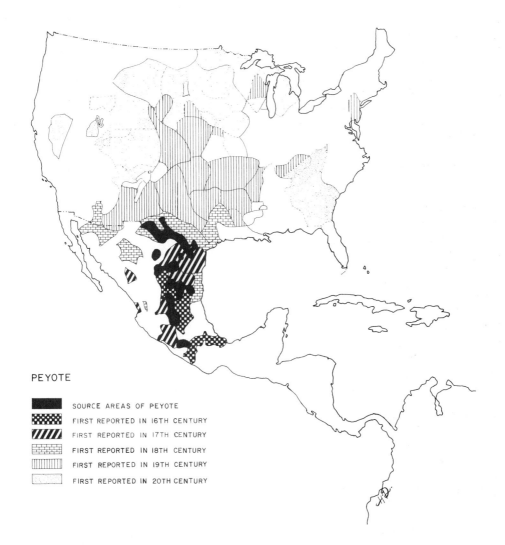

PEYOTE

■ (solid black)	SOURCE AREAS OF PEYOTE
▨ (checkerboard)	FIRST REPORTED IN 16TH CENTURY
▧ (diagonal stripes)	FIRST REPORTED IN 17TH CENTURY
▤ (brick)	FIRST REPORTED IN 18TH CENTURY
▥ (vertical lines)	FIRST REPORTED IN 19TH CENTURY
░ (stippled)	FIRST REPORTED IN 20TH CENTURY

This form of Peyotism lasted until about 1850. Near the turn of the Twentieth Century the second form surfaced. The *Peyote Religion* emerged in various tribes. A more specific date or place of origin is obscure.

> ...This form of Peyotism consists of a voluntary association whose rite is one of singing, prayer and quiet contemplation, centered on Peyote both as a symbol of spirits being worshipped and a sacrament. It is quite distinct from the older form of collective Peyotism which consists of tribal participation in a dancing rite with Peyote as a mere component. There are significant differences be-

> tween the two, both in form and function. (Slotkin, 1975:28)

How and why Peyotism diffused among tribes and evolved into a "fully developed" Peyote Religion is a complex story.

> *Peyote*, I was told, *was acquired by the Oto since their arrival in Oklahoma.* Today it is eaten by nearly all Oto men and women, and is one of the few ceremonies in which most of the tribe participate. *Those who follow the "peyote road" call themselves members of the "Native American Church."* At first anyone could put up meetings who had the necessary provisions. He was leader

for that meeting only. Now the right to lead meetings belongs to certain individuals who have inherited or purchased their fireplaces.

There are five or six peyote leaders among the Oto, but not all of them hold regular meetings or practice their powers. *Their "fireplaces" were purchased from the southern Plains Indians, chiefly the Kiowa and the Comanche.* Only one Oto, White Horn, a member of Eagle gens, obtained a peyote fireplace by personal vision. This was about the year 1908. I was told that White Horn's meetings were very similar to the Kiowa, but that there were a few minor differences in ritual. Exactly what these differences were I could not discover.

Meetings are held whenever the group wishes. Each leader has his own tipi and his special followers, but members from other groups can be present if they wish. The food is provided by the Peyote members. Special meetings are held for the sick, and occasionally these are held indoors and not in the tipi.

Peyote is a great force for good according to my informants, but even more important than this is its curative value. Most of the Oto with whom I talked had great faith in the healing power of the sacred ceremony.

The Peyote fireplace can be passed on to son, grandson, or brother-in-law. The following description of the Oto Peyote ceremony is by B. D., one of the Oto Peyote leaders.

"There was a Kiowa Indian by the name of White Buffalo who was a leader of Peyote. The Oto had been using peyote before that. I had been using it since 1887-88. We did not know anything about it, but we used it. But that year, 1914, I called that old man. I wanted him to give me his fireplace and all. I wanted to join the regular Peyote members. We put a tipi up and had a meeting that night. He taught me how to use peyote and how to run the meeting.

"He said, 'When you take this peyote, if you want to use this peyote, you must love everybody, treat everybody right. Pray to God to guide you in this way of life. He is the power who guides through this lodge. You must try to give up all the bad habits you have, try to keep faith. You have got to have God in your heart; Jesus' name in your heart.'

"I was a great drunkard and gambler before this peyote. It was kind of hard for me, the first five years. Many times as I came to meetings I wished I had kept out of this society. Well, I got by that. Peyote must be the only power which makes a man try to be good.

"This peyote, Indians had been using a long, long time ago. It started in Arizona somewhere, *before white people ever knew it.* At that time the old Indian prayed to god in his tipi. In those days Indians hated other tribes. In those days they killed one another. But those Indians using peyote asked everybody to have peace and shake hands.

"In the first part of the ceremony when you go into the peyote tipi, the fireplace is made. They put a peyote button on the west side of the fireplace. There has to be one peyote button. When they put the peyote down, everybody takes a smoke from his own cigarette. You smoke a cigarette and ask a blessing from God. *I talk to God just the way I want to.* Everybody talks for himself. When we are through the peyote is passed. Everybody takes four peyote pieces and passes them all around. You eat and chew and swallow. When you get through, the leader begins singing. There is a drum, a gourd, and a stick. The stick represents the bow. *The first song is a special opening song.* When you sing it, you have the cane in the left hand, the gourd in the right.

"The drummer and the leader sing together. Everybody can sing if they want to. When the leader is through singing he gives the cane to the drummer. Then the cedar man sings. *The songs pass to the left.* The cane and gourd are passed round till midnight. When midnight comes, the cane returns to the leader. He says, 'We are going to rest and drink water.' *He sings the water song.* When he gets through he sings three other songs as well. Then the fireman comes in with the water. He sets it before the fireplace and puts the bucket down in front. Then we give him tobacco and he makes himself a cigarette. He prays to God to help him and his family, to help everybody and the sick. What is this water? Jesus was baptized in water. This is holy. We call it Ni* Waxobini.** There must be some power in this world. We all ask God that way. We can't live without water.

"When he gets through praying he gives part of his cigarette to me and I pray. I use the same tobacco. We have to pray to God. This power must be from God. God made everything on the face of this earth at one time. Everything He made He blessed and said it was good. This peyote must be good. It was blessed by God Himself.

"So when we are through praying, we put tobacco beside the fireplace† mound —to the west where the peyote button is.

---

* *Ni*, Water

**Waxobini, holy, sacred, powerful

† fireplace, in this case—a raised earth mound of a crescent moon.

Kiowa man building mound for the ceremony, 1891. James Mooney. (Courtesy of the Smithsonian Institution, National Anthropological Archives)

When we put tobacco down, the fireman pours water on the ground. Then he passes it to the first man on the south side of the tipi door. He drinks first, then passes it round. Everyone is supposed to drink. After water has been drunk, when they put the bucket down, it is taken out. Then they put cedar on the fire, and smoke it. That is the time the leader takes his whistle, it is on the fireplace, and the drum and drumstick and gives them to the drummer. Then he picks up the whistle and goes out. When he goes out he passes the cane and gourd to cedar man to sing. When he goes out he stands at the south side of the tipi and prays again. Then he blows the whistle four times again. Then he goes north and east in the same way.

"When he gets through, he comes back to the tipi and they put cedar in the fire for him and then he smokes. After a while he sits down in his place. After he returns, the door is open to everybody. Anybody can go out if they want to and come back in. The singing goes on until morning. About daylight the leader calls for water again. His wife has to bring in the water that time. If his wife can't, some other close female relative takes her place. When she comes in with the water she takes a seat, and is given a cigarette. When she smokes, she prays for all children, friends, everybody. She asks God to bless them, white and black. When she gets through she gives the cigarette to the leader and he has to pray for her. This woman represents man's helpmate. You can't keep a home without a woman. She does the cooking and everything.

"When everybody is through smoking, they put the tobacco down. The woman pours out water, then takes a drink, and then gives it to the others. This takes place in the morning between four and five. If there is any left, she takes it back round the fireplace, picks up the bucket and goes out.

"After that it does not matter whether we sing or not. When the time comes, we say it is pretty nearly quitting time. Food is coming in. Squaw corn is in the lead, fruit or candy follows and last comes meat. When grub comes in, we put it before the fireplace. When that meat comes in, it is closing time. All right, we are going to finish. The sun is peeping. The leader picks up the stick, gourd and feather, the drummer his drum. They put cedar on the fire and begin the quitting song. Four songs, then quit. The grub is Waxo'bibi. The drum has to be untied and the drummer does this. Everything has to go outside. Somebody must pray over this grub we are to eat—any old man may be appointed. He asks God's blessing. When he gets through, the fireman takes the food and hands it out one spoonful at a time. It is passed round to the left, it has to go round again. When everything is eaten, the dishes go out. About that time everything is over. They give the cedar to the boys and pray the dismissal prayer. They put cedar in the fire, and everybody goes out of the tipi.

"If anybody is sick, the ceremony is carried out the same way. We give the sick peyote and pray. Anybody can make up a peyote song. That is why peyote has more songs than any society in the world. Some have visions through peyote. Visions differ. Sometimes you dream a vision sitting up. We are told we have to be good. We have to go that way." (Whitman, 1969:127-139)

PEYOTE ORIGINS

The originations of peyote are described differently by different tribes. In some cases explanations come from the oral traditions.

1) There is a story from long ago about the origin of peyote. It goes back to the times the Indians were fighting each other. On the other side of New Mexico a group of Indians were camped, and they were attacked... The mountains there were very high. The tribe that was attacked got scattered. There was just one woman and her boy left. They were Lipan Apaches. It was very hot and dry there. All the water had dried up. They had no food or water and there was none around them.

The woman told her boy, "I am tired and hungry and thirsty. We will rest here. Maybe I will die here. You go on. If you can't find anything, maybe you will die somewhere." It was early in the morning. The boy went out in the mountains. She told him to look around to see if he could see anyone. He walked around. Then something above spoke to him. It said, "I know you are hungry. Look down ahead of you. You will see something green. Eat it." He saw a green plant and dug it up and began to eat it. He looked around and saw many more. He ate some. Soon his hunger was gone, as if he had eaten a lot of meat. He dug some more of the plants up and took them to his mother. He told her of the voice that had spoken to him. She ate some of the plants, and felt as if she had eaten a big meal of meat. Her hunger was gone.

In the middle of the afternoon it was very hot. She said, "I do not know who gave us this. I am going to pray to him." She prayed for water and to find their people again. Later on, a cloud began to darken the sky and it thundered. Rain fell and there was water running through the mountains. They drank and rested there that night.

During the night the woman dreamed. Someone came to her and said, "Look over there and you will see a certain mountain." She looked and saw people moving along the hills. There was a creek nearby. It was east of where she and her boy were lying. In the dream she was told to go up on a high mountain in the morning and look out, and she would see her own people. She was told to take peyote to her people and a way would be made for it.

In the morning they washed and ate some peyote. She told her son of her dream. They went to the mountain and looked out, as she had been told in her dream. She saw people settling down and camping. She knew from her dream that they would be Indians. She and her boy started toward them. One man met them. He recognized them as the lost ones. They were glad to see each other. When they reached the camp he told all the people about them.

The boy had the peyote with him. After they got settled the boy asked his mother to fix him a tipi, off by himself. He said he would go into the mountains and lie down. He sat down inside the tipi and put the peyote on the ground, just as it looked when he first saw it. He prayed to the spirit that had shown him the peyote. "You have helped me. When I eat peyote tonight I want you to help me to find a way for it." He had a bow and arrow, and he drummed on the bowstring with the arrow. He sang two songs. He smoked a pipe made of bone from a deer's leg. He drummed and sang all night long. Early in the morning he went to the mountains and stayed there all day and night. The following morning he came back.

He did this several times. He put up a tipi and sang and drummed all night, and then went alone to the mountains.

Soon the men began to talk among themselves. They said, "That young man is doing something." One time one old man went over to the boy's tipi. He called him and asked, "Are you afraid for me to come in? I want to come in." The boy told him to enter, and the old man sat down beside him. The boy gave him the pipe and he lit it from the fire. Then the boy gave him peyote to eat.

Early in the morning they went to the mountains and returned to camp just before dark. His mother had taken the tipi down in the meantime.

After that, people asked the old man what had happened. They said they were all going into the tipi next time.

Not long afterward the boy put up the tipi again. The old man came. Another man came by and asked to enter. He was told to enter clockwise and to attend to the fire. The next morning the three of them went to the mountains and stayed until sundown. The boy's mother took the tipi down.

The next day the boy told them he was running short of peyote and would go for more. He went where it was growing and brought back more of it.

The next time they put up a tipi and had a meeting a fourth man came. They told him to sit on the south side. Next day they all went to the mountains, as before. That man asked if others could come, and he was told they were welcome.

When there was a meeting again, all those men came and seated themselves, beginning on the south side, and on around the tipi. As meeting after meeting took place, more men came, until the tipi was full.

All the time the boy wondered about improving the sound of his bow and arrow. He cut a long stick and thought, "I will use this to pray with." He took a horn and put stones in it to make a rattle. At the next meeting he used those things. As he held the staff and shook the horn, he sang some songs he had made.

Then he found a container of wood, already formed. He put water in it and tied a hide over it. He made a drumstick from a yucca stalk. At the next meeting he gave the drum to the man next to him, to drum for him while he sang. In the morning he told the man next to him to untie the drum. He said, "Maybe because of this horn we will get meat. The sound of this drum reminds me of the thunder I heard, and the water in it reminds me of the rain that came. Think of things that will be good to have here." The others learned songs of their own, and soon everything began to fit right in the meetings. Different ones added new things. The rocks and the drum were to represent tipi poles; the rope represented the rope holding the tipi poles at the top.

Later, Nayokogal learned of Peyote and brought it to us. In time it went north into the Dakotas. To this day it is our religion. Even today different men add things to make it better. The boy told them long ago to think to add to make it better. Nowadays it is held on holidays like Thanksgiving and Easter, and the feast has been added to it. (Whitewolf, 1969:123-126)

2) According to the story, two young men had gone upon a war expedition to the far south. They did not return at the expected time, and after long waiting their sister, according to Indian custom,

Comanche Peyote bag and necklace. (Courtesy of American Indian, Heye Foundation)

foot and hungry in the far off passes of the Sierra Madre. A strong party was organized to penetrate the enemy's country, and after many days the young men were found and restored to their people. Since then the Peyote is eaten by the Indians with song and prayer that they may see visions and know inspiration, and the young girl who first gave it is venerated as the "Peyote woman." (Mooney, in Slotkin, 1975:23)

The Kiowa were recorded as one of the earlier tribal groups to adopt the Peyote Religion, sometime before 1890. They have been credited with inventing the Peyote Religion. Other sources differ saying the Kiowas acquired Peyote from other tribes in the Southwest. One account even states that it was acquired from "Whites." In any case, the Kiowas did have the Peyote Religion at an early date. The preceding story was collected by Mooney, an anthropologist. He did research in Oklahoma among the Kiowa for five years. He was also instrumental in organizing a Peyote "church."

retired alone to the hills to bewail their death. Worn out with grief and weeping, as night came on she was unable to get back to the camp, and lay down where she was. In her dreams the Peyote spirit came to her and said, "You wait for your brothers, they still live. In the morning, look, and where your head now rests, you will find that which will restore them to you." The spirit gave her further instruction and was gone. With daylight, she arose, and on looking where she had slept found Peyote, which she dug up and took back with her to camp. Here she summoned the priests of the tribe, to whom she told her vision and delivered the instructions which she had received from the spirit. Under her direction the sacred tipi was set up with its crescent mound, the old men entered and said the prayers and sang the songs and ate the Peyote—which seems to have been miraculously multiplied—until daylight, when they saw in their visions a picture of the two young warriors, wandering on

Later on the trouble began here. They said it [Peyote] made the Indians worthless and lazy. They were the same bunch that caused the trouble with the Cheyennes and Arapaho. It was two years after that when they came down here. There were three of them. The agent told us to stop using Peyote down here and then it would stop among the Cheyennes and Arapaho. But he told the missionaries they would have to handle the matter between themselves and the Indians. The agent said that Quanah Parker, Apache John, and Ahpeahtone had explained Peyote to him as their church and he didn't want to interfere. The missionaries sent a report to the Indian Office in Washington against Peyote. There was no signature on the complaint when it was sent. In Washington they sent a man out to investigate Peyote. *That was James Mooney. He had been here before and had attended peyote meetings.* They had a meeting and he attended it. A lot of the strong believers in Peyote came to it. Old Man Hunting Horse was the chief of it.

Mooney wrote down everything that he saw. I was at that meeting. Mooney did everything the Indians did in the meeting. He ate the food they brought in the morning, too. He came to the feast the next day. *In the afternoon they spread out some blankets and sat down with Mooney to tell him what he wanted to know about Peyote.* They asked him what he wanted to do and what he wished to say to them. *Mooney said he had come to learn about Peyote and now that he had attended he would send a report to Washington on it. He said he had read many reports on Peyote that were against it, but that he now believed they were wrong.* He said the meeting that night was good and he hoped we would carry on this Indian religion. He brought along four bottles of medicines that had been examined in Washington. He said that one of them contained mescal and that it was found to be intoxicating. There were two more that contained herbs that were no good. The fourth contained Peyote and he said they had found nothing harmful in it.

Mooney said he was going to the Comanches and then would later attend a meeting to be given by Apache Ben. After that there would be a meeting to discuss Peyote at El Reno. I went to the Comanche meeting and heard Mooney say it was good. It was the same at Ben's meeting.

At the meeting in El Reno *Mooney told us to organize, choose officers, and name our church.* He said we should pay two dollars a year dues and respect it as a church. *He said to call it the "Native American Church.* To this day it still stands...

We got a charter for the "Native American Church" for Oklahoma in 1918. (Whitewolf, 1969: 129-131)

In contrast to the many stories of the Plains tribes, most written records indicate that the Navajos were introduced to Peyote only recently. Since 1920, a half-dozen Navajo men have been almost solely responsible for carrying the Peyote "teachings" to other interested Navajo individuals in remote areas of the vast Navajo Reservation. Today the Navajoland Native American Church boasts a very high membership in that organization. It estimates that fifty percent of the adult Navajo population are members of the Native American Church. At this time the officers of the organization are making more attempts to verify membership. The Peyote Religion was introduced to the Navajos in several ways. Their neighbors to the north were the Utes. They acquired Peyotism before the Navajo and an effort was made to extend the Peyote Religion into the Navajo Reservation. The Navajos hosted several "meetings" in which "teachers" from other tribes could demonstrate the ritual and power of Peyote.

But, the Navajos had previously anticipated the coming of Peyote in their oral tradition. It

Comanche man, Na-no-che, with rattle and staff, 1893. James Mooney. (Courtesy of the Smithsonian Institution, National Anthropological Archives)

241

is said that there were four or seven plants (herbs). One left, going south. It was also said it would return to the Navajos when the time was right, when the Navajos would be in need of such. This story was recalled by Larry Etsitty. John Walters added to it by noting that the plant spoke. He said *he* would return. Manual Watchman pointed out that this occurred in the "first world" of the Navajo. (See Navajo Chapter.) He also stated that medicine men knew about this "medicine" plant (Peyote) through the legends before it made its return in this world at the present time.

Ron Barton also relates another story told by the Navajo:

My mother, she told me a story like a creation myth. Twelve warriors were getting ready for war, far off. Then, men, when going to war, didn't take any women along with them. One lady, she begged to go. The warriors refused, but the woman kept pleading persistantly. She promised she would cook for them, mend their clothes for them and take care of them because she belonged to them. Finally the warriors agreed to let her go. The journey took a long time and then finally they got there. The woman did everything she said she would do. At a certain time, all the warriors were killed after they fought for a long time. The woman, she cried. She shed tears for them. She didn't have any purpose for being where she was so she started to go home. She was taking her time, thinking about her loss. While she was taking the long journey back home, *Coyote* met her and told her there was a prayer meeting going on and described it. He understood her loss and wanted to help her, so he said to go over to the prayer meeting, to observe and to listen. There was a tipi set up by a hill. As soon as she got there a man was waiting for her. He said we have something to teach you, to take home to your people. When she went in and sat down, she looked around and saw that her twelve warriors were in there (the tipi). All night, she looked, she learned. *To give her respect, the men asked her to bring in water in the morning and pray.*

When the peyote meeting was over her twelve warriors turned into Peyote buttons. She was instructed to pick them up, to take them home and teach her people what she had witnessed that night. That's the story my mother told me.

Tom Ration, Navajo medicine man, says that the Navajos always knew about drug-like herbs, similar to Peyote, *'A zee'*. He is familiar with the myth told by Ron Barton. He himself first heard it in 1912. In about 1926, he heard another similar to it, but it was related to him by a Taos man married to a Navajo woman. Tom Ration says his great grandfather told him that Navajos have known about these herbs as early as 1100. Even before Kit Carson came into Canyon de Chelly, the Navajos used them. It was necessary for an offering to be made to them before they could be used. There were also known antidotes for them. *Coyote or Mai, introduced these four sacred herbs to the Navajo according to their story.*

PLAINS DIFFUSION OF PEYOTISM

The impact of Peyotism in the form of the Native American Church upon Native American communities, urban and reservation, in the past and present has been a subtle and steady movement. In attempting to understand the diffusion of Peyotism, it is necessary to understand the people and their backgrounds.

We will discuss the Plains Indians because they obviously were visibly attracted to Peyote. Many Peyotists feel the influence they exerted on other tribes can be seen and felt today, though this cannot be proven. It is important to remember that not all tribes yielded to Peyote and were cautious in their approach to Peyote and the followers of Peyotism. It is also a generalization to imply that whole tribes became "Peyote People" because that is not true. With that in mind, we may begin to think about the situation the Plains Indian found himself in, in the last century.

J. S. Slotkin, at one time Menominee delegate to the Native American Church of North America Conference (1954), wrote of the conditions confronting the Plains Indians. He wrote how he felt these conditions led to the acceptance of Peyote in the daily lives of Plains Indian people.

A human society adjusts to its environment (*both external and internal*) *by means of its culture*. It follows that when the environmental conditions change, the culture changes correspondingly in terms of the previous culture, if the society is to readjust. The thesis of this chapter (Chapter II, 19th Century Background, *The Peyote Religion*, 1956) is that during the second half of the 19th century the Plains Indians were confronted by catastrophic changes in their environment, and the history of Plains societies and cultures during that period can be viewed as responses to this situation.

From the beginning of the European invasion of what is now the United States social interaction between Whites and Indians resulted in marked changes in the latter's environment. Geographically, their lands were taken over by invaders and the Indians were either restricted to a fraction of their former territories or transported to new localities with different environmental features. Biologically, the ecological balance of plants and animals upon which the Indians depend for subsistence was upset by White technology, and the Whites also brought diseases to which the Indians had little resistance. Socially, the Indians not only were confronted by a White culture very different from any known to them previously, but also subjected to forced acculturations once they were conquered by the invaders who posessed superior weapons.

This pattern was repeated successively in each region as the invaders spread over the country. When the Plains became the last frontier of White society, it was the turn of the Plains Indians to suffer the fate which previously had overtaken the aborigines in other regions. The precipitating factor was White expansion after the close of the Civil War in 1865 (Slotkin, 1975:12).

The Plains Indians attempted to readjust.

John Wilson, Delaware-Caddo, Peyote leader of the Delaware, died in 1922. G. W. Parsons. (Courtesy of American Indian, Heye Foundation)

Slotkin notes that "a *profusion** of *syncretistic*** religions appeared in the Plains during the second half of the 19th Century." He also noted that four of these movements had many common features. Perhaps most importantly, all four "were Pan-Indian social movements, i.e., they were intertribal and widespread, rather than tribal and localized." He felt this was a result, direct or indirect, for these reasons:

In the first place... ...Since the dominant Whites categorized all Natives, irrespective of tribe, as Indian and subjected them to the same discrimination, the subordinate *Indians developed an ethnic group identity and solidarity*. Socially the movements included in their ethics the beliefs that all tribes should be at peace and participants from different tribes should treat each other as

---

* profusion—abundance.

** syncretistic—reconciliatory.

brothers; concomitantly, intertribal visiting was a feature at all the rites. *Culturally the religions were conceived as belonging to all Indians*; the paraphernalia and ceremonial details diffused with the movements themselves... In the second place, insofar as the Plains tribes follow the same culture patterns and found themselves confronted by similar reservation problem situations, they were similarly maladjusted. And innovations, either invested or diffused, which were compatible with the traditional culture of any tribe from that culture area were probably also compatible with the culture of other tribes from that same area. Besides the obvious inadequacy of traditional tribal cultures, plus increased nonconformity and breakdown in social controls, meant that it was difficult to maintain traditional tribal customs. Now, all these are preconditions for extensive diffusion. (Slotkin, 1975:19)

The Peyote Religion was one of the four religions described, as was the Ghost Dance. White the importance of the other three diminished, the Peyote Religion grew significantly. Slotkin felt it was because:

The Peyote Religion was *nativistic*, but not militant. Culturally it permitted the Indians to achieve a cultural organization in which they took pride. Socially it provides a supernatural means of accommodation to the existing domination-subordination...

Perhaps the word dignity could be substituted for the word pride, as was particularly indicated to the author by Peyotist people. Perhaps Slotkin and other Peyotists provide insight to statements such as, "The Peyote Religion is the only thing left to us Indians." "When I join a church, it will be a Peyote Church because it is Indian." These statements and similar ones can be overheard today.

THE PEYOTE CEREMONY

The Peyote Religion has been examined by several people who usually have documented only the ceremonial side. The Peyote Religion is attractive to Indian People for several reasons. A few were identified by Slotkin and other researchers. But, primarily, the Peyote Religion is attractive because of its teachings and beliefs held by its followers. And because of the material and psychological security offered an individual. One is provided for by one's own means and always with support from others.

"I don't know how long we will have this," he said. "I gave up my old Indian ways. I have only this way. It is good, I think."

"Maybe we won't have this in 50 years; maybe it will be gone when you come to visit my people again. But, now they have this and they believe in it. You never learn all there is. Each time in here, I learn more and more."

"It is no plaything. This peyote helps you out when you call upon it, with sincerity and love inside you. We are fortunate people, and we pray to peyote and God to have pity on us. Maybe all this will be gone some day. We don't know; but now we have it, and it is ours." (Nabokov, 1969)

Many Indian people see Peyotism as a favorable alternative when more familiar tribal religions break down. Larry Etsitty gave a vivid description of Peyote and the directions it might take at any time. He sees Peyotism similar to a bird in flight. The bird is flexible, fluid, and may easily fly with the wind. He personally feels that the Native American Church could easily fit into and complement any American Indian religion. The Peyote Way and traditional ways to him are equal in importance and relevance. They could be compatible.

"Indian people can relate to it (Peyotism)," says Ron Barton, because the means advocated and the goals strived for are familiar to Indian People. Peyotism uses in the ritual the four elements of life: earth, water, fire and air, which are symbolic in most Indian rituals. This point is made by Shirley Etsitty who also stresses that the elements and herbs are all "native," the result of natural phenomena or cycles.

Four herbs are used in the Peyote ceremony. The four are Peyote, Tobacco, Cedar and Sage.

Without exception all these plants have been used prehistorically by Indians of the Americas, usually for medicinal purposes. Every part of the Peyote "meeting," no matter what the variation or how minute the detail, is extremely important and is done exaggeratedly and elaborately. Most Peyotists will emphasize attention to details.

General Description of the Ritual

The ritual developed by the Plains Indians has roughly the following form. A crescent shaped mound is raised in the back of a teepee, especially constructed for the purpose, and in front of this a small fire, ignited with flint, is kept burning. A dozen or so participants sit in a circle around this, and behind the crescent sits the agreed ceremonial leader, the Road Chief. He is chosen by reason of his experience with Peyote, and while he has no authority, he initiates the singing of songs, the prescribed midnight and dawn breaks for water, and it is to him that members address requests to have a special prayer offered or to be allowed to leave the teepee. On either side of the Road Chief are two assistants, the cedar-chief, and the drum chief who begins the beating of a drum that is passed along the members and is kept up throughout the night. A meeting begins about 8 P.M., usually on a Saturday night, and continues until noon of the following day when the individual sponsoring the meeting provides a small feast. During the whole of this time the participants are to center their gaze upon a Peyote plant placed atop the crescent and, in turn, to sing certain appropriate songs and to beat the drum as others sing.

Prayers are offered to the Great Spirit, through his mediator, Father Peyote, and are made while smoking a pipe or cigarettes specially prepared with Indian tobacco. Visions and hallucinations are definitely discouraged, as they are thought to indicate a lack of the purity of spirit with which it is necessary to approach Peyote. Similarly, excessive nausea or vomiting upon eating the plant is taken as implying that the subject is not as acceptable to Father Peyote as he might be. Meetings are usually held under the sponsorship of an individual who desires that special prayers be offered on behalf of an illness or misfortune in his family, although they are also regularly held on Christian and Indian holy days. To some degree the meetings are limited to adult males, and as far as possible, non-Indians are prevented from attending.

Following the invocation offered by the Road Chief, four dried peyote buttons are passed to each participant, but after a suitable interval for these to be eaten, one may take as much Peyote as he wishes. Peyote is regarded as having powerful medicinal qualities, if only by reason of its great spiritual sanctity, and a Peyote tea—the usual form in which Peyote is offered to women and children —is given to such afflicted persons as it may have been the purpose of the meeting to assist. No remarks are passed during the meeting about the effects of the plant nor about any individual's experience at the time.

The rules regarding use by the Indians are brief and simple. In the legendary account of how Father Peyote made himself known to the Indian he is made to say: "There are several different ways that you can use me, but unless you use me in only one way, the right way, I may harm you. Use me the right way and I will help you."

The only way to learn about the Peyote Religion, about the right way to use Peyote, is to eat the plant. It must be approached in a reverent contemplative frame of mind and accepted as a great power through which one may reach the great spirit. Perhaps the only real rule is that one must surrender himself completely and unreservedly to Peyote if he is to use it at all. (Flattery & Pierce, 1965:13-16)

The Peyote experience is one of individual meditation and consequently, revelation. Prayer and contemplation provide reasonable access, through Peyote, to satisfying revelations about one's self. Shirly Etsitty explains further, "The fundamental teaching is as a

245

sacrament..., it (Peyote) is the mediator, When you take the medicine, you learn from inside out." Change is inevitable, according to one's conscience and confrontation with himself. Change for the better becomes possible, necessary, and worthwhile. However, the *change must be within the individual, as his environment does not visibly alter.* While he cannot usually control conditions that affect him, *he can influence and exercise more controls within his own life.* His outlook, philosophically, and behavior adjusts accordingly.

There it was that we ate peyote. My husband never thought much of the Indian customs and whatever there was he mocked. But there he ate peyote and he realized something. Whatever the peyote was, he understood, and from that time we ate peyote. I had two children at that time and I was going to have my third child. When I had children I used to suffer. I used to have a hard time and really suffered until I finally gave birth. There in Nebraska in the wintertime when we were with my sister I was about to give birth. I told her, "I think I am going to be sick." She said, "Little sister, when people are in that condition they use peyote. They have children without much suffering. Perhaps you can do that. You always suffer so much. This way you will have it easily."

"All right, whatever you say, I will do." That was the first time I was to eat peyote. My sister did that for me. She prepared it for me and gave me some and I took it. Then I soon had the baby. I had a boy.

From that time on whenever they held peyote meetings we all attended. Mother, father, we all used to attend the peyote meetings. One time something happened to me. I had three children then and I used to be rather shy. In the evening if I sat in the meeting, that would be all I did. I would just sit there. I would sit there all night. In the morning when they went outside, then I would go out too. It used to be hard for me. Some got up any time and went outside. But I used to think if I stood up, everybody would look at me. I used to respect people. Once when I was

eating peyote—I ate quite a bit, perhaps twenty buttons—this is what happened to me.

I was sitting with bowed head. We were all sitting with bowed heads. *We were supposed to ponder. We prayed.* We were all doing this. We were having our peyote meeting. In the west the sun thundered and made terrible noises. I was hearing this sound. Oh, the sky was very black! I had my head bowed, but this is what I saw. The sky was terribly black. The storm clouds came whirling. When the storm clouds came the sky would become black. Big winds came. The ground kept caving in. This is the way I saw it. It thundered repeatedly and the sky was dark. The storm was approaching and people came running. The women had shawls about them and they had bundles on their backs. They were carrying something on their backs, and they came running. There was a mighty wind and their clothes were blowing about them. They stumbled and rolled over and over. They they would get up and run again. And there they came by. It did not seem to me as if it were windy. That is what I was seeing. And I thought to myself, "Where are they fleeing? Nowhere on this earth is there any place to run to. There is not any place for life. Where are they saying that they are fleeing to? Jesus is the only place to flee to." That is what I thought.

Then I saw Jesus standing there. I saw that He had one hand raised high. The right hand, high in the air. I saw that He was standing there. Whatever He was doing, I was to do also. I was to pray, I thought, I stood up. Though I was in the midst of all those people my thoughts were not on that. I stood up because I saw Jesus. I will pray to Him, I thought. I stood up and raised my arm. I prayed. *I asked for a good life—thanking God who gave me life.* This I did. And as the drum was beating, my body shook in time to the beat. I was unaware of it. I was just very contented. I never knew such pleasure as this. There was a sensation of great joyousness. Now I was an angel. That is how I saw myself. Because I had wings I supposed to fly but I could not quite get my feet off of the ground—I wanted to fly right away, but I could not because my time is not yet completed.

Then the drummers stopped singing. When they reached the end of the song they stopped. Then I sat down on the ground. I knew when I ate peyote that they were using something holy. That way is directed toward God. Nothing else on earth is holy. If someone speaks about something holy he does not know what he is talking about. But if someone sees something holy at a peyote meeting, that is really true. They are able to understand things concerning God. I understood that this religion is holy. It is directed toward God. (Lurie, 1961:40-42)

For most Indian people, prayer is an ancient form of communication. John Emhoolah, Kiowa, says, "Always, our people are a praying people." On Indian religion, he stated eloquently, "Our church is the world." The two in his mind are inseparable and blend complimentary with Peyotism. Sam Gardipe, Jr. (Pawnee/Sauk-Fox) who identifies "Indian"

religion with Peyotism says religion (Indian) was or is encompassing, and is not a "once a week 'feeling solemn.' "

Indian religion is interwoven into your life. Everything, the way you live, the way you sleep. Indian religion is a way of life. To call it a 'religion' is wrong (misleading). Everything is close to Mother Earth, in accordance to the way we are taught. It is something we know (for a fact or from experience). Other people don't look at Mother Earth as such. The concept is hard for them to grasp. (Ron Barton)

CHRISTIANITY AND THE PEYOTE RELIGION

Emhoolah who has spent part of his life from childhood with "Peyote People" says, "I've gone to Christian Churches. I always come back. There must be something about that herb that appeals to the Indian." Ron Barton echoes the sentiment, "I've been involved in the Native American Church all my life, since I was born. It's in me. It will always be in me. I like the Peyote Way. I pray that way.

Kiowa man holding rattle and wand. James Mooney, 1891. (Courtesy of the Smithsonian Institution, National Anthropological Archives)

I eat that way. I sleep that way. I live that way. It puts back the dignity." Sam Gardipe talking about tradition and its place in a fast-moving technologically oriented world, shared his philosophy as a Peyotist, and as an Indian. "I have a philosophy. One of the ways of rebelling, is to be traditional, to really know your own way (*Peyote Way*)."

To reiterate, Larry Etsitty also acknowledges that the bird he envisions can also go in the direction of Christianity. He sees Peyotism as being adaptable, supplemental and not detrimental to any other religion, including Christianity. It is acknowledged that the Native American Church in its contemporary form contains seeds of Christianity, incorporated either recently or in some cases before the 20th century.

The Peyote Religion functioned as separate independent groups prior to the organization of specific groups into the affiliated Native American Church. In doing so, some groups also introduced characteristics and the concept of Christianity. Other groups did not attempt to introduce change or did not reorganize themselves.

> A lot of people, such as myself, do not put Christianity into the Peyote Religion, but we do have our respect for it. Christianity is a good religion, but our concepts of it with the Peyote religion will not mix. Many people put the two together and it is their way and we respect that. (Ron Barton)

John Emhoolah discusses the influence of Christianity upon Indian religions, and not necessarily only on Peyotism.

> Indians have always been religious. Way before the Whiteman, they saw a vision. A man was coming with a book under his arm. Our people are always praying people. But the Indians had certain things before the Whiteman came. They added to their own songs and their own way of expression.

> Slotkin states: Most Peyotists consider themselves to be Christians, for they conceive Peyotism to be the Indian version of Christianity. Their proof of this is that they accept the Christian Trinity and Christian ethics.

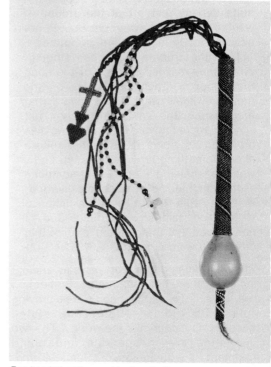

Fox beaded rattle used in Peyote Ceremony. (Courtesy of American Indian, Heye Foundation)

The influence of Christianity upon Peyotism or perhaps vice-versa, came about in several ways. Obviously missionary zeal and *proselytizing* had some effect on Peyote followers. Slotkin implies that anti-Peyotists applied pressure on Peyote practices and the result was suppressed Peyotism. Christianity was introduced to justify Peyotism and partronize anti-Peyotists, though this was not always the case. Many Peyotists really do conceive of Peyotism as the Indian version of Christianity and as the essence of Peyotism. *It is significant to state that most "INDIAN RELIGIONS" do not practice proselytizing.* There was a period of time when possession of Peyote was illegal and followers were prosecuted by law, but the law varied from state to state and from time to time the possession of peyote by designated people was championed by political groups. As Peyotism became more respectable in the eyes of critical opposition and anti-Peyotists more tolerating, the law was amended for the benefit of Peyotists. In part, this was due to the reorganization of Peyote groups. As they identified and affiliated themselves, their umbers became clear and politically influential. Also as they became stronger, they became less intimidated by criticism on the use of Peyote. This is particularly obvious on the Navajo Reservation. As church charters were drawn up beginning in 1918, the nationwide Native American Church of North America was inevitably born.

SUMMARY

The *Native American Church* practices the *Peyote Religion*, which is the newest form of *Peyotism*. Slotkin identifies three fundamental traits of Peyotism found in all religions: a doctrine (philosophy), ethics (rules of behavior), and ritual (ceremony, or the Peyote "meeting"). Though he states that, "No official *promulgated** Peyotist doctrine can be presented, for the religion is relatively individualistic..., ...Peyotism consists of a belief in existence of power, spirits, and *incarnations*** of power."

The Peyote Way or Peyote Road stresses four main teachings one must conform and adhere to. "Peyote People" may supply the instruction, or after Peyote is consumed it may be directly responsible for teaching. The teachings are: (1) Love for your fellow man or brotherly love; (2) responsibility for one's family; (3) self-reliance; and (4) refraining from use of alcohol.

Slotkin adds: Traditionally, the Indians' more customs were reinforced by various supernatural sanctions applied both in this life and the next. If a person follows the Peyote Road faithfully—with Peyote always ready to guide, help, and comfort him on the way—it will lead him to tranquility in this life (and such material goods as health, long life, and the well being of children and grandchildren), and bliss in the next world (in association with his loved ones and God).

There are many variations to the Peyote "meeting, ceremony, ritual or rite." References to "fireplaces," indicate variants in altars which are commonly called "fireplaces."

Fireplaces may be purchased or may be exchanged as gifts. All fireplaces are meticulously constructed as their purpose is to serve as altars. A certain man is designated to care for an altar in the course of a meeting. His place is also designated inside the entrance. He takes his job seriously and keeps the altar immaculate. Usually he is called a "fire chief."

A meeting usually begins sometime after sunset and lasts past dawn when "Dawn woman" or "Peyote woman," or "Water woman" brings the morning water. Water comes first as it is very sacred. It comes before life. Shirley Etsitty explained, "That is why when a baby is born, the water comes first." Water is followed by corn, meat, and fruit, which are considered to be substances of life. They represent a person, an entity, and they are all human necessities for life. Corn represents the heart, the very insides of life. Meat represents flesh, and fruit (preferably vine fruit), the blood stream, source of life. One is gently reminded that if one is sick, these four sacred needs can restore health.

In the course of the rite, several things happen that have not been mentioned previously.

The participants arrive at the place of the meeting, customarily held in tipis, in the past. However, presently meetings are held in hogans and other dwellings including apartments in urban areas. The participants may be elderly or infants, men and women, and children.

Larry Etsitty stated with regard to children that he had been told by other members of the Native American Church (not of the Navajoland chapter or branch) that it delighted them to see children participate. Their age ranged from infants to expectant parents. Larry Etsitty continued, "They said they felt that's where they went wrong. At times when there were too many participants, the young ones were requested to leave to make room for older participants." He indicated that these people regretted that their young ones have not responded in the desired manner. As to the women in Peyotism, depending on the area and the time, it was once recorded they were sometimes not allowed to participate. Most tribes, as oral tradition indicates, gave the woman a very high place in the Peyote Religion

---

* promulgated—declaration

* incarnation—embodiment

249

Kiowa Peyote Ceremony, near Ft. Sill, Oklahoma, 1892. James Mooney. (Courtesy of the Smithsonian Institution, National Anthropological Archives)

The Road Man has the honor of singing the opening song. He is accompanied by a rattle or a drum. The drum is usually held by a man to the side of him. Thus, the singing is underway. Intermittently it will continue with prayer and Peyote solitude. Anyone who desires to sing or pray may do so when the opportunity arises.

At midnight, there may or may not be a recess. Certain people may be allowed to leave but usually only at this time. An eagle bone whistle is blown four times, symbolic of a bird. This bird has also been related as the Peyote Bird, messenger between the Peyote follower and Father Peyote. The midnight song is offered. The meeting continues until after dawn when the road man brings the meeting to a close.

The ritualism of Peyotism is obviously the most impressive to "non-Peyote people." The symbolism in the ritual of the Peyote Religion is probably the most difficult part of the Peyote Religion to comprehend. It is inaccurate to assume that the whole of Peyote Religion is incorporated in the rite. It is true, Peyotists claim, that all the teaching is there in the fireplace. However, members of the Peyote Religion, the Native American Church, insist the Peyote Religion does not end when a ceremony concludes. The Peyote Way or the Peyote Road begins, and one should strive to keep in order (on the Peyote Road).

In the Summer of 1975, the author met an elderly man at The Navajo Tribal Fair in Window Rock, Arizona. He was a golden man, all sparkly, dark skin and eyes, in the sun. He was obviously not wealthy in ways of money and extravagent finery. He and his clothes were all wrinkly and worn. Both had bags in them. He stepped up to negotiate a purchase he planned. He wanted the man's robe or sheet, half red and half black, worn in the Peyote meeting. He said he was a road man, had been one for forty years. He said he'd been to jail for Peyote, was there when Peyote followers were harrassed. He said it simply and matter-of-factly. "Peyotism had endured." He said that softly, gently in Navajo. He said he would do it all over again.

In conclusion, Shirley Etsitty, in her own words, defines religion as she interprets it. "...All religion is, is trying to understand what the Creator wants you to do..."

and usually credit her for the bringing of Peyote. The Navajo tribe is one of the very, very few who allow women to sing during the meeting.

One enters the dwelling, from left to right, or clockwise. (For all Navajo ceremonial purposes, one enters in this manner. It is symbolic of the sun's pattern and represents balance and harmony.)

Participants usually sit on the ground or floor and arrange themselves in a circle. In the center of the circle is a fireplace, constructed of earth into a shallow mound. The mound may take one of several shapes, a crescent moon is common. A fire is in process and the fire chief tends it. Directly across from the fire chief is the "road man." He will conduct the rite. He begins as speaker, talking about the reasons for the meeting which might vary from a birthday to a healing function. He will offer the first prayer and Peyote to the participants. Each man will accept Peyote in the form of a button, tea, or powder, *when the formalities*

Suggested Additional Readings

BENITEZ, FERNANDO
1975 *In The Magic Land of Peyote*, John Upton (tr.), Austin, Texas: University of Texas Press

FURST, PETER
1973 "Indian Journey to Life's Source: Huichol Indians' Peyote Rituals," *Natural History*, 82:34-43 (April).

MYERHOFF, BARBARA G.
1974 *Peyote Hunt: The Sacred Journey of the Huichol Indians,* Ithaca, New York: Cornell University Press.

STEWART, O. C.
1972 "The Peyote Religion and the Ghost Dance," *Indian Historian*, 5:4, Winter, pp. 27-30.

CHAPTER ELEVEN

11 Sacred and Secular: Seminole Tradition in the Midst of Change

In this chapter we will briefly examine the Seminole of Florida and Oklahoma and the two contrasting sacred ways in their present-day society: the Green Corn (Stomp) Dance and the Christian Church. The Seminole People are unique in the sense that there are two major geographical divisions of Seminole (Mikasuki language-speaking) Peoples—groups in Florida and groups in Oklahoma—and their acculturation experience has been distinct. The Oklahoma part of the Seminole (Mikasuki-speaking) People have been involved in the acculturation process as a tribe for over one hundred years. The Seminole of Florida, however, only incorporated as a tribe in 1957 (Seminole Tribe) and 1961 (Miccosukee Tribe), with over 200 of the 1,500 plus Seminole People in Florida *refusing* membership in any tribe.

In Oklahoma, part of the acculturation process involved conversion to Christianity through the leadership of non-Seminole missionaries. Many Seminoles are Christians and, in the old days, their participation in the Stomp Dances and Green Corn Dance celebrations was strictly forbidden. That is changing now. There are complaints that fewer people are going to Church and there seems to be a revival of the Stomp Dance. Younger people show an interest and a new Stomp Dance ground may be dedicated sometime soon in Oklahoma, Seminole country. Some Christians now attend the Stomp Dances. There are very few "medicine men" or specialists in medicine, in general, among the Oklahoma Seminole; but there are young men becoming Stomp Dance leaders and Medicine men, connected with the Stomp Dance itself.

In Florida, around 60% of the Seminole People are non-Christians, and most of these attend the two Green Corn Dance ceremonials held in the summer. Only non-Christians attend the Green Corn Dance in Florida. However, though there is a strong effort on the part of the non-tribal affiliated Seminole People to teach their children environmental/ecological knowledge, herbs, and other sacred knowledge, there are only two "Medicine Men" who know the specialized knowledge that belongs to the Medicine Bundle and its renewal procedures in the Green Corn Dance. In Florida Christianity was first preached to the People in the 1930's—only 40 years ago—*by Seminole People who spoke, preached, sang, and taught the Bible in their own language.* Because of the trust that was established between the Seminole missionaries and The People, and because of the radical changes that were coming to the Seminole in Florida around this time and continuing to this day, a large part of the Seminole population of Florida converted to Christianity during these years. These same people are now the leaders in the newly-incorporated Tribal Governments. Political functions that used to be carried out by the Medicine Men and the community during the week of the Green Corn Dance in the past, are now carried out by the leadership of the Tribe who, for the most part, are church-goers. Of course, they are still sensitive to the ancient traditions of decision-making—how The People are accustomed to settling problems and engaging in debate. But these leaders, too, are dedicated to the task of 20th century government as well.

What we see is that, as in many Native American communities today, the sacred life of The People is part of a new *context* of environment, economics, politics, and education. Acculturation processes and the pressures from the dominant society have made it necessary to *separate* the sacred from the non-sacred—or the *secular*. Stomp Dance is sacred; Tribal Council is secular. School is secular; obeying the traditional instructions after giving birth* is sacred. Learning to prepare *sofki*** is sacred; buying canned milk and corn meal at the store is secular. These are divisions in the life of The People that, aboriginally, did not exist in North America. But, now that they do, we have the ability to understand conceptually—or "think about"— how this separation of daily life changes the way people live and some of the ways The People deal with the change.

In this chapter we will mostly be looking at the main features of the Green Corn (Stomp) Dance and Christian Seminole-style doctrine, in the context of the community and the natural environment or eco-system. For further research into "why" and "how" traditions are altered over time, the student is directed to other readings. Very little has been written by Seminoles about Seminoles, or by non-Seminoles about the Seminole People. The Seminole ways of life remain among The People of the communities in Oklahoma and Florida.

BACKGROUND OF THE SEMINOLE PEOPLE AND THEIR HABITAT

During the Stomp Dances, the Seminole women wear turtle-shell rattles on their legs that form the rhythmic sound that keeps the men singing in time, as they answer the Song-phrases of the Leader. The Earth, to the Seminole people, was formed from the back, the shell of a Great Turtle. A Seminole man from Oklahoma told part of the story:

---

* See Chapter Fourteen, **The Wandering Ground**.

** *Sofki* is a drink made from corn meal which has gone through the liming process of hominy.

...and there were ants and then this round thing (they didn't know what it was) came out of the sea. It was floating out in the big sea. Finally the Mighty One gave this big round thing to land and while he was resting it started cracking and while he was cracking he was trying to breathe; and then he made a loud hiss and this giant ant came over and said, "What will you do for me if I put you together?" And he said, "The only thing that I can give you is inside of me. And there is no way that I can survive; but the only thing is that the Earth Children must crawl over me." And the giant ant (there were four of them, four brothers) put this giant turtle back together and they sang, *"chotoelaylay, chotoelaylay"*—they said that four times. That means "rock layer." That's the reason why the turtle has squares on his back. That's where he was put together and that's the symbol of the Earth. And then there's a mound, and then the Earth Children did come out under it, and we're living on it.

There are many different versions in the oral tradition of the Seminoles concerning their migrations on their way to their present locations in Florida. Apparently, since it is emphasized in the histories and stories, the Seminole People lived near the shores of Lake Okeechobee (see map). Due to a long history of pursuit and harassment by Spanish, French, English, and finally American colonists; The People's harboring of run-away Black slaves, and the need to hunt; the Seminole People soon populated various areas of the Florida Everglades. The Seminole, it is said, were a group of people that broke away from the larger Creek tribe. Seminole is sometimes said to mean, "run-away," sometimes "lover of freedom," or "of the wilds."

Nowadays the division between the two tribes is a matter of language, though half of the incorporated Seminole Tribe (1957) speaks Creek. The Seminole Tribe (1957) includes people from Brighton, Big Cypress, and Hollywood reservations. There are about 237 people in Brighton and they speak *Creek*. In Big Cypress, there are about 259 people who speak *Mikasuki* (the language of the Oklahoma Seminole). The Hollywood reservation has a population of about 332 and the people there

FLORIDA SEMINOLE AND MICCOSUKEE LOCATIONS

usually speak both Creek and Mikasuki. In 1961 the Miccosukee Tribe was organized, with a membership of 243, including about one-half of the people who live along the Tamiami Trail, leaving about 200 people who refuse to belong to any tribal corporation or reservation. The people both in and outside of that tribe are *Mikasuki* speakers.

In Oklahoma there is a definite separation between Creek and Seminole even though their ceremonial life comes together in the Stomp Dances, the Ball Games, in some medicine specialization, and occasionally in the Church, though the Seminole speakers have a hymnal of songs written in their own language.

As for "government," as we have discussed in other chapters, the necessary balances that have to be maintained between people in the community, and the community and the environment are what constitutes "government" in sacred aboriginal tradition. Forty years ago, a Christian Church or a Tribal Government did not exist. The Green Corn Dance was a time of decision-making. A time when the people discussed legal, criminal, and other questions that had to do with the well-being of The People:

In those days, too, the elders held a court and council meeting; judgements were made upon criminal acts and other misbehaviors; weddings were performed; the state of the tribe was seriously discussed; and the traditions and values by which decisions were made were all validated and reinforced by the sacredness of the occasion. (Buswell, 1972: 69-70)

The other "hidden" form of government was, of course, the kinship system, or system of clans and extended families. Today, even though a family may attend church instead of the Green Corn Dance, the family and kin have a large role, especially in the conservative communities; in settling disputes; carrying on some traditional sacred or medicinal practices; and seeing to the early education of the children. The clan system is still important to the Seminole, both in Florida and Oklahoma. And, in Florida, the traditional clothing is embroidered with the symbolic design of the mother's and father's clan.

The Habitat

The natural environment, or habitat, that the Florida Seminole hid within, learned to adapt to, and maintained a good life in, are called the Everglades. There are no other Everglades in the world except those in Florida. One hundred miles long from Lake Okeechobee to the Gulf of Mexico, and seventy miles wide, the Everglades have been called a "river of grass"—that refers to the saw grass, a sharp-edged vegetation that grows like tall grass in the water. Scattered throughout the Big Cypress Swamp and the Everglades are "islands" of rock, soil, and trees. Here, pines, cypress trees, and oak grow. On these islands, too, the Seminole People live in their dwellings called *chickees*. Some Seminole People still live in these well-adapted dwellings, tending their pigs and chickens, but many more have moved to settled areas near the reservation centers and are living in government cinderblock houses so that they can have plumbing and electricity. Some people live in *chickees* and have electricity brought into them.

Among the islands, within the glades and swamps, live many different kinds of plants, herbs, roots, birds, and animals. These include various types of fish, frogs, turtles,

H. DENETSOSIE

snakes, and alligators, as well as otter, quail, rabbits, opossums, wildcats, black bear, and jaguars. The white crane, one of which is shot for its feathers for the "feather dance" of the Green Corn Dance ceremonial, lives in this habitat. From these animals and plants the Seminole People got their clan names: turtle, fish, alligator, deer, sweet potato, tiger, bear, wind, and bird.

The seasons in the Everglades consist of a rainy season from May to November, and a dry season for the rest of the year. The rainy season is hot and humid. Between the rainy and dry seasons is a time of hurricanes and cyclones. Then the dry season comes with its cool weather, and especially nowadays, occasional forest fires.

In the old days travel was by canoe only. Now most camps can be reached by roads. The building of highways and roads, in fact, has changed the way of life for the Seminole people of Florida. Highways mean outside civilization and economic contacts outside the immediate community. What has happeed to the Everglades habitat in Florida is but one of the tragic stories of ecological disaster in North America. Much of the Everglades and swamps have been landfilled and "dried up" to make land on which to build the suburbs of Florida's large cities.

Another ecological shift in the balances of human survival and animal life was the outboard motor and the rifle. Nowadays, very few Seminole men hunt and fish for their daily food or for income. These are sports now. They do not hunt because there is not much to hunt anymore. One of the first events that radically changed the Seminole way of life, or, to be more exact, made the Seminole dependent on the "outside" for economic goods and trade, was when they no longer could compete with outsiders for the fur and skin trade. Even when hunting and trapping were still the principle occupations that brought in income, only 35% of the trade with dealers went to the Seminole People; the majority of trade was with outsiders who employed motor boats and reflectors, instead of canoes and torches for nighttime alligator hunting.

Recently, in an effort to keep people employed on the reservation the Seminole Tribe began a cattle industry, and individual families still grow corn and raise pigs and chickens. When one has to go out of one's village or camp to find work, and when one is buying one's food instead of catching it or growing it, other networks of life and customs change also. Tribal government, in a way, is a communications center with the "outside world." Schools also serve as communications centers. As we shall see, for the Seminole, the Christian Church, too, has served as a center for people to gain a different perspective on modern life and the new problems it presents to the Seminole People.

In Oklahoma the habitat is very different from that of Florida. Most of the Seminole People live on small farms, or small acreage. The Seminole People farm and hold jobs in the nearby towns of southern Oklahoma. Reservation lands were set aside for the Seminole who were forced to go to Oklahoma in the 1830's, but during the Allotment Act period many Seminole People sold their lands, or part of their lands, for income. Oil was, at one time, a source of income for some Seminole People on whose land oil was discovered. Throughout the countryside oil well towers and pumps are visible, standing out in the middle of corn fields.

The land is good for farming and many people have cows, pigs and chickens; they grow grains, corn, and vegetables. The growing season is a long one, beginning in March. Because lands were sold or given up during the Allotment Act period, farms are separated by great distances sometimes. The land of rolling hills, streams, and swamps, is criss-crossed by many county roads, and, now a couple of highways.

In the past, the centers for community get-togethers and discussion were the Churches, and to an extent, the Stomp Dances, centrally located near the populated areas of the Seminole community. Now, the focus of attention is on education and community development through bi-lingual bi-cultural education programs and other programs coordinated through the Tribal Council. The sacred life of The People is focused mainly through the weekend camps at the Stomp Dance Grounds, or the Sunday and Wednesday night worshipping at the Churches. The People are aware, however, of the mysteries and strengths of the land. They will tell many stories of encounters with wild animals whose powers have served to teach Medicine people or specialists. They know of the sacred places located near creeks or in the woods; and daily The People observe certain rules of behavior. These are taught through oral tradition and generations of practice— ways of acting towards kin, of picking plants and herbs, and of remembering one's dreams.

THE GREEN CORN DANCE AND STOMP DANCE

Old generation, old folks was playing —that's part of it that makes you forget. Well, and otherwise you'd be saying, when you be thinking about it, then you cry. That's what it is; you think about your grandpa and this and that, some- times you sit there and think about it. You'd be start crying, that's what it is. These sticks (ball sticks) keep you from crying but it'll make you think. That's what your generations back, what they been doing. Back in the days of them old folks, they knew how to make medicine. *

The Green Corn Dance is an ancient gathering, described in the oral histories for hundreds of years. Aboriginally, the coming together for the Green Corn Dance, which is the largest and most important of the Stomp Dances for Oklahoma Seminoles and an annual ceremonial for Florida Seminoles, served many different functions in the lives of The People.

---

* Oklahoma Seminole Stomp Dance Leader talking about the Ball Game.

259

First, the Elders held "council" meetings. These functions are now, as we said earlier, divided between the civil authorities, Tribal Council, and Christian Churches.

Second, the Green Corn Dance was, and still is, a time for *cleansing*, for renewal. The men take sweatbaths, fast, and drink "Red Root," or Black Drink, a boiled drink which makes them vomit. Children and adults are "scratched" and their blood is revitalized in this way. (We will describe this later.) Renewal is also made for the Medicine Bundle which is representative of the Seminole cosmology and sacred knowledge. The Medicine Bundle is an object of power for The People, for in it are each of the elements specialists know to be necessary for the life of The People and for the functioning of the world.

The Medicine Bundle itself is kept in the care of a "Medicine Man," the central leader of the Green Corn Dance gathering. Its contents are "medicines for the health of the tribe; for warfare; and for peace; numbering up to six or seven hundred items wrapped variously in buckskin or white cloth, the whole wrapped up in a deerskin with the hair side out." (Buswell, 1972:68) The Medicine Bundle is taken out in the final 24 hours of the Green Corn Dance (in Florida). It is blessed as part of the blessings, prayers, and other sacred activities that take place in the moments before sunrise on the final morning. It is said that if the Medicine Bundle were not renewed, The People would die and the tribe disappear.

Third, the Green Corn Dance and often Stomp Dances, in general, are a time for the ball games. There are two kinds: one with the men against the women, which is entertaining and relaxing for the afternoons; and one with men teams picked from different communities or sometimes from different tribal groups—these teams then compete as East against West.

The game with the men against the women is played in Oklahoma on Sundays, the Stomp Dance taking place on Fridays and Saturdays, or just Saturdays. Some distance from the Stomp Dance circle, and within the camping grounds, a pole is erected, about 30 feet high. The object of the game is to hit a marked-off area near the top of the pole with a ball made of grasses wound with hide. Says George B. Harjo, a Stomp Dance leader from Oklahoma,

"We got a horse head on the pole out there. We play every Sunday, men and women play together. Men use the stick (the Ball Game Stick)—they are not supposed to touch it [the ball] with their hands. The women touch the ball, play the game with their hands." Points are scored for hitting the horse's head at the top of the pole.

The game of men against men is a rougher game seen almost in terms of a ritualized warfare. It requires stamina since the object, as in La Crosse, is to send the ball into the goal of the opposing team at the end of the playing field. The ball is passed from player to player down the field and cannot be touched with the hands, only with the small net-like scoop at the end of the ball stick. The players wear special clothes, mostly consisting of a loin-cloth and ribbons or yarns wound a special way around the waist. The women sing songs before the game, teasing the men about their strength and bravery, and urging them on to the game. Then the two teams meet on the field and a special leader gives a speech—in special poetry, talking about the game, the teams, and the men. Then they play. George B. Harjo tells us:

The time that the women are going to sing is when you are going to play ball sticks—they call it "man to man" East and West. I'm West; I've played a few times. No women, only two women at both ends; they serve water or sofki, or whatever it is. There are five lines of forty men—forty men East, forty men West. They come together. It's like football—like a football field, each side's got a pole. They have to be naked and they wear diapers, and they use those ball sticks. Before they come in together they'd be out there and go around that pole, hollerin' and hootin'. When they get through they come together. They play "at the end of the season" (the Stomp Dance season), when the fall comes. Every year they have one game, until next year. You dance all night, and then the next day you play ball...

The Ball Game is played by many tribal people in the Southeastern part of North America, including the Cherokee, Choctaw,

Seneca boy dressed for the ball game (Lacrosse) Cattaruagus Reservation, New York, 1901. (Courtesy of Museum of American Indian, Heye Foundation)

and Creek and in the Northeast among the Seneca and Iroquois. In earlier times the game became a focus for specialists to use magic against the other team. There is a Cherokee story that tells about the origin of these "spirit wars" in the Ball Game:

According to the Cherokee, the animals once challenged the birds to a great ball play. The [challenge] was accepted, the preliminaries were arranged, and at last the contestants assembled at the appointed spot... The animals on the ground, while the birds took position in the tree-tops to await the throwing up of the ball. On the side of the animals were the bear, whose [heavy] weight bore down all opposition, the deer, who excelled all others in running, and the terrapin, who was invulnerable to the stoutest blows. On the side of the birds were the eagle, the hawk, and the great Tlaniwa...all noted for their swiftness and power of flight. While the latter were preening their feathers and watching every motion of their adversaries below, they noticed two small creatures, hardly larger than mice, climbing up the tree on which was perched the leader of the birds. Finally they reached the top and humbly asked to be allowed to join in the game. The captain looked at them a moment and, seeing that they were four-footed, asked them why they did not go to the animals where they properly belonged. The little things explained that they had done so, but had been laughed at and had been rejected on account of their [small] size. On hearing their story the bird captain

261

[wanted to] take pity on them, but there was one serious difficulty in the way... How could they join the birds when they had no wings? The eagle, the hawk, and the rest now crowded around, and after some discussion, it was decided to try and make wings for the little fellows. But, how to do it? All at once, by a happy inspiration, [somebody thought] of the drum used in the [ball game] dance before the throwing of the ball. The head was made of ground-hog leather, and perhaps a corner would be cut off and [used] for wings. No sooner suggested than done. Two pieces of leather taken from the drumhead were cut into shape and attached to the legs of one of the small animals, and thus originated Tlameha, the bat. The ball was now tossed up and the bat was told to catch it, and his expertness in dodging and circling about, keeping the ball constantly in motion and never allowing it to fall to the ground, soon convinced the birds that they had gained a most valuable ally. They next turned their attention to the other little creature; and now [discovered] the worst difficulty! All their leather had been used in making wings for the bat, and there was not time to send for more. In this dilemma it was suggested that perhaps wings might be made by stretching out the skin of the animal itself. So, two large birds seized him from opposite sides with their strong bills; and by tugging and pulling at his fur for several minutes succeeded in stretching the skin between the fore and hind feet until at last the thing was done and there was Tewa, the flying squirrel. Then the bird captain, to try him, threw up the ball, when the flying squirrel, with a graceful bound, sprang off the limb and catching it in his teeth, carried it through the air to another tree-top, a hundred feet away. When all was ready, the game began, but at the very [beginning] the flying squirrel caught the ball and carried it up a tree, then threw it to the birds, who kept it in the air for some time when it dropped; but, just before it reached the ground, the bat [grabbed] it, and by his dodging and doubling, kept it out of the

way of even the swiftest of the animals until he finally threw it in at the goal, and thus won the victory for the birds. Because of their assistance on this occasion, the Cherokee player invokes the aid of the bat, of the bird spirits as well as the flying squirrel and hangs a piece of the bat's wing on his stick to bring him swiftness, sureness, and victory. (Mooney, 1890:105)

During the period of religious suppression from the 1870's to the 1920's, the Ball Game was banned because it was "too tough," but it has been reinstated again.

Finally, the Green Corn Dance is held to mark the height of the new growing season—the new moon of the "Everything Growing Moon"—the last of June or the first of July. It is a celebration of a maturing new year of life, signified by the ripening of the corn. At the same time the special roles of men and women, girls and boys, in this cycle of growth is celebrated: "the coming of age" for girls, the "naming" of the boys. Likewise, their special duties in the life process is made clear: the sowing and cultivating of the corn by the boys, the making of sofki by the girls. Andrew Harjo from Oklahoma told the way it was, about the ripening of the corn and the Green Corn Dance:

Them tassels, like sometimes its purple...the tassels—the corn silk. When they see that on the stem they can tell the girls to take that and rub it and put it on their hair so that it could be so silky. They have to wash their hair with it and press it down and anytime they do like that, it'll stay that way. Their hair is so silky because they use that. They call it a hair purifier—and in this period of time, all the young girls use it—because later on in the future they're going to be making sofki. It's a broth of boiled corn—dry corn, hominy. See, the girls are going to be doing that. And the men, boys—they planted the corn and it was really a ceremonial occasion. And the boys were really so proud because when they saw the corn came up with their silk sticking up and they go out and look and, of course, the father would be so proud of them because he had planted the corn and, boy, he's gonna have good ears of corn. They do not eat any corn before then. If a boy plants it, then when the time for them to pull come—to pull roasting ears—then, of course, the boys or men have to go out and pull them and the ladies have to do the preparing.

When to have the first meeting of the year in Oklahoma is decided in different ways, depending on the particular Stomp Dance Ground, each of which has its own set of rules and leaders. George B. Harjo tells us:

Now, we have to go by the leaf and grass; how high grass and how big a leaf. Then we know that's the time to start. Each ground has different rules. This one here, in July, we call it Green Corn. That's our big ceremony. We call it "Christmas— "Indian Christmas." Each ground, they got different rules. This one here, for the "Christmas" we feed the fire with green wood and corn; that's a ground rule. And like Alabama, when they have a buffalo dance, a Green Corn, something like that, when they have one, their ceremony is with dry wood. Now all the grounds are

not alike. Just like church, got different denominations, different ways. We can't go down there and tell them what to do, and they can't come down here and tell us what to do. We have to go our way and they have to go their way. And when we go there we have to go their way. That's the way it is...But we dance (Stomp Dance gatherings) once a month only. Gives us a chance to go down there and help our friends dance for the ground— help them out dancing. And they have one each a month too. We depend on each other getting help, back and forth.

In Florida, the Green Corn Dance takes about seven days, with some days of preparation and four days of the main gathering when all the people have arrived and the central events of a sacred nature take place. These include wood gathering: steer butchering; the hunting of the white Egret for feathers for the Feather Dance; the preparing of the Black Drink; the sweat bath; the "scratching" of the boys and men; the blessing of the Medicine Bundle; and the serving of the final meal. These events, with the exception of the sweat bath and scratching, take place in the day time.

Seminole dancing, ca. 1956. Florida. (Courtesy of the Smithsonian Institution, National Anthropological Archives)

In Oklahoma, a Stomp Dance takes place at night. The camp is set up in a circle, with the different clan families situated in the camp in different directions, just as they sit, within the Stomp Dance Circle, in specific places. Cooking takes place in *chickees*, or, in Oklahoma, under branch arbors, on the edge of the clearing. In the center, off to the side somewhat, is the Mens-Womens Ball Game Pole. The Stomp Dance Circle itself is only occupied during the dancing, and has certain rules which belong to it alone.

The dancing itself attracts The People in Oklahoma. Each ground has its own leaders, but dance leaders—those men who know the songs or make up songs and can lead the dances well—come from different grounds to "help out," as George B. Harjo told us. Stomp Dancing is hard work, both for the men who sing, and for the women who follow wearing the turtle-shell rattles, keeping the rhythm. Throughout the night the leaders change and the dances change—Buffalo Dance, Feather Dance, Duck Dance, Ribbon Dance—dances for different occasions.

Another leader is ready. They ask him, "Can you lead?" If he says yes, well, then when he comes back and another leader quits, they announce it. They say, "We gonna have another leader coming in..." It's like in church, when one person starts singing, they all singing. That's the way the men sing—"Everybody come on out and enjoy themselves!" They say when the other leader comes in—it's like church songs.

The Stomp Dance songs do not sound the same as church songs, but the leading and the following is a tradition of gospel singing as well as Stomp Dance singing. In fact, the way the people dance, and the entire atmosphere of the Stomp Dance, is frowned upon by the Christians. In the old days, and today in Florida, they will not let their members attend the Green Corn Dance or Stomp Dances. One Seminole woman was brought to Stomp Dances by her father, a Medicine Man; she trained in his knowledge for a few years. She was later prevented from going by her mother, who was a Christian (Baptist), and began taking her to church. She tells us:

The men that go to the Stomp Dance, you'll find them a lot stronger than our men who do not go to a Stomp Dance. They are more physically stronger. I don't know if it's because they stomp all night, or what. But they still...purify themselves. They drink herbs—"cleaning out." And you know, as a rule, your ones that go to the Stomp Dance are your most healthiest, because they take care of themselves. Your leaders have certain rules they have to follow; because if they don't follow this, they claim, every person that leaves and has not taken care of him/herself—everybody that dances with that person gets tired. And the one who really takes care of himself can go in there and dance, keep on dancing. Sometimes one leader will take over and dance for 3 hours straight—no resting or anything.

I went over there once—I hadn't danced for years and years, and I thought, well, boy, I'm going to have to learn. And I started dancing. For some reason, I wanted to get in there and start dancing; and it seemed like my whole body just came back to life—I can't explain it. I danced for about 3 hours and I came out and my mother said..."And you must be a christian?"

One of the most important procedures of the Green Corn Dance is the drinking of the Black Drink, or "Medicine" which is prepared with Red Root, a medicinal herb used by the Seminole People. It is prepared on the first day of fasting, and drunk at various intervals for two days until the sweat bath, or swimming, as is the case in Oklahoma. George B. Harjo explains:

If we are going to eat medicine, I can eat all I want today, but at 12:00 I quit. And I won't eat anything till I go into that ground except that medicine. All morning. At evening they have a call again between 7 and 8, and when they call, we go back into that ring, and when you're back in that ring you can't drink pop, coffee, chewing gum, candy—you have to stay with that medicine. If you get thirsty, you go out there and drink that medicine. If you get hungry, you go out there and eat that medicine. We dance all night till the next morning around 7 or 8. Then we go swimming. When we come back, we're free.

Another procedure which was both part of the Green Corn Dance and a general procedure throughout life was and is "scratching." We are told that young Seminole boys and girls were, traditionally, scratched regularly. It was a form of discipline done by the mother's brother and elders on the mother's side of the family, to teach the importance of "proper conduct and behavior." (Buswell, 1972:183) A Seminole man from Florida describes this process:

The father taught the children. He taught them who their elders were. When an elder of the clan visited the camp he had not seen them for a long time. He would needle them. They took off their shirts and wet themselves on the calves. The elder administered the needling and went on his way. The children washed off the blood and went on. They did not get mad too much. They regarded and obeyed the elders—what they had been taught. The badness in their blood would be spilt . . . But when there is no needling, the people have heavy blood. They steal, they get mad, and they destroy things.

Another Seminole man explains that scratching was also done to adults, as it is in the Green Corn Dance:

When they came to the home sometimes even an adult who felt he was getting too lazy or perhaps irritable or short-tempered—because of having too much blood—would ask such an elder to scratch him. Afterwards he would feel *good* again! (Buswell, 1972:185)

At the Green Corn Dance there is a special sequence to the scratching of the boys and men—in the old days girls were included in the scratching of the final day—perhaps two strokes down the length of the right then left calf; a single stroke down each forearm, and two parallel strokes on the breast bone, slanting down to the left and to the right. Andrew Harjo, telling of a particular sequence of events in the Green Corn Dance gathering, says:

Everybody has to be scratched, with the owl claws (nowadays needles are used)—the women and girls not as much. They can't twitch, they can't—even the little boys, they told them not to cry. They have to be brave. It's painful—even the little girls.

At the end of the Green Corn Dance, the leading Medicine Man thanks The People for coming, and "sums up" the feeling of the purpose for the Dance. It is a *meditation*, Andrew Harjo tells us:

It's just like a prayer, (in church), just a real prayer, but the only thing is he doesn't say "Life Giver"—he doesn't say that. The only thing he'll say is, The Mighty One. He uses the word, Mighty One, and only one and you are the Life Giver. And then he returns thanks to the corn, since he is the medicine man and leader of the whole tribe, so he says this thanks—the corn that we have received from you, for giving us this so that my children will survive through this year, another year.

In Florida, as we have said, until very recently the Green Corn Dance was the time when the entire tribe came together to discuss important matters as well as reaffirm the sacred and mystical roots of The People and their cosmology. The Green Corn Dance was not a special society. In Oklahoma there is more of a "membership." Perhaps because the church criticized the Stomp Dancers for so long, to go to the Stomp Dance Grounds was more of a private, perhaps even secret thing. One had to show a special interest. George B. Harjo explains how his ground receives new members:

We watch him year by year, and we say, "That guy, he likes that medicine." So, we make him a member; we call him. They come to us; we call his name, then when he comes to us, we give him another name, a "ground" name. That's the way we go.

Marie Hall, a member of the Tribal Council in Oklahoma, gives us a clear idea of how a sacred way like the Stomp Dance is something that is also "passed on" from generation to generation, and how important the continuity of seeing, hearing, and doing the dances, songs, and other procedures is to each new generation:

...when you go to the Stomp Dance you start your children, if you're a real Stomp Dance believer, you raise your children in that and everything they do at the Stomp Dance you teach your children and the children go there all the time. Just like your pop music, you expose your child to the radio, to the pop music they like—they learn the songs on their own, well, your children will learn it. I have seen kids as little as four get out there and lead with their father, dance on their knees, and I seen a small child, a mother will make a small turtle shell for it and get out there and shake. You just grow up in it and you just learn.

The Florida Green Corn Dance and the Oklahoma Stomp Dances have differences regarding drinking, and the Christian church-goers do too. George B. Harjo, a Stomp Dance Leader, speaks of the rules at his Ground:

that's why we here, we like to stop the drinking—and the girl's monthly period, we call it. We can't allow them to dance inside the ring. We aren't stingy with our ground but we try to have love for one another. We can't have white people dance inside, that's a rule from way back, generations back, and we are going to try and stand by it close as we can. We don't want anybody down and making fun, make a fool out of this ground. That's why we always tell The People, "We love the People"—we try and tell them the rules. If you come out there half drunk, you raise hell, you answer back this and that—you get sickness.

In Florida, however, drinking is one of the main features of the Green Corn Dance, with even the Leaders drinking, sometimes heavily. It happens that these individuals do not drink

in ordinary daily life, *only* at the Green Corn Dance—so that here, at this time, even drinking can become sacred. Even though there is drinking, it is made clear that the Grounds are sacred ground and fighting or disruption is not wanted.

And finally, Marie Hall talks about the meaning of the Stomp Dance and the meaning of the ground rules:

It was healing and giving thanks. Your drunks could go to church but they couldn't go to the Stomp Dance—*sacred ground*. Well, you know what I think? (Everybody says I'm a little off.) You know when Moses went up there on that Mountain for God—that was a holy and sacred place, not everybody could go there. The Stomp Dance—to the one who really believes in it—it's a holy place for them, they do not allow any violation, any violence, and they can't tolerate anyone who violates their rules; and their rules are a lot stricter—their laws remind me of Moses.

THE SEMINOLE ADAPT CHRISTIANITY

One afternoon as the wind began blowing through the woods and over the fields towards the house, Webster Wise, a Seminole man from Oklahoma who has studied many things in his long life, began speaking. He was talking about human nature—what the scripture* tells us about human beings and the natural world:

We must study nature.
I've seen the scripture. The scripture tells us we don't have to work
we have our daily bread, clothes, we don't have to work. Jesus said,
*"Ye are more val'ble** than the bird."*
You don't see no bird plowin, sowin the seed, reapin, buildin the storage. And when he gets hungry goin up to the storagehouse and get the food, plow some more. God takes care of you.
"Ye are more val'ble than the birds."

---

* The words in the Bible.

**Valuable, pronounced with a Southern accent of Oklahoma.

You don't have to be seekin the job. You start selling your energies, turning to the commercial for your energies. You not a commercial person. Your energies not commercial. Your soul not commercial. But your the one that's turning yourself into commercial. That's the way the scriptures refer.

"Ye are more val'ble than the birds."

You don't see no birds sowin the seed, plowing the fields, reapin, building the storehouse. He's enjoyin the glorious merciful God. He don't work for his clothes. He don't work for his food. He don't PLAN in the future, in the next day. When the day's over, that rooster in the trees, and the next day he start enjoyin himself. But we the one. We are very intolerant, opposite, deceptive, and we do have to work.

That's why I have to go to the employment office tomorrow at eight. That's so that I'll just put myself in the commercial, suckin my energies, for two dollars an hour. You see the point? But: if we start seeking the righteousness of God in his kingdom, all those things will be added unto you. You don't have to work.

"Ye are more val'ble than the birds."

That shows how stubborn people we are.

"Ye are more val'ble than the birds."

We never did see birds workin, workin for someone. But he enjoyin, singin, flyin up in the air. That shows how stubborn people we are. I'm not professin myself "I'm not stubborn," but I am after all. I'm not professin myself "I'm a righteous man." "I'm a Christian man." "I go to church every Wednesday night, every Sunday—I'm a Sunday school teacher!" If I'm working for someone I'm showin how stubborn I am—puttin myself in the commercial. The birds is not commercial; they work, they enjoyin, but it's not commercial.

"Ye are more val'ble than the birds."

But even what I professin I am, what I am still shows I'm stubborn, how stubborn I am. We don't have to carry a money bag, extra clothes, extra shoes, but we do. We take up things, we take all these things. When we complete our destination we open our bag . . . God says all things will be added unto you. You don't have to spend no money. If I'm in the commercial, if I want a place to sleep, I have to spend money. That shows how stubborn people we are. Therefore, I have to bring extras. You never did see a bird carryin a lunch bag, seed bag, carryin seed with him when he flies. That's the nature that teaches how stubborn we are. We are more val'ble than the birds, but we put ourselves way less than the birds. We know we don't enjoy it. We don't sing in the glorious singin, we don't do that. But the bird does. 'Cause we're stubborn.

Webster Wise, in his talk here, touches on one of the critical ideas or concepts in the Christian doctrine as it was taken and accepted by the Seminole People recently in Florida: *the effect of a modern, dominant society's economy on the lives of The People.* In this section we will be discussing these effects and examining briefly the background of Baptist and Christian adaptation among the Seminole of Oklahoma and Florida.

Historical Background

After the second Seminole War in 1843 and the removal of part of the Seminole communities to Oklahoma, the missionary activity among The People began in Oklahoma. In Florida, The People just went deeper into the interior of Florida, and resisted any contacts with the outside world until the 1940's. In Florida, then, conversion into the Baptist Church has followed directly from the amount of outside contact each community has had recently and the effect of this contact on individuals and families.

In Oklahoma, missionizing, especially from Baptists, began with the first arrivals. The missionaries were "white" but the preaching and converting was done in the Seminole language, orally transmitted, since most of The People at that time could not read, nor had the Seminole language developed into a written form. Often, a few individuals who had frequent contact with the missionaries would learn certain key concepts and phrases, and bring these back to their communities—the settlements where the Seminole People lived. They would talk about the things they had heard and The People would listen and learn. Of course, the key concepts and phrases were interpreted in the light of what The People already knew about the world, and, as we saw in the Chapter, **The World Out of Balance**, in the light of any prophecies or dreams The People or the community might have had. James Cully, a former Preacher and founder of one of the Baptist Churches near Seminole, Oklahoma, explains how The People learned the hymns they now sing in the Churches—hymns in the Seminole language and with unique melodies:

> Yes, they had Indian songs, but everyone had their own song seems like; just like today, you know, so when you're ready to sing, you went ahead and sung. They didn't have any books...they was led by the Holy Spirit, because they used to go fast and pray. I know a lot of places where they used to go fast and pray, to learn the song and carry on the work—you don't see them now no more. The songs were written from the heart and spirit. They didn't know how to read, couldn't even write nor read, but they preached. But when you compare it today, they were in the Bible when they were preaching—that shows that the spirit had preached through them. They thought they were doing the preaching but it wasn't them, it was the Holy Spirit preaching through their service.

He goes on to explain that in the early days of the Church, The People used to go out into the woods, as in a vision quest, and fasting, they would meditate and pray until they had had a vision. Songs or sermons would come in these visions. Sometimes the entire congregation would do this, in order to meditate on problems they had in common as a people:

> Back in those days they all went out in the woods. They had a date set of their own. They have a fasting day at the church too and they do that also, but the day of their own they have to be out in the woods there—I guess they prayed and found their locations too. That's what they used all the time. They used to have rocks, two or three rocks sitting there against a tree, so when they pray well, they kneel against those rocks, and when they get through they can sit down, rest, concentrate—half a day if they want to, longer, as long as they want. They didn't have to be told to do that. That was done for the spirit I imagine. Its the only way. You could see the little hole where they had been kneeling. Womanfolk had their own, menfolk had their own.

> I guess it's either mind or through their prayers that this happens. The Bible talks about fasting and praying too you know—sure does. Go out, found their place, fasting place; if they had anything coming up in the church that was to be settled or anything that comes up they wanted to know which way, they'd have to go out there and ask Him for help, telling Him to lead that business, whatever it may be. Some of them used to go a day. They didn't have much trouble like they do today. You take it today, some of them aren't doing the right thing, what the Lord wants, that's what they try to do, they, that bunch, they bring in something else, create a confusion amongst themselves. That's why these churches just not going—it's going down.

CHRISTIANITY AND GREEN CORN DANCE: A CONTRAST

> The head chief told us that there was not a family in that whole Nation that had not a home of its own. There was not a [poor man] in that Nation, and the Nation did not owe a dollar. It built...its schools, its hospitals. Yet the defect of the system was apparent. They have got as far as they can go, because they own their land in common...under [this] system there is no enterprise to make your home any better than that of your neighbors. *There is no selfishness, which is at the bottom of civilization*. Till the people will consent to give up their lands, and divide them among their citizens so that each can own the land he cultivates, they will not make much more progress.*

---

* Senator Henry Dawes (of the Dawes or "Allotment Act" of 1887) speaking in 1885. Italics are ours.

Christianity, in the form of concepts preached by Seminole Baptist preachers, made its entrance in Florida Seminole communities at the same time as their economic isolation from the "outside" dominant society ceased. The Tamiami Trail community, for example, which is still more "crafts-economy"-oriented, speaks little English, is basically mistrustful of "outside" ways, and continues to treat the Green Corn Dance as a central renewing event in the cosmology of their sacred system. There are few Christians in this community, and those who have converted have often left to go to one of the more Tribal-oriented communities— Brighton, Big Cypress, and Hollywood. Of these three, Hollywood is most acculturated.

Christianity first, and the new Tribal Government second, brought the Seminole People a new kind of leadership—that is, a different *style* or way of dealing with the problems of everyday life. For Baptist-style Christianity, as we have discussed briefly in the Chapter, **The World Out of Balance,** * a dynamic *preacher* is the central figure in introducing that faith. In the case of the Seminole People, the preacher made all the difference. The People, those who eventually converted, accepted the new style, the unfamiliar role of the preacher, and in doing so, opened themselves up to what he was saying—they followed his lead. As we have suggested earlier, what the preachers were saying made new sense with the changing times.

When the new Tribal Government was formed, it took as its model the dominant society's style of governing; one or two dominant leaders. The Green Corn Dance had aboriginally been the focus for "consensus" governing with the elders taking the lead in the discussions, and everyone ultimately agreeing or disagreeing with the decisions under discussion. The preachers fit into the new position of *Tribal leader* and through the Tribal Government, also helped The People move into the 20th century world with its pressures for assimilation. They did not criticize those who did not want to follow; they only made it

easier for those who did. Below are two examples of the histories of preachers, from their conversions, to their taking positions in the Tribal Government.

The first preacher is the minister of the First Seminole Baptist Church (Southern Baptist) which was founded by Willie King in 1936. He was among the first group of five to attend the Baptist Bible Institute at Lakeland in 1946 and to start preaching. It was he who founded the mission work at Brighton in 1951 and was the minister there at the dedication of their building in 1952. He is good-looking, good at meeting people, and owns 230 head of cattle.

[This] preacher had moved to the Brighton Reservation in 1939. From there he worked for a white man. Consequently he was able to learn both Creek and English. At twenty he married a Mikasuki woman, and in 1941 they moved to Big Cypress where he worked at road construction for the Government. His wife was converted under Stanley Smith's ministry in 1944 and under her influence he accepted Christianity.

The details of his conversion experience are noteworthy...One night in November 1945, when he had gone to bed in his chickee, he saw a bright light as if under the edge of the roof, and heard a voice calling his name and saying, "Arise and take my message to your people." On the following two nights the vision was repeated, the same bright light and the same words following. At the third occurrence of the vision he responded in prayer and could hardly wait to make his formal acceptance of Christ at Stanley Smith's invitation the following Sunday.

This preacher's knowledge of Creek, Mikasuki, and English, his exposure to the white man and his training at the Bible Institute enabled him to represent his people on many public occasions. Thus one fellow Seminole student at the B.B.I. remarked that this Preacher did not attend classes regularly because he was often out on speaking engagements.

[The second preacher] on the other hand, had no education. He has a literate

* See, for example, the discussion of Pentecostalism and evangelists.

269

and talented wife to help him, however, and he himself [has a] strong motivation and desire to get things done. "I don't just want to think about it; I want to do it!" Furthermore, he [learned] from Stanley Smith and is a dynamic preacher in his own right. Persuasive but at ease on the platform, he is a speaker who zeros in on practical problems such as money, and weighty matters such as the appeal to young people.

In 1957 the second and first preachers became, respectively, the first President of the newly constituted Board of Directors, and the first Chairman of the newly constituted Tribal Council of the Seminole Tribe of Florida. In 1959 they were each re-elected President and both men then held their respective offices until 1965. The second remains as a representative on the Tribal Council. (Buswell, 1972:417-418)

One of the central differences in the traditional sacred system, whose spiritual renewal took place with the community-at-large, is that the emphasis in the Seminole Baptist-style Christianity is on the *individual* whereas the aboriginal system on the *group*. In other words, problems in the Seminole Baptist system are personal problems; aboriginally, they were a communal problem involving clan, kin, extended family, and so on.

In the Baptist system a person's relationship to God is the focus of attention; in the Green Corn Dance the involvement in the ritual is what is important. The Seminole Baptists insist on a personal commitment to God; whereas in the Green Corn Dance, there is no missionary work or attempt to change a person's ways. In the Baptist system the emphasis is on personal salvation: life after death, and a fear of "Satan" and sin. In the Green Corn Dance there is a reaffirmation of basic cosmological principles—the personal discipline of the child, The People's responsibility to the Earth.

In addition, people in Florida who have had a drinking problem turn to the Church because they require the constant help that a weekly or twice weekly Church meeting can give them. Since drinking is preached against in the Church, these meetings help the drinking individual to keep from "back sliding" into

drink again. A chart appears on the facing page comparing the character and main purposes of the Church and the Green Corn Dance.

As we have said, in the past the Green Corn Dance involved an individual in an entire ritual network. In the Green Corn Dance "clan membership structures leadership roles, camp arrangement, certain sequences of dancers, the naming ceremony, and is a crucial aspect of the celebration from beginning to end. In the church, however, clan membership carries no function whatever...Christianity cross-cuts clan, family, tribe, language, reservation, and visiting patterns..." (Buswell, 1972:394) Conversion to Christianity is by individuals, for one reason because its message quite often appeals to an individual's personal worries and problems. When new economic problems and situations began separating individuals from each other, forcing individuals and families out of the customary and traditional networks of communication and economics, Christianity became a much more influential force in the lives of many Seminole People. Earlier, in the beginning of the chapter, we cited the statistics for hunters and trappers, showing that even when there was trade between the Seminoles and outside traders, non-Seminoles made up a greater percentage of the trade, using different "modern" methods of hunting and trapping. The colonizers who began moving into Florida, who now make up the populations of the big cities, were rich compared to the Seminole who had previously not been involved with making money or living the life-style of the dominant society. Suddenly, things changed. Suddenly, it became clear to some people that a compromise, a change in customs and habit might be necessary.

As The People began modifying and changing their economic customs—the ways of their lives in general—it happened that, as in the case of so many people in the dominant society, the "dream" or reward of the economic system was not everybody's reward. Many people remained poor. One can see that the sermons of the Seminole preachers focus on this "problem," on this worry. And as we mentioned in the Chapter, **The World Out of Balance**, the gospel of "the Poor will enter the Kingdom of Heaven" appealed to individuals who were having a difficult and bitter time of

	Church	Green Corn Dance
1. Location	Reservation	Off-Reservation (Florida)
2. Type of calendar	Weekly and monthly	Annual event (Florida) Summer months (Oklahoma)
3. Membership	Open to all believers. Appeal made to all.	Open to Indians who wish to participate; closed to outsiders; no appeal made.
4. Participation	Greater responsibility upon leaders as directors.	Greater responsibility upon individuals as participants.
5. Leadership	Individual initiative important to direct program.	Initiative less important than the ritual tradition.
6. Things that are condemned.	Emphasis upon behavior outside the church: drinking, smoking, breaking the Sabbath, and participation in the Stomp or Green Corn Dance.	Emphasis upon behavior in the Green Corn Dance or on the Stomp Dance Grounds; any violation of sacred ritual.
7. Ultimate goals	Conversion, salvation, permanent renewal.	Cleansing; annual renewal.
8. Orientation	Afterlife, Heaven, Hell.	The here-and-now; sanctity of the entire system.
9. Social group	Denomination	Clan
10. The sacred	Personal deity, religious service and worship.	Medicine bundle and other ceremonial procedures and prayers. (after Buswell, 1972:395)

living on earth. Recall Webster Wise's talk in the beginning of this section. He tells us that "putting ourselves in the commercial" is making us forget our kinship with the natural world, the flow of life and survival as a "natural" thing, like the bird's life. We hear other people talk about this same subject in the final chapter of this textbook, **The Wandering Ground**. It's a difficult question: civilization of The People was supposed to mean a good life, a wealthy life. Instead, for many people, the new way made life more difficult and more confusing than before. Following is part of a sermon that the second preacher, written about earlier, gave July 6, 1969, in the Mekesuky Baptist Church near Hollywood, Florida:

I don't know why Christians are poor, but the Bible says He is going to give to us riches. Everytime I see this one I've been thinking, when I read this.

You know, lot of us asking the Lord, this is Christians, talking about Christians. Father's working, mother's working, oldest son working, daughter's working, seems not enough money coming in. Everybody's working. Looks like money's not enough. So, we just keep on. We work, work, work, work, and I think Satan, he wants us to be busy. And he don't want us to be busy spiritually. That's why he give us bills at Sears Roebuck and big stores that say, "Come and get it! No money, no down payment." We look at the beds and they're still good, but we throw it out and go get a new one, because no down payment. But you have to pay every month. It doesn't say every month, but no down payment gets in our eye. Chair look good, just a little scratch. We just throw it out. Go get new one. And we look at the television. We don't have no color. We need color. And we need something else. And pretty soon bills pretty high, and hard to pay. And that way we're so busy trying to pay these bills. Car payments coming, house payment coming, grocery bills, everything...

Next thing I did, I asked my wife to go out and find work and she did. She worked and fed me and she had a hard time. But she kept working, and she got disgusted with me. And then, when you are too old it would be hard, so this was the case. You quit working. We just have to depend on the Lord to feed us. Our son works, and everybody worked, but it seems like it is not enough money. There's lot of people like that. The father works, the mother works, the son works, and then, if there is a daughter, she works. But still, not enough. What is wrong? We get letters saying, "Come get things," but they don't tell you that you have to end up paying every month...

So take Simon Peter.* He must have had a lot of bills, and maybe people he owed it to were pressuring him to pay. So he was a fisherman. So he went back to fish. So the other disciples went with him when he said he was going to go fishing. Then they went and got in the boat. Then they went out and did as they always did, dropped their nets and tried to get fish all night. They didn't catch one by morning, and they were so tired and cold, just like when you go out hunting for deer all night. That's the way they came back.

When they came back, Jesus was walking by the sea. He told them to drop their nets onto the right side, but before they did that, Simon Peter said, "I've been throwing nets all night." Simon Peter had been a fisherman all his life, and that's all he knew.

Joseph was a carpenter, and when He was a little boy He (Jesus) used to help His dad. Jesus helped His father build houses.

"But I'm a fisherman, and I've been dropping nets all night, yet I can't catch one," he could have told Jesus. But instead he told Him, "I'll do what you tell me." When he dropped the net he got a lot of fish, enough to pay bills with. When I think about this story how come I can't get enough money to pay for these things, and turn all these things over to the Lord and let Him take over. Then these bills we wouldn't have to bother us.

My wife works, I work, my daughter works; yet we still don't have enough to pay the bills. Then we go out and borrow money to pay the bills. Then we get deeper in debt. Then we wonder why we have so many bills.

If we listen to Jesus we could have a lot of fish. And just like they said, "Come help us." He could do that for us. He'll give it to you. Now that is all. You've made it through the week so we will dismiss early. Get ready, whatever your job is, and look for strength. Work and let us try to do the Lord's work. Now everybody stand and we will have prayer. Joe will pray and we will dismiss. (Buswell, 1972:476-483)

In addition to this aspect of the Baptist-Christian appeal to the Seminole People, there have been some other factors which have made it easier for Seminoles in general to accept Christianity compared with many Native American communities in North America. For one, the Gospel was presented in Florida through the interpretation of original key concepts *by Seminoles*, and transmitted *by Seminoles* in Florida and Oklahoma.

Second, Christianity was eventually and importantly advocated by traditional leaders—the Medicine Men of the Green Corn Dance who converted.

Third, in the beginning there was preaching about the differences between the Church and the Green Corn Dance—that they were incompatible (they could not get along

---

* A disciple or follower of Jesus in the New Testament.

together). *But*, in general, there has not been a negative attitude (in Florida and except for the drinking aspect) on the part of the Christians toward the Green Corn Dance or other traditional customs and practices. For example, herb doctors and herb women who are Christians continue to serve both non-Christians and Christians as specialists in this area. One non-Christian Medicine Man, leader of the Green Corn Dance, goes to a converted Medicine Man for treatment. Most other routines go on as before, with such new elements as schooling and tribal laws affecting both Christians and non-Christians alike.

Some of the potential weaknesses in the Seminole Churches are first, the lack of a Bible in the Seminole (Mikasuki) language. Without a Bible the Christian doctrine cannot be studied. Key concepts cannot be interpreted in the light of Seminole experience and world-view. Young people who want to study to be preachers and whose congregations are Seminole-speaking, must not only go to Baptist Bible School, but they must learn English.

Second, the concepts and themes of the sermons are still the same ones that the missionaries in Oklahoma brought with them into the newly settled Seminole communities a hundred years ago. Because the Bible is not studied, new themes cannot be presented. Some people, young people especially, lose their interest, as one individual put it: "I know what that man is going to say; he has been preaching the same thing for ten, fifteen years." (Buswell, 1972:443)

Third, the factions of different denominations might weaken the Church by putting denomination ahead of Christian doctrine and practice.

The strength of any system of ideal behavior is in its adaptability or viability. Christianity has been strongest where its basic elements have been incorporated into a culture's already-existing cosmology and adapted at the same time into a culture's acculturation processes, for example, like the Pomo Bole Maru and the Native American Church. This way is advocated by a 96 year-old Seminole woman in Oklahoma, who one night after church, got in a discussion with the lead singer of the congregation. He was asked:

Woman: You a Baptist clear through then?

Lead singer: Yes, Baptist, and my wife is a Presbyterian.

Woman: It's all the same anyhow—different baptisms, they don't baptize alike...

Lead singer: It's what they believe in—just so whatever you got will save you...

Woman: But then of course, this Baptism it's not what saves you, it's the way you live daily isn't it?

SUMMARY

In this Chapter we examined the transition one culture (the Seminole) made from the *sacred* to the *secular*, separating, out of necessity, sacred knowledge and practices from daily life. We saw how the Seminole have managed, to a degree, to preserve much of the aboriginal core of their culture, including the sacred ways connected with herbal knowledge, childbirth, clanship, naming, scratching, story-telling, the oral histories, and practices connected with the Green Corn Dance and the Stomp Dance.

In addition, we examined what changes have entered the lives of the Seminole People of Florida in the last 30 years, and how these changes are requiring certain adaptations on the part of the Seminole community and Seminole individuals. One of these adaptations has been, apparently, the conversion to Baptist Christianity in the Florida communities. Christianity, along with the Tribal Council, has absorbed many of the functions the Green Corn Dance and related ceremonies used to perform, including weddings; political and criminal matters; and family problems. The Church has also provided a vehicle for mystical experience as we saw in the conversion experience of the first preacher.

The sacred among the Seminole is slowly narrowing its focus to include mainly the annual Green Corn Dances; the Stomp Dances with their ball games; the specialists' field of knowledge; conversion experiences and mystical experiences within the setting of the Church, and a few family networks of conservative traditional day-to-day life. Mystical experience and oral tradition do not govern such aspects of life as economics, politics, and education—these are now considered secular. Despite this separation of sacred and secular, which did not exist aboriginally, the Seminole are attempting to carry on their lives in the 20th century without forsaking the basic roots of their traditional culture. And these roots are strengthened during sacred reunions and with the continuation of sacred practices.

Suggested Additional Readings

CAPRON, LOUIS
   1969   "Florida's Emerging Seminoles," *National Geographic*, November, pp. 717-734.
CARR, ARCHIE FAIRLY
   1973   *The Everglades*, New York, Time-Life Books, (The Everglades habitat)
GARBARINO, MERWYN S.
   1972   *Big Cypress: A Changing Seminole Community*, New York, Holt, Rinehart and Winston.

INDIAN HOUSE
            Songs of the Muskogee Creek, Indian House Records. Taos, New Mexico. (Stomp Dance music)
STURTEVANT, W.C.
   1971   "Creek to Seminole," Chapter 4 in Leacock and Lurie, *The North American Indian In Historical Perspective*, New York, Random House.

CHAPTER TWELVE

12 Navajo Traditional Knowledge

PART 1

"I AM THE ESSENCE OF LIFE WHICH IS OLD AGE..."*

There were several prominent events that used to mark a Diné** person's life, but this is generally not true for most young people (Diné) today, especially since formal education began for Diné children throughout the Navajo land (reservation). Why are not these certain ceremonies experienced by the present-day young people? One reason is the effect of government policy on early childhood education—"Early formal education programs for the Indians, beginning with some groups in colonial times and extending to the late 1920's and early 1930's, [were] aimed at 'civilizing' and 'christianizing Indians.'' (Thompson, 1975:25) Children were taken away from their homes to boarding schools, and some children daily left their *hooghan* to go to day school in their community. These "schools" were, and still are, foreign to the *ways* of our grandparents and their ancestors who are our forefathers. Despite the amount of time Diné children spend in schools there are ceremonies or rituals a child has a chance to participate in, to be a part of, in early childhood when parents take care of the child. Ceremonies sponsored by the parents, grandparents, or relatives, are given for the children.

The Diné dine'é believe that these events of early childhood and along the path of a Diné person's life are set by the *diyin dine'é*.†

Several activities in early childhood are like those in the original events told in the stories and myths. In the present day they are sponsored by a parent or guardian, in which the child is *the main person.*

Aside from these formally sponsored events, it is believed that there are major mythical figures that set examples for the personal growth of a female, and a male Diné dine'é, from their babyhood and adulthood to parenthood. When mythical stories are told there are many sacred beings—among them are major figures that significantly deal *with Diné dine'é, the People*:

...When First Man came to the top of the mountains he heard a baby crying. The lightning striking all about and murk caused by the hard rain made it difficult to see anything. He discovered the baby lying with its head towards the west and its feet towards the east. Its cradle consisted of two short rainbows which lay longitudinally under it. Crosswide, at its chest and feet, lay red rays of the rising sun. The baby was wrapped in four blankets—dark cloud, blue cloud, yellow cloud, and white cloud. Along either side was a row of loops made of lightning and through these a sunbeam was laced back and forth.

First Man, not knowing how to undo the fastenings, took up the baby cradle and all, and started home. When he arrived he called out, "Old Woman, it is a baby, I found it there where it is black

---

* T. Ration, Smith Lake, New Mexico, 1976.

** The Navajos' name for themselves in their language.

† Diyin dine'é—All the sacred beings mentioned in the myths, stories of Diné are called diyin dine'é. These are the beings from the underworlds and after the (Diné dine'és) emergence.

277

night with rain clouds." He put the baby on the ground back of the fire, pulled the string and the lacing came free in both directions. "The cradle shall be like this, thin pieces of wood shall be placed underneath. There will be a row of loops on either side made of string. The bark of the cliffrose shredded and rubbed fine, will be used under the child for a bed." It was a girl...

A day was the same as a year. The second day the girl was up, and when two days had passed, she looked around, and when these days had passed she danced...and on the tenth day, at dawn, she was named Yolkai Estaan, White Shell Woman. (Goddard, 1933:148-150)

In this description White Shell Woman's basic character and what she did, from her childhood to womanhood to motherhood, sets an example of what a Diné female will personally experience. When White Shell Woman was found as a baby, she was bedded in a cradle board; in the present day many Diné women still bed their babies in cradle boards. When White Shell Woman menstruated she was given the Puberty rite, which many young girls have a chance to go through. Following that White Shell Woman gave birth to her twin boys who became great warriors.

Likewise with the Diné male role, a male baby grows up doing what the Twins—Monsterslayer and Born-for-the-Water—did. These two sacred beings, as young boys, demanded weapons be made for them... (Today young Diné boys ask for toy weapons they see displayed at stores.) Then the Twins traveled to their father and on the way they got into many mishaps, until they reached their father. There they received special knowledge and great weapons, and they returned to kill all the dangerous monsters. They became warriors. But following their victories they became ill from slaying the many monsters, so a curing ceremony was done for them by the diyin dine'é.* So, whatever the Twins did while growing from their babyhood to adulthood, are experienced by Diné men today.

Thus it is said that the sacred beings set a pattern for the Diné dine'é. For instance, we always hear our elder relatives say that such and such is not for the Diné át'éi.** This set pattern is best shown by sampling the prominent events in a Diné person's life, both female and male. When we examine our grandparents' lives, oral tradition is the main core of their beliefs and practices. Many, many restrictions, speech patterns, and concepts radiate *from the Beauty Way† stories.*

You are yearning for them (legends and traditional ways) all of you. These Beauty Way songs that is what you are yearning for. The old people they have all gone with them. The Beauty Way songs are priority to all...merits above all. It is like Washington, D. C., President's position. It is number one. We think about these songs that way on this Earth and among this human race. That is the way we know it is the best. And that has vanished with the old people and that is what you are missing the most. The ceremonial corn (naadą́'ást'ą́ą́n) is what you are yearning for, and the white corn meal, the yellow corn meal, these are what they are missing. Because of this they are traveling everywhere, they are looking and digging in the Earth for these things. They are trying hard. I do not know if the young people will acquire them (the knowledge) again, I do not think so—that is how I think about it. Except for those people that know about these things (Beauty Way songs and prayers), they are the ones to carry on for now. (E. Lee, Crownpoint, New Mexico 1976)

Stressing these prominent events in a Diné person's life also shows what rituals occur in that person's life. These rituals are significant

---

* Diyin dine'é—Holy Beings—...the reader will probably have to ask a knowledgeable Diné person which particular beings are represented or responsible for these events.

**Diné át'éi—could also be used "for those who are Navajo."

† *From the Beauty Way stories*—there are several versions to these stories, there is one from the underworld and another one beginning with the Emergence. In this particular case, the Beauty Way stories is after the emergence.

in the sense of understanding the *Dinéji binahagha'* (Diné's way). They are rituals because these events have an origin story which usually has songs, sayings, prayers that go with them, and these rituals are considered to be a very strong influence on one's life.

It is important to know that the central Navajo's (Diné) religious ideas are concerned with health and order; very likely to the Navaho (Diné) mind, these two concepts are in fact inseparable. Moreover, the kind of order conceived of is primarily of ritual order, that is, order imposed by human religious action, and, for the Navaho (Diné) this is largely a matter of creating and maintaining health. Health, on its part, is seen as stretching far beyond the individual: it concerns his whole people as well as himself, and it is based in large part on a reciprocal relationship with the world of nature, mediated through ritual. The world is seen as an essentially disordered place which may bring to many at any time bad dreams, encounters with unhealthy animals and situations

© E. Singer

(lightning, ants), and all sorts of unnamed hazards. Man himself may run afoul of nature by not being under control; that is, his own natural desires, if allowed full rein, can cause disease (the best example is, of course, excess of any sort). In fact, one common way of envisioning evil among the Navaho (Diné) is to describe it as the absence of order, or as something which is ritually not under control. (Tolkein, 1969:229)

Pregnancy begins this pattern. When a child is conceived and still a fetus, the carrying mother must take care of herself and her unborn. The father of the unborn must also, like his wife, be careful in whatever activity he is doing. After the child is born, her/his pre-natal history is important, because The People say that the fetus of the unborn is very vulnerable to the world.

Outside of the womb (its mother), if the parents are careless, The People say that that baby "will be a copy of" whatever the carrying mother (and parents) has done, has seen, or has witnessed; for example, if the parents do something like kill a frog; if the parents see a dead frog; or if the parents witness a ceremony in which the frog is important.* It is believed that a healthy child is born to careful parents. The parents of the unborn child must not attend any major curing ceremonies or sings, nor must they participate in them. They must not attend funerals, nor must they kill animals that have a secret power, because the unborn is still forming and is easily subjected to injury. The actions of careless parents will cause ill-health in the child later in life.

Years back I was stricken with a big sore here (showing her thigh to me I saw

---

* It is true that my own relatives are always finding a way to be cured of their ailment. They hire a medicine man, a herbalist many times when they need them. And it is always said that "one made a mistake with or for himself."

280

a scar more than two inches long). I was twelve years old and the sore became worse. One day a medicine man named Baali who was of the Redhouse clan was a prominent diagnostician or a Hand Trembler. My uncle, my father's brother, brought him home to help me. I was dying; I hadn't eaten for days and I was very weak. I was all puffed up from my ailment. He (the uncle) begged the man to find out what really was the cause of my sickness, which was killing me. All my immediate family were hovering over me as I was suffering and struggling for life, for survival. Then, we, or my family found out what was wrong with me. *The Hand Trembler told my father the following story. The lightning had struck the whole herd of sheep fold a few days before I was born and my mother saw what all happened then. I was afflicted with this evil effect.* The man advised my parents to hustle before it was too late. His prescription was to have a special ceremony. He recommended the Lightning Way ceremony. (Amy Kindle, Shiprock, New Mexico, 1975)

A special offering (*K'eet'áán*—prayer stick) and certain curing rituals are done for a child who has been afflicted. If the diagnostician finds that the child is ill because of "something that he/she is a copy of," the parents are the ones to have ceremony done for their child. Sometimes an aunt or other concerned relative will only suggest to the parents that maybe some "sings" or a ceremony has to be done for the sickly child.

Before a Diné woman gives birth to her baby, sometimes she requests that a blessing way "no sleep" is done for her. It is even done in the present day (*Díishjíigi*) before the pregnant woman leaves for the hospital. It is done so that the delivery and laboring will be bearable, and that there will be a normal childbirth. Life is a whirling with many unexpected events—it happens at times that a woman unfortunately has a miscarriage, a still-birth. It is believed that when this happens the grieving woman should have a special prayer done for her, for it is said that her womb is the place of death. Long ago when this happened, women disposed of the lifeless with rituals but without grief. The disposal was referred to as "disposing of the unspoken." If the special prayer was not done, it affected that woman later in her life.

However, if there is a normal childbirth, another Blessing Way "no sleep"* is done for the mother and child. From this time until the child is old enough to sit for his/her ceremony, the mother must sit** for the baby.

In the days before pick-ups, cars and hospitals, the whole process of having a baby was a ritual—with the help of a Hat'aalii (singer or medicine man) and a midwife—there were songs sung; spreading of fresh soil; sprinkling of corn pollen; stretching of the sash belt; and untying of tied knots; letting hair down. Long ago, childbirth was a real-life, beautiful struggle and a ritual with the sacred beings watching on.

When a baby is born, it is the creation of a human being, the most beautiful gift from the sacred beings (diyin dine'e). The life the baby receives is sent by the sacred beings. The wind† is sent into the newborn baby. That is why there are whirls on the tips of human hands and the hair grows in whirls on the head.

He has no mind before he is born. When he is born the Holy People (*Diyin Dine'é*) send the wind into him and then he has a mind. It goes into your heart and stays there. It directs the movement of the person like a lawyer or boss sitting inside him telling him what to do. The whirls on your fingers are the marks of the wind in them. The first finger has Black Wind, the second finger has Blue Wind, and the middle one has Yellow Wind, the fourth finger has White Wind, and the little finger has Pinto Wind.‡ Something else is inside you, too. I can't

---

* No sleep—Dine term, *dooii gaash*, it is a one-night sing when a medicine man sings from late evening until early dawn, "until dawn has a white stripe."

** The main person or patient in a ceremony must sit on the north side of the singer. So the mother sits with the baby and that is what is called sitting for the baby child.

† In the creation of man and woman, the different winds are the ones that entered them. (A. Yazzie, Ft. Defiance, Arizona, 1976)

‡ This is referring to the right hand going clockwise.

remember all of it. There are four or five things inside your heart. The Dawn gets into your body. He speaks, "I'll stay in you for so many years, then I'll get out." At the end of the specified time, when the Dawn comes, you will die. You can't live any longer than he told you at your birth.

After death the body [decays] but the soul returns as a screech owl, or a coyote, or a piñon jay (ts'ánídílzhi'í). As nothing else, that is why people are afraid of an owl at night, or to stay home. (Bailey, 1950:21)

The beginning of a baby's life is when he/she begins breathing. The breath of mankind is sacred—and so long as the breath is wet, moist, the words that are spoken are sacred and alive. (So, if a person speaks very harsh words against you, your family/ relatives, usually a protection prayer is done for you/your family.)

Another traditional custom our elders did which we practiced, is when a child is born, a man of wisdom is chosen to consecrate the newborn child. This chosen man is there with the relatives during the delivery. This was a very

special occasion. When born the infant is given the sap juice of the inner white skin of the piñon tree to extract all the foreign substance from the stomach, then corn pollen diluted with water is fed to the infant. Right at high noon the father of the infant takes the infant to a peaceful, quiet, nice place. Here the man of wisdom offers a blessing prayer for a long time. (T. Ration, Smith Lake, New Mexico, 1975)

Mr. Ration would like to share that blessing prayer Diné say when a child is being blessed; it is called a person "speaks" for the baby (Awéé' yá haadzíí'). *And what is said in the prayer is the blessing.* This is how a newborn baby is spoken for, and how a strong leader comes about:

Today we are blessed
With this beautiful baby
May his feet be to the East
His right hand to the South
His head to the West
His left hand to the North.

May he walk and dwell on Mother Earth
    peacefully.

May he be blessed with assorted soft
  valued goods.
May he be blessed with precious
  varigated stones.
May he be blessed with fat sheep in
  variation.
May he be blessed with nice swift horses
  in variation.
May he be blessed with respectful
  relatives and friends.
I asked all these blessings with reverence
  and holiness.
My mother, the Earth, the Sky, the Sun,
  the Moon,
      Together, my Father.
I am the Essence of Life which is old age.
I am the source of happiness in beauty.
All is peaceful, all in beauty, all in
  harmony, all in happiness.

(With such a blessing the child will grow
up healthy and strong. Later he will have
all the good things that he has been
blessed with. This is not practiced
anymore.) (T. Ration, Smith Lake, New
Mexico, 1975)

And from this day on it is thought that the
baby is in the presence of the diyin dine'é,
especially in their protection. The Dine say
that these sacred beings love the People,
mankind, five-fingers more than we love our
own children. They look upon this baby with
love, protection and blessings. In this
particular form of the prayer, the wording is
usually not the same for the female baby.
Different items are mentioned. For example, in
place of references to livestock, etc., household utensils—stirring sticks—articles for
weaving, are mentioned. Because of this
blessing, it is said that a father of a child must
not say that the child is not his, for the diyin
dine'é will see to it that this baby is taken back
to them.

Within our whole family (which includes
most relatives living near by, clan relatives) a
newborn child is accepted and everyone
attends to the child's needs. Like someone—
an aunt, maybe, ánalí* would gather cliffrose
('Awééts'áál) from the foothills of mountain
hills and teach the young mother how to shred

---
* Father's mother

it and fix it for the cradle board. Also, a young
mother is shown how to prepare the cradle
board bedding for the newborn baby. In the old
days, a cradle board was made directly from
the growing living tree. A small prayer is said
while annointing the cradle board with red clay
(chííli) mixed with raw fat, before the baby is
placed in the cradle board. This applies to all
cradle boards—newly made or old ones. A
cradle board has to be bought (or paid for)
from another person who has one, but
sometimes it is borrowed for a while and
returned. The People say that after you get
through using a cradle board, if it is left pieced
together you are asking for another child. So,
very soon after the child weans his/her cradle,
you will be blessed with another baby.

A newborn baby must not be decorated with
silver buttons (hard possessions), beads, or
precious stones, neither should these be put
on the cradle board yet. A baby is young and
her/his heart is still soft and not ready to take
possession of things. At first, when we want
to show our deepest love for our children we
do not do it materialistically. A child is given
hard possessions when she/he bursts out
laughing.

When a baby bursts out laughing it is a
joyous event for the family. Then, the baby is
given a "give away" celebration. It is said that
when a baby bursts out laughing, she/he will
cry for long periods until this "give away" is
done for her/him. Babies laugh about anything
they might think ticklish or see. Sometimes
another person might help them laugh. And it
is this person, who helps the baby laugh, that
sponsors the "give away." She/he honors the
baby with a celebration. This person is given or
allowed four days after the baby laughs to
decide what the people will have to eat, and
what riches will be given away.

On the day of the give-away, sometimes a
sheep is butchered and made into a big meal,
and what is left of the mutton is divided into
pieces to be given away. (If a child has helped
a baby laugh, it is the parents or guardian of
the child who will assist in honoring the
first-laugh baby.)

Nowadays, the "give away" gifts are usually
candies, fruits, cookies, cakes, and pennies.
But the main object that is to be given away is
rock salt. (It is the mythical Salt Woman—a
sacred being who presents the first give-

away for a baby.) The rock salt is poured into a ceremonial basket, and placed on top are the gifts to be given away. The sponsor holds the baby in the sitting position, holding out the baby's tiny palm. Then, the sponsor picks up one rock salt—a small piece from the basket along with the fruit, or cake or cookie or penny, and then the sponsor touches them to the palm of the baby. Meanwhile, the people accepting these gifts walk by taking the gifts while making ironic statements like "I will be a cry baby. I will live to be young. My teeth will all fall out. I will be ugliest." So, it is said that if these statements are made, the child will be contrary to them. The People say that if this give-away is not done for the baby, she/he will be a selfish person, unwilling to share her/his opulence.*

> ...during the wintertime, I was told when I was four months old, I was being held outside in the warm sun and the sheep were being brought home; I was looking at two little billy goats (tł'ízíchǫǫh yázhí). They were rearing up with their horns, clashing into each other when suddenly, I laughed my first laugh. Right away, they said, let's have a little feast for him. The only reason why one had a dinner at that time of their first laugh is because in the future one will not be selfish. They (relatives) butchered a goat, then it was cut into small portions to give to the neighbors that heard the news. I passed out the mutton to the people while they helped me, held it together while pressing my hand along with the rock salt. Right away, the people built fires and started charcoaling the meat (that was given away). So this was done for me. (M. Hanley, Sr., Tuba City, Arizona, 1976)

After the baby has laughed he/she is allowed to wear bracelets, necklaces, silver buttons, etc.; a small turquoise dangling from the head band of a craddle board, if the baby is male; a white shell or bead if the child is female.** In most cases a special amulet is used. The amulets are not just charms for the baby, they have a meaning—just like the cradle board is a very sacred bedding for the child. It must not be placed on a bare earth, or be left without the blanket covering the head band. Dine' say that the head band of the cradle board is the rainbow; the lacings are the sunbeams; the loops through which it is laced are the lightning; the blankets are the clouds; and the base board are short rainbows.

There are several amulets that are used. Not just ordinary corn pollen but corn pollen that has been sprinkled on certain animals that have desirable habits, traits. The different corn pollen is wrapped separately. The animals used are flying squirrels, the humming bird, the bear, and the mocking bird. Also, parts of a flying gray squirrel are used—the tail, or the tanned pelt of this squirrel is used. The miraculous abilities these animals are blessed with can help a baby be likewise. For instance, the flying squirrel jumps from the highest branch to another tree; sometimes it fails and falls to the ground; however, it still manages to get up and climb up the tree. If an amulet of pollen sprinkled on this squirrel is used, the secret power this squirrel has will be with the baby—he or she will not be injured falling. If the pollen that has been sprinkled on a bear is used, the baby becomes in likeness of the bear's nature—strong physique, but ill-tempered. It is told in the stories that after Changing Woman moved to the west she created the human beings who were to become the different clans to which the Diné now belong. Then she gave them pets or guardians that would travel back ith them to the land between the sacred mountains. The bear is one of those four pets who were guardians; and, it is said that the *bear* was not vicious but became vicious by making its own songs and singing them. This is when the bear became ill-tempered; this is the song which gives the bear its miraculous power.

---

* See Chapter Thirteen, **Sacred Fools and Clowns**, for more examples of this "backwards talk" bringing power and good to The People.

**This is done if the child had a five-night ceremony done on her/him. The medicine man makes a bead for his/her patient, which the patient keeps for the rest of his/her life. The same goes for the turquoise for the male and white shell for the female.

284

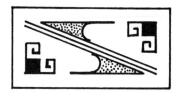

© E.Singer

SONG OF THE BLACK BEAR*

My moccasins are black obsidian,
My leggings are black obsidian,
My shirt is black obsidian.
I am girded with a black arrowsnake.
Black snakes go up from my head.
With zigzag lightning streaming out from
    the ends of my feet I step.
With zigzag lightning streaming from my
    knees I step.
With zigzag lightning streaming from the
    tip of my tongue I speak.
Now a disk of pollen rests on the crown
    of my head.
Gray arrowsnakes and rattlesnakes eat it.
Black obsidian and zigzag lightning
    stream out from me in four ways.
Where they strike the earth, bad things,
    bad talk does not like it.
It causes the missiles to spread out.
Long life, something frightful I am.
Now I am.
There is danger where I move my feet.
I am a whirlwind.
There is danger when I move my feet.
I am gray bear.
When I walk, where I stop, lightning flies
    from me.
Where I walk, one to be feared I am.
Where I walk, Long Life.
One to be feared I am.
There is danger where I walk.

                    (Goddard, 1933:176-178)

If the pollen that has been sprinkled on a humming bird is used, the baby grows to be a fast runner. The corn pollen that is sprinkled on a mocking bird is placed in the mouth, and that is the only pollen that is placed in the mouth they say. It is done so the child will be talkative, linguistic. Another amulet that is used is a small bug** that is a parasite of the tree called k'a, the red bark cottonwood. This small bug dwells in the seed or shell for at

---

* *Song of the Black Bear*—This song of the bear mentions how the bear speaks of himself as a frightful being. Our grandmothers tell us not to curse the name of the bear in the mountains. It is said that the bears can sense your anger (they know you are talking about him, it is said).

**The informant who told about the small bug and the mud clowns is M. Mitchell, Many Farms, Arizona.

least two years without dying. If this bug is tied to the child's cradle board, she/he will have endurance against hunger, cold weather, and be a quiet baby. The mud that falls off the mud clowns from the Enemy Chant Way (the war dance), called *jaashzhiní* is used, too. If this is used, the baby will be immune to common colds, leg aches, and any injury. The People say that the mud these clowns paint themselves with is taken from a sacred stream or well. These are a few of the amulets (there are others) that are commonly used and suggested to young mothers to use. *It is to help her raise a strong healthy child, and help the child become a strong adult.*

To have a child is a big responsibility. That is probably true in any culture or society, but we Diné dine'é are proud people to know our grandparents and their parents have been raising children with all these particulars (to have a healthy child become a healthy adult). The children are carefully watched in their growth, to be secure from injury. Any ceremonial items—paraphernalia of any chant way are not to be handled by young children and babies. They are easily afflicted by what they have handled. The chant way (to which the item that is handled belongs) will have to be performed on him/her. For example, when a ceremonial basket of a chant way (Mountain Chant Way, for instance) is left in reach of a child, the unattended child, not knowing the uses of this basket, begins playing with it—playing with it in a way that he/she places it over his/her head. The People say that this act will definitely affect the child, or it might affect him/her later in life. It will affect the speech or speaking of the child such as stuttering. It will affect the growth of the child's mind. The Mountain Chant Way will afflict the child. Definitely, these ceremonies or rituals will have to be performed on the child to be cured.

The child is watched. Any subtle changes in the child's forming habits are seen. Sometimes, when the child's spirit is low and the coloration around the eyes of the child is dark, it is said that the child is not feeling well. Diné say, "around the eyes of the child is dark. Is the child feeling sick?" And because a baby or child cannot speak up for himself/herself usually a diagnostician is consulted. This hand trembler called Gila monster (*Tiníleí*), determines what is causing the baby to be ill. *Often the pre-natal history trauma is brought up in the diagnosis.* The hand trembler usually recommends what type of curing ceremony is needed, or which "singer" or medicine man could help the ill child. The hand trembler makes this diagnosis in a special ceremony and by use of a trance state. Often it is found that the illness is a minor ailment and a hospital is recommended.

Haashch'éilti'í (Headsman for a group of sacred beings) was the one who accepted the Twin Boys (sons of the baby who was found on the clouded mountains—later called White Shell Woman) as his grandchildren. They say that he taught the boys many things. He made them items to play with, which the Twins toyed with, as weapons—bows and arrows. They shot at the buzzard. It's not mentioned what method of teachings this Headsman used, but it is said that he was with the Twins mostly. Nowadays the People don't have a traditional form of education for their children, but children have active minds and they learn from their relatives and from their environment:

A person who has self-respect and has a well-stimulated mind is more likely to succeed. He/she listens to all the lectures and puts them in his/her mind. (T. Ration, Smith Lake, New Mexico, 1976)

The ways *Diné Dine'é* taught their children were not formal classes in school but lessons that supplemented the daily living of the People. It was the person who knew and had experienced his/her lessons who taught others, including children, about what happens to people who do such and such... excesses of those things that are prohibited, or restricted from the *Diné a't'éí*. David Kindle of Shiprock, New Mexico, was asked what the traditional teachings at home in the *hooghan* are. He explained what lectures were made to young people. He mentioned many important teachings that a Diné person should know but, he urged that there are do's and don't's that his mother had taught him during his childhood:

I would strongly use the words *yíiyá* again to the young people. You must not do all this. If you listen to what I have to say, you might live a long life like I did.

My children, grandchildren, I always use these words when I speak to my people everywhere... You will have a better life. The words of wisdom your mother and father taught you are very precious and you listen to them. That is for your own benefit. Keep away from evil things and not do anything wrong. It is dangerous. Some do's and don't's as taught to a child are: You should never abuse or kill any kind of reptiles (*Na'ashǫ'ie*). It is not allowed for it is dangerous (*bááhádzid*). The effects will not afflict you until you are over fifty years old, but not when you are young. Snakes are very dangerous, especially rattlesnakes, they have fangs, poison to strike you with. When you pass your young stage of life your wrist and ankles will begin to swell, these are the first symptoms. Sometimes you ache around the waist and chest. This one (snake) is the worst enemy which must be left alone. Another is the eagle (*atsá*). I knew this (leaving the eagles alone) but once I brought down two eaglets (young black eaglets) when I was a boy. I suffered the consequences hard. Several times I had the abscess of the esophagus or a boil. Sometimes it almost choked me. My folks worked hard to help me with all kinds of ceremonies to cure me but it (the boil) kept coming back. Finally, I found the right medicine herb to cure it.

As soon as the children start talking and can recollect events, figures and stories, they are told many stories and lectured to for best manners, and behavior. Stories are told to stimulate the mind and restrictions are told to form the basic habits and concepts of beliefs. Some of these concepts are taught for a person's self-respect as an individual, a clan member, a tribal member. When an adolescent is lectured to, this is what is said:

Our forefathers struggled for survival so that we may enjoy what we have now. I should think the least we can do is *to be grateful to them and remember what they stood for*. We look back and see how they suffered and here we are comfortable and have all the wonderful opportunities

287

knocking on our doors. Be ready to accept these, your future is what you must think about. (T. Ration, Smith Lake, New Mexico, 1976)

...It is told that the human beings they were not decorated or created awkwardly or aimlessly...(E. Lee, Crownpoint, New Mexico, 1975)

...All the values of riches is in your body. Whatever we are adorned with like turquoise necklace, turquoise pendants, bracelets, rings, beautiful clothes, all these are just ornaments to admire like values. Our body is more valuable above all these. This is why we must not destroy one another or make fun of (mock) anyone. You cannot tell a person he/she is a pauper. (J. Dick, Rough Rock, Arizona, 1976)

The Coyote, who is a sly person, has started the people to become drunk and stuporous. Now, we have a sickness called "alcoholism" which has spread widely among the People both young and old. This horrible sickness can destroy you, your physical being, your dignity and make you an unwanted person and dangerous. I hope you contemplate on

this very carefully, someday you may remember what I told you and say, "Grandfather told us about this"...it will make me very happy that you have listened, then again your children will say my parents taught me these and you too will be proud and happy. I know because I had this experience myself. My parents taught and lectured this to me, how else can I be telling you these. Our children are very precious to us and we want the best for them. I have this kind of feeling to all young people, no matter who they are. I do not want them to destroy themselves. Life is too short and precious to take for granted. Especially while you are young you have much to live for. (T. Ration, Smith Lake, New Mexico, 1976)

When a child abides all his/her valuable lessons and lectures, it is said that *child is becoming wise*. (In the story of the White Shell Woman and her twin boys, they became wise in one day...for each phase of growing to adults, there was one day.) When the child is accepted as being alert and wise, he/she is thought of as being ready to take on bigger responsibilities in ceremonial events and community events.

Before an individual becomes a wife or a husband,* there are certain responsibilities that are endowed upon him/her. That is, children from the ages of five years old to twelve, fourteen year olds, and through adolescence.

A child has a role in the Enemy Chant Way (War Dance). Here a child who is alert and willing to participate is chosen. *The male child takes the role of the person who sits between the two main patients who are of the same clan; or between the woman who is blackened and the other person (male) who is blackened. The female child is chosen to take the role of the young maiden that carries the sacred stick.*

Another event we take part in as children is a minor ceremony called "to see the Yei." A child volunteers to see this rite. But an offering of money or corn pollen (a tablespoonful) is given to the singer (*hataalii*) and he is asked to set up the time to see the Yei ceremony. (This is part of the Night Chant way.) *Biyeel* is made to the singer or medicine man. This is when the child is initiated to see the person behind the mask of the *yei'ii'b i chei*. (A person has to see this ceremony before becoming one of the dancer of the *yei'ii'bi chei* team.) When a child participates, he/she must remember the sequences of events, how to sprinkle corn pollen toward and up the person who portrays the sacred beings —*Haashch'ééh dine'é*. And that person who portrays these beings is the person a child *must always remember.* We are told to remember who our "grand-father" is. Our elderly relatives say that whenever we meet with that man later anywhere; and any time we are to greet him as "grandfather"—*Shichei we will say.* This particular event "to see the Ye'ii" is not strictly for the children, but if an older person who has not seen or been initiated into this ceremony may join the children.

By the time children become adolescents they are considered grown and are changing to adults. At this time young people begin taking on different attitudes toward their once-play world; seriousness comes. By now many lectures are remembered and are becoming reality for them. So it is the time when many young people start being independent from their parents' constant advice and lectures. Being independent, some young people begin marriage life and start growing a family. Of course, there are certain ceremonies for first marriage, and beginning menstruation for girls. And when marriage occurs it is understood by the community that the two, male and female, are husband and wife. The sacred beings even set the ways of being a husband and wife.

A marriage ceremony is also a ritual that was done long ago. It was part of the White Shell Woman's life. Many stories tell how White Shell Woman was made pregnant by the Sun and Water; and she had twins. It is also mentioned that the Sun instructed White Shell Woman to tell her father that he was to prepare a circle arbor lodge for his step-daughter. When the instructions were followed the Sun did visit White Shell Woman four times, aside from meeting her daily.

Sun's Instruction

Go home and tell your father to build a brush hogan to the south of your home. Make ready a meal out of the seeds of grass that you have gathered. Put this meal into a white bead basket. Have the pollen from a pair of blue birds (pollen which has been sprinkled over them) and use this pollen to draw a line from east to west across the basket on top of the meal. Turn the hand and make a line from north to south, and a line must be drawn around the outer edge of the basket. Set the basket inside the brush hogan. You and your father must sit there late into the night. He will then go home to his wife and you must stay there alone. (O'Bryan, 1956:76)

This is also the instruction for the present *Diné át'eí marriage ceremony.* This was done four times in the legends, but it is only done once for the mortals or Diné. After a male and female have become husband and wife, they complement each other's well being. The sacred beings also set ways of being a husband and wife according to which many Diné dine'é are living today.

---

* Before becoming a wife or husband is usually referring to still being innocent of sexual acts.

Then they (*diyin dine'é*) planned how a husband and a wife should feel toward each other, and how jealousy should affect both sexes. They got the yucca and the yucca fruit, and water from the sacred springs and dew from all the plants, corn, trees, and flowers. These they gathered and they called them *tó'-ałtaashchíín*, sacred waters. They rubbed the yucca and the sacred waters over the woman's heart and over the man's heart. This was done so they would love each other, but at the same time there arose jealousy between the man (husband) and the woman, his wife.

After that they (*diyin dine'é*) planned how each sex would have its feeling of passion. A medicine was for the organs of sex. The organ of the man would whistle; and then the organ of the woman would whistle. When they heard this each organ gave a long, clear whistle. After that they come together and the sound of the whistle was different. That is why the voice of the young boy and maiden are different; and it is why their voices change. (O'Bryan, 1956:33)

As husband and wife, a couple are allowed to do certain ceremonial activities together. When a woman, who is married, has a ceremony done on her, the Ha taali, the singer, tells her to keep in peace and harmony with all things around her; for her not to poke the fire or cook; and not to sleep with her husband or a man for four days. And on the fourth day after the ceremony she has to take a bath and clean off the markings from the ceremony. There is a phrase some medicine men use for a young man or just other men: he tells him "do not bother the 'rabbit' my grandson." And it means for the man not to have a sexual relationship with his wife or woman for four days. The People say that a man and wife must not have the same medicine man or singer sing on them. It is considered the same as putting the two mates in the same bedding with the ceremonial paintings on them. They say is is very dangerous. Also, a man and a woman are not to have intercourse in certain places because this would result in some kind of affliction. One of these places is the sweat house. Men and women are not supposed to meet in or enter the sweat house at the same time. The People say that it is only for the sacred beings to do that. Another place where intercourse is forbidden is the corn field, since it is related to the "mating of the corn" story. There are curing ceremonies for these types of afflictions, but they are scarce and they are not being done anymore.

By practicing the teaching of the medicine man and the elderly people, we are showing respect for ourselves. When we know our clanship, our paternal grandparents, and all the related kinsmen and greet them as such, "we respect ourselves" we say. How does a Diné woman think of herself? If she knows the meaning of what a woman is and is responsible for, she will respect herself and others. And many other people will respect her; the same goes for a man.

This is all traditional education. One must never laugh at a woman. She is the seed of the Mother Earth. She was the first one to be placed on the earth or (she was the first to be made) planted. She reproduced as a seed. She bore a child. From this a new generation existed.

When you are making fun of (mocking) a woman, it is told you are really making fun of your own mother. She *is a woman* you know. In fact, never laugh at your sisters, your brothers, and father. (J. Dick, Rough Rock, Arizona: 1976)

A woman is the child bearer, she conceives the greatest value of this world which is human life. It is said that the Earth was made to menstruate and that is where the reproduction originated. When the Earth and Sky were being created they both were dressed or decorated with certain elements. Dew was one of the elements aside from trees, mountains, etc.

...You see, the dew of the horizontal skyblue was a male, while that of the darkness was female. These two were mixed together and the one named Calling God (Hashche'é hooghan) performed over them. After placing a spread over them he tremble-ran towards it from the four sides, which caused it to move nicely. It became known that this (dew) was to be the menstrual flow of the Earth by means of which vegetation will

become possible and by the same means reproduction would be possible...
(o'Bryan, 1956:345-346)

White Shell Woman was found by the Sacred Beings. They took it upon themselves to raise her. She grew in four days, and when she had grown she had her menses. The Sacred Beings didn't know how to deal with the flow of the blood. Because of this they made the Puberty Rite for her. (See Chapter Nine: **Girls' Puberty Ceremonies**) Today, the Puberty Rite ceremony has a strong influence on a young girl's life. It gives her the strength to be a strong woman, and it gives her the protection of the Sacred Beings.

The Puberty rite is a gift given to Diné women. If a woman is concerned about her daughter's well-being and the prosperity of her clan, she sponsors the Puberty rite for her daughter's first and second menses. If it is not done, the girl grows to adulthood not knowing the significance of childbearing (fertility), and herself as the diné'asdza'ni meant for a woman to know herself. She should know, be aware of the weapons given to her by the diyin dine'é. The People say that there are weapons given to a woman. The weapons are not ordinary weapons—weapons to harm with, or to protect oneself—they are weapons to survive, to give life and prosperity. It was the time when the Earth and Sky were being created; they were decorated with various clothing like vegetation, mountains, dew, rain, clouds:

> ...That (Earth) woman spoke, "What about my left hand, what will lie there?" she asked. "Whatever will be placed in the hands of both of you (Earth and Sky) is already known," they were told. *"This collected mirage stone (striped aragonite), which is called old age cane, will be your cane and will be placed in your left hand.* That is for the sole purpose of strengthening you in the event you are to be useful by means of it," she was told. "You in turn will hold zigzag lightning and the straight lightning, and sunray, and rainbow, and rainray, five all told, in your right hand," Sky was told. "With these you will punish occurrences on the surface of this one who is the woman which, as it were, may not be as they

should; you will keep watch over them by means of these," he was told. These it seems proved to be what in time became arrows. *The things placed into the woman's hands, as mentioned, were to become stirring sticks whose purpose was to enable her to provide for herself.* That (all) took place in this manner.
(Wyman, 1970:352)

One of the weapons that was given to woman (Earth) before the birth of White Shell Woman was stirring sticks. The stirring sticks (ádístsiin) were commonly used by our grandmothers, great aunts, and *análi* (our father's mother). Our grandmother or a great aunt would say that these things, stirring sticks, are the woman's weapon, a weapon against hunger and poverty. If one has these stirring sticks in one's home, hooghan, one's food will never be scarce. The stirring sticks are used to cook meals, like boiling corn meal, mush for an everyday meal, or mush for the Puberty rite cake. It is also used for stirring many other meals, such as preparing yucca fruit roll (*neesdoig*) and in any ceremony that requires cooking cornmeal or anything mush-like. When one cooks with the stirring sticks, after using them, they are cleaned with a humble prayer of thanksgiving. The prayer is said while cleaning them. The fingers are run along each stick, from the root to the growing end, gripping the single stick with the index finger and thumb, all the while blowing with the motion of wiping off.

There are other weapons given to a woman; they are the items that decorated the hooghan. These include long life and happiness, and the blessing of the sacred beings.

PART 2   HOOGHAN A'T'EI (THE HOGAN)

Chief Hooghan Song

Of origins I have full knowledge...
   gooiaghai
Of Earth's origin I have full knowledge
Of plant origins I have full knowledge
Of various fabrics' origins I have full knowledge.

Now of long life's, now of happiness' origin I have full knowledge, *goolaghai.*

Of Mountain Woman's origin I have full knowledge.

Of Rain Mountain's origin I have full
knowledge.
Of various jewels' origin I have full
knowledge.
Now of long life's, now of happiness'
origin I have full knowledge, of their
origin I have full knowledge,
goolaghai.
Of Water Woman's origin I have full
knowledge.
Of collected water's origin I have full
knowledge.
Now of long life's now of happiness'
origin I have full knowledge, *goolaghai.*
Of corn woman's origin I have full
knowledge.
Of pollen's origin I have full knowledge.
Now of long life's, now of happiness'
origin I have full knowledge, *goolaghai.*
(Wyman, 1970:113)

The hooghan dwelling has always been of
special significance and great value to our
grandparents; their parents and previous
generations; and presently to those who know
the meaning of a dwelling belonging to Diné
Dine'é, the People. The dwelling is popularly
knows as the "hogan." The People pronounced
it "hooghan" literally meaning home. And
hooghan dijooli is a descriptive phrase
meaning the round (circular) home. Other
hooghan dwellings have descriptive names of
their own; they all have origin stories and have
songs of their own; each type of hooghan has
certain activities take place in it.

Diné Dine'é, the People, say that the
hooghan dwelling has a meaning because,
from the legends, there are hooghan songs
(*hooghan bi yin*) and there were origins of
certain prayers that were spoken in the First
Hooghan. It was the hooghan that was created
first—and then the order and planning of all
creations. The first hooghan was different
from the present day *hooghan dijooli* that we
see in our communities on the Navajo land:

There are many legends and traditions
of wonderful houses made by the gods
(Diyin dine'é), and by the mythic pro-
genitors of the tribe. In the building of
these houses turquoise and pearly shells

were freely used, as were also the transparent mists of dawn and the gorgeous colors of sunset. They were covered by sunbeams and the rays of the rainbow, with everything beautiful, or richly colored on the earth and in the sky. It is perhaps on account of these gorgeous mythical hogans that no attempt is now made to decorate the everyday dwelling; it would be *baha dzid* (Diné word meaning dangerous), tabooed, (or sacriligious). (Mindeleff, A.R.B.A.E. 17th:488)

In these stories told only during the winter season, an uncle or grandfather (*shei*) who might be a knowledgeable man would tell of many incidents involving the sacred beings called *Diyin dine 'é*; he would tell of what these people did. Listening to the stories being told by a relative was informing and interesting. His descriptions were picturesque and beautiful. (*Nizhónígo yaa halni' leh*.) In these stories, it is told the *Diyin dine'é* told the people how to build their houses in future times which is nowadays:

> The traditions preserve methods of house building that were (taught) to mortals by the gods (Diyin dine'é) themselves. These methods, as is usual in such cases, are the simplest, but they are still scrupulously followed. Early mention of house building occurs in the creation myths. First Man and First Woman are discovered in the first or lowest underworld, living in a hut which was the prototype of the hooghan. (Mindeleff, A.R.B.A.E., 17th:488)

The description of the hooghans in the Underworld gives mystical images and power to an ordinary *hooghan* and knowing these stories provides the very meaning of what a *hooghan* is. Because the origin stories of the hooghan have been orally passed on from times before the "white" colonial people came to North America, there are variations— different versions told to the Diné dine'é (Navajos) today:

> Some versions of the myth hold that First Man's hut was made of wood just like the modern hogan, but it was covered with gorgeous rainbows and bright sunbeams instead of bark and earth. At that time the firmament had not been made, but these first beings possessed the elements for its production. Rainbows and sunbeams consisted of layers or films of materials, textiles, or at least pliable in nature, and these materials were laid across the hut alternately, first the rainbows from north to south, then the sunbeams from east to west. According to this account the other four houses at the cardinal points were similarly made of wood, the different substances mentioned being merely used for covering. Other traditions hold that the houses were made entirely of the substances mentioned and that no wood was used in their construction because at that time no wood or other vegetal material had been produced. (Mindeleff, A.R.B.A.E., 17th:489)

Hooghan literally means "home." It is from the hooghan environment the Dine dine'é beings learn their beliefs and begin living a set pattern of their beliefs. Hooghan is where their daily living takes place. "You hardly see the round hooghan anymore; only a few of the Diné dine'é still live in these. The round hooghans are now being built for ceremonial purposes only." (Ration, Smith Lake, New Mexico, 1975) Presently the uses of the hooghan have been changing through modifications and ignorance of what the meaning of a hooghan is, or for economic reasons.

A hooghan is built in a carefully chosen spot. Because of the significance of this dwelling, a suitable place has to be found for its construction. The tiny surroundings are considered, such as ant mounds, gravesites, battle grounds of the enemy's, and places where lightning has struck. In the woodlands the builder has to see that there are no trees that were struck by lightning near the place where the hooghan is to be built:

> He (builder) must be careful to select a place well-removed from hills of red ants, as aside from the perpetual discomfort consequent on too close proximity, it is told that in the underworld these pests troubled First Man and the other gods

(*diyin dine'é*), who then dwelt together and caused them to disperse. (Mindeleff, A.R.B.A.E., 17th:489)

Even the materials that are used for building a hooghan are carefully chosen. The non-lightning struck logs are used, for those that were struck are already the property of the Lightning. And when a hooghan is being built it is not made aimlessly but constructed according to what the *diyin dine'é* had blueprinted for the People to follow:

> After mankind had ascended through the three underworlds by means of the magic reed to the present or fourth world, Talking God (*Haashch'éílti'í* the Talking headsman for the sacred beings), the God of Dawn, the benevolent nature god of the south and east, imparted to each group of mankind an appropriate architecture—to the tribes of the plains, skin lodges; to the Pueblos, stone houses; and to the Navajo (Diné dine'é), huts of wood and earth and summer shelter. Curiously enough, nowhere in the Navajo tradition is any mention or suggestion made of the use by them of skin lodges. (Mindeleff, A.R.B.A.E., 17th:489)

When a hooghan is being made the people making it build it with the entrance to the east. There is a reason. *Haashch'éílti'í*, the Heads-man for the sacred beings was the one who set the custom of building the hooghan entrance *always* to the east:

> Long ago at the Emergence place it is told Haashch'éílti'í performed a "no sleep" ceremony or a vigilance. There at this "sing" the people could not find anyone to do the bathing of the client or patient. Haashch'éílti'í gathered the sand from where the ground is black, blue, red and white. He made a picture of a round shaped pan like thing with the colored sand and designed it—to be a ceremonial basket, (with) the finishing out-let to the east. It was very beautiful. Later again at Huerfano Mountain, the *First Blessing Way* was held there too, at a place called Mating-of-the-Corn (*Naadą́ą́' alt'ánáályaági*). Here again it was asked who

is going to do the bathing and in what (container) and how (it's going to be done).

> *Haashch'éílti'í* was told to go back to the Emergence place, to the hooghan there and get what he had hid in the far end of the hooghan inside. He ran there and brought it back. This was copied, and today the ceremonial basket is used in the "Blessing Way sing." We used the basket to bathe in, with the outlet of the basket facing to the east, and *the door way of the hooghan faces the east always. All good things enter with the dawn from the east.* (Ration, Smith Lake, New Mexico, 1975)

The People say that the entrance of the hooghan will always be to the east. Another important aspect of the building of a hooghan was the setting of the logs. The logs, which are the main beams of the roof in the *hooghan dijooli*, in the round-top-house, were set a certain way. For instance, the person who cut the main beam kept in mind which was the root end and which was the growing end.

> There were two ceremonial hooghans long ago. One is a "dugout" hooghan, the other was the round-top house. The hooghan was made round like *Haashch'éílti'í* made the round basket. All the main beam longs were placed with the growing end clockwise to the east, next on to the south clockwise, the west clockwise, the north the same. (Ration, Smith Lake, New Mexico, 1976)

The material to be used was decided upon by the sacred beings too. After the Sun, and the Moon were created, they [Sun and Moon] were instructed by First Man on what properties they would protect or control on the woman Earth:

> "The Sun will chiefly control the trees which are found on the surface of the Earth," he [First Man] said. "The Moon too will be next in charge of trees found on Mountain Woman (representative of all mountains); Talking God [Hash-ch'élt'i'í] between others, will be in charge of trees found on Water Woman [referring to mountains as sources of

water]; Calling God, as youngest chief, will be in charge of trees found on original Corn Woman [referring to mountains on which the trees are found which can serve as the main poles of the hooghan]. In this manner [the hooghan] will now be made [of trees], and there will be fillings [between the main poles] for it [smaller timber from the mountains and tree bark], and the layer [of soil] over it," he [First Man] said. (Wyman, 1970:384)

It is during the blessing of a new *hooghan* that these main beams are annointed. The beams are annointed going clockwise. When a new building is finished, the owner-to-be uses white corn meal to bless the main beams, or a *Hat'aalii* is hired to do that. There are times—when a family has moved out of the house for a long period and moves back again—then they use white corn meal or corn pollen (whichever is available) to bless their home.

Another time the main beams are annointed is when the medicine man is to perform a prayer, a Blessingway "no sleep," or a major ceremony (all these events are ceremonies to cure or help a person.) The annointing is done before the singing begins. White corn meal is used if the patient is a male, and Yellow corn meal is used if the patient is a woman.

In the present day, the *hooghans* are built for ceremonial purposes only. The *hooghan* was once the home to live in and often it became a shrine for ceremonial events, whether for one night, five nights, or nine nights.

When a sing is being done in a *hooghan* there are certain manners that a person should have. For instance, if a person speaks loudly or laughs aloud, nothing is said about the person except that the individual is showing a sign of disrespect to the patient, the medicine man, and the people helping. In all the "sings," i.e. ceremonial events, the women tend to sit on the North side and the men sit on the South side. The People say it was set that way long ago, during the time when the sacred beings met to create the Sun and the Moon, and other things.

First Man seated himself facing them [Sun and Moon] along the south side of the interior (where the singer usually sits). Talking God [Haashch'éłtı'í] too took a seat there... Next to him along that [south] side toward the exit men only took seats. Along the north side of the interior, First Woman sat down and on that north side toward the exit, women only were seated. "Now then, the so-called chief of hooghan songs will come into being, and chief songs will come into being. You see, this Sun will be the leading one (First Chief), while the Moon will be second chief, between, and Calling God will be the youngest chief..." he (First Man) said. (Wyman, 1970: 384)

The structure and shape of a hoogan originated from the Beauty Way stories. It is said that the hooghan has taken on the shape of the mountains. It was the time after the fixing of the mountains that the complete shape of the hooghan building was decided upon. That is the hooghan shape, the way of entrance, the interior decorations and their purposes, and the belongings were completed at this time.

The first of the two mountains [Godernador Knob] had a fine tapering shape, the second [Huerfano Mountain] was somewhat round at the top. There, the decision was made that, "in future times the home of these Navajos [Diné Dine'é] will have these shapes." The hogan [hooghan] in the shape of the first one we call pointed-towards-each-other [conical] that is what it is [like]. That hooghan in the shape of the second one is what it is [now] called under-around-top [round roof] hooghan. "In future times Blessings way ceremonials will be held in the first kind [Interlocked forked-pole type]. Nothing to jar it shall be planned with it."

"In the second one [round-roof type] the several lines of chant-way ceremonials will all, without exception, be conducted as well as all injury way ceremonials. For these that kind [of hogan] will serve," was said, they say. (Wyman, 1970:361-362)

Thus, in the present day, the hooghan take on the shapes of the two sacred mountains; they are to be respected for this.

There are different types of hooghans and they have their genders too: a male hooghan, a female hooghan, and each have their own use. The forked (conical) hooghan is male; the round-top (roof) hooghan is female. The sweat lodge is male. The many-legged hooghan is female. The logs hooghan is female, and the square of "sun" house is male:

All of the male hooghans are made in certain way of ceremonial purposes. Inside the male hooghan, usually ceremonials, prayers and other chants that deal with healing are conducted. Especially, *the sweat lodge*, there is usually a planning session and telling of sacred stories during the sweat lodge bath get together. Also many religious ceremonies are learned in the sweat lodge. In the female hooghans, there is usually a social gathering for laughing, joking and babies crying. But not in all of the male hooghans. (B. Mitchell, Curriculum Material, 1976)

The hooghan is the home and very much a part of the environment on different parts of Navajo land. There are geographical differences and they affect the moving habits of our grandparents, and us nowadays. The climate is not the same either. The weather is quite different, when comparing Shiprock and Wheatfield areas, Tuba City area and Black Mountain area. Spring comes earlier in Shiprock, during the time when the snow has just begun thawing in the Wheatfield area. The climate affected the moving of our grandparents so that they had a summer home and a winter home. As a home, our grandparents thought of these shelters as places where we, the young people, could gain knowledge for our future. There in the hooghan they constantly stressed to the young men the importance of learning how to build a hooghan, and how to tend to the outside work, (chores) to the livestock; and to the young ladies the importance of learning to care for the home. They urged them (grandchildren) to understand the importance of maintaining a hooghan.

It was after a person had learned the different stories relating to the hooghan that he/she would look at an ordinary hooghan with awe, reverence and respect. The Diyin dine'é decided that a hooghan would be decorated with various items for use by the Diné dine'é (Navajos):

In its interior too, everything will be found, (i.e., known by name), there will be a name for all. There will be the entrance (mat) woven toward each other, and the entrance uprights with the curtain. There will be the fire with the food, the pot with the stirring sticks, the earthen bowl and the gourd ladle, the metate and the whicker broom. There will be a sleeping place and the under (bedding) spreads, and clothing, various fabrics, and earbands, and various jewels. There will be long life and happiness (existing) there. Now in this manner living will continue within it, and thinking about it, getting them fixed up and bringing them [thought and discussion] together. Planning things and making them strong will be done there, (i.e., the hooghan will become a center of strength and sound planning). Moving into it [by the Holy People (diyin dine'é)] will take place and they will have lasting homes in it in the future. And entering into it in a holy way will occur and [life] will continue on in blessing within, just as it was originally [intended]. (Wyman, 1970:385)

The People say that there is an early morning surveillance by the sacred beings of dawn on the home. Tom Ration says Haashch'éílti'í and his follower, Haasch'é wan are the two people of Dawn. Some Diné parents today will remember hearing their parents say to them when they were youngsters, "Rise early in the morning, when morning stars are out to see you. Be active outside the hooghan. Let the sacred beings bless you well!"

Our parents would say to us, "Arise. Wake up! What are you sleeping for! Take out the ashes! Clean around the outside, we do not want trash around the hogan!"

This is done so that the dawn people do not see any trash. They will know they are welcome to this place. "There is no wealth here, let's go in and give them some," they (Sacred Beings) will say (by wealth, they meant trash). Where the place is dirty and trashy, they will ignore the place and say, "too much welath there, let's go to another place." (Ration, Smith Lake, New Mexico, 1976)

In the present day, among our own people (diné dine'é) we know special leaders, spokesmen and women who have been raised from the hooghan. These people probably have learned and know the significance of a hooghan, and they know of many other leaders that have been raised out of a hooghan lifestyle. We believe that life as a human being (that comes from hooghan lifestyle) has a meaning. If a person is raised in the whole environment of a hooghan, through all seasons of the year, he/she definitely has a unique lifestyle and perception of what a diné's life is. This itself has that meaning of what is "traditional Diné (Navajo)."

Suggested Additional Readings

1910, 1968 *An Ethnologic Dictionary of the Navajo Language*, St. Michaels, Arizona: The Franciscan Fathers.

LOUIS, RAY BALDWIN
1975 *Child of the Hogan*, Provo, Utah: Brigham Young University Press.

MITCHELL, EMERSON BLACKHORSE
1967 *Miracle Hill*, Norman, Okla: University of Oklahoma Press.

NEWCOMB, FRANC JOHNSON
1964 *Hosteen Clah, Navajo Medicine Man and Sand Painter*, Norman, Okla.: University of Oklahoma Press.

1967 *Navajo Folktales*, Santa Fe, N.M.: Museum of Navajo Ceremonial Art.

CHAPTER THIRTEEN

Mimbres pottery bowl design from New Mexico, A.D. 1100-1250 (Courtesy of the Taylor Museum of the Colorado Fine Arts Center)

13 Sacred Fools and Clowns

Innocent and wise; painted in their stripes, their lightning streaks, fantastic masks, or naked from head to toe; the Clowns catch our attention whenever and wherever they appear. They are called *heyoka, chifone, koshare,* "banana ripener," *kwirana*, "blue jay," and many other names. These are the characters that follow behind the neat rows of dancers, dancing out of step, singing one beat behind. These are the confusing individuals, men dressed as women; old men acting young, young acting old. They are lovers, teasing the young women, the tourist ladies taking pictures, the unmarried women or other men. So obscene are their actions at times that the crowd watching them gasps in horror; minutes later people from the crowd are giving them food—melons, squash, corn, tortillas, fried bread, and chiles. They are the brave hunters shooting the deer dancers with miniature crooked bows and sticks for arrows, or "counting coup" to a pot of boiling dog meat; they plunge their arms into the water to grab the meat without getting burnt. They are the serious Clowns of the medicine society maintaining the continuity of fertility, rain, crops, health, and the various orders of Creation. They are the guardians of the ritual, ready with their whips, their yucca plant lashes, ready to catch a child to throw him in the river.

Whenever the Clowns enter the stage of drama in a ritual and wherever they are found in the oral histories, stories, or songs, the Clowns have something in common with each other. A sacred Clown from one tribe would recognize a sacred Clown from another tribe, and, without a word passing between them, they would know who the other one was; what he represented, and what he was placed on earth to do. Clowns and foolish characters are part of the oral tradition of most Native

American peoples. When Clowns appear in the Creation histories they often play very important roles during the *emergence* of The People into this present world. We have already seen how foolish figures like Coyote created death; in other instances, these figures bring light and fire to humans, and give creatures their behavior characteristics and tools for survival. In these early histories of oral tradition we are first introduced to the concepts and the techniques of clowning.

Sacred Clowns often have a special relationship to the sun—almost like sons—particularly in the Southwest of the Continent. Often there is more than one Clown society. In the Rio Grande, for instance, Pueblos divide the Clowns into Summer and Winter Clowns. Sometimes Clowns are associated with the World of Souls or the Land of the Dead and are guides to individuals whose dreams or visions take them there (as among the Chiricahua Apache), or to the souls of the dead on their way to their final resting place. The most widespread association the Clowns make is with watery places: mist, drizzle, rain, the clouds, storms, streams, water holes, damp places, thunder, and lightning.

The Clowns are *mediators* for rain. They bring rain and thus bring fertility to crops, growth and life to The People. In San Juan Pueblo the Clowns usher in the Cloud Beings during the Cloud Dance. In the Hopi dance we will describe later, the Clowns are referred to as "The White Cloud" Clowns and at different points in the two-day dance they are *mediators* for rain. The "watersprinkler" (To nei nili) of the Navajo Night Chant Way has his origins in the Grey (San Francisco) mountain to the West. His other name is Grey God (Hash ch'el Bahi) and he is associated with rain, for West is the direction of storms and clouds. The "watersprinkler" appears in certain parts of the

Group of clowns, Zuni. (Courtesy of the Smithsonian Institution, National Anthropological Archives)

Night Chant Way, and does not appear in others. Barney Mitchell, speaking of the dramatic role of the "watersprinkler" remarked, "Having a 'watersprinkler' in the ceremony means you will have a hard winter, and therefore, one Singer from the Tsaile area does not use the 'watersprinkler' in part of the Night Chant ceremony." Another Navajo sacred Clown is "mud clown" (Chaazhini); the "mud clowns" are found in the Enemy Way ceremony (Squaw Dance). The Enemy Way ceremony has a "rain ceremony" within it. The ones who help with this are the "mud clowns." Sometimes, similar to the "watersprinkler," if there has been a lot of rain, the "mud clowns" do not appear. Otherwise, they do and they help attract rain.

The Sioux *heyoka* receives his powers from the Tunderbeings, or *wakinyan*. Lame Deer describes in detail the Thunderbeings and the sacred power of lightning and helps us understand why sacred Clowns might be associated with these powers:

A clown get his strange powers from the *wakinyan*, the sacred flying-ones, the thunderbirds. Let me tell you about them. We believe that at the beginning of all things, when the earth was young, the thunderbirds were giants. They dug out the riverbeds so that the streams could flow. They ruled over the waters; they fought with *unktegila*, the great water monster. It had red hair all over, one eye, and one horn in the middle of its forehead. It had a backbone like a saw. Those who saw it went blind for one day. On the next day they went *witko*, crazy, and on the third day, they died. You can find the bones of *unktegila* in the Badlands mixed with the remains of petrified sea shells and turtles. Whatever else you may think you know that all this land around here was once a vast ocean, that everything started with the waters.

When the thunderbeings lived on earth they had no wings, and it rained without thunder. When they died their spirits went up into the clouds. They turned into winged creatures, like *wakinyan*. Their earthly bodies turned into stones, like those of the sea monster *unktegila*. Their remains, too, are scattered throughout the Badlands. There you also find many *kangi tame*—bolts of lightning which have turned into black stones shaped like spear points.

High above the clouds, at the end of the world where the sun goes down, is the mountain where the *wakinyan* dwell. Four paths lead into that mountain. A butterfly guards the entrance at the east, a bear guards the west, a deer the north, and a beaver the south. The thunderbirds have a gigantic nest made up of dry bones. In it rests the great egg from which the little thunderbirds are hatched. This egg is huge, bigger than all of South Dakota.

There are four large, old thunderbirds. The great *wakinyan* of the west is the first and foremost among them. He is clothed in clouds. His body has no form, but he has huge, four-jointed wings. He has no feet, but he has claws, enormous claws. He has no head, but he has a huge beak with rows of sharp teeth. His color is black. The second thunderbird is red. He has wings with eight joints. The third thunderbird is yellow. The fourth thunderbird is blue. This one has neither eyes nor ears.

When I try to describe the thunderbirds I can't really do it. A face without features, a shape without form, claws without feet, eyes that are not eyes. From time to time one of our ancient holy men got a glimpse of these beings in a vision, but only a part of them. No man ever saw the whole, even in his dreams. Who knows what the great thunderbeings look like? Do you know what God looks like? All we know is what the old ones told us, what our own visions tell us.

These thunderbirds, they are *wakan oyate*—the spirit nation. They are not like living beings. You might call them enormous gods. When they open their mouths they talk thunder, and all the little thunderbirds repeat it after them. That's why you first hear the big thunder clap being followed by all those smaller rumblings. When the *wakinyan* open their eyes the lightning shoots out from there, even in the case of the thunderbird with no eyes. He has half-moons there instead of eyes, and still the lightning is coming out.

These thunderbirds are part of the Great Spirit. Theirs is about the greatest power in the whole universe. It is the power of the hot and the cold clashing way above the clouds. It is lightning— blue lightning from the sun. It is like a colossal welding, like the making of another sun. It is like atomic power. The thunder power protects and destroys. It is good and bad, as God is good and bad, as nature is good and bad, as you and I are good and bad. It is the great winged power. When we draw the lightning we depict it like this,

as a zigzag line with a forked end. It has tufted feathers at the tips of the fork to denote the winged power. We believe that lightning branches out into a good and a bad part.

The good part is the light. It comes from the Great Spirit. It contains the first spark to illuminate the earth when there was nothing—no light, just darkness. And the Great Spirit, the Light God, made this light. Sometimes you see lightning coming down in just one streak with no fork at the end. This light blesses. It brightens up the earth; it makes a light in your mind. It gives us visions. This lightning is still another link from the sky to the earth, like the stem and the smoke of our sacred pipe. That light gave the people their first sound, the first word, maybe.

The lightning power is awesome, fearful. We are afraid of its destructive aspect. That lightning from the south spells danger. It heads against the wind. If it collides with another lightning— that's like a worldwide car smash-up. That kills you. A lawyer, a judge, or preacher can't help you there. That flash from the south, that's *tonwan*, the thunderbolt—the arrow of a god. Sometimes it hits a horse. You see all the veins burn up, like an x-ray. Afterward you find one of these black stones embedded in the earth where the lightning struck. The old people used to say that the damage caused by the lightning was done by the young, inexperienced thunderbirds. They did all the mischief. They were like pranksters, clowns. The old thunderbirds were wise. They never killed anybody (Lame Deer, 1972:238-241)

Black Elk says it more simply and also gives us a feeling for the "balancing" role of the sacred Clown—the relief the Clown provides us with his pranks and mischief. Black Elk explains it this way:

I will say something about *heyokas* and the *heyoka* ceremony, which seems to be very foolish, but is not so. Only those who have had visions of the thunder beings of the west can act as *heyokas*. They have sacred power and they share some of this with all the people, but they do it through funny actions. When a vision comes from the thunder beings of the west, it comes with terror like a thunder storm; but when the storm of vision has passed, the world is greener and happier; for wherever the truth of vision comes upon the world, it is like a rain. The world, you see, is happier after the terror of the storm. (Black Elk, 1932:192)

The following origin stories give us a glimpse of the important roles sacred Clowns play in the creation and emergence of The People. In these stories we also see other elements and powers with which the sacred Clown is associated, for instance, the Sun Father (Acoma). The two stories have certain things in common since the two tribes from which they come, Zia Pueblo and Acoma Pueblo, are related linguistically and culturally. For example, the creative powers are a parent and two daughters. The *koshare* and *kwiraina*, different kinds of Clowns, are also found in both tribes.

The first story from Zia Pueblo describes the principle roles *koshare* and *kwiraina* play in the emergence of The People into the second and third worlds—the Blue-green world and the Red world.

The two daughters, Utetsiti and Naotsiti created the medicine society, various other societies, Kachinas, and many different animals:

They lived in the Yellow world for 4 years. Then it was time for the people to ascend to the upper world. They wondered how they would go up. Early in the fourth morning Tsityostinako, Utetsiti, and Naotsiti got together. They created a ha'a'kak (Douglas spruce) seed and planted it. It sprouted at once and grew rapidly. By sunup it was 4 feet high. They sang songs to make it grow faster. By mid-morning the top of the tree was out of sight. By noontime the tree had reached the next world. They told Koshairi to make the tree firm and strong. He climbed the tree, doing funny things, shaking the branches as he went up. He was painted then as he is nowadays. When he reached the top he saw the Blue-green world. But all there was there on the land was *henati* (clouds) and *heyac* (fog). Koshairi came down and told the *yayas* (mothers; what he had seen. He told them the tree was now ready and strong.

They started to ascend. Koshairi went first. Then came the three mothers and all of the societies and the people in the order in which they had been created. It took only a short time for everyone to get to the Blue-green earth.

They stayed in the Blue-green land for 4 years. The people were fed miraculously by Utetsiti and Naotsiti. Then a (unidentified) tree seed was created and planted. It grew up to the Red world. Kwiraina was sent to try out the tree. He acted funny as he climbed up the tree. He got to the Red world. He thought it was nice. He said to himself: "This is the place my mother sent me to see, so I am making the tree firm." Then he came down and told Utetsiti what he had seen. She thanked him. Then everyone ascended to the Red world, with Kwiraina leading the way. (White, BBAE 184:116-117)

The following story from Acoma describes specifically the creation of the sacred Clown *koshare*. He began as a mysterious object in the basket of Iatiku, one of the sisters who helped create all the beings on the Earth:

Iatiku had three more things in her basket. She knew that there were two eggs, parrot, and crow, but the third thing she did not know, so she decided to bring it to life, and see what it was. So she said, "Come alive! Let us see what you are like." And at her words it came alive. It said "Why have I come alive: Am I wanted?" Iatiku said, "Do not ask. You will be useful." It came to life in the form of a human (male). Koshari was kind of crazy; he was active, picking around, talking nonsense, talking backward, etc. Iatiku did not think much of him, so she sent him to the Oak Man to see if he would be of any use there. So Koshari went, saying, "I know everything." Sure I'll go and I'll do everything for him, I'll be a big help." (This is said though he was just born and had no experience.)

Koshari rushed to the pueblo, climbing the wall to get in, asking everyone where the altar of the Oak Man was. He spoke very loudly around the altar, even though it was supposed to be very quiet there. After he had finally bumped into Country Chief, who was guarding the altar, Koshari asked, "Where is the Mauharo Kai'ye (kiva of the medicine man)?" He tried to go in directly, so Country Chief caught him. "But," he protested, "I have been sent here. I am allowed everywhere by Iatiku." So Country Chief let him go, saying, "Well, he may be of some use." So Koshari yelled into the kiva, "I'm

coming down," and without awaiting response or permission, he went down. As soon as he reached the bottom he said, "I came here as your partner." I have been sent to help you. I can do anything." The Oak Man was glad to have someone help him. But Koshari waited for nothing but went right to work and placed the different objects in front of the altar, saying, "Let me do it! I can do it." So Oak Man did not keep him from doing anything. He caused Oak Man a lot of amusement, in his heretofore solitary life, with his garbled speech and wisecracking and his self-confidence. (Stirling, BBAE 135:33)

Then later on, after *koshare* had been initiated into the knowledge and practices of the *chayani* medicine society he was sent away, to the Sun.

Iatiku turned to Koshari and said, "You have done your work faithfully but you are not acting normally enough to be here with the people." *He was different from the other people because he knew something about himself,* so Iatiku told him to go and live at ha-kuai'ch (the house of the Sun). "You are to be a help to the Sun. You will be called at times to help here. You are not going to be afraid of anything or to regard anything as sacred. You are to be allowed everywhere." So Iatiku painted him white with black stripes around his body and said, "This is your costume."

She took some of the things from the altar and gave them to Koshari saying, "You will use these." He thanked her but said, "I can make more to it and get what I want." So he went and lives today with the Sun, whom he helps. (Stirling, BBAE 135:37)

And in one version of the Zuni histories concerning the origin of the sacred Clown societies *newekwe* and *koymemsi* the Kok'ho who is the overseer of the *newekwe* society, a Holy Being, was talking to Bi'tsitsi, the first Clown, who was telling him about some of his clowning implements. Kok'ho is pleased and says to Bi'tsitsi, "That is well, that is well!

The Koshare before a dance, Cochiti Pueblo, New Mexico. (Courtesy of Museum of American Indian, Heye Foundation)

Come and live with me and you shall be musician and jester to the Sun Father." (Stevenson, 1904:430)

SACRED CLOWNS: THEIR RELATIONSHIP TO SACRED KNOWLEDGE

The sacred Clowns of North American tribal people are direct evidence that the sacred ways of tribal people are not inflexible, self-important and without humor. As we have seen throughout this textbook most sacred teachings and practices contain humor: the stories of Trickster heroes such as Coyote, Rabbit, and Raven; the curing songs of the Pima Shaman; and the admonitions to "have fun" and "enjoy yourself" during the dances, by the Elders. One of the unique features of Native American sacred ways is the important place of humor and laughter in this aspect of the Peoples' lives.

Sacred Clowns portray and symbolize all the aspects of the sacred that we have discussed,

chapter by chapter throughout this book. But they do so in a special way, a way in which their teachings get through to us without our even "thinking about" them. The Clowns in their actions do not seem to care about "concepts." They are not concerned with definitions, but at the same time Clowns do define the concepts at the root of tribal cosmologies, the guidelines for moral and ethical behavior, and the theories of balance and imbalance.

In Chapter Three: **Learning The Way: Traditional Education**, we heard a number of individuals say that to learn you should not "ask why." By asking "Why" you limit your chances of *experiencing* sacred knowledge. Another reason people say you should not "ask why," is that the subject being asked may be too dangerous. Without proper instruction beforehand the person asking "why" might be harmed. In Native American communities the Clowns are the ones that "ask why." They are often the only ones that may "ask why" in reference to dangerous objects, or "ask why" of those people who are specialists in advanced sacred knowledge. They ask in their backwards language, through their satire, and their fooling around, the questions we would like to ask. They say the things we might be afraid to say to those we might be afraid to speak to. Even though they may not or cannot *conceptualize* their knowledge, the answers to our questions—the truths, the philosophy, and the wisdom—comes through to us.

Jokes, puns, satire—these different forms of humor are important teaching tools. In general, with Clowns, we, the audience, have to "read between the lines" to understand their dramatic message. By making us read between the lines, the Clowns make us think about things we do not usually think about in ways we do not usually think; or look at things in a way we do not usually look. That is what jokes do to people in conversations.

A Joke takes your thoughts, ties them in a knot and then, at the punch line, the joker takes the two ends, pulls them, and the knot is untied. Many times we might even feel as though we had been part of the joke all along just by listening to it from beginning to end. The sacred Clowns do the same thing. They teach by not teaching; they make us see by stumbling around; they make us laugh by frightening us; and they can take the heart of sacred knowledge and ridicule it before our eyes.

In terms of portraying and symbolizing other concepts that we have been discussing throughout this textbook, the Clowns' role is an important one.

In Chapter Four, we discussed the boundaries of the world. Such boundaries are often *symbolized* in rituals, in the sacred pipe ceremony, for example, or in San Juan Pueblo by the directions from which the Holy Beings enter the Plaza where the drama and dances are held. In most Native American ceremonies, boundaries and directions are usually strictly observed in dancers' movements, the movements of the characters in the drama, and the manner in which lodges, tipis, hogans, and other ritual structures are placed and entered.

Clowns often turn these directions inside out and backwards. Instead of moving clockwise they move counterclockwise. Instead of using the right hand, they use the

left. The Clowns may also enter realms where ordinary people are not allowed to go or would be afraid to go, for instance, into the symbolized worlds of the Holy People. In this way the Clowns portray the limits and boundaries of the world by going beyond them, acting in a non-ordinary way while doing so, and in this way they contrast their own contrary behavior with the orderly ritual directions and sacred worlds.

Fundamentally, the sacred Clowns portray the Path of Life with all of its pitfalls, sorrows, laughter, mystery, and playful obscenity. They dramatize the powerful relationships of love, the possibility of catastrophe; the sorrow of separation and death; the emerging consciousness of human beings entering into life—into this world as ordinary beings with non-ordinary potential. They show the dark side; they show the light side; they show us that life is hard; and they show us how we can make it easier. If death takes everything away when it robs an individual of life, then the Clowns must be able to combat death in mock battle and wrestle life back again. Just as the Baffin Bay People say that "evil will shun a place where people are happy," so do the Clowns; they hold the fourth enemy away from our thoughts by making us laugh. And if catastrophe is always just around the corner, the Clowns must prepare us for the worst by portraying it...and then...stabilize everything in the end of the drama. If we are there watching the Clowns, if we are perhaps the subject of the Clowns' ridicule and teasing, we will learn. Because the Clowns are just reflecting what could happen to any of us, at any time of day or year, at every turn along the Road of Life.

And last, where there are still sacred Clowns in tribal societies, they have been able to integrate modern-day elements into aboriginal rituals. This, of course, makes their dramas effective from year to year, whereas, in many instances, ceremonial dramas and healing rituals have lost their meaning for young people. Symbolic dramas, rituals, and ceremonials often lose their effectiveness in the lives of The People without the leadership of specialists and without educating the young people in their rules and symbols year after year. The Clowns, since their message is basic to every human being in every society, (and

The Kwakiutl *Noo'nlemala* or "fool dancers." Franz Boas, 1895. (Courtesy of the Smithsonian Institution, National Anthropological Archives)

has been for thousands of years) can usually manage to reflect the problems and jokes of today as well as of the past. An example of this is the weekly cartoon in the Hopi newspaper *Qua'toqti*, published at New Oraibi, which features the striped Hopi Clowns in an editorial page cartoon of contemporary significance.

Lame Deer, a Sioux man who has narrated his autobiography, summed up the most important role of the Clown, in this case the Sioux *heyoka*, when he said:

> For people who are as poor as us, who have lost everything, who had to endure so much death and sadness, laughter is a precious gift. When we were dying like flies from the white man's diseases, when we were driven into the reservations, when the Government rations did not arrive and we were starving, at such times watching the pranks of a *heyoka* must have been a blessing. (Lame Deer, 1972:237)

THE CONCEPT AND CHARACTERISTICS OF THE RITUAL CLOWNS

> He was different from the other people because he knew something about himself.*

The most obvious characteristic of sacred Clowns is that they are full of contradictions. One of the contradictory qualities people use to describe sacred Clowns is their mixture of *innocence* and *wisdom*. On the one hand they act foolishly, apparently without any thought, without any conscience; and, on the other hand, the creation histories say that the Clowns speak like "wise priests," speaking the truth, speaking prophecies.

Children, too, are considered *innocent*. To grow older is to grow wiser. Often the rituals that mark a person's growth reflect this learning process from being empty of wisdom as a child to becoming filled with experience and knowledge as one grows older. A young man strips naked and fasts in the wilderness for a vision or power dream. He cries like a baby with the pain and the loneliness, and if he is fortunate, a vision comes to him. Then afterward he is cleansed, given a new name perhaps, and allowed many new privileges that only an initiated man can have. During the Zuni ceremonies in the 1930's the *koyemsi* Clowns stripped naked, and one individual was recorded as explaining, "It is alright for the *koyemsi* to take off their covering, because

---

* Referring to the original *koshare*, or Clown of the Acoma (Stirling, 135th:37).

they are just like children." They are like children sometimes and other times they display a knowledge far beyond that of childhood. They have knowledge of sexual relationships, the specialized knowledge of rituals, and about the inner workings of human nature and human society.

For example, the Acoma *koshare* are members of the Acoma Medicine Society along with the society's specialists, the *Chaianyi*, some of the most powerful individuals in the tribe. In the origin story of the *koshare* when the *koshare* group was first given its privileges and duties, "the Chaianyi told the koshare they were to know no sadness and were to know no pain even if hurt. They were to know no sickness." (Stirling, 135th:65) On the one hand they were joining the powerful medicine society and, on the other hand, they were innocent of pain, sickness, and sadness. The "Water Sprinkler" or *To'nei nili* of the Navajo who is the Clown in the Night Chant, "Has no knowledge of love and no knowledge of being serious."

To know love and to have love break your heart is to know sadness and pain. To know sickness is to know the fear of death. For a Clown to bring laughter he/she must be innocent of these things, and it is the Clowns' duty to not only make people aware of the origin of their pain and their sorrow, but also to relieve them of the thought of it. In order to combat the pain of heartbreak and sickness, in order to take away seriousness, the Clown must know about them but he must not let them touch him. This is why the Clown is both wise with ancient knowledge and innocent of its pain. In the Creation histories the Clown emerges with the knowledge of things, and in the rituals of today the Clown acts innocently of them. Lame Deer, speaking again of the *heyoka* tells us that "Being a Clown brings you honor, but also shame. It gives you power, but you have to pay for it."

It seems that in dreams we can imagine many things that in ordinary life could not happen, for one, because it would create mass

Hopi "pointed" clowns next to a line of dancers in the "Long Hair" dance. (Courtesy of Museum of American Indian, Heye Foundation) Emory Kopta, 1912.

confusion—at least that is what people say. One can imagine if everyone acted like Clowns non-stop every day of the year, order and growth could not be maintained. In dreams, in our non-conscious, non-mindful behavior, we sometimes behave like Clowns. At the beginning of this section we heard that *koshare* was described as "different from the other people because he knew something about himself." He knew something we do not ordinarily think or ask about—sacred things perhaps, dangerous things, shameful things. Of course, during the course of one's life, one asks about troubling problems, dreams, experiences, and it is good to know that there are specialists around who can help answer questions. Clowns also act as instructors and counselors in their dramas about matters of sex, love, death, pride, shame, selfishness, and many other powerful feelings. In the emergence and creation stories and in other parts of oral tradition are found the origin of the Clowns' particular wisdom.

The following story* tells the origin of the Zuni *koyemsi* clowns. It is from the Zuni emergence history at the time The People were searching for The Center or The Middle, as the right place to begin their lives as The Zuni. This particular segment begins when the leader of The People (who were Holy People in that period) chose one of his own sons to go and seek "the middle"—the final resting place of the Zuni People...

The father chose his oldest son, for he was wise, but the son, after setting out did not return. The father and the people were worried, so he sent the second eldest son and he left and did not return. Then he sent his third oldest son and the same thing happened. Finally the father decided to send his youngest son who was a handsome young man, and his daughter who was a beautiful young woman.

They journeyed far and late in the day they saw a mountains before them. The brother spoke, "Let us hurry my sister because you are tired from traveling. We will rest in the shade of that mountain over there. I will build you a shelter of cedar and hunt for small game for our food, and you shall rest happily my sister." He spoke gently to her because he loved her and her beauty. And so they hurried, and when they reached the mountain, the brother built a shelter of cedar branches under the shade of a tree. Then he went out to hunt for some game. When he returned, his sister was sleeping in the shelter. He came in and sat down gazing at her for a long time with his chin in his hand. The wind was blowing gently through the shelter, lifting slightly now and then her light clothes. Her brother became filled with desire and when he could no longer contain his feelings, he slept with her. He lay with her and made love with her without thinking of the consequences of his act. When his sister woke up and realized what had happened she fled from him, afraid. And as she fled her fear turned to shame, and then to anger. She came back to where he was shouting furiously at him for what he had done. And as she scolded him her eyes grew large and glaring and her face spotted and pale. And as he listened and watched her, he grew dazed and stood senseless before her, his head bowed, his eyes red and swollen, his forehead bent and burning.

"You shameless man," she cried, "You shall never return to your people, never, and neither will I. With my power I will make a deep river dividing this mountain. Alone on one side I will live, and alone on the other you shall live. I will draw a line and make the water swift between us and between our people!" She stomped with her sandle as she spoke and the sound echoed through the mountain. Then she ran down to the westward end of the mountain and drew her foot along the sands from south to north making a gully as she went. And her brother, seeing her run away, ran after her, calling hoarsely. But, as he neared her he stopped and stared. Then he grew crazy again—this time in fright and anguish at her anger and the way her face was

---

* Adapted from Frank Cushing, "Outline of Zuni Creation Myths" 13th ARBAE, 1891-1892:398-403.

becoming changed and distorted. As she turned again away from him he lifted his arms high and beat his head and temples and tore away his hair and clothes and clutched his mouth and eyes wildly, until great welts and knobs stood out on his head. His eyes puffed up, and his lips blubbered and puckered. Tears and sweat and wet blood drenched him and he rolled in the dust until he was coated with the color of the earth from that place. And when he staggered to his feet, the soil stuck to him and his ugliness hardened.

The sister stared in wild terror at him and she too was filled with sorrow and grief and ran around shrieking in despair —so much so that her hair turned white. And so she cried, and sometimes she pitied him and yearned for him with love, and sometimes they laughed at one another's ugliness, other times in love. When he laughed she laughed too; and when he was silent and bowed she cried and called to him. From then on it was like that with them. They talked loudly to each other; they laughed or they cried. *Sometimes they were like silly children playing on the ground; then suddenly they were wise as priests and high beings and preached as parents to children and leaders to people.* And as the water in the river grew deeper and swifter they ran away together, away from their people. They lived in caves forgetting the faces of human beings and not thinking about their own ugly condition.

In time there were born to these two, twelve children. They were neither man-children or woman-children, but both mixed together. The first three were girls, the rest were boys. They were big boys and earth-colored like their father. *They were silly yet wise as the gods and high priests. Because fools and mad people speak from the things seen in the instant, uttering wise words and prophecy, so they spoke that way and became the wise people and interpreters, attendants, and guides of the ancient dance dramas of the Kachinas.*

[These nine boys] had names but they were not ordinary names—they were instead "names of mismeaning," or contrary names.

First, *Priest Speaker of the Sun*. He meditates in the middle of the day and does not say much at all. When he does speak it is something without sense or without use.

Second, *Bow Priest Warrior*. He is a coward, so much that he dodges behind ladders thinking that they are trees and stays back after the others, frightened at the smallest leaf or spider—and looks in every direction but the straight one whenever danger threatens.

Third, *The Bat*. Who can see better in the sunlight than any of them but would injure himself in a shadow and will avoid a hole in the ground even if it were the size of a beetle hole.

Fourth, *Wearer of the Eyelets of Invisibility*. He has horns like the catfish and is knobbed like a squash. He never disappears even when he hides his head behind a ladder rung or turkey quill— though he thinks he is out of sight then.

Fifth, *The Pouter*, who does nothing but laugh.

Sixth, his younger brother, *Aged Buck*, who is the biggest of them all. He looks as ancient as a horned toad, but is as frisky as a fawn and giggles and cries like a small boy playing games.

Seventh, *The Glum One*.

Eighth, *Suckling*.

Ninth, *Old Youth*, the youngest and most willfully important of the nine. Always advising others and strutting like a young priest in his first dance or like a youthful warrior who has gone sour with self-importance.

And while their father stands dazed with his head bowed and his hands clasped before him, like broken bows hanging by his sides, these children romp and play (as he and his sister did when they turned childish). And their children are like idiots and crones turned young again, laughing, startled to a new thought by every flitting thing around them. But in the Presence of the Old Ones and serious Kachinas they are themselves more serious. And they are like oracles of all the sacred "sayings" of deep meanings; and so they are called *koyemsi*, husbandmen of the ko'ko or sacred drama-dance. And they are spoken of as the *Wisemen of the Ancients.*

That is the story of one group of sacred fools who knew shame, came to "know themselves" and through this knew wisdom. Today these same characters appear in Zuni dance dramas.

Another group of Clowns found among the Sioux also derive their power and wisdom from an experience of shame. Unlike the *koyemsi*, the Sioux *heyoka* originates at least part of his/her characteristics from an *individual* vision or dream uniquely his/her own, and not recorded in oral tradition. Similar to the *koyemsi* and other sacred Clowns, however, the relationship of sacred Clowns to thunder, lightning, rain—water in general—is made explicit with the *heyoka*. (Some say that the *koyemsi* Clowns of the Zuni derive their

"knobby" appearance from the association of those knobs with certain stones found in the area through which the original Zuni wandered on their way to The Middle or The Center. These stones are associated with rain, torrents, and high mesa watery places.)

With the Sioux, the concept of shame is tied to a fear and respect for the *wakinyan* or thunder beings. The *heyoka* has to "pay for his power" by being threatened with punishment by the thunderbeings if he/she does not follow the rules of becoming a *heyoka*. For example, Lame Deer tells us:

A clown in our language is called a *heyoka*. He is upsidedown, backward-forward, yes-and-no man, a contrary-wise. Everybody can be made into a clown, from one day to another, whether he likes it or not. It is very simple to become a *heyoka*. All you have to do is dream about the lightning, the thunder-

Zuni Koyemsi clowns. (Courtesy of the Smithsonian Institution, National Anthropological Archives)

A painting done by Rain-in-the-face, a Hunkpapa Sioux man from the Standing Rock Reservation. In a dream, the lightning tells him that, unless he gives a buffalo feast, the lightning will kill him. He gives the feast, one part of which consists of filling a kettle with hot buffalo tongues and eating some in order to save his life. (Courtesy of Museum of American Indian, Heye Foundation)

birds. You do this, and when you wake up in the morning you are a *heyoka*. There is nothing you can do about it.

If the thunder-beings want to put their power on the earth, among the people, they send a dream to a man, a vision about thunder and lightning. By this dream they appoint him to work his power for them in a human way. This is what makes him a *heyoka*. He doesn't even have to see the actual lightning, or hear the thunder in his dream. If he dreams about a certain kind of horse coming towards him, about certain riders with grass in their hair or in their belts, he knows this comes from the *wakinyan*. Every dream which has some symbol of the thunder powers in it will make you into a *heyoka*.

Suppose you have such a dream. What happens then? It is very unpleasant to talk about. What I mean is that a man who has dreamed about the thunderbirds, right away, the next morning, he's got a fear in him, a fear to perform his act. He has to act out his dream in public.

If I had a heyoka dream now which I would have to re-enact, the thunder-being would place something in that dream that I'd be ashamed of. Ashamed to do in public, ashamed to own up to. Something that's going to want me not to

perform this act. And that is what's going to torment me. Having had that dream, getting up in the morning, at once I would hear this noise in the ground, just under my feet, that rumble of thunder. I'd know that before the day ends that thunder will come through and hit me, unless I perform the dream. I'm scared; I hide in the cellar; I cry; I ask for help, but there is no remedy until I have performed this act. Only this can free me. Maybe by doing it, I'll receive some power, but most people would just as soon forget about it.

The wise old people know that the clowns are thunder-dreamers, that the thunder-beings commanded them to act in a silly way, each *heyoka* according to his dream. They also know that a *heyoka* protects the people from lightning and storms and that his capers, which make people laugh, are holy. Laughter—that is something very sacred, especially for us Indians. (Lame Deer, 1972:236, 241-242, 237)

This power that the *heyoka* receives in his/her vision has to be cleaned of its wildness, its unharnessed force. This is done in a cleaning ceremony. Black Elk, the Oglala man of knowledge, had a series of important visions from the time he was young. In these visions he was taught sacred knowledge which was to eventually prepare him to be a sacred practitioner among his people. One of his last visions was a *heyoka* vision. He tells us that after he came back from his lonely vision quest:

> We brought the sacred pipe back home and I went into the sweat lodge after offering the pipe to the Six Powers. When I was purified again, some very old men who were good and wise asked me to tell them what I had heard and seen. So, after offering and smoking the sacred pipe again, I told it all to them, and they said that I must perform the dog vision on earth to help the people, and because the people were discouraged and sad, I should do this with heyokas, who are sacred fools, doing everything wrong or backwards to make the people laugh. They said they did not know but I would be a great man, because not many men were called to see such visions. I must wait twenty days, they said, and then perform my duty. So I waited. (Black Elk, 1932:191)

He was then counseled by the old men to have a cleansing ceremony. To prepare for the ceremony he and his *heyoka* helpers had to kill a dog and put it to boil in a big kettle. Every person in camp was called to join in the ceremony around the area where the stew was cooking. Lame Deer with his version of a "dog" ceremony, goes on to explain:

> Well, the *heyokas* dance around that steaming kettle, sing and act contrary. If the dreamer says, "A good day to-morrow," well, it will be a hell of a day next day. And if he says, "Tomorrow will be a bad day, thunderstorms from morning to night," why, you can leave your umbrella at home. You won't need it, because it will be beautiful. And if the *heyoka* sees a sick person and says, "He's going to die," that sick person will be all smiles because he knows he's going to live. But, if the *heyoka* says, "You are going to get well," the poor thing, he might as well start writing his will. (Lame Deer, 1972, 244)

Black Elk adds from his own experience:

> During all this time, thirty heyokas, one for each day of a moon, were doing foolish tricks among the people to make them feel jolly. They were all dressed and painted in such funny ways that everybody who saw them had to laugh. One Side and I were fellow clowns. We had our bodies painted red all over and streaked with black lightning. The right sides of our heads were shaved, and the hair on left side was left hanging long. This looked very funny, but it had a meaning, for when we looked toward where you are always facing (the south) the bare sides of our heads were toward the west, which showed that we were humble before the thunder beings who had given us power. Each of us carried a very long bow, so long that nobody could use it, and it was very crooked too. The arrows that we carried were very long and very crooked so that it looked crazy to have them. We were riding sorrels with streaks of black lightning all over them, for we were to represent the two men of my dog vision. (Black Elk, 1932:194-195)

The climax of the ceremony is when the *heyokas* dance around the kettle and prepare to take out the dog meat. At this time the *heyokas* are doctors since the meat is sacred now through the prayers and songs that have been sung, and they can strengthen people by feeding it to them. Lame Deer describes this scene:

> The fourth time around the *heyoka* runs up to the bucket and at the precise moment plunges his whole bare arm into that boiling water, searches around in there and comes up with the head, holding it up to the four winds. He will run with it, and he is guided in this by the spirit, by what he has dreamed, to whom to give this dog's head. He will give it to a certain sick man or woman. That person will be scalded. He will quickly throw it to another man, and he will get burned, and he will throw it to the one next to him and so on. Five or six people will throw that head, because it is too hot for them

to hold. And this comes from the thunder power; it is not a cheap, magic trick.

After this the other *heyokas* charge that bucket, put their arms in and get the rest of the meat out. They don't care how hot it is. They give this meat to the poor and the sick. Their dreams told them whom to give it to. That's a good medicine and a hundred times better than all your pills and antibiotics or whatever you call them, because it cures all their sicknesses right there, during the ceremony. This happens every year and I have witnessed it many times.

What is it that makes a *heyoka* not get scalded? You can go up to him and examine his hands and arms. There's not a blister on him. It wouldn't even show color as when you dip your hand in really hot water and it gets red. It's not even pink. There is a special herb that I know of, a kind of grayish moss, the root of it, called *heyoka tapejuta*. When you chew that and smear your arms with it the boiling water won't burn you. But you have to be a *heyoka* for that herb to do you any good. A man who isn't a *heyoka* could never stand that boiling water. He'd have no arm...(Lame Deer, 1972: 245)

The combination of the vision, the acting out of the dream, and the final cleansing ceremony are good examples of where shame becomes transformed into wisdom by a person coming to "know himself." The individual who becomes a *heyoka* begins in innocence like a child. He learns shame, and then transforms it into power—both by using the gift of making people laugh which is a powerful gift, and by acting out the deeply hidden emotions of human beings—the emotions that make up the Path of Life itself. Black Elk summarizes the *heyoka* cleansing ceremony by saying:

In the heyoka ceremony, everything is backwards, it is planned that the people shall be made to feel jolly and happy first, so that it may be easier for the power to come to them. You have noticed that the truth comes into this world with two faces. One is sad with suffering, and the other laughs; but it is the same face, laughing and weeping. When people are already in despair, maybe the laughing face is better for them; and when they feel too good and are too sure of being safe, maybe the weeping face is better for them to see. And so I think that is what the heyoka ceremony is for. (Black Elk, 1932:192-193)

In Chapter One, Part II, we discussed basic ways of "thinking about" the sacred, concepts at the root of the sacred. We also heard many people comment on the fact that the sacred was part of everyday life. These sacred concepts were, aboriginally, important to The People because they aided or prevented the survival of a community. Clowns are directly involved in the educational process; that of dramatizing relationships basic to ecology and the continuity of the society and the life of each individual. Such relationships would include, for example:

health	— illness
cleanliness	— uncleanliness
order	— disorder
responsibility	— irresponsibility
eating	— defecating
humility	— arrogance
sharing	— selfishness

Of these and other relationships, food, reproduction, health, sharing, and language are very important. Every child must learn the concepts at the root of the sacred to fully participate in the sacred life of the tribe—not specialized knowledge, but the basic balances of life. The Clowns, as we said earlier, teach the children and remind the adults about these survival tools. As we said, they teach backwards, through nonsense, jokes and threats.

The language the Clowns use is backwards contrary speech. For example, Lame Deer describes the action of a *heyoka* after he has had his "shameful" dream and must act it out in public. Since our actions in dreams are often confusing, backwards, without a sense of time, the actions of the *heyoka* are also like this. Lame Deer explains:

A *heyoka* does strange things. He says "yes" when he means "no." He rides his horse backward. He wears his moccasins or boots the wrong way. When he's coming, he's really going. When it's real hot, during a heat wave, a *heyoka* will shiver with cold, put his mittens on and cover himself with blankets. He'll build a big fire and complain that he is freezing to death. In the wintertime, during a blizzard, when the temperature drops down to 40 degrees below, the *heyoka* will be in a sticky sweat. It's too hot for him. He's putting on a bathing suit and says he's going for a swim to cool off. My grandma told me about one clown who used to wander around naked for hours in subzero weather, wearing only his breechcloth, complaining all the time about the heat. They called him Heyoka Osni—the cold fool. Another clown was called the straighten-outener. He was always running around with a hammer trying to flatten round and curvy things, making them straight, things like soup dishes, eggs, balls, rings or cartwheels. (Lame Deer, 1972:237)

Among the Zuni, it has been recorded that the Clowns imitate Satataca, the Bow Priest, in his Night Chant prayer (see end of Chapter Two)—they make obscene remarks in place of the original lines, for example:

Now that those who hold our roads, night priests, have come out standing to their sacred place, we have passed you on your roads. Our daylight fathers; our daylight mothers, after so many days, eight days, on the ninth day you will copulate with rams. (Bunzel, 47th ARBAE:952)

Newekwe Clowns at Zuni, New Mexico. M. C. Stevenson, 1898. (Courtesy of Museum of American Indian, Heye Foundation)

One man from Acoma remarked that perhaps the Clowns speak their contrary language to remind us of the precious gift language really is for us; without it we could not communicate abstract ideas, compose curing songs, pass on oral tradition and, of course, many other essential things.

Other ritual Clowns perform in a similar way, for example, the "Blue Jay" Clown from the Plateau tribes (Sanpoiel, Gros Ventres, Spokane). Running around the lodge acting like Blue Jays, perching now and then on the rafter beams, shooting miniature arrows from miniature bows, the "Blue Jays" hoard feathers, holding them in their arms. Then they begin to throw them into the air, around the room, shouting at the same time the precious feathers disappear, "I am rich, I am rich!" We are told in an account of various clowning activities that the

> Arapaho "Crazy Dancers" are said to "act as ridiculously as possible and annoy everyone in camp;" the Cahuilla "Funny Man" of Southern California "annoys people by throwing water on them or dropping live coals down their backs;" and the Iroquois "False Faces" on entering a house, scoop up handfuls of smoldering cinders from the fireplace and spray everyone in sight, sending them screaming in all directions. (Tedlock, 1975:107)

The Clowns teach by "bad example." That is, the Clowns do just the opposite of what a child should learn. They mock the order of the ritual, they mock the prayers, the songs, the Holy Beings, and the sacred objects. The Clowns momentarily create an unbalanced and disordered world in the midst of ritualized social order. The student will recall previous discussions of *disease and imbalance** in the

textbook. One of the Clowns' roles is to prepare us for *catastrophe*—the possibility at any moment of disorder, sickness, separation, death. Social order, first constructed in the Creation histories, is designed to maintain order in the midst of the world's "essential disorder." Collaboration by everyone is needed to maintain life which is threatened always by catastrophe. In the end, at the conclusion of the ceremonies, the Clowns are brought into the balanced world again in cleansing ceremonies. All the frenzy, obscenity, and terror is calmed and dispersed at this time. The Clowns' imbalance, their dancing at the edge of limitations, and their mocking of order, helps contrast imbalance and balance, order and disorder, in such a way that even a child can understand the basic concept of balance. Without the Clowns' disorder, order would not, in the end, be so obvious and so justified.

Personal responsibility is at the heart of social order and survival—many individuals have said this throughout the pages of this textbook. The following Hopi dance drama portrays among other concepts, the consequences of irresponsibility. In the end the Clowns go through a cleansing ceremony in which they are forgiven for their misbehavior and trouble they have caused. They are also, at this time, given the opportunity to share their "shame" with the public and release it from their thoughts.

The Clowns are chosen before the day of the dance. At noon on Saturday the Kachinas come from the sponsoring kiva and arrive in the plaza to begin the dancing. The Clowns have been preparing themselves in another kiva, planning how they are going to entertain the People, preparing prayer sticks, fasting, talking. When they come out they first go up on the top of the roofs of the house on one side of the plaza. They lift up their arms and shout, fooling around, so that the people know that they have arrived. Here on the roof, they also symbolize clouds, which will bring rain for the crops.

The first thing they do when they jump off or come down off the roof is to "build their house." Groups of clowns go off into each of the four directions to get materials with which to build their "house"—sand, sticks, and so on—not big pieces of wood, but wood chips, etc. They also have in their possession a doll

---

* For example, in Part I of Chapter Eleven,
  The world is seen as an essentially disordered place which may bring to man at any time bad dreams, encounters with unhealthy animals and situations (lightning, ants), and all sorts of unnamed hazards. Nature may turn on a person by their not being under control; that is, his own natural desires if allowed full rein, can cause disease (the best example is, of course, excess of any sort). In fact, one common way of envisioning evil among the Navajo (Diné) is to describe it as the absence of order, or as something which is ritually not under control. (Tolkein, 1969:229)

whom they call the "girl clown." When they are done building their house they place the girl doll in the west corner of it. The house is divided into rooms and during the course of the day, when the Clowns receive gifts of food from their aunts, they place everything they receive in this house.

Then they begin their joking and clowning around. Later on in the day another group of Clown-like Kachinas comes out of another kiva. These are the "imitators"—they are Kachinas who help carry out the plans of the Clowns. For example, they play the roles of individuals the Clowns want to imitate or satirize, like the tourist man in his shorts taking pictures; the missionaries trying to convert the People; and so on. Some Clowns tease people in the audience—young girls for example—propositioning them, teasing each other about them. The tourists are the subject of many jokes. Some are requested to come into the plaza to dance, others to join in a planned contest in which they bid for a doll. After every one of these skits and jokes, the person whom the Clown has teased receives a gift from the Clown. Sometimes the Clowns demand things from people in the audience and these are given without hesitation.

Demanding food from the audience is one of the characteristics of sacred Clowns in many places in North America. Teaching about hoarding, greed, selfishness is difficult unless you can set an example. The Clowns do just that. They are gluttons; they stuff down food; they pretend to urinate where people are eating. It has been said that during certain Acoma dances, "the *koshare* always grab the food the Kachinas bring to the people and then demand some themselves—for example, biting a piece out of a melon before giving it over." (Stirling, 35th BBAE:34) And at Zuni, we are told,

One must never refuse anything to the Koyemci, because they are dangerous.

Anak'china Dance; clown antics (Hopi). (Courtesy of Museum of the American Indian, Heye Foundation)

Last year around Ca'lako my mother received a present of a box of apples. She was wondering whether she should give it to our "child" when he was washed.* She was thinking it would be nice if she would keep that box of apples. While she was white-washing the house she fell off the ladder and bruised her leg. Then she knew that she must give that box of apples to the Koyemci. She was hurt because she had withheld it from them even in her thoughts. The Koyemci are dangerous. (Bunzel, 47th ARBAE:947)

And among the Papago, too, the Clowns ask for food. Maria Chona tells of the time she went to the Harvest ceremony where her second husband was one of the Clowns:

This husband was one of the clowns who makes the people laugh at our great harvest ceremony. The clowns wear masks, you know, great white bags of deerskin, pulled down over their faces with tiny eyes painted on them and just little holes to see through.** They talk in a squeaky voice because we think the clown is a magic person who comes from far in the north and talks a language we do not know. So when we went to the harvest festival and I saw the clown, I never knew it was my own husband.

In the evening, when we were getting supper ready, the clowns would come running to all the camps squeaking in their sacred voices and holding a basket out for food, to feed the men in the Big House. Then we all gave them food, and we were afraid of them, too, because clowns have much power. Once I put tamales in the clown's basket, and there, under the white blanket that was tied around him, I saw a piece of my husband's trousers. "I'm not going to give you anything more," I said. "I know you now." The other women said I must not speak like that. They were afraid. So I kept on giving him food. (Underhill, 1936:59)

The performances and fooling around of the Hopi Clowns is inspired, obscene, playful, serious, and goes on all day. On Sunday, the next day, two dances from the end of the whole ceremony, people bring buckets of water onto the plaza and put them down in various places. The imitators come and catch the Clowns; they whip them and dump the water over their heads. This is the first punishment and cleansing; the pouring of water is also for rain.

At the end of the dance the Imitators line up in two rows and the Clowns group together at one end of the plaza. Each Clown moves up to the head of the line of imitators, one at a time. Here he begins a song that he has composed. He must sing about some personal event— something that is shameful inside of him or that makes him feel bad, like a bad dream, or something about a relative that is disturbing— some way he or she had misbehaved. He sings this song, moving down the row of imitators until he is finished and can join the clowns again. After each of the clowns has sung his song he may then pick up all the food he has

Hopi Clown sprinkling pollen on the "Long Hair" dancers, Hopi, 1912. Emory Kopta (Courtesy of Smithsonian Institution, National Anthropological Archives)

---

* A sacred initiation ceremony.

** See illustration of this Clown on p. 325.

received that day from a pile near where they have been singing. At this time, too, he can join his relatives and eat with them.

One of the main themes of this ceremony is the importance of individual responsibility—to share, to be humble, to be thoughtful. One of the main objectives is to make people happy— "the Clowns open you," "they make you happy," the people say. And the Clowns "tame"—they unbalance things and balance them again. "When they feel too sure or too safe, maybe this is good for them," says Black Elk. The Navajo *mud clown* of the Enemy Way ceremony does this too—it is one of his powers. By throwing a well-dressed man (who is showing off his clothes) in the mud, the man is tamed. And, as we saw, the Clown is fair about this. After he has teased his victim he gives him/her a gift. This is behavior which helps a community survive.

THE SPECIAL POWER OF CLOWNS

One of the roles of sacred Clowns is to serve The People against excesses by practitioners or leaders who might wrongly use their special knowledge: the power of magic; secrets or oral tradition; sacred practices; and other special techniques or prayers. The Clowns, as allies and friends to ordinary people, some-times mock the practitioners (as we heard in the Sayataca Night Chant parody) by dancing behind the dancers and mocking their steps; interrupting speeches by dance leaders as the Clowns did in the aboriginal Winter Hesi Ceremony; or mimicking shamans in their work.* Like all excesses, the Clowns serve to neutralize them; to return excesses to a balanced state.

But we have already seen that Clowns are also considered to be powerful in their own way, and different from ordinary people. One Zuni individual stated:

The Koyemci are the most dangerous of all the kachinas. If anyone touches a Koyemci while he has his paint on, he will surely go crazy. They carry the

sacred butterfly, *lahacoma*, in their drum to make people follow them. That is why they are so dangerous. Anyone who follows *lahacoma* will go crazy. (Bunzel, 47th ARBAE:947)

The Contrary Society of the aboriginal Cheyenne, for example, was a warrior society of great power, reputation, and strict regula-tions. Its members were highly respected, its arms and implements feared. Though the members lived alone, ate alone, did not engage in sex, and lived a simple life, their actions were the opposite. They did things backwards; they gave orders backwards; they rode into battle without thought of their own lives; and they carried a lance that was half spear, half bow.

The Clowns in oral tradition, as well as during rituals and ceremonies, are often given duties and responsibilities equal to the specialists and sacred practitioners. For example, in Acoma oral tradition, one account tells us the story of how *koshare* was given the responsibility to invent a dance because The People did not have one:

Country Chief told the people to make their own songs, that this dance was to be danced by everyone who wanted to dance—boys, girls, men and women. Katsinas dance with just one foot so when the people suggested that they dance like katsina—which was the only dancing they had ever seen—Country Chief said, "No! This is your dance and you must do it a different way." But he knew no way to do it. They decided to spend 4 days preparing for the dance, making up the songs and rehearsing. Everyone was happy, full of anticipation; the whole pueblo was stirred up.

So the War captain, Country Chief, kept suggesting that they call Koshari, that he was going to call him. This was because he knew of no new way to dance and he wanted to leave it to Koshari to arrange the dance and instruct the people in it. Koshari had power to do this. Country Chief said to his two helpers, "I'll try out Koshari and see if he will come. He talks a lot and seems to know everything." So he made a prayer stick and prayed and made a cigarette for him.

---

* See, for instance, Crumrine, N. Ross, "Capakoba, The Mayo, Easter Ceremonial Impersonator: Explanations of Ritual Clowning," *Jrl. For the Scientific Study of Religion*, 8:1-22, 1969.

This prayer stick reached Koshari at hakuaich. On the morning of the fourth day Koshari arrived, still painted in stripes, with his hair tied up on top of his head. He asked for Country Chief, "Am I needed here? I have been called to this place." He was brought to the kiva where Country Chief was. Country Chief said, *"Yes, I want you here. I believe now that you are real and have power.* My people are going to have a dance and I am leaving it all to you to arrange as you may wish." He explained to Koshari the purpose of the dance. Before he had stopped telling him about it, Koshari knew all about it and said, "Yes, I will arrange it for you." So Country Chief told the people that they were to obey Koshari.

Koshari went out, going from house to house telling the people to hurry up and come out. They were much interested in him and obeyed him. He said, "All who want to dance come on to the kiva." He was the one to show them how to paint themselves and put on their costumes. While going from house to house, Koshari spied the drum belonging to the Chaianyi [Medicine Society] (The drum, of course, was only for a very sacred purpose, but without asking permission, Koshari took it.) (Stirling, 135th BBAE: 43)

Sacred Clowns have a special relationship to the specialists—the shamans, the curers, and the medicine people. Often Clowns are considered to be able to cure illnesses, often they have access to the same knowledge or societies as the medicine people. For instance, the Acoma *koshare* is part of the *Chayaini* medicine society. In the oral tradition, when the first *koshares* were being initiated into the Clown society as was the first and original *koshare*:

Chaianyi told them they were to represent the real Koshari, who had the habit of going wherever they pleased, and they would be allowed to go even in the most sacred places. *"You will also have the power of a chaianyi. Even if the chaianyi has made medicine, you can go in and take it without permission and go out and cure anyone you wish with it."* (Nowadays the Koshari will sometimes go to the medicine bowl, suck up some of the medicine, and administer it to the patient through his mouth.) *The chaianyi told the men they were to know no sadness and were to know no pain even if hurt. They were to know no sickness.* (If someone in a household is unhappy or sick, frequently they prefer to call on a Koshari rather than on a medicine man.) (Stirling, BBAE 135:65)

And, among the Papago, when Maria Chona described her life, she told about the powers of her husband who was a sacred Clown:

At the festival, my husband cured the sick people. Everybody who feels badly sits in a row at that feast and they call to the clown: "Cleanse me!" So he comes and blows over them and then they are well. People used to come to my husband even when we were home again at Standing Rock. Anyone who had done wrong at the harvest feast would come to him; those who had danced or sung wrong or, maybe, fallen down when they were carrying some sacred thing. That can make you very sick, perhaps, so that you cannot walk any more.

My husband would put on his white mask, with the big bunch of turkey feathers on top. He kept that mask in a jar, far out in the hills behind our house. You must not keep such things near you. They are too strong. Perhaps you would die from their power. But he would go out all alone and get it, and come back from the north, wearing it. Then he would blow on the people. If they were very sick indeed, he had to have singers to sing the harvest songs and make the harvest feast again for that sick man. That is the way to get well. (Underhill, 1936:59-60)

Though often Clowns are considered to be very powerful as curing specialists, like everything else, they cure in a kind of backwards, joking around way. They prefer to focus on "preventive medicine"—everyday ordinary things such as eating and defecating—and how important these acts are to us

Beggar dancer of the Seneca, Cattaraugus Reservation, New York, 1905. Joseph Keppler. (Courtesy of Museum of the American Indian, Heye Foundation)

daily. In the past, it has been recorded among many communities, that the Clowns would pretend urine and feces were "medicine" as well as making reference to the power of menstrual blood—in addition to the other basic instincts and functions common to human beings and animals.

Earlier we discussed the relationship of shame to wisdom, or "knowing oneself." In the Mountain Chant of the Navajo, the sacred Clown, "Yucca Fruit Grower" or "Banana Ripener" (*Hashk'aan Neinilt'a'i*) together with his "wife" (a man dressed up as a woman) performs a small skit for the people attending the Sing. It concerns a theme that is found in every society in the world: jealousy. More than that, however, the skit portrays, in front of children as well as adults, the sexual act, and it may also portray other kinds of behavior ordinarily not talked about nor performed in public. The following portion of the skit performed by the Yucca Fruit Grower is taken

from *The Mountain Chant** This kind of dialogue is still dramatized today during the Mountain Chant (Fire Dance) of the Navajo People.

> *CHARACTERS:* The old hunter and the man dressed as a woman, who will be referred to as He and She.

He: Come, my wife, I have found something good. This [yucca fruit] is what I have long looked for. Are you not glad I have found it?

She: Yes, I am very glad, my sweet.

He: It tastes like you. (He gives her a piece to eat.)

She: It is sweet, but not as sweet as you.

(After this compliment he draws close to

---

* 5th ARBAE, 1888, p. 441, recorded by Washington Matthews, but kept out of that publication, and placed in the National Anthropological Archives, ms. 4834.

322

her and begins to dally, not over decently. One act is to put his hand under her clothes, withdraw it and smell it. At length he puts his hand in at the neck of her dress as if to feel her bosom and draws forth a handkerchief hidden there. He becomes furious.)

He: (Squealing in feeble wrath) Where did you get this?
She: My aunt lost it in the spring and, when I went for water, I found it there.
He: I don't believe you! You have been cohabiting* with someone else. This is your pay.
She: No, truly, my aunt lost it.
He: (Still in jealous fury, lights a cigarette and tries to smoke, presently throws cigarette peevishly away.) I will go away and never see you again.
She: Don't leave! Don't leave! You are a fool!
He: Yes, I know it, but I will be one no longer. Now I go away. (He moves off.)
She: (Pouts a moment, then takes a pinch of dust in her fingers, blows it toward him and says,) Thus, do I blow away my regard for you. I will follow you no more.

(With head averted, and sitting, she watches him furtively till he shuffles off out of sight, among the crowd of spectators; then she runs after him and soon reappears dragging him back.)

He: You were not strong enough to blow me away, I am so sweet. (Again they sit side by side and indulge in [teasing] and loud kisses)
He: I don't like you to cohabit with others while I am away hunting. I find you food and sweet things to eat, but you are bad.
She: Do not leave me. I will never touch another man again. (They eat together of the yucca fruit.)
He: How sweet this fruit is! Let us see which is the sweeter, this or [making love] (Each puts a piece in the mouth and they proceed with the most complete realism of action, but without

_____
* Sleeping or living with someone else.

exposure, to imitate the sexual act. When through, he tumbles off with a groan as if completely exhausted.)
She: (Spitting the fruit from her mouth) The hosh-kawn is sweet, but not half so sweet as what we have been doing.

The skit is most important, ultimately as a curing technique. The patient is inside the hogan with the Singer (Hat'aalii), the Clown is outside making jokes, saying strange and funny things, as well as performing with his "wife" in the skit. "It's the way he talks," explained one Navajo man, "What he says helps cure the patient who is inside with the Singer. The patient, in other words, is guilty of all these things he (Yucca Fruit Grower) says. The patient works out his/her problems through the jokes and ways of the Yucca Fruit Grower." In this case then, the Clown is a "psychologist" working through the problem feelings of the patient.

Other Navajo sacred Clowns have curing powers. "The Watersprinkler," Barney Mitchell tells us, "has more power over all the dancers than the Talking God. He is like Coyote. Talking God has his limitations but Coyote has his ways of getting around them." The Mud Clowns of the Enemy Way ceremony can also cure, Barney Mitchell explains, "They can cure by putting a special black mud on a sick child, for instance. Sometimes they also bounce the sick child in the air and sing."

Lame Deer sums up the special relationship of Clowns to sacred power when he says:

To us a clown is somebody sacred, funny, powerful, ridiculous, holy, shameful, visionary. He is all this and then some more. Fooling around, a clown is really performing a spiritual ceremony. He has a power. It comes from the thunder-beings, not the animals or the earth. In our Indian belief, a clown has more power than the atom bomb. This power could blow off the dome of the Capital. I have told you that I once worked as a rodeo clown. This was almost like doing spiritual work. Being a clown, for me, came close to being a medicine man. It was in the same nature.
(Lame Deer, 1972:236)

Mud clowns in the Enemy Way ceremony of the Navajo, Kayenta, Arizona, 1920. (Courtesy of Museum of the American Indian, Heye Foundation)

SUMMARY

In this chapter we have discussed the origin, concept, and ritual behavior of the Native American sacred Clown. We discussed the relationship of *shame* to *wisdom*, or "knowing oneself." The role of the Clown in carrying out the educational process for children and the rest of the community was explained— particularly the Clowns' ability to create disorder and order or balance it again, leaving behind a message for the audience on what constitutes personal responsibility in respect to a community's survival. We also talked about the special language and dramatic techniques the Clowns use to communicate their message: backwards talk, jokes, satire, and contrary behavior.

As a final word on Clowns, we present a story that comes from the Papago. It concerns an old man and his dream about the Papago Clown—the same Clown that Maria Chona described earlier. The Clown, even in the dream, leaves the People with the gift of knowledge and thoughfulness.

One of the northern villages has an ancient Keeper of the Smoke who at one time was very ill. In his delierium he dreamed a series of songs to which the youths and maidens of his village have been dancing for two years.

The old man found himself in a city "far under the east" where the streets were like rocky canyons. [New York City] There he saw the clown who dances at Papago ceremonies, wandering lost. The clown said he had been spirited to this strange city because someone had taken his photograph and transported it [there].

Of course, the body of the clown then had to follow, even against his will. But, with the old man there, the clown felt strength to return.

The clown went, singing, back to the west, and the old man followed. "There wonderful things were seen." Among them was an ancient rain house, made of brush and hung with all the [decorations] of a Papago ceremony. There were the masks of the harvest singers; there were the cotton "clouds;" there, too, were the woman's grinding slab, and the man's bow and arrow.

"Look at these things," said the clown. "Our people are ceasing to use them. It may be that this is right and that they should take over the white man's ways. But, before you decide, come here. Look once more at the old things. Be sure." (Underhill, 1938:157-158)

Suggested Additional Readings

CATLIN, GEORGE
1967   *O-kee-pa: A Religious Ceremony and Other Customs of the Mandans*, New Haven, Conn., Yale University Press.

EVANS-PRITCHARD, E. E.
1967   *The Zande Trickster*, Oxford, Clarendon. (The West African trickster figure and the tales in which he is hero.)

LEWIS, THOMAS
1970   "Notes on the Heyoka: The Teton Dakota 'Contrary Cult'," *Pine Ridge Research Bulletin*, No. 11 (Jan.), pp. 7-19.

OPLER, MORRIS
1938   "The Sacred Clowns of the Chiricahua and Mescalero Indians," *El Palacio*, 44, nos. 10-12, pp. 75-79.

RADIN, PAUL
1972   *The Trickster*, New York, Schoken Books. (Tales of the Winnebago trickster figure.)

CHAPTER FOURTEEN

14 The Wandering Ground

I was raised by my grandparents until I was school age. I was very observant watching the world [environment] and people [grandparents] around me.

I began thinking about "life" when I was about five. The subject impressed and hit me hard enough that I recollect to this day, where I was in our house and what I was doing at the time.

I remember asking (in my head) what was life for, why did anyone live, and why did *I* live. At that point death to me was a word that represented very little fear. I had seen things die; animals and such, and heard of people dying and saw evidence of it. I remember thinking that from what I could tell or see, there were only two things that were "real" and the wonder of both: life and death.

Comically too, I also remember thinking that since I was "alive" (as far as I knew), I would try my best to "live" and if things didn't work out for me then I would simply die. (Incidentally, today I have altered that thought only a little, to read, "die, simply.")

The point is that I have been grasping at life and death, the unfathomable meaning of each, since then. They still impress me as the two things that are "real."

This brings me to another point. I decided, somewhere along the way and only for myself that these two things in their reality, are the "truth." I also questioned (in my mind and my heart) whether or not "truths" ever change. I came to decide that if a certain thing altered it would not, could not be the truth. Do truths change?

Of course, I ran into problems with this one [question]. In everyday life, one sees alterations and indeed is a part of continual transition. There is a paradox here, somewhere.

As I grew, I was introduced more and more to aspects of "religious" life, Indian and non. Perhaps because of my grandparents' major influential part in my life, surfacing in my perception of things, I assumed that "religious" life had to do with coming to terms with one's "truth," whatever that truth might be.

Again on assumption, I thought the "truth" (if it were the truth) would be the same for everybody.

I was overwhelmed to learn that many, many people had other truths, not these truths. I was amazed to discover that a few had no truths at all. Then there were people like me...

But the most upsetting thing that I heard was that some peoples' truths could become outdated and therefore erased. And I heard too, of certain truths being more lucrative than others.

This new information went against everything I have ever been taught.

My grandparents were people with honest simplicity in their approach to life and death. They communicated to me certain truths, which I could not alter and that I must come to terms with; responsibility, with profound respect, sincere humility and by myself, alone. No one could do it for me.

The most important person in my world died before I was eight. I was there with him at the last, saw him pass away before my eyes. There was no fear of him, or for him. There was loss as if for a part of myself.

When I was nineteen, I gave birth to a boy child and another when I was twenty-one.

These three incidents, though seemingly at opposite sides of the world, have something in common. On each occasion, I came face to face with a "truth." Each was a tremendous emotional experience which intensified my respect for life and death, made me more humble and responsible for myself; for my life and my death.

Now great changes have occurred on this earth since its beginning. We live at a time when people are more preoccupied and impressed by those changes that have occurred at the hands of men.

But it seems to me that in the light of life and death, the incredible wonder and awe of each, that every act of a human being can be measured and put into perspective, and therefore, any plan that we [human beings] can devise and make functional, and any magnificent dream that we can imagine, will not be comparable.

This is what I believe. Until there is no more life and no more death, anywhere, there will always be a "truth," and the unspeakable wonder of it. (A.L. Walters, 1976)

SOME CONTEMPORARY PROBLEMS

In preceding chapters we have discussed various ways of living and the utilization of sacred knowledge by tribes, from prehistoric times.

Anishnabe people, parching wild rice, ca. 1940. (Courtesy of Minnesota Historical Society)

From the earlier ways of sacred knowledge, until Christianity was introduced, we have discussed and described how each way was adapted by tribal people; how and where each fit into a peoples' perception of things, and why each might have flourished.

We have seen how the newer practices were incorporated by individuals into the life of the tribe and the resulting modifications people, ways of living, and sacred knowledge underwent.

We also have described and given examples of how native beliefs were interlocked, how they functioned. We have shown that some customs have remained more stable than others.

In this chapter we will be discussing some contemporary insights by native people about social, environmental, and economic problems that affect most peoples' daily lives. We will be discussing how these elements relate to what one worships today, in contrast to the past, and the manners of worship.

In *Land of the Spotted Eagle* (1933), Luther Standing Bear, the author, summarized his feelings about the new contemporary "civilization." He experienced it and compared it to his older Lakota way of life and what he believed as a Lakota person, to be sacred.

> Regarding the "civilization" that has been thrust upon me since the days of reservation, it has not added one whit to my sense of justice; to my reverence for the rights of life; to my love for truth, honesty, and generosity; nor to my faith in Wakan Tanka—God of the Lakotas. For after all the great religions have been preached and expounded, or have been revealed by brilliant scholars, or have been written in books and embellished in fine language with finer covers, *man—all man—is confronted with the Great Mystery.*
>
> So if today I had a young mind to direct, to start on the journey of life, and I was faced with the duty of choosing between the natural way of my forefathers and that of the...present way of civilization, I would, for its welfare, unhesitatingly set that child's feet in the path of my forefathers. I would raise him to be an Indian! (Standing Bear, 1933: 258-259)

Standing Bear makes an important point that has caused conflict and anxiety for many native people when he says, "If...I was faced with the duty of choosing..." This is exactly what many native people feel they must do. They feel that they must choose between the implications of "civilization" and the older, more familiar ways of living that have always sufficed.

It is very, very important to remember that a few tribes continue today to live in ways that have remained virtually unchanged for centuries. Their concepts of living have not changed. Their identity has not been taken from them, or their territory (environment) drastically altered. They are on the same familiar path of life all their ancestors have travelled and foretold. We see this survival among the Pueblo people whose culture is healthy and rich.

In Chapter One, recall how the word "religion" was defined. Many Indian people have always objected to the word when it is applied to their way of life. They feel that it is inadequate to justly encompass the mystery of life itself and also because (as Allen Quetone, Kiowa, put it), "...it has too much a connotation of present-day denominations as we know them in this country."

Remember that it was and still is now this mystery of life which many native peoples built their life-styles around, because they were in awe of that mystery and recognized their vulnerability. These life-styles of Native Americans are indirectly referred to when anyone discusses beliefs and practices (or customs) of Native Americans.

CHANGE AND RECONCILIATION

Obviously most Native American tribes have experienced a dramatic social change in the last century. Change has influenced their perception of themselves. Change causes us to make evaluation of our place, ideas, beliefs and customs. We live in a world mainly oriented toward technology. This world was far more sophisticated than early Native Americans imagined it to be. Later upon examination, their fears were confirmed.

Vine Deloria wrote about tribal religions vs. modern technology, or what technology represents.

In the college classroom, the student body is often composed of young and older native people. (Courtesy of Navajo Community College, Title III)

The important aspects of Indian tribal religions however, has been their insistence on developing and maintaining a constant relationship with the spiritual forces that govern the lives of humans. As ceremonies have lost their content, with the changing of life styles, they have been forgotten or abandoned. The recent efforts of Indian activists, to reclaim tribal ceremonies have highlighted the dilemma of today's religious Indian. A traditional Indian finds himself still experiencing the generalized presence of spiritual forces; at the same time he finds himself bound by the modern technology of communications and transportation, which speed his world far beyond its original boundaries. (Deloria, 1974)

There have been several attempts by contemporary native people to reinstate sacred ceremonies, customs, and practices into their personal lives. This is usually done with support and help from tribal organizations. Ted Means (of the We Will Remember School in Rapid City, South Dakota) describes such an attempt below. He is describing a "new trend in education of native children."

The whole basis of the Survival School concept is centered around our spirituality as Indian people. In order for us to survive as a people, we must maintain the religion of our forefathers. We must maintain the language, the songs, the respect for our brother's vision. Our young people must develop within themselves a sense of who they are as Indian persons.

In the Survival Schools, we do not teach hand-to-hand combat or guerilla warfare—but we do teach respect. (Akwesasne Notes, Winter, 1975)

The following is another revitalization attempt, but in another area. It is representative of the unique problems to be resolved.

In an attempt to "wake up" certain Wintu sacred places and revitalize her doctoring activities, Flora in 1973 approached the U.S. Forest Service, which now controls much of former Wintu lands, for permission to carry out doctoring, ceremonies on public lands. Cautiously cooperative, the Forest Service advised that, "by means of this letter you are hereby authorized to utilize approximately one acre of land...to carry out your Indian doctor practices. This does not authorize the violation of any County, State, or Federal laws." (Knudtson, 1975)

The woman called Flora was a practicing Wintu "doctor." Below she further explains her role today and what it means in terms of the conflicts she has had to rectify.

"Nowadays," Flora stated solemnly, "we have to live almost half in the white man's way and half in my own way. I will never forget my own way, but I have to steer myself with the white ways. The spirits understand that...I was told by the spiritual one time when I was doctoring that I must help my white brothers as well, if I am to be a thoroughly spiritual doctor."

Treatment of whites, however, seems to demand different techniques. Diagnosis takes place without an interpreter and involves only a brief trance. Like some sort of transient X-ray image, the trance permits Flora to visually scan the patient's internal organs for the source of his discomforts. (Knudtson, 1975)

Technological, social, economic, and philosophical circumstances are all described as areas of reconciliation. At a Denver Conference with Indian Elders, Allen Quetone had this to say about "the Indian way of life in today's world."

Today Indian people who are still holding on to the remnants of their Indian way, at least try to find a manner of expressing this Indian way of life in today's world. They have done it in their own native way.

This is a method or idea that has to be worked out if a new way is found to strengthen and perpetuate our Indian life. It's difficult for young people. For instance, Kiowa people—and I'm sure all Indian people teach their young people to be patient, especially among their elders. It's a quality that has high importance in Indian life. You're taught this from the very beginning. But then today, the young Indian has to go out into the world and compete. The outside world is a competitive, aggressive world which will leave behind the man that has patience, that stands back and lets the next man have the way. So in the modern world there has to be a balancing, a reconciling of ways.

These are the things that need to be deliberated on by Indian people. Some of these are realities that have caused our Indian way of life to suffer, because it's hard, especially for the younger Indians, to practice some of these things in a different setting. (Morey, 1970:49)

"So in the modern world there has to be a balancing, a reconciling of ways." More examples of the areas to be reconciled sooner or later and examples of problems in maintaining balance are given below. Also, there are explanations of the "different setting" (described by Quetone) some tribes and individuals find themselves in. Though some descriptions are humorous, there is an over-all poignancy in the dilemma of Native American groups who cannot balance or reconcile the old with the new.

(1) Comes from the Eskimo (Baffin Bay area), before 1927. The speaker was in New York City, on the roof of a skyscraper "looking out over the stony desert of New York."

Butch Felix, Sioux, 1975. (Courtesy of Navajo Community College, Title III)

"Ah," sighed Anarulunquaq, "and we used to think Nature was the greatest and most wonderful of all! Yet here we are among mountains and great gulfs and precipices, all made by the work of human hands. Nature is great; Sila, as we call it at home; nature, the world, the universe, all that is Sila; which our wise men declared they could hold in poise. And I could never believe it; but I see it now; Nature is great; but are not men greater? Those tiny beings we can see down there far below, hurrying this way and that. They live among these stone walls; on a great plain of stones made with hands. Stone and stone and stone—there is no game to be seen anywhere, and yet they manage to live and find their daily food. Have they then learned of the animals, since they can dig down under the earth like marmots, hang in the air like spiders, fly like the birds and dive under water like the fishes; seemingly masters of all that we struggled against ourselves?

"I see things more that my mind can grasp; and the only way to save oneself from madness is to suppose that we have all died suddenly before we knew, and that this is part of another life." (Rasmussen, 1928:386)

(2) From the Navajo medicine man, Tom Ration:

Long ago it was a traditional custom to return to your birthplace now and then and roll around there. Today no one practices this custom anymore. Recently many babies are born in the hospitals so this makes it impossible. Imagine one rolling around in the obstetrician ward. They would think you were crazy. (Interview, 1975)

(3) Also from Tom Ration, regarding "soft goods."

Many Navajos became silversmiths, and all the stores are filled with Indian-made jewelry. Instead of the Indians making their profits, we have made the white traders rich with our jewelry. This has all happened because we have forgotten the songs of the soft goods (Yo Di Bi Yin) and sacred stone songs (Nitl'iz Bi Yin). We are deprived of these riches by our own carelessness. This also goes for sheep and horses. It was told when a person sings these songs with reverence he is gifted with all the goodness and blessed with goodness. (Interview, 1975)

(4) This example comes from Deloria, though it is about the Hopi. (Deloria is a Sioux.)

The most persistent problem of the Hopi and other Pueblo people is the degree of adaptation that will be allowed inside the villages. Often the conflict is framed in practical terms, such as the question of allowing refrigerators inside the village. Younger people, having attended Bureau of Indian Affairs boarding schools, are accustomed to having cold milk to drink, but a Pueblo without refrigerators precludes the preservation of foods and drinks that are dependent upon cold. The conflict is sometimes heated and represents a challenge of no small proportion to traditional Indians. Does one forsake a philosophical and religious tradition in which things "happen" for the sake of bodily comfort? (Deloria, 1974)

(5) Miccosukee, often identified as Seminole: Our informant was the young mother of a six-month-old baby boy, her first child. Her Mikasuki* home life had been conservative.

Her mother's mother's brother was a Medicine Man and she followed the rule which forbade young people to call old people by their Indian name. She never knew the names of her grandparents. When her father was young he was punished if he was found in possession of a pencil. Nevertheless he was not opposed to his children going to school so that eventually she achieved the unusual distinction of completing Junior College at a time when there was only one young man in the entire Seminole and Miccosukee population who had a four-year college degree. This man later became her husband.

When they were first married he tried to continue the custom of the husband walking in front of his wife. This did not last very long. His wife told us, "He did that until I kicked him one time. I walk beside him now. I broke the spell on him. He doesn't trust me back there any more."

Their son was not born in a traditional birth shelter, but in a hospital. They gave him an English name with his father's surname at birth. About three months later, however, he was given his first Indian name by his father's uncle (mother's brother). I was told that the name could have been given as well by the father, his brother, or a grandfather. Early in the morning before either the baby or the naming elder had eaten they visited him and he gave them two Indian names from which to choose. The name

they chose for the baby became "his everyday, given name."

As soon as possible after the baby was born, (in this case "just a few days"), the mother visited an old (past menopause) medicine woman in the company of an aunt to receive her traditional postpartum treatment. She presented certain specified gifts to the medicine woman through her aunt. These were a live chicken, some red ribbon, two yards of red cloth for sewing. [A skirt]...was also supposed to be red, but a skirt of another color was accepted, earrings (these were made from coins instead of from the old-fashioned medals or pounded medal pieces), and four sewing needles stuck through a piece of red cloth.

Out some distance away from the medicine woman's dwelling the old lady had brewed herb medicine, boiling it over a fire. The young mother was placed over this medicine, seated on a wooden support so that the vapors could cleanse and heal her womb. Over her head was placed the old skirt, tied at the waist to make a cone which could contain the hot vapors she was supposed to breathe.

Although the medicine woman prepared the medicine, only one woman, in this case, the aunt, could conduct the treatment. Had her aunt been a medicine woman, her mother might have been the one to transmit the gifts and conduct the treatment.

This procedure was supposed to last for about ten minutes each morning for four days, but she adapted the ritual by shortening the period to two days, undergoing the treatment both morning and evening of each day. She "nearly passed out" with the first morning's experience but grew stronger and held out.

The new mother also had to drink a portion of the dark red medicine. It was warm and very bitter. She admitted that she could hardly swallow it, but drank it twice, each time, just before undergoing the vapor treatment. The concoction affected her milk so that the baby got diarrhea and they had to feed him from a bottle temporarily.

---

* Mikasuki—spelling refers to the language. (See Chapter Eleven)

These and the taboos which follow were all matters about which a young girl could neither ask nor be instructed in advance.

Attached to this medicine ritual is the rule stated...that the parents may not sleep together in the same chickee or room for four moons, nor eat at the same table. In this case our informant asked her husband for permission to undertake the entire ritual sequence, for without the husband's cooperation the wife's medicine vapor treatment will be of no avail.

The new father readily agreed to his wife's request. Then came the most drastic adaptation to modern times. No tiny birth chickee was available—nor could any distant chickee be utilized; for this Seminole family lived in a house-trailer in the town where the father taught in the local high school.

Nevertheless, they stuck to the ritual demands as far as possible. Since she was the only one present to prepare their food, she did so. But they ate separately and she kept all of the baby's dishes and utensils and her own separate from his for four moons. And she and the baby slept in their bed, but the father slept on the couch for four moons.

As if this was not enough to manage, she also had to observe certain food taboos during this period. For four moons she could not eat any cooked, large-boned meat. This included venison, beef, pork, and turkey, but not chicken. Chicken bones were not big enough to matter. The taboo extended to all entrails, such as liver, chitterlings, and sausage. It also included fried pork rind and fat—and all leavened bread and cake.

One other taboo was mentioned: the mother could not attend a funeral or visit a graveyard during that period. Had she done so, there would have been sickness.

Thus, a modern Seminole couple, educationally perhaps the most advanced husband and wife in the two tribes, accomplished a feat of conservative conformity to a degree limited only by their physical circumstances. The fact that they did so suggests that the ritual

sequence is still carried out by other families even though many young people no longer observe such customs. (Buzwell, 1972:54-58)

(6) From the Lakota:

Long ago, the Lakota young men and women amused themselves all night long with these dances. They had fun with them. At the time no one got drunk. So soberly these were done. The first song is sung slowly, then the beat picks up, the men and women both bounce with their feet in the air. Now, in our life, a song like that would cause one of us to have a heart attack.

(7) From the same Lakota informant (preceding), regarding New Year's songs and the new lifestyle of the Lakota.

Then, three New Year's songs are sung (at the New Year), and there are more songs but these three are sung. Long ago, when the Lakota came to the New Year, there was great rejoicing. Even the

Mae K. Begay, Navajo, teaching moccasin making, 1975. (Courtesy of Navajo Community College, Title III)

elderly said, "Great! I have luckily arrived at the New Year!" For three or four days during both the days and nights, they had fun, they ate, and they rejoiced. Without drinking (alcohol) these traditions were fun. Now, in our lifestyle, no one cares about these. Now, it seems we would want to die. The years come for a long time so whoever lives long gladly receives them. So, because of those, many with strong wills and strength used to rejoice. Now, our lifestyle is very different. So be it. (Theisz, MS n.d.)

PROPHECIES AND HISTORY

With the coming of the "white" man, great change occurred for the native people. Native people did not object to change, for they had been prepared for change by observation and first-hand experience on life's path. Some tribes had even prepared for the arrival of this man, by way of prophecy and according to their oral tradition. Incidentally most stories forecast a gloomy picture of this newcomer and what he represented. Here are some interpretations taken from stories and songs, concerning this newcomer.

(1)   *Wintu Dream Song*

When Red Cane [white man] comes
We Wintu shall forget our songs.

(Knudtson, 1975)

(2)   *Pima Prophecy*

The prophetic content consists of a prediction that other people, who may be understood to be Anglo-Americans, will do that which the Pimans must not do, namely to kill the earth. The Pimans told that they will not kill the earth. They are ordered to be "deferent," *ba bagid*. If they are deferent,* they will experience propriety—enjoy health and avoid sickness—and they will live to witness the earth's death at the hands of non-Pimans.

(Free translation)

I'm going back
since I've already died.

---

* Defer—to yield to. Deferent—yielding.

I'm going back
and my corpses will be doing what I have been doing.
And you [Pimans] will defer to it

and down here on earth will be your propriety.
Should you not defer to it,
Quickly you will see your impropriety [improperness].

...And you will not be the ones to kill the staying earth
I will leave it to them [non-Pimans]

and they will do it.
And these will kill the staying earth,

and even if you don't know anything [about it],
and you will just be feeling fine,

and you will see it,
when it happens.

(Bahr et al., 1974: 46-47)

(3) Navajo story of "The Great Gambler" told by Tom Ration.

I will tell you another story. This happened at Chaco Canyon (Tse' Biya'a Nii' A Hi). There was a man named One-Who-Wins-You (Na'whiil Bii Hi). He was a wizard with all the gambling games. He won everything from his opponents and even won his opponents, and made them slaves. I do not know what he did to have such incredible luck. Maybe it was just by mere instinct. He was born as a twin. No one told exactly who he was. Just thinking to myself he must have been an angel of some kind according to what he said to the people. Someone had a dream one night about the gambling wizard. All the people he had won were his slaves. They also worked very hard. They carried limestone slabs on their backs from a rock quarry to Chaco Canyon. The rocks were masoned into blocks to make stone houses with many rooms. One-Who-Wins-You lived above the canyon. Below the slaves built these houses. The people who built these houses were called the cliff dwellers

('Anasazi). His brother and he were identical twins. The only way to tell them apart was the fact that his brother was an honest man. His brother lived at Bird Knoll (Tsi Di Yik'id). The people all said, "Let his own twin be his next opponent, that will change his luck, you'll see." It is told that twins are extraordinary beings. I will tell you where his brother came to him. It is told a real brother can win from his brother after he has sex relations with his sister-in-law. This is what happened here when Na'whiil Bii Hi's brother came to his home.

The visiting brother was advised by the people not to greet his brother as "my dear brother." He was not supposed to shake his hand either. The only greeting expression was to be, "My opponent," and then to immediately sing a song in [from] the Prostitute Way. After this he was supposed to say, "let's play a game and see who wins." Na'whiil Bii Hi knew that he always wins. They started their gambling games with the shinny game. One after the other, the gambling wizard lost. The last game was the tree breaking. The only possessions Na'whiil Bii Hi had now were his wife and children. "We will bet on our wives," said Na'whiil Bii Hi. The two trees were at the far end of the race track. They got all set and the race was on. About half way Na'whiil Bii Hi shot a witch missile at the bottom of his brother's feet but missed. This is how he had won all the games and races from his opponents before. His twin brother had caught the witch missile ('adigash) and returned the shot aiming at his brother's feet. The twin brother was ahead now. Before he got to the finish line a horned toad (Na 'ashoii Dish ch'ihii) was running beside him. Horned Toad told the man the two trees ahead were One Can Reed tree and a hard oak tree, and told him which was the hard oak tree. (Usually one who breaks the tree wins.) Na'whiil Bii Hi was still struggling with the oak tree when his twin brother got to his tree and broke it off without a struggle. We all know that hard oak cannot be broken. Na'whiil Bii Hi had lost everything now, even his wife, children,

and his home. His twin brother had redeemed all the people with their belongings, their children, and their wives.

Everyone was happy, only Na'whiil Bii Hi was downhearted. He told his twin brother to take good care of his family and began to speak to the people. The people only ignored him. "Send him away," they shouted. "Put him on the strong swift, black arrow (E tiihi Dil hi l) and shoot him up yonder into space," they shouted. Na'whiil Bii Hi stood on the arrow. Before he left he yelled, "Even if you send me far into space I shall return. I will see you and I will be alone, you wait and see."

This is what I meant. He must be a white man. The President of the U.S. is an Anglo and we live under the government. Na'whiil Bii Hi said to the people, "There will be round objects the people will play with to win. This is a reminder of me." We know there are balls that are round like baseballs, volleyballs, basketballs, and golf balls that people play with to win. There are many round objects that remind us of the once gambling wizard who became a loser. Whatever is round belongs to him. Na'whiil Bii Hi also said, "The lightning flash will be his power and also the wind. When I return everything that is round will roll beneath you with the wind. We will travel on the rainbow arc." Today this is all very obvious. We do travel on the highways with yellow streaks and white streaks. The highways remind us of the rainbow as it curves. The round objects under us are the wheels of whatever we travel in: trucks, cars, trains, bicycles and others, and we travel with the wind. The lightning we also know has to do with electric currents. We have lights in our homes, business places, and all kinds of electrical devices. We have electricity everywhere today. All these put together, Na'whiil Bii Hi must have been a whiteman. We call the radio, "The Wind That Talks." This too is a whiteman's invention.

All the stories have their significance and it is wonderful to be able to know

them. (Interview, 1975)

From the three preceding descriptions, one might be able to understand why native peoples looked upon this aggressive newcomer with fearful premonition and with cautious warnings. And, of course, history has shown that this newcomer was indeed ambitious and aggressive. History has also shown that he did bring drastic change to the American Indian, to his lifestyle, and to his beliefs. In addition, we know from experience that he expected immediate transformation by native peoples, to accommodate his aggression and ambition. We see the results of these imposed transformations today. We also hear and see the opposition of native peoples to these impositions now.

Luther Standing Bear also wrote of this change that swept over native peoples, what the change reaped and for whom.

> True, the white man brought great change. But the varied fruits of his civilization, though highly colored and inviting, are sickening and deadening. And if it be the part of civilization to maim, rob, and thwart, then what is progress?
> I am going to venture that the man who sat on the ground in his tepee meditating on life and its meaning, accepting the kinship of all creatures, and acknowledging unity with the universe of things was infusing into his being the true essence of civilization. And when native man left off this form of development, his humanization was retarded in growth. (Standing Bear, 1933:249-250)

Another view of what change brought is described by David Kindle, Navajo from Shiprock, New Mexico. Though it is a more positive stance, he also discusses its relationship to worship, which might be repetitive of what many native people have been saying.

> I think we owe a credit to this white race because they came from across the sea and moved into this new world. They have come with the skill, ingenuity and scientific development. What has been placed here by the Great Spirit for the Indian people—for instance, take the trees—these white people come in and they made a lot of useful things out of them. They have built sawmills, boards to build houses and homes, bridges and conveyances of every kind. I think we owe a great gratitude to this white race from the standpoint of Indian philosophy.

Moving day, Leech Lake, Minnesota (Anishnabe). (Courtesy of Minnesota Historical Society)

Even with this ingenuity and his inventiveness of everything of every shape and form, the white man is lacking one thing. He has lost track of his Creator. He has forgotten his Maker. I think that the Indian people have not lost that respect for their Creator, the Great Spirit, and what has been placed to govern our lives in this new world. The Great Spirit has left certain fundamental laws for us that we have to go by and live accordingly.

Among the things that govern everyone's lives in North America or influence them in some manner are newer concepts to most native people. They include capitalism which is a new form of economy to tribal people: competition, and "making a living," which has to do with supporting oneself economically vs. "seeking life." That has to do with acknowledging the sacred and maintaining a constant relationship between the sacred and oneself. At one time, most native people were capable of doing both simultaneously. This is one reason why many native people have objected to calling their lifestyles a "religion." But times have changed and the emphasis seems to be "on making a living." This is not true only with Native Americans. It is probably more so with the dominant society.

Previously native people understood from observation these "certain fundamental laws" Kindle described. They understood the system of checks and balances in nature that are necessary in order to maintain continual renewal of life, whether it applied to the seasons, to the trees, or to people. Oral traditions often speak of people in their pasts who attempted to change these fundamental laws. The results according to the stories did not make conditions better, in fact, they often were catastrophic. Through such stories came better understanding of those fundamental laws that were evident everywhere. The stories encouraged people to be responsible before making alterations that they might not be able to call back or correct.

Dr. Peter Paul, Malecite, tells of such an attempt by Glooskap (a coyote-like character).

Glooskap, Good Man, it does not mean liar. We use the wood Glooskap for anyone that lies. I think the reason in that is, anyone telling a lie changes the story. And that was what Glooskap did with all things. *He changed them. He's Changer*, you might say, of all things.

In the old days the people complained about so much wind. Too much wind, they said. There shouldn't be any. Glooskap goes and visits the creator of the wind, which was a big bird. So he ties his wings down, so he could not flap them because of wind. The waters did not move. The wind didn't move such things as bad odors, coming from decayed things and so on. Water gathered on the lakes and shores of the ocean. Everything lay still and nothing moved. Everything lay right as it fell on the water, therefore leaving sickness and so forth. When Glooskap realized what was happening, he went back and untied one wing of this bird. That made some wind which helped things out considerably. There were no hurricanes but there was a gradual wind which was helpful to conditions. (Taped Interview, 1974)

As further example of stories that concern contemporary problems is the following, told by Tom Ration. It is the story of alcohol and Coyote, who became intoxicated.

A person who does not drink looks at the person who is always drunk. He wonders how he became an alcoholic. We hear many stories about the coyote who gets involved in many mischievious actions. I will tell you another brief story about the coyote who got intoxicated. I want you to think about it.

It is told the Coyote was the first person who suggested getting drunk. In those days it was called Spitting the Medicine into the Mouth of Another (' Azee' Aza Dit' a x). They used all the plants that are poisonous like poison ivy, sow thistle, big thumb, vine plant, and jimson weed, and others that make people go loco. The Coyote advised the people who had such plants to bring them to a special suggested location called Mancos Creek. This happened long ago. The people came with the plants they had. All the plants were put together into a large container and put on to boil. After it had cooled the juice was separated into a water bag (animal skin). A gourd ladle set by it. The people waited for the Coyote who was late in arriving. After a while he finally appeared. His name was First Scolder. When he arrived he said, "I thought you were all celebrating by now. What are you waiting for?" They replied, "You are the one who suggested this, so we waited. You have the first dip." The Coyote quickly grabbed the dipper...and got a dipper full. He gulped it all down fast, some dripping from his mouth. Not too long after this, his eyes got crossed and he began to stagger as his mouth began to foam. The Coyote said, "I am about to scream." He was drunk. He jabbered senselessly and partly screaming. The people all stared at the Coyote and said, "He is crazy. Give him a neutralizer." There was another Coyote called White Tail who knew the cure or remedy. "Don't just stand there. Do something. He will pass out soon." said someone. "What is the neutralizer?" asked another. "Grind some sacred stones fine and add cool, clear water." said White Tail. The people quickly ground the sacred stones and put that mixture into a vessel of water and poured it down the Coyote's throat. The sacred stones contained White Shell, Turquoise, Abalone Shell, and Obsidian. The Coyote became himself again. Thereafter this neutralizer has been used when someone is loco with poison plants...as I said before, many of our people go loco with alcohol and do not know how to control it. (Interview, 1975)

This story is relevant today in that alcoholism is another contemporary problem with which native peoples must contend.

In the past, native peoples' ways of life were determined by the natural environment and the natural elements. These lifestyles satisfied the sacred knowledge and sacred traditions of a tribe. They were therefore compatible, or capable of existing together in harmony.

Today the ways of living for native peoples have altered considerably because they have experienced cultural, material (land and natural resources), and religious exploitation, all in a relatively short time. As a result, the new way of living, while definitely more convenient, cannot yet be compatible with traditional sacred knowledge of life. This new lifestyle is not compatible with former practices of our people. We naturally desire to preserve the older practices. The two often cannot be reconciled because they seem to advocate different concepts of living.

But in spite of all these new elements that native people must deal with, there are some very basic things which have not changed. These things have always made up the core of most aboriginal beliefs and practices. The Road of Life had not changed all that much. It is still there and maps the way to long life. People still live and die. We are still faced with the four enemies described by the Navajo: Poverty, Sickness, Old Age, and Body Lice.

Floyd Westerman, Sioux musician, in the classroom. (Courtesy of Navajo Community College, Title III)

Some Navajo people substitute Hunger and Fatigue for Sickness and Old Age. But that doesn't matter. What matters is that these "enemies" are familiar to all people. They have not been eradicated or changed. They are still with us. Many native people still live in awe of the Great Mystery. Many native people still believe in the sacred ways of knowledge. Many native people still practice sacred traditions which are the source of their life. Tom Ration is one and this is what he, and countless others, believe and teach.

> I am quite aware of the statement often used, "nothing is holy now." We who still have faith in our religion know everything is holy. How else can we be alive? The air we breathe is holy, the natural spring is holy, childbirth is holy. Just think of all the wonderful things nature provides, it is all holy. (Interview, 1975)

THE WANDERING

We have called this chapter the Wandering Ground. There is some similarity in the Anishnabe story of the Wandering Ground and to where many native people find themselves in today's world.

> The wandering ground was supposed to be the place where the spirit of the departed had to abide at least one year as a restless wanderer, doing penance for past transgressions during life, and sometimes the spirit could find no rest until relieved by the mashkikiwinini [man with knowledge of herbal medicine] who was kept informed of the wanderer by the supposed visitations of the manito [Spirit of the Anishnabe people] in his dreams. The happy hunting ground, of course, was looked upon as the home of rest—the abiding place of the just and worthy. (Vizenor, 1970:61)

There are indeed many problems that must be faced by Native Americans today. Most native people realize these problems are all related, not independent of one another.

The attempted transformation of the Indian by the white man and the chaos that has resulted are but the fruits of...disobedience of a fundamental and spiritual law. The pressure that has been brought to bear upon the native people, since the [stopping] of armed conflict in the attempt to force [obedience] of custom and habit has caused a reaction more destructive than war and the injury has not only affected the Indian, but has extended to the white population as well. Tyranny, stupidity, and lack of vision have brought about the situation now [referred] to as the "Indian Problem." (Standing Bear, 1933:568)

Over the years, the "Indian Problem" has been defined in several ways, usually by non-Indian people. Luther Standing Bear gave his opinion on the reason for it.

Perhaps because the focus has often been almost entirely on the problems of the Native Americans, many people who are unfamiliar with the American Indian assume that he will and must eventually yield to acculturation and capitalism. He will put away his identity, the source of it, and cease to exist. Luther Standing Bear also had something to say about this.

> When the Indian has forgotten the music of his forefathers, when the sound of the tomtom is no more, when noisy jazz has drowned the melody of the flute, he will be a dead Indian. When the memory of his heroes are no longer told in story, and he forsakes the beautiful white buckskin for factory shoddy, he will be dead. When from him has been taken all that is his, all that he has visioned in nature, all that has come to him from infinite sources, he then, truly, will be a dead Indian. *His spirit will be gone*, and though he walk crowded streets, he will in truth be—dead! (Standing Bear, 1933:255)

The assumption now, by non-Indians and a few Indian people, is that all sacred knowledge of most native peoples has deteriorated, been destroyed, or is lost. For some groups or tribes, this is partly true. A great deal of sacred knowledge has been misplaced and can never be exactly reinstated or practiced as it once was. However, among several tribes, what was sacred knowledge a century ago remains so today, true and uncompromising. Native North American sacred knowledge is still the only source of life for those who seek it.

Suggested Additional Readings

FEIT, HARVEY A.
1973 "Twilight of the Cree Hunting Nation: James Bay Cree Indians," *Natural History*, 82:48-57, (August)

GALLAGHER, H.G.
1974 *Etok: A Story of Eskimo Power*, New York: G.P. Putnam.

MCNICKLE, D'ARCY
1973 *Native American Tribalism: Indian Survivals and Renewals*, New York: Oxford University Press.

MALAN, VERNON D. (Revised by James L. Satterlee)
Acculturation of the Dakota Indians, 2nd Edition, Pamphlet No. 123, Agriculture Experiment Station, Dakota State University, Rural Sociology Department, Brookings, South Dakota.

MANUAL, GEORGE and M. POSLUNS
1974 "Indian World and the Fourth World," *Current History* 67:263-267 (Dec.)

SHEFFE, NORMAN (ed.)
1970 *Issues For the Seventies: Canada's Indians*, New York: McGraw Hill.

344   Nowadays, the Pow-Wow dancer. (Courtesy of Gallup Independent)

REFERENCE SECTION

Glossary

aboriginal native to a region; indigenous; from the Latin, *ab origine* (from the beginning).

abstract not concrete; a model of an idea; intangible; insufficiently factual. [4]

acculturation the process by which one culture is modified by another, specifically a group of people in the minority with respect to a dominating culture.

amulet an object or objects worn to maintain a person's strength or to guard against misfortune, danger, and weakness.

Anishnabe the original name of The People, renamed Chippewa or Ojibwa by the colonizers.

Arctic Circle the region around the North Pole; a circle enclosing this region that is parallel to the equator and lies at approximately 23°-27° from the North Pole.

areole a small area between things or about something; a colored ring.

aristocracy government by a small privileged class; the "upper" class.

bass the low notes of a scale; a low, deep voice or tone.

bisect to separate, divide.

cache a place where food, clothes, weapons —any items—are hidden over a period of time so that they can be dug up or taken out of hiding when the owner returns. A French word.

capitalism an economic system based on the accumulation of wealth, private ownership of the means of production, and concentration of wealth and capital by private corporate ownership; motivated by profit and capital gains, not by public welfare of community well-being.

carnal bodily; corporeal; marked by sexuality. [127]

circumpolar *circum* (around)—around the North Pole. (See **Arctic Circle**)

circumscribe to define or mark off. [151]

classic "of the highest class;" most representative of the excellence of its kind; having recognized worth.

collective a cooperative unit or organization; group effort; doing things together.

colonialism a policy by which a nation maintains or extends its control over foreign dependencies. (262)

colonize to establish a colony or colonies; to occupy as a colony; to establish a settlement. (263)

compatible capable of existing together in harmony. [169]

conception (a) act of becoming pregnant; (b) beginning, (c) the function or process of forming or understanding ideas. [171]

conjunction connection; coming together.

contemplation to view, consider, regard with continuing attention. [180]

copulate to engage in sexual intercourse. [184]

cosmology a specific theory or model of the structure and dynamics of the universe; a philosophy dealing with the origin, processes, and structure of the universe.

counting coup *coup* is a French word meaning to hit someone, or touch someone neatly, gracefully, and courageously. To "count coup" was a French word given to the Plains Indian custom of "touching" the enemy—getting close to the enemy and taking something from him perhaps, but without killing him.

deities sky beings; heavenly beings; sacred beings not of this world.

deity one exalted or revered as supremely good or powerful. (127)

derive to trace from a source; to show the derivation of; to get by reasoning.

detrimental harmful; damaging.

dimension the range over which or the degree to which something extends; size; measurement; the scope of something.

NOTE: The page numbers in parenthesis are from the *American Heritage Dictionary*, New York, American Heritage Publishing Co., Inc. 1973. The page numbers in brackets are from the *Websters Seventh New Collegiate Dictionary*, Springfield, Mass., G & C Merriam Co., 1965.

divine sacred, holy, supremely good, being or having the nature of a *deity*; being an expression of a deity. In the service of worship or a god. (385)

ecology the science of the relationships between organisms and their environments. From the Greek word *oikos* (house).

eco-system an ecological community together with its physical environment considered as a unit.

ecstasy (ecstatic) a state of exalted delight in which normal understanding is felt to be insufficient to explain the feeling. A state of any emotion so intense that rational thought and self-control are erased.

epidermis skin; a thin surface layer of primary tissue in higher plants. [279]

essence the most significant property of something; the most important quality of a thing.

ethics a system of values or teachings (philosophy) that teach social behavior or the way individuals construct their behavior among one another.

ethnologist a specialist in a science that deals with the division of humankind into races—their origin, distribution, relations and characteristics. [285]

falsetto a normally male voice which is able to reach the very high notes of the scale with a forced or artificial quality.

fanatic excessive enthusiasm and intense uncritical devotion.

fathom to penetrate an idea and come to understand. [304]

figurative representing something by a figure or resemblance, expressing one thing in terms of another. [311]

gruel a thin soft food made by boiling meal of grains in milk or water. [369]

igloo a structure built to live in made by placing snow blocks on top of each other to form a simple dome-like building, with an entrance way, and ice blocks in the ceiling to let light in. The structure is finally covered with water which freezes. Inside there are snow benches covered with skins and furs. The snow and ice make an excellent insulator.

imperceptible not capable of being perceived by the senses.

incarnation a concrete or actual form of a concept or abstract idea; a deity or spirit in an earthly form.

innovation introduction of something new, method or idea, etc. [436]

intangible not able to be defined, perceived, or precisely identified.

intrusion the entry of some foreign object into a body (see Chapter Five). Entering without asking or without warning; interrupting. (intrude)

invocation act or process of asking for help or support; beginning prayer. [446]

kin a group of persons of common ancestry; one's relatives. [466]

maladjusted lacking harmony with one's environment from one's failure to reach a satisfactory adjustment between one's desires and the conditions of one's life. [511]

malleable capable of being fashioned into a different form or shape. [512]

mediate to act by means of communication between two groups or two individuals, or between an individual and a group. A mediator is someone who is inbetween, who acts as a "go between" in the affairs of two parties.

mediator one who acts as a middle agent in bringing, affecting, or communicating; an individual who is a channel of communication between the earthly world and the world of spirits.

menses the menstrual flow.

meticulous extreme or excessive care in the consideration of details. (534)

migratory coming and going with the seasons; changing one's home from one place to another with the change of seasons.

morals teachings that set the limits and boundaries of personal behavior.

modify to change or transform.

movement the activities of a group of people to achieve a specific goal; a tendency or trend which includes a number of people.

multi-faceted many sides or aspects.

mythology a collection of myths about the origin and history of a people and their deities, ancestors, and heroes. **myth** a traditional story originating in a pre-literate society dealing with supernatural beings, ancestors, or heroes, as well as fundamental relationships, that serve as primordial types. [868-869]

nativistic revival of or perpetuation of an indigenous culture especially in opposition to acculturation.

nodules a small mass of rounded or irregular shape. [572]

nonconformity refusal to conform to an established or conventional creed, rule, or practice. [573]

objective (a) something toward which effort is directed; an aim or end of some action; goal, object. (b) expressing or involving the use of facts without distortion by personal feelings or prejudices. [581]

pachivat Luiseño and Cupeño word for a kind of brush used for beds.

pan-tribal involving or encompassing many tribes—"applying to all."

paraphernalia personal belongings; a bunch of things.

permeate to spread or diffuse through.

phenomenon an observable fact or event. Any occurrence or fact that is directly perceptible by the senses. (plural: **phenomena**) (983)

pictograph a picture representing a word or idea; hieroglyph. A record in hieroglyphic symbols. (991)

pilgrimage journey to a shrine or a sacred place. [641]

precipitate to bring about especially abruptly; result or outcome of some process or action; to cause. [668]

prohibition (prohibit) something that is forbidden; to forbid; not allowed.

promulgate (promulgation) to make known by open proclaim; declaration. [682]

proselytize to convert from one religion, belief, or party to another; to recruit members. [684]

recurrance to occur again.

reiterate to say or do over again; repeat. [722]

revitalization to bring to life again; to revive; to make vital **(revitalize)**.

sacrament bond; a formal religious act that is shared as a sign or symbol of a spiritual reality. [757]

sacrilege violation of something sacred.

seance a meeting of people at which spiritual beings become present or spiritual *phenomena* occur, or communication with spirit(s) takes place.

second-sight the ability to see future events or remote (distant) events.

sects a group of people forming a distinct unit within a larger group of people because their ideas, beliefs, or practices are different. A group of people breaking off from a larger group for the same reasons.

secular not sacred; referring to the temporal (time) or ordinary.

self-effacing retiring, reserved, shy, modest, humble.

shaman (See Chapter Five, **Shamans and The World of Spirits: The Oldest Religion**).

solidarity unity; a community of interests, objectives or standards in a group. (831)

terrestrial of or relating to Earth or its inhabitants. *Terra* (earth), Latin. Relating to land as distinct from air or water; earthly. [911]

traditional the passing down of elements of a culture from generation to generation, especially by oral communication, cultural custom or usage. Any time-honored practice or set of practices. (1360)

trance a hypnotic, cataleptic, or ecstatic state. A state of detachment from one's physical surroundings. From the Old French, *transir* (to pass from life to death).

tranquility being calm, quiet. **(tranquil)**

transcendental beyond the limits of ordinary experience; to be beyond the universe or material existence. (939)

tundra a level of slightly rolling treeless plain in Arctic and sub-Arctic regions. Consists of black, murky soil with a permanently frozen sub-soil which supports a dense growth of flowering dwarf plants, flowers, herbs, and shrubs.

validate to make valid, to make official, to make correct.

viable "likely to live;" able to live; able to take root and grow.

wamkish Luiseño and Cupeño word for a ceremonial shelter where the menstruating women go.

wikut Luiseño and Cupeño word for juniper.

Bibliography

AGINSKY, B.W.
1944   "An Indian Soliloquy," *American Journal of Sociology*, 46:43-44.

AKWESASNE NOTES
1975   "How to Use the Bible to Justify Manifest Destiny and Genocide," Vol. 7, No. 5, pp. 28-29, Early Winter.

ALLEN, T.D.
1974   *Arrows Four: Prose And Poetry By Young American Indians*, New York: Washington Square press.

ARMSTRONG, VIRGINIA IRVING
1971   *I Have Spoken: American History Through The Voices of Indians*, 1st Edition, Chicago: Sage Books.

ASTROV, MARGOT
1962   *American Indian Prose and Poetry*, New York: Capricorn Books.

AVENI, ANTHONY (ed.)
1975   Archaeo-Astronomy in Pre-Columbian America. Austin: University of Texas Press.

BAILY, FLORA L.
1950   "Some Sex Beliefs and Practices in a Navajo Community," Cambridge, Mass., *Papers of the Peabody Museum of American Archeology and Ethnology*, Harvard University, Vol. 40, No. 2.

BAHR, DONALD
1974   Juan Gregorio, David Lopez, and Albert Alvarez, *Pima Shamanism and Staying Sickness*, Tucson: University of Arizona Press.

BARNES, NELLIE
1925   *American Indian Love Lyrics and Other Verse*, New York.

BARRETT, S. M.
1970   *Geronimo: His Own Story*, New York: Dutton.

BARRETT, S. A.
1972   "The Stewarts Point Maru of 1958," Appendix D, **in** *The Maru Cult of the Pomo Indians: A California Ghost Dance Survival,* Clement W. Meighan and Francis Riddel, Los Angeles: Southwest Museum Press.

BASSO, KEITH H.
1970   *Cibeque Apaches*, New York: Holt, Rinehart and Winston.

BLACK ELK, *with* JOHN G. NEIHARDT
1932   *Black Elk Speaks*, New York: W. Morrow and Co.

BOAS, FRANZ
1969   *Religion of the Kwakiutl Indians*, New York: AMS Press.

BOWERS, ALFRED W.
1950   *Mandan Social and Ceremonial Organization*, Chicago: University of Chicago Press.

BRITT, CLAUDE
1975   "Early Navajo Astronomical Pictographs," **in** *Archaeo-Astronomy in Pre-Columbian America*, Anthony F. Aveni (ed.), Austin: University of Texas Press.

BUNZEL, RUTH L.
1932   *Zuni Origin Myths*, Washington, D.C., ARBAE 47th, pp. 611-837, Smithsonian Institution, 1929-1930.

BUSWELL, JAMES O.
1972   *Florida Seminole Religious Ritual: Resistance and Change*, Ann Arbor, Michigan, University Microfilms. (PhD Dissertation, St. Louis University).

COOK, S.F.
1943   "The Conflict Between the California Indians and White Civilization," Vol. III, The American Invasion, 1848-1870, *Ibero-Americana*, 23.

COOPER, J.M.
1957   *Gros Ventre of Montana, Part II, Social Life*, Washington, D.C.; Catholic University of America, Anthropological Series, No. 14.

COPE, LEONA
1919   "Calendars of the Indians North of Mexico," *California Publications in Archeology and Ethnology*, Vol. 16, No. 4, pp. 119-176.

COYOTE MAN
1973   *Old People of The New World, Vol. 1, Sun, Moon and Stars*, Berkeley, Calif.: Brother William Press.

DE ANGULO, JAIME
1973   *Indians In Overalls*, San Francisco: Turtle Island Foundation.

————
1926   "Background of a Religious Feeling," *American Anthropologist*, Vol. 28, No. 2, (April-June).

DELORIA, VINE
1974   "Religion and the Modern American Indian," *Current History*, Dec., pp. 251-253.

DENSMORE, FRANCIS
1918   *Teton Sioux Music*, Washington, D. C., BBAE 61st.

————
"Music in its Relation to the Religious
1916   "Thought of the Teton Sioux," *Holmes Anniversary Volume*, pp. 67-69.

————

NOTE: The following abbreviations are used in this bibliography: ARBAE (Annual Report of the Bureau of American Ethnology), APBAE (Anthropological Papers of the Bureau of American Ethnology), BBAE (Bulletin of the Bureau of American Ethnology.)

The Bureau of American Ethnology is part of the Smithsonian Institution, Washington, D. C. The Bureau publications are printed by the U.S. Government Printing Office, Washington, D.C.

DILLARD, ANNIE
    1974   *Pilgrim At Tinker Creek*, New York: Harper Magazine Press.

DORSEY, JAMES O.
    1970   *Omaha Sociology*, New York: Johnson Reprint.

DOWNS, JAMES F.
    1966   *The Two Worlds of the Washoe: An Indian Tribe of California*, New York: Holt, Rinehart and Winston.

DUBOIS, CORA
    1939   "The 1870 Ghost Dance," *Anthropological Records*, Berkeley, California.

    ———
    1908   "The Religion of the Luiseno Indians of Southern California," *University of California Publications in Archeology and Ethnology*, Vol. 8, No. 3, pp. 69-186, Pl. 16-19.

ELLIS, FLORENCE HAWLEY
    1975   "A Thousand Years of the Pueblo Sun-Moon-Stars Calendar" in *Archaeo-Astronomy in Pre-Columbian America*. Aveni, A (ed.), Austin: University of Texas Press.

ERDOES, RICHARD
    1972   *The Sun Dance People*, New York: Alfred Knopf, Inc.

    ———
    1971   and John Fire, *Lame Deer: Seeker of Visions*, New York, Simon and Schuster.

FARRAND, LIVINGSTON and THERESA MAYER
    1917   "Sahaptin Tales," *Memoirs of the American Folklore Society*, Vol. 11.

FLATTERY, DAVID S. and M. PIERCE, M.D.
    1965   *Peyote*, Berkeley, California: Berkeley Press.

FLETCHER, ALICE C. and FRANCIS LAFLESCHE
    1911   *The Omaha Tribe*, Washington, D.C., ARBAE 27th, 1805-1906.

FRISBIE, CHARLOTTE JOHNSON
    1967   *Kinaalda: A Study of Navajo Girls' Puberty Ceremony*, Middleton, Conn:, Wesleyan University Press.

FUCHS, ESTELLE and ROBERT J. HAVIGHURST
    1973   *To Live On This Earth*, New York: Doubleday Anchor Press, 1967.

GIBBON, WILLIAM B.
    1972   "Asiatic Parallels in North American Star-lore," *Journal of American Folklore*, 85:236-247, (July-Sept.).

GODDARD, PLINY E.
    1933   *Navajo Text*, New York: American Museum of Natural History.

GRINNELL, GEORGE BIRD
    1972   *The Cheyenne Indians: Their History and Way of Life*, Vols. I and II, Lincoln, Neb.: University of Nebraska Press.

    ———
    1904   "Cheyenne Woman Customs," *American Anthropologist*, ns, Vol. 4, No. 1, (Jan.-March) 1902, pp. 13-16.

HAILE, BERARD OFM
    1947   *Starlore Among the Navajo*, Santa Fe, N.M.: Museum of Navajo Ceremonial Art.

HARRISON, E.S.
    1892   *History of Santa Cruz County*, San Francisco: Pacific Press Publishing Co., pp. 45-48.

HILL, JANE and ROSINDA NOLASQUEZ
    1973   *Mulu'wetam: The First People*, Banning, California: Malki Museum Press.

INDIAN HISTORIAN
    1975   "The Denial of Indian Civil and Religious Rights," Vol. 2, No. 3, Summer, pp. 43-44.

KEESING, ROGER W.
    1976   *Cultural Anthropology: A Contemporary Perspective*, New York: Holt, Rinehart and Winston.

KEMP, W. B.
    1971   "The Flow of Energy in a Hunting Society," *Scientific American*, Vol. 225, No. 1, Sept., pp. 104-115.

KNUDTSON, PETER N.
    1975   "Flora, Shaman of the Wintu," *Natural History*, May, pp. 6-18.

KRAUSE, AUREL
    1971   *The Tlingit Indians*, Erna Gunter (tr.), Seattle: University of Washington Press.

KROEBER, ALFRED
    1972   *Handbook of the Indians of California*, Vol. 2, St. Clair Shores, Michigan: Scholarly Press (Reprint of BBAE 79th, 1925).

    ———
    1908   "A Mission Record of the California Indians," *California Publications in Archeology and Ethnology*, Vol. 8, No. 1, May, pp. 1-27.

LAME DEER
    1972   See Erdoes, Richard

LASKI, VERA
    1959   *Seeking Life*, Austin, Texas: University of Texas Press.

LEE, DOROTHY D.
    1959   *Freedom and Culture*, New Jersey: Prentice Hall.

LEVITAS, GLORIA
    1974   *American Indian Prose and Poetry: We Wait in Darkness*, New York: G.P. Putnam and Capricorn Books.

LITTLE COYOTE, JOE
    1973   "The Cheyenne Response," *Wassaja*, Vol. 1, No. 7, October.

LOEB, EDWIN MEYER
    1926   *Pomo Folkways*, Berkeley, California: University of California Press.

LUCKERT, KARL W.
    1975   *The Navajo Hunter Tradition*, Tucson, Arizona: University of Arizona Press.

LURIE, NANCY OESTREICH
    1961   *Mountain Wolf Woman, Sister of Crashing Thunder: The Autobiography of a Winnebago Indian*, Ann Arbor, Michigan: University of Michigan Press.

MARRIOTT, ALICE LEE and CAROL K. RACHLIN
    1971   *Peyote*, New York: Thomas Y. Crowell Co.

MAYER, DOROTHY
    1975   "Great Basin Petroglyphs" in *Archeo-Astronomy in Pre-Columbian America*. Aveni, A. (ed.), Austin, Texas: University of Texas Press.

MCALLESTER, DAVID
1961   Field Notes for July 19-20, 1961, in *Kinaalda: A Study of Navajo Girl's Puberty Ceremony*, by Charlotte Johnson Frisbie, Middleton, Connecticut: Wesleyan University Press.

MCLUHAN, T. C.
1971   *Touch The Earth: A Self-Portrait of Indian Existence*, New York: Outerbridge and Dienstfrey.

MEIGHAN, CLEMENT W. and FRANCIS A. RIDDLE
1972   *The Maru Cult of the Pomo Indians: A California Ghost Dance Survival*, Los Angeles, Calif.: Southwest Museum Press.

MINDELEFF, COSMOS
            Navajo Houses, ARBAE 17th, Washington, D. C., 1895-96.

MONSEN, FREDERICK
1907   "Festivals of the Hopi: Religion, the Inspiration, and Dancing, an Expression of Their National Ceremonies," *The Craftsmen*, No. 12.

MOONEY, JAMES
            Myths of the Cherokees, ARBAE 19th, 1897-98, Pt. 1, pp. 3-568.

1890   "The Cherokee Ball Game," *American Anthropologist*, Vol. III, pp. 105-132.

MOREY, SYLVESTER M.
1970   *Can the Red Man Help the White Man?*, New York: The Myrin Institute, Inc.

NABOKOV, PETER
1969   "The Peyote Road," *New York Times Magazine*, March.

NEQUATEWA, EDMUND N.
1931   "Hopi Hopiwine: The Hopi Ceremonial Calendar," *Museum Notes of Museum of Northern Arizona*, Vol. 3, No. 9., Flagstaff.

NEWCOMB, FRANC J.
1967   *Navajo Folktales*, Santa Fe, N.M.: Museum of Navajo Ceremonial Art.

O'BRYAN, AILEEN
1956   *The Dine: Origin Myths of the Navajo Indians*, BBAE 163rd, Washington, D. C.

OPLER, MORRIS EDWARD
1964   *Childhood and Youth in Jicarilla Apache Society*, Los Angeles, Ca.: F.W. Hodge Anniversary Fund Publications.

1956   *Apache Life-ways: The Economic, Social and Religious Institutions of the Chiricahua Indians*, New York: Cooper Press.

ORTIZ, ALFONSO
1973   "Look to the Mountaintop," in *Essays on Reflection*, E. Graham Ward, ed., Boston, Mass.: Houghton-Mifflin.

1972   *New Perspectives on the Pueblos*, ed., 1st ed., Albuquerque: University of New Mexico Press.

1969   *The Tewa World: Space, Time, Beings and Becoming in a Pueblo Society*, Chicago, Ill.: University of Chicago Press.

PAUL, DORIS A.
1973   *Navajo Code Talkers*, Philadelphia, Pa., Dorrance and Company.

RADIN, PAUL
1970   *The Winnebago Tribe*, Lincoln University of Nebraska Press. (Originally published in ARBAE 37th, 1923)

1945   *The Culture of the Winnebago as Described By Themselves*, Baltimore: Waverly Press. (Indiana University Publications in Anthropology and Linguistics, Memoir #2)

1945   *The Road of Life and Death*, New York: Pantheon Books.

RASMUSSEN, KNUD
1932   *The Intellectual Culture of the Copper Eskimos*, Vol. 9, Copenhagen, Report of the 5th Thule Expedition.

1931   *The Utkutlsaling Eskimos*, Vol. 8, No. 2, Copenhage, Report of the 5th Thule Expedition.

1931   *The Netsilik Eskimos*, Vol. 8, No. 1, Copenhagen, Report of the 5th Thule Expedition.

1930   *The Intellectual Culture of the Caribou Eskimos*, Vol. 7, No. 2, Copenhagen, Report of the 5th Thule Expedition.

1930   *The Intellectual Culture of Iglulik Eskimos*, Vol. 7, No. 1, Copenhagen, Report of the 5th Thule Expedition, 1929.

1927   *Across Arctic America*, New York, G.P. Putnam and Sons.

ROGERS, JOHN
1974   *Red World and White*, Oklahoma City, Okla., Oklahoma University Press.

SIMMONS, LEO W. AND DON TALAYESVA
1942   *Sun Chief, The Autobiography of a Hopi Indian*, New Haven: Publishing for Inst. of Human Relations by Yale University Press.

SLOTKIN, J.S.
1975   *The Peyote Religion, A Study In Indian-White Relations*, New York: Octagon Books.

SMITH, MARION WESLEY
1969   *The Puyallup-Nisqually*, Reprint, 1940 edition., Columbia University Contributions to Anthropology, Vol.. 32; New York: AMS Press.

SMITHSON, CARMA LEE
1971   *Havasupai Religion and Mythology*, University of Utah Anthropological Papers, No. 68, Salt Lake City, Utah: University of Utah Press, 1964; Johnson Reprint, 1971.

STANDING BEAR, LUTHER
1933   *Land of the Spotted Eagle*, Boston, Mass.; New York.

STIRLING, MATTHEW
1942   *Origin Myth of Acoma and Other Records*, BBAE 135th, Washington, D. C.

SWEEZY, CARL
1966   *The Arapaho Way: Memoirs of An Indian Boyhood*, as told to Althea L. Bass, New York: Potter.

TEDLOCK, BARBARA and DENNIS
1975   *Teachings From the American Earth*, New York: Liveright Press.

TEIT, JAMES A.
1917   "Thompson Tales," *Memoirs of the American Folklore Society*, Vol. II.

THEISZ, RONALD
         Lakota Music and Dance, South Dakota, Sinte Gleska College (Unpublished manuscript).

THOMPSON, HILDEGAARD
         The Navajos' Long Walk for Education, A History of Navajo Education, Tsaile, Az.: Navajo Community College Press.

TOLKEIN, BARRE
         "The Pretty Languages of Yellowman," *Genre*, 2, pp. 211-235.

TUNDRA TIMES
1976   Vol. 14, No. 3 (Jan. 21), Fairbanks, Alaska, pp. 1-2.

UNDERHILL, RUTH
1938   *Singing For Power: The Song Magic of the Papago Indians of Southern Arizona*, Berkeley, Ca.: University of California Press.

──────── and MARIA CHONA
1936   *The Autobiography of a Papago Woman*, Memoirs of the American Anthropological Association, No. 46, Menasha, Wisconsin: Krause Reprint Co., 1974, 1936.

VIZENOR, GERALD
1970   *Anishinabe Adisokan: Tales of The People*, Minneapolis, Minn.: Nodin Press.

WATERMAN, T.T.
1971   "Yurok Geographical Concepts," in *The California Indians* by R.J. Heizer and M.R. Whipple, ed., Berkeley, Ca.: University of California Press.

────────
1910   "Religious Practices of the Diegueno Indians," *University of California Publications in American Archeology and Ethnology*, Vol. 8, No. 66, pp. 271-358, pl. 21-28.

WHITEWOLF, JIM
1969   *Jim Whitewolf: The Life of a Kiowa Apache Indian*, Charles F. Brant (ed.), New York: Dover Publishing.

WHITMAN, WILLIAM
1969   *The Otoe*, New York: AMS Press.

WYMAN, LELAND C.
1970   *Blessing Way*, Tucson, Arizona: University of Arizona Press.

YAZZIE, ETHELOU
1971   *Navajo History*, Many Farms, Arizona: Navajo Community College Press.

Films and Filmstrips

Below, under each chapter, are listed some of the films and filmstrips that can supplement the chapter texts. This is only a list of titles. Following this basic listing is an annotated film guide which reviews films mentioned; states the film length, type, and the film distributor and producer. In addition, the names and addresses of the distributors are provided in a section following the film and filmstrip guide.

Chapter One: Seeking Life: Definitions of Religion and the Sacred
The Hopi Way
Indian Family of the California Desert
Ishi of Two Worlds
The Longhouse People
Look What We've Done to the Land
Silent Enemy
These Are My People
Three Stone Blades

Chapter Two: Ritual Drama and Prayer
Calumet: Pipe of Peace
Circle of the Sun
Hopi Kachinas
Ka ke ki Ku
The Loon's Necklace
Okan: Sun Dance of the Blackfoot
Totem Pole
Ways of our Fathers

Chapter Three: Learning The Way: Traditional Knowledge
Coyote and the Lizard (in Navajo)
Coyote and the Snake (in Navajo)
The Hands of Maria
Indian Mainstream

Chapter Four: The Boundaries of the World
In Beauty I walk
Ishi in Two Worlds
Home
The Long Walk, Pt. I
Look What We've Done to the Land
You Are On Indian Land

Chapter Five: Shamans and the World of Spirits: The Oldest Religion
Annanacks
Attiuk (The Caribou Eskimo)
Eskimo Artist Kennejuk

Netsilik Eskimo Series
Fishing at the Stone Weir, Pt. I & II
Winter Ice Sea Camp, Pts. I, II, III, IV
Autumn River Camp, Pt. I & II
How to Build an Igloo
Three Stone Blades
Alaska Speaks
Pomo Shaman
Sucking Doctor
Spirit of the Navajo
The Living Stone

Chapter Six: The Changeable Earth: The Colonizers and Genocide
The Meek Shall Inherit the Earth
Ballad of Crowfoot
Charlie Squash Goes to Town
End of the Trail
47 Cents
Ishi in Two Worlds
Home
The Last Menominee
The Long Walk, Pts. I & II
The Longest War
You Are On Indian Land
Look What We've Done to This Land
Now That the Buffalo's Gone
Song for Dear Warriors

Chapter Seven: The World Out of Balance
Bryan Beavers: A Moving Portrait
Dream Dance of the Kashia Pomo
Kashia Men's Dance
Ishi in Two Worlds
Hupa Indian White Deerskin Dance
Acorns
Sucking Doctor

Chapter Eight: The Path of Life
Bryan Beavers: A Moving Portrait
Indian Family of the California Desert

The Hopi Way
The Long Walk, Pt. I
Longhouse People
The Washoe, Pt. I
Zuni Today

Chapter Nine: **Girls' Puberty Ceremonies**
The Washoe, Pt. II
When Boys Encounter Puberty
(Non-Indian material)
When Girls Encounter Puberty (includes
non-Indian material)

Chapter Ten: **The Peyote Spirit**
To Find Our Life

Chapter Eleven: **Sacred and Secular: Seminole Tradition in the Midst of Change**

Chapter Twelve: **Navajo Traditional Education**
In Beauty I Walk
In Beauty May I Walk
The Long Walk, Pt. I & II
Spirit of the Navajo
A Visit to the Father (4 parts)

Chapter Thirteen: **Sacred Fools and Clowns**
Hopi Kachinas

Chapter Fourteen: **The Wandering Ground**
The Ballad of Crowfoot
Alaska Speaks
Bitterwind
You Are On Indian Land
Circle of the Sun
Home
Indian Mainstream
The Indian Speaks
Ishi of Two Worlds
Ka ke ki ku
The Last Menominee
The Longhouse People
The Longest War
Look What We've Done to This Land
Ways of Our Fathers
Song for Dead Warriors
These Are My People
Long Walk, Pt. I & II
Ten Thousand Beads for Navajo Sam

General Tribal Background
Blunden Harbor
Indian Family of the California Desert
Little White Salmon Indian Settlement
Native Alaska
The Washoe

Film and Filmstrip Guide

Most of these films can be obtained from the University of California Extension Media Center, Berkeley, California.

Acorns—Staple Food of California Indians (1962) 16 mm Film Optical Sound Color, 30 min., University of California Extension Media Center (PR) Dist: UCEMC "Demonstrates the traditional harvesting, storing and processing methods of acorns."

Alaska Speaks 16 mm Film Optical Sound Color, 15 min., Arthur Mokin Productions (PR) Dist: Holt, Rinehart & Winston, New York. "Narrates the history of Alaska, from the side of the Native Alaskan, including Eskimo, Aleut, and Indian until the present day and discovery of oil." 1970

The Annanacks (1962) Color, 60 min., Crawley Films Ltd. (PR) Dist: Canadian Broadcasting Corporation. "It deals in a sociological manner with the history of a group of Eskimos who have been living in and around the George River District on the Hudson's Straits."

Attiuk (*The Caribou*), 17 min. National Film Board of Canada (PR), Dist: McGraw Hill Contemporary Films, Inc. "Deals with Montaignis Indians, on the north side of gulf of St. Lawrence, who are caribou hunters. They believe all hunting is accomplished first in dreams, and who still follow ancient rituals of the hunt."

Autumn River Camp, Part I & II (1964) Color, 30 min., Educational Development Center (PR) Dist: Universal Education & Visual Arts, Inc. "Documents, without narration, one part of the Nesilik Eskimo's nomadic cycle of establishing camps according to hunting and weather conditions." (Netsilik Eskimo Series)

Ballad of Crowfoot, 16 mm Film Optical Sound, B/W, 10 min., National Film Board of Canada (PR), Dist: McGraw-Hill Textfilms. "Film by young Canadian Indians. Presents graphic history of Canadian West. Words and music, the film's commentary by Willie Dunn."

Before The White Man Came, 16 mm Film Optical Sound, B/W, 50 min., Dist: Films Classics Exchange. "Made in 1920's in Big Horn Mountains of Montana & Wyoming. Original Crow Country."

Bitter Wind (1963) 16mm Film Optical Sound, Color, 30 min., Brigham Young University (PR), Dist: B.Y.U. "Dramatization of breakdown of American Indian family because of alcoholism."

Blunden Harbor, 16 mm Optical Sound, B/W, 20 min., Orbit Films and R. G. Gardner (PR), Dist: Univ. of Calif. Ext. Media Center. "Documentary of Pacific Northwest Indian Life. Kwakiutl Indians as they lived in Blunden Harbor in 1950."

Bryan Beavers: A Moving Portrait (1968), 16 mm Film Optical Sound, Color, 30 min., KVIE TV(PR), Dist: Indiana University. "Camera follows Bryan Beavers, a Maidu Indian, around. Shows his lifestyle, discusses his heritage, etc."

Calumet: Pipe of Peace (1964) 16 mm Film Optical Sound, Color, 23 min., National Science Foundation (PR), Dist: Univ. of Calif. Ext. Media Center. "Historical accounts and oral tradition (stories, ritual uses) are used in narration of origin of tobacco and pipes among Great Plains People."

Caribou Hunting at the Crossing Place, Part I & II (1970), Color, 30 min. each, Education Development Center (PR), Dist: Universal Education & Visual Arts, Inc. "Documents, without narration, one part of the Nesilik Eskimo's nomadic cycle of establishing camps according to hunting and weather conditions." (Netsilik Eskimo Series)

Charlie Squash Goes To Town, 16mm Film Optical Sound, Color, 5 min., National Film Board of Canada (PR), Dist: University of Michigan. "Animated. Film by Duke Redbird, Ontario-Cree."

Circle of the Sun (1960) 16 mm Film Optical Sound, Color, 29 min., National Film Board of Canada (PR), Dist: McGraw-Hill

Coyote and the Lizard, 16 mm Film Optical Sound, Color, 7 min., Navajo Curriculum San Juan School District, Dist: Indian Education Center. "Animated. (In Navajo—to be shown only in winter.)

Dream Dances of the Kashia Pomo (1964), 16mm Film Optical Sound, Color, 30 min., National Science Foundation (PR), Dist: Univ. of Calif. Ext. Media Center. "Bole-Maru Cult of the Pomo. Pomo women dance the Bole-Maru of today."

End of the Trail: The American Plains Indian (1967), 16 mm Film Optical Sound, B/W, 53 min., Part I & II, N.B.C. TV (PR), Dist: CF McGraw-Hill. "Covers the period between 1860 and 1890, showing the inevitable clash between the white and red, over encroachment and destruction of the Plains Indian's physical and spiritual environment."

Eskimo Artist—Kenojuak (1964), 16mm Film Optical Sound, Color, 20 min., National Film Board of Canada (PR), Dist: McGraw-Hill Textfilm. "Eskimo woman artist, Kenojuak, shows the art center of Cape Dorsey where the stone cutter Iyola and the printers use her design to make prints on rice paper for sale in galleries of the South."

Explorations in Southern Ute History, For more information, write: Mr. Leonard Burch, Chairman, Southern Ute Tribe, Tribal Affairs Building, Ignacio, Colorado 81137.

Fishing At the Stone Weir, Parts I & II, Color, 30 min. each, Educational Development Center (PR), Dist: Universal Education & Visual Arts, Inc. "Documents, without narration, one part of the Nesilik Eskimo's nomadic cycle of establishing camps according to hunting and weather conditions." (Netsilik Eskimo Series)

Forty-seven Cents (1973), 16 mm Film Optical Sound, Color, 25 min., University of Calif. Ext. Media Center (PR), Dist: UCEMC. "Tells how the Pit River Indian Nation of Northern California wound up with a land settlement of 47 cents an acre for land taken from them in the 19th Century."

Haida Carver (1964), 16mm Film Optical Sound, Color, 12 min., National Film Board of Canada (PR), Dist: International Film Bureau. "Features craftsmanship of Haida carvers."

Hands of Maria, The, 16 mm Film Optical Sound, Color, 17 min., Coleman E. Enterprises, Inc. (PR), Dist: RMI Film Producers. "Maria Martinez of San Ildefonso Pueblo, world famous potter demonstrates her craft."

History of the Norther Paiutes of Nevada, 16mm Film Optical Sound. For more information write: Mrs. Winona Holmes, Project Director, Inter-Tribal Council of Nevada, 98 Colony Road, Reno, Nevada 89502.

Home (1972), Color, 29 min., Univ. of Calif. Ext. Media Center (PR), Dist: Southern Baptist Radio and Television Commission. "Shows contrasting scenes of pollution and beauty in America today while presenting an 1859 speech by Chief Seattle of the Duwamish Tribe."

Hopi Way, The (1972), 16mm Film Optical Sound, Color, 23 min., Shoshoni Production Inc. (PR), Dist: Films Inc. "The effects on the Hopi People by the Coal Mines on their traditional lands. The reaction of both young and old to the invasion is negative; most Hopis want to preserve their way of life."

How To Build An Igloo, B/W, 10 min., National Film Board of Canada (PR), Dist: McGraw-Hill Contemporary Films, Inc. "Demonstration of Igloo building."

Hupa Indian White Deerskin Dance (1958), 16mm Film Optical Sound Color, 11 min., Arthur Barr Productions. "Shows how ancient cultural patterns are still retained by the Hupa Indians of Northwestern California. Includes scenes of a ten-day Deerskin Dance Ceremony."

In Beauty I Walk (1972), 16mm Film Optical Sound, Color, 30 min., United Presbyterian Church (PR). "Carl Gormon talks about his paintings, Navajo weaving, the Twins of Navajo legends, corn pollen, the four Sacred Mountains, and 1, 2, 3, 4 worlds."

In Beauty May I Walk, 16mm Film Optical Sound, Color, 17 min. Greenburg Production "Contrasts old ways with the new in Navajoland. English/Navajo."

Indian Family of the California Desert (1967), 16 mm Film Optical Sound, Color, 16 min., Educational Horizons (PR), Dist: Encyclopedia Britannica Educational Corporation.

"Cahuilla woman of California recalls childhood, lifestyle of the Cahuilla."

Indian Mainstream (1972), 16mm Film Optical Sound, Color, 25 min., L. R. Korb (PR), Dist: Univ. of Calif. Extension Media Center. "A narrative of the accomplishments and goals of a cultural revitalization program for Northern California Indians — Hoopas, Yuroks, Karoks, through Humboldt State College."

The Indian Speaks, 16mm Film Optical Sound, Color, 41 min., National Film Board of Canada (PR), Dist: McGraw-Hill Textfilms.

Ishi in Two Worlds (1967), 16mm, Film Optical Sound, Color, 19 min., Contemporary Films (PR), Dist: McGraw-Hill Textfilms. "Describes Ishi's life as last of the Yahi Indians of California."

Ka ke ki ku (1960), B/W, 27 min., Canadian Broadcasting Corp. (PR), Dist: Crawley Films, Ltd. "A poetic insight into the problems of education of the younger generation on one of the most primitive tribes in Canada—the Montagnais Indians."

Kashia Men's Dances (1963), 16mm Film Optical Sound, Color, 40 min., Univ. of Calif. (PR), Dist: Univ. of Calif., Berkeley Media Ext. Center. "Four Pomo dances are performed in Kashia Reservation near northern California coast."

Last Menominee (1966), 16mm Film Optical Sound, B/W, 30 min., National Educational Television, Inc., (PR), Dist: Indiana Univ. "Menominee Indians speak, on their status since termination."

Little White Salmon Indian Settlement (1972), 16mm Film Optical Sound, Color, 28 min., Univ. of Calif. Extension Media Center (PR), Dist: Tricontinental Film Center West. "Examines aspects of Native American life, past and present, in the Pacific Northwest, interspersing historical material with a report, from the Indian's point of view, on their current struggle for fishing rights on the Columbia River."

Living Stone (1959), 16mm Film Optical Sound, Color, 33 min., National Film Board of Canada (PR), Dist: McGraw-Hill Textfilms. "Aspects of Eskimo life and explanation of an Eskimo belief in that a spirit exists in every stick and stone, bird and beast."

Longhouse People, The Color, 23 min., National Film Board of Canada (PR), Dist:

McGraw-Hill Contem. Films, Inc. "Iroquois"

Long Walk, The (1970) 16mm Film Optical Sound, Color, Part I-30 min.; Part II-29 min., KQED, San Francisco (PR), Dist: Univ. of Calif. Ext. Media Center. "Part I—narration in Navajo/English. Perspectives on historical events and contemporary trends." "Part II focuses on the Rough Rock Demonstration School and a discussion of Navajos asserting themselves in order to gain control over their destiny."

Longest War, The 16 mm Film Optical Sound, Color, 30 min., Soho Cinema (PR), Dist: Soho Cinema. "Dennis Banks gives commentary on American Indian Movement."

Look What We've Done To This Land (1973), 16 mm Film Optical Sound, Color, 20 min. Central Clearing House (PR), Dist: Central Clearing House. "Discusses ecological and spiritual questions concerning mining and burning of coal, production of electricity on Hopi and Navajo Reservations for benefit of big cities."

Loon's Necklace (1949), 16mm Film Optical Sound, Color, 11 min., Crawley Films, Ltd., (PR), Dist: Encyclopedia Brit. Ed. Corp. "Legend of how the Loon, a water bird, received her neckband. Ceremonial masks establish character of story."

Native Alaska (1961), 16 mm Film Optical Sound, B/W, 29 min., National Educational TV, Inc. (PR), Dist: Indiana University. "Problems of Indians and Eskimos in Alaska, destruction of hunting and fishing grounds."

Navajo Fight For Survival (1972), 16 mm Film Optical Sound, Color, 47 min., British Broadcasting Co., TV (PR), Dist: Time-Life Films. "Documents the destruction of Indian civilization since the days of the first conquistadores and chronicles current attempts to preserve Navajo culture from the insidious forces of modern society."

Navajos and Annie Wauneka, The (1965), 16 mm Film Optical Sound, B/W, 30 min., Columbia Broadcasting System (PR), Dist: CCM Films, Inc. "Documents the work of Mrs. Annie B. Wauneka, recipient of Freedom Medal of President J. F. Kennedy for her achievements in Public Health and Education."

Now That The Buffalo's Gone 16 mm Film Optical Sound, Color, 7 min., Dist: Creative Film Society, U.C.L.A. (PR)

Okan, Sun Dance of the Blackfeet, 64 min., Glenbow Foundation (PR), Dist: Glenbow-Alberta Inst.

Photographic History of Zuni, A For more information write: Zuni Cultural Project, Zuni Pueblo, P. O. Box 5, Zuni, New Mexico 87327.

Pomo Shaman (1964), 20 min., Univ. of Calif. Ext. Media Center (Dist). "A shortened version of the film "Sucking Doctor," with repetitive elements eliminated." A curing ceremony held by the Kashia group of the Southwestern Pomo Indians.

Pride And The Shame (1968) 16mm Film Optical Sound, B/W, 30 min. British Broadcasting Co., TV (PR), Dist: Time-Life Films. "Sioux Indians of Black Hills, North Dakota, American Indians on the reservation."

Silent Enemy, 16mm Film Optical Sound, B/W, 50 min. Films Classic Exchange (Dist). "This film is about thunder and the Ojibways of Canada."

Song for Dead Warriors, A (1975) 16mm Film Optical Sound, Color, 25 min., Tri-continental Film Center (PR) "Russell Means, Dick Wilson, Senator Abourezk: Hearings on Wounded Knee."

Southern Paiute, Filmstrip—For more information write: Mrs. Winona Holmes, Project Director, Inter-Tribal Council of Nevada, 98 Colony Road, Reno, Nevada, 89502.

Southern Paiutes: A Filmstrip Narrative. Filmstrip. For more information write: Mrs. Winona Holmes, Project Director, Inter-Tribal Council of Nevada, 98 Colony Road, Reno, Nevada 89502.

Southern Ute Today: For more information write: Mr. Leonard Burch, Chairman, Southern Ute Tribe, Tribal Affairs Building, Ignacia, Colorado 81137.

Southwest Indians of Early America (1973), 16 mm Film Optical Sound, Color, 14 min., Coronet Films (PR), Dist: Coronet Films. "Shows Indian occupation in Southwestern United States over a thousand years ago: Hopi, Pima, and Papago."

Spirit of the Navajo, The (1972), 16mm Film Silent, B/W, 21 min., Center for Mass Communication (PR), Dist: Center for Mass Communication (From Navajos Film Themselves) "Shows medicine man preparing for a ceremony."

Sucking Doctor, 16 mm Film Optical Sound, B/W, 45 min., Univ. of Calif. Ext. Media Center (PR), Dist: U.C.E.M.C. "Remarkable documentary presents, in its entirety, the second and final night of a curing ceremony held by the Kashia group of the Southwestern Pomo Indians."

Tahtonka, Plains Indian Buffalo Culture (1966), 16mm Film Optical Sound, Color, 28 min., Nauman Films, Custer, South Dakota (PR), Dist: ACI Films. "Tahtonka is the story of the buffalo period and the Plains Indians' dependence upon the buffalo from the pre-horse days to the time of the Wounded Knee tragedy of 1890, an era representing over 300 years in early American history."

Ten Thousand Beads for Navajo Sam, 16mm Film Optical Sound, Color, 25 min., "Has to do with the relocation program, features a Navajo family in Chicago."

These Are My People, 16mm Film Optical Sound, B/W, 14 min., National Film Board of Canada (PR), Dist: McGraw-Hill Contemp. Films Inc. "Akwesasne (St. Regis) Mohawk Reserve; Indian view of religion and culture, effect of coming of white man, and revival of the Longhouse Culture."

Three Stone Bands, 15 min., Dorothy and Orville Goldner (PR), Dist: International Film Bureau, Inc. "Eskimo legend that shows that 'spirits help those who live by the rules of the people and that in the Arctic to share is to survive' ..."

To Find Our Life: The People Hunt of the Huichols of Mexico (1968), 16mm Film Optical Sound, Color, 65 min., Peter Furst (PR), Dist: Latin American Center, UCLA. "Documentary of the annual peyote hunt of Huichol Indians, who live in the Sierra Madre of Northwest Jalcisco, Mexico."

Totem Pole, 16mm Film Optical Sound, Color, 27 min., Dist: Univ. of Calif. Ext. Media Center. "All types of totem poles are shown with an explanation of their purpose, origin, etc., Pacific Northwest Coast area between Puget and Alaska."

A Visit To The Father, Filmstrip. Part I: The Twins Set Out; Part II: Journey to Sun Bearer's House; Part III: At the Home of Sun Bearer; Part IV: Killing the Moster Giant. Centron Education Films, 1621 West Ninth St., Lawrence, Kansas 66044.

Washo, The. Filmstrip. For more information write: Mrs. Winona Holmes, Project Director, Inter-Tribal Council of Nevada, 98 Colony Road, Reno, Nevada 89502.

Water So Clear A Blind Man Could See, The (1970), 16mm Film Optical Sound, Color, 30 min., Indiana University (PR), Dist: U.C.E.M.E. "Features Taos People (New Mexico), ecological problems faced today, and how the new exists alongside the old. Blue Lake is discussed."

Ways Of Our Fathers (1968), 16mm Film Optical Sound, Color, 30 min., Humboldt State College (PR), Dist: U.C.E.M.C. "Involves Hupa, Hoopa, Tolowa, Karok, Yurok Peoples of California. Focuses on contemporary education of these people as opposed to traditional education."

When Boys Encounter Puberty, 30 min., National Education Television (PR), Dist: Indiana University. "Uses dance routines and originally scored music to portray male adolescent rituals as a means of passing boys to manhood. Compares Americans, the Pokot of Kenya, and the Nupe of Northern Nigeria."

When Girls Encounter Puberty, 30 min., National Education Television (PR), Dist: Indiana University. "Compares the rituals of Americans, Apache Indians, and the Andaman Islanders."

Winter Sea-Ice Camp, Part I, II, III, IV, Color, 30 min. each, Educational Development Center (PR), Dist: Universal Education & Visual Arts, Inc. "Documents, without narration, one part of the Nesilik Eskimo's nomadic cycle of establishing camps according to hunting and weather conditions." Netsilik Eskimo Series)

Zuni Today—For more information write: Zuni Cultural Project, Zuni Pueblo, P.O. Box 5, Zuni, New Mexico 87327.

Addresses of Distributors

ACI Films
35 West 45 Street
New York, NY 10036
(212) 528-1918

Arthur Barr Productions
3490 E Fothill Blvd.
Box 5667
Pasadena, Ca. 91107
(213) 793-6153

Brigham Young University
Green House
Provo, Utah 84602
(801) 374-1211

Canadian Broadcasting Corp.
354 Jarvis Street
Toronto, Canada

Central Clearing House
338 E. DeVargas Street
Santa Fe, New Mexico 87501
(505) 982-4349

Creative Film Society
14558 Valerio Street
Van Nuys, Ca. 91405
(213) 786-8277

Encyclopedia Brit. Edu. Corp.
425 N. Michigan Ave.
Chicago, Ill. 60611
(312) 321-6800

Film Classic Exchange
1926 South Vermont Ave.
Los Angeles, Ca. 90007
(213) 731-3854

Films Incorporated
144 Wilmette Ave.
Wilmette, Ill. 60091

Glenbow-Alberta Institute
902 11 Avenue, S.W.
Calgary, Alberta, Canada

Indiana University
Audio-Visual Center
Bloomington, In. 47401
(812) 337-2103

International Film Bureau, Inc.
323 South Michigan Avenue
Chicago, Ill. 60604

Latin American Center—UCLA
405 Hilgard Avenue
Los Angeles, Ca. 90024
(213) 825-4321

McGraw-Hill Contemporary Films Inc.
Princeton Road
Hightstown, N.J. 08520
(609) 448-1700

828 Custer Avenue
Evanston, Ill. 60202
(312) 869-5010

1714 Stockton Street
San Francisco, Ca. 94133
(415) 362-3115

Soho Cinema
Shoshoni Productions, Inc.
225 Lafayette Street
New York, New York 10012
(212) 966-1416

Southern Baptist Radio
  and Television Commission
6350 W. Freeway
Ft. Worth, Texas 76116
(817) 737-4011

Time-Life Films
Time and Life Building
Rockefeller Center
New York, New York 10020

Tri-Continental Film Center
333 Ave. of the Americas
New York, New York 10014
(212) 989-3330

Tri-Continental Film Center West
P.O. Box 4430
Berkeley, Ca. 94704

Universal Education & Visual Arts, Inc.
221 Park Avenue South
New York, New York 10003
(212) 677-5658

University of California Extension
  Media Center
2223 Fulton Street
Berkeley, Ca. 94720
(415) 642-0462

University of Michigan
Audio-Visual Education Center
416 4th Street
Ann Arbor, Michigan 48103

Crawley Films, Ltd.
19 Fairmount Avenue
Ottawa, Ontario, Canada

Index

COPYRIGHT CITATIONS AND ACKNOWLEDGEMENTS continued from page ii

DeAngulo, Jaime, *Indians in Overalls*, reprinted by permission from the *Hudson Review*, Vol. III, No. 3 (Autumn, 1950) Copyright © 1950 by the Hudson Review, Inc.

Dubois, Cora, *The 1870 Ghost Dance*, Anthropological Records, Vol. 3, No. 1, published in 1939 by the Regents of the University of California, reprinted by permission of the University of California Press.

Heizer, R.F. & M.A. Whipple, *The California Indians: A Source Book*, published in 1951, 1971 by the Regents of the University of California, reprinted by permission of the University of California Press.

Knudtson, Peter M., Excerpts from *Flora: Shaman of the Wintu*, reprinted with permission of the author and *Natural History* Magazine, May 1975. © The American Museum of Natural History, 1975.

LaBarre, Weston, *The Peyote Cult*, fourth edition enlarged 1975 © 1959, 1964 by the Shoe String Press Inc., Hamden, Conn. 06514.

Levitas, Gloria, *American Indian Prose and Poetry*, (We Wait in Darkness) reprinted by permission from Capricorn Books, 1974.

Luckert, Karl W., *The Navajo Hunter Tradition*, by permission from Tucson: University of Arizona Press, © 1975.

Lurie, Nancy O., *Mountain Wolf Woman, Sister of Crashing Thunder*, University of Michigan Press, Ann Arbor, 1961.

Marriott, Alice L. & Carol K. Racklin, *Peyote*, © 1971. Reprinted by permission from New York, Crowell Company, Inc.

McNickle, D'Arcy, *Native American Tribalism: Indian Survivals and Renewals*, Maps: *Present Indian Reservations* and *Approximate Location of Native Tribes at the Time of Discovery*. Reprinted with permission by Oxford University Press, Inc. © 1973.

Mimbres Bowl, TM 4589, (B & W), Courtesy of the Taylor Museum of the Colorado Springs Fine Arts Center.

Morey, Sylvester M., *Can the Red Man Help the White Man?*, New York, The Myrin Institute, Inc., 1970.

Parrish, Essie, "Speech by Essie Parrish," transcribed by George Quasha March 14, 1972, reprinted with permission by the editors and by the Trustees of Boston University. © 1972.

Rasmussen, Knud, *Across Arctic America*, reprinted by permission from G. P. Putnam Sons, 1927.

Rasmussen, Knud, *Report of the 5th Thule Expedition*, reprinted by permission of the heirs of Knud Rasmussen.

Whitman, W., *The Oto*, reprinted by permission of New York:Columbia University Press, 1937, reprinted by AMS Press, 1969.

Wyman, Leland C., *Blessingway*, by permission from Tucson: University of Arizona Press, © 1970.

Underhill, Ruth. Material from *Autobiography of a Papago Woman*, reprinted by permission from the author and the American Anthropological Association.

Bass, Alphea, *The Arapaho Way*, © 1966 by Alphea Bass, used by permission of Clarkson N. Potter, Inc.